PERSONAL
AND
PUBLIC
SPEAKING

FOURTH EDITION

By
DONALD W. KLOPF
West Virginia University

RONALD E. CAMBRA
University of Hawaii

Morton Publishing Company
925 W. Kenyon, Unit 12
Englewood, Colorado 80110

The "Shannon-Weaver Model," page 12, is from C. E. Shannon and W. Weaver, *The Mathematical Theory of Communication* ((Urbana: University of Illinois Press, 1949), p. 98. The Schramm Model, page 13, is from "How Communication Works" in *The Process and Effects of Mass Communication* (Urbana: University of Illinois Press, 1955), p. 8. Reprinted by permission of the University of Illinois Press. Figure 2.4, page 13, "A Model of the Ingredients in Communication,' is from *The Process of Communication,* Third Edition, by David Berlo. Copyright © 1960 by Holt, Rinehart and Winston. Reprinted by permission of the publisher.

Preface

The United States is a pluralistic nation made up of people representing a variety of racial and ethnic backgrounds, religions, socioeconomic levels, and native languages, in addition to natural diversities based on gender, age, and physical and mental abilities. These differences are cultural, and they surface in the daily communicative interactions of the country's population. In this fourth edition of *Personal and Public Speaking*, we have modified the content to take into account these cultural variations. Whenever necessary, especially in the chapters presenting an overview of the communication process and the factors affecting that process, the influence of cultural dissimilarities on communication is emphasized.

Millions of migrants from the Caribbean islands, Mexico, and countries of the Orient have changed the nation's complexion. No longer is the United States a largely white Anglo-Saxon country. By the century's end, about 40 percent of the population is expected to be non-Caucasian, and the country's institutions will be dealing with people raised under totalitarian or authoritarian regimes, who were educated to appreciate the advantages of collectivism. Many of the migrants are not prepared to express themselves orally in the American way of life, where the ability to verbalize with fluency is highly prized — and anticipated.

The fourth edition of *Personal and Public Speaking* is designed to open the minds of its readers to the communicative diversity in the fifty states and possessions. The book is meant to be a start — the beginning of greater student understanding of the communication problems that exist now and will confront the nation more and more as time goes on. Perhaps the book also will make students aware of the dangers of ethnocentrism and prejudice that often creep into intercultural interactions.

The bulk of the book remains grounded in the communication skills necessary to succeed in the workplace. Abilities in interviewing, discussion, and public speaking are necessary for people who expect to function orally in the workplace. Because many students lack those skills, *Personal and Public Speaking* was created to introduce students to the theory and practical knowledge needed to function at work. The same skills are vital to most communicative situations in everyday living, so the book's scope is broad and encompasses most speaking experiences.

The book is divided into three parts. The first two are largely descriptive, giving an overview of the oral communication process and descriptions of the factors influencing the act of speaking. The third part is largely prescriptive, offering instruction in the arts of interviewing, discussing in groups, and public speaking — important communication areas in achieving effective interpersonal relations on the job and in life in general.

Thousands of students have read previous editions of *Personal and Public Speaking*. Most reacted positively to its content. We continue to benefit greatly from their evaluations and suggestions, and we appreciate their support.

D.W.K.
R.E.C.

Contents

Communicating Competently

In a class exercise, the instructor played the role of an employer interviewing applicants for a job. The applicants were the instructor's students, learning the art of applying for jobs.[1] One of the applicants, Dick Vandenberg, caught the instructor's eye. He looked older than the average student and seemed more mature. In fact, at twenty-eight, he was older and, more important, held a bachelor of science degree in electrical engineering, had worked briefly, served three years in the U.S. Air Force, and now was back in school. The instructor was curious about Dick's return to school and his interest in speech communication.

"Why," the instructor inquired, "are you working on another bachelor's degree, and why are you taking this course?"

Dick replied: "Why am I getting another bachelor's? Well, I'm not sure I will. I want to take as many liberal arts courses as I can, though, and that's why I'm back in school. My undergraduate work was all math and engineering. After being out of school a while and working, I knew I'd missed something. I knew nothing about art, literature, history — I was really one-sided."

"I see," the instructor nodded. "The B.S. training prepared you for a job but not really for life."

"That's about it. I want something more than just working."

"I understand," the instructor said. "But why speech communication?"

"You know about jobs. To get ahead, or just do your job well, you need a couple of skills. One is how to do the work. Right now, while going to school, I support myself by working in a copying and duplicating service. We do photocopying, duplicating, instant printing, and stuff like that. I operate

various machines, and I had to learn how to do that. Actually, it took me a couple of weeks. The other skill I need on the job is how to communicate — how to talk with people. That's why I'm taking speech.

"For myself, I think the communication skill is more important than knowing how to operate the machines. I'm talking to people all day long on the job. But every day I'm talking to people off the job, too. I talk to my friends, parents, people I meet, besides customers and the people I work with. I belong to a couple of clubs and do several things for them that are really important to me. And occasionally I have to give a speech. Talking is a big part of those interests."

The instructor asked, "How are you doing? I mean, are you getting your ideas across?"

"Well, I'm doing okay, I guess," Dick replied, "as well as most people. I just don't think I'm doing as well as I could. I'm not coming across like I really want."

"Oh? What's wrong?"

"It's little things. On the job I screw up every once in a while. The boss gives me a special task something I haven't done before. We talk it over and seem to agree about what needs to be done. When it's done, it's all screwed up. I didn't understand him. Or he didn't understand my questions. The job's all wrong, and time and money went down the tubes. Take the other day. The boss is out. A lady rushes in to pick up an order. She didn't have enough money, so I couldn't give it to her. She got excited. We argued. It didn't turn out too well."

"You felt you should have handled her better?"

"Yes," Dick said quickly. "She was a customer. I was out of line."

1

"Most of us have had experiences like yours," the instructor reassured him. "They're common. Is there something else that makes you concerned?"

"A couple of things. For one, when I meet people, it's hard for me to carry on a conversation — I mean, a genuine one."

The instructor laughed. "Not too many of us are great conversationalists."

"I'd like to do better. After all, I am a college grad. Then, too, I have trouble selling myself — selling anything, for that matter. In the air force the guys who got promoted quickly knew their job but knew how to sell themselves as well. I knew my job, but I couldn't sell myself. It was the difference between being an Airman and an Airman first class. I even have trouble applying for a job."

"This speech course can't overcome habits years in the making," the instructor reminded him.

"I know. But the course can give me the know-how. I understand that it's up to me to practice, to try on my own. I learned the hard way that the oral skills count."

This exchange between Vandenberg and the instructor points out that speech communication is a common activity. It is one to which most human beings devote a lot of time.

SPEECH: THE PRINCIPAL COMMUNICATION FORM

Dick did much talking each day. A typical person, he engaged in other forms of communication as well, like most of us do. We live and function in a society based on communication. Almost everything we do with other people involves communication in one form or another. We communicate how we feel, what we know, and how we think. In the same fashion, others communicate with us. Actually, we spend nearly 75 percent of our waking hours communicating with our fellow citizens, at home, at school, on the job, at play, or in community activities.[2] As we go about our daily business, we communicate with family, friends, co-workers, customers, fellow students, teachers, store clerks, and a multitude of other people. Living without communicating is next to impossible. Without the ability to speak, listen, read, write, or gesture, we would exist in virtual isolation, cut off from society, unable to interact with people.[3]

Of the three-quarters of a waking day an adult spends in communication activities, a large portion is oral. The communication practices of people in all walks of life have been researched carefully, and the results substantiate that more than half of the communication time is spent in speaking and its companion activity, listening, as Figure 1.1 shows graphically. The remaining time is shared among television viewing and radio listening, reading, and writing.[4] Oral communication consumes more of the communicative day than the other forms combined.

Among the types of people contacted in the research, college students communicate the most. The average student's school day is a day of communication; almost all of it involves communication in some form. Speaking and listening are the principal forms, but reading also has a large role, and students tend to write a lot.[5]

Of the other types of people researched, the highest paid, best educated, and most highly trained people do the most communicating. In the professional, administrative, engineering, and sales occupational groups, communication consumes the major part of the day. Within these groups are business managers, department heads, supervisors, architects, physicians, lawyers, dentists, teachers, social workers, accountants, engineers, business personnel, and salespeople, among others — all of whom, by the nature of their work, interact with people regularly. In contrast, those doing skilled and unskilled work spend the least amount of time communicating. Laborers and tradespeople are examples. Their work is apt to be tool- or thing-related. Their interaction with others is limited, and they deal more directly with the objects used on the job.[6]

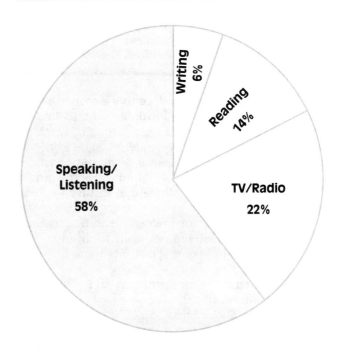

FIGURE 1.1. Daily time spent in various communication activities.

TYPES OF SPEAKING

In his interview with the instructor, Dick Vandenberg mentioned the types of speaking he used. He talked about giving and getting information, selling himself, making speeches, conversing, and interviewing for jobs. And, of course, Dick talked to himself, as we all do. These types are common to everyday communication and usually are classified as intrapersonal, interpersonal, and public speaking.

Intrapersonal Communication

Intrapersonal communication is the *process through which we share information, meanings, and feelings with the self*. We talk to ourselves almost continuously. Although we are more easily absorbed when we are alone, we can be communicating intrapersonally even in the presence of others. We might be thinking about what the others are saying or doing. When listening to a lecture, we could be pondering what is being said — or daydreaming about that beautiful girl or handsome hunk sitting next to us. While watching television, we work hard at trying to make sense out of the unfolding action.

Extremely complex, intrapersonal communication involves our central nervous system, including the functions of the left and right hemispheres of the brain, our thinking facility, and other physiological properties. Gathering, storing, and retrieving information is part of the process, and we use this information in internal problem solving, resolving internal conflicts, planning for the future, releasing emotions, criticizing ourselves and others, and engaging in interpersonal relationships. Intrapersonal communication revolves only around the self, but it forms the basis for all other communication.

Interpersonal Communication

Interpersonal communication is the *process through which we share information, meanings, and feelings with at least one other person* and as many as are in a small group of people. Two forms of interpersonal communication assume important roles in our lives: person-to-person and small-group.

Person-to-Person

Person-to-person talk involves two parties (a dyad), who alternate in speaking and listening. The typical person spends much time each day conversing in this fashion. In the working world, for example, millions of these transactions occur daily.[7] Included among them are giving and receiving instructions, selling ideas and products, appraising performances, handling grievances, and solving problems. They take place between physician and patient, lawyer and client, teacher and student, employer and employee, social worker and ward, supervisor and subordinate — to name but a few.[8]

To that number of dyadic transactions we add those that are not work-related — occurring at home, in school, at play, and in community activities. With these people we share feelings, tell stories, discuss future plans, gossip, seek guidance, and socialize.

Types of Speaking

Person-To-Person   **Small-Group**   **Public**

Small-Group Communication

Communication in small groups is ever present in the working world. Staff meetings, committee sessions, conferences, discussions, small-group laboratory classes, negotiations, bargaining sessions, workshops, and seminars, involving small groups of people, occupy a significant part of the work week, and the trend is toward more of this activity.[9]

Meetings of small groups are not just occupationally oriented, though. Community and social groups meet for purposes of learning together, solving common problems, and carrying out neighborhood improvement projects. Less formal groups of family, friends, and neighbors gather also, meeting to socialize and have fun.[10]

Public Speaking

Although the average person devotes less time to public speaking than to the other types, public speeches demand more careful preparation. In the public speaking situation the speaker takes the floor and hopes to command the listeners' attention for the length of the speech whether it is a short oral report or a major address. Maintaining audience interest and attention requires skill and effort.

For business executives and professional people, public speaking opportunities abound, either within their work institution or with outside audiences. When they do speak, the speaking situation normally is important for themselves as well as the business or profession they represent. The stakes are apt to be high when they seek to persuade an audience to accept their ideas or proposals.[11]

As in the other types of speech, public speaking is not confined to the working world. Students occasionally present oral reports, and people from all segments of society address the membership of clubs, organizations, and associations.

MULTICULTURAL COMMUNICATORS

Dick talked a lot on his job, with different kinds of people. "In my city, Milwaukee, where I work," he told the instructor, "you meet all kinds. It used to be just the locals — blacks and persons of European background like Poles, Germans and Italians — but now there's Mexicans, Haitians, Cubans, Koreans, Japanese, Chinese, and Filipinos. Miss Wisconsin a few years ago was Korean. Trouble is they all act differently. Usually we get along all right, but I've got to be careful. A wrong gesture, the wrong word, and I've cost the boss a customer."

"Doesn't that happen with the old-time locals as well?" queried the instructor.

"Oh sure. I'm more familiar with their customs, though. With all the new people settling in Milwaukee, I need some help. Are there courses I can take to help me with the newcomers?"

Speech and communication departments in most universities have classes in intercultural communication — classes in which students learn to become aware of the communication problems that arise when individuals from different cultures interact. In recent years the United States has become such a mixture of races and ethnic groups that the nation's academic leaders realize the need for specialized speech training.

The country is undergoing cultural change. Once a largely white Anglo-Saxon nation based on political and social institutions influenced by western European traditions, the millions of migrants from the Caribbean islands, Mexico, and the countries of the Orient have altered the nation's complexion. By the year 2000 the population is expected to be roughly 35 percent non-European. Meeting the expected population diversity is going to be a challenge for old-timers and newcomers alike. To speak successfully will require special knowledge and training.

COMMUNICATING COMPETENTLY AND SKILLFULLY

Our ability to communicate through spoken language distinguishes us from other living things. This ability does not benefit us much, however, unless we speak with reasonable success. Often a breakdown in communication over a minor problem can create bitterness and hostility between close acquaintances. On the other hand, successful communication in a casual meeting between two people ultimately may lead to a lifelong relationship or friendship. Some people believe that only certain people — for instance, politicians, lawyers, and priests — have to speak with care. But whatever our role in life, we have to sell ourselves to others, to speak as successfully as we can.

To speak successfully, we ought to speak with competence and skill. *Competence* comes with knowledge and understanding. It is a cognitive quality derived from studying the communication process and learning how it operates with different kinds of people in different speaking situations. *Skill* comes with mastering the expressive behaviors required in speaking and listening. It is a psychomotor quality derived from practicing the oral communicative behaviors under expert guidance and subsequently applying them in real situations.[12]

What competencies and skills foster successful oral communication is an issue of continuing investigation. Among them, task forces of the national speech communication association have studied the issue, as have agencies representing state and local governments.[13] Lists of recommended competencies and skills are available for various educational levels.[14] One of these lists is directed at the competencies and skills college students should have.[15]

COMPETENCIES/SKILLS FOR COLLEGE STUDENTS

The following set of competencies represents the minimum requirements for a successful college communicator at the sophomore level. The items that make up the list should be meaningful and comprehensible to individuals with high school or college speech training. Those lacking that background will find the necessary explanations in this book.

Speaking Competencies and Skills

Speaking is the *process of transmitting ideas and information orally in a variety of situations.* Successful oral communication ideally involves generating messages of any length and delivering them in standard American English with attention to vocal variety, articulation, and nonverbal signs.

Speaking Competencies

To be a successful speaker, a student must know how to compose a message that provides ideas and information suitable to the message's topic, its purpose, and its listeners. In achieving this goal, the student must know how to:

- Determine the purpose of oral discourse.
- Choose a message topic and adapt it to the purpose and the listeners.
- Formulate a point or thesis for the message.
- Provide adequate support material.
- Organize the message in a suitable fashion.
- Use proper language.
- Supply necessary transitions.
- Demonstrate appropriate interpersonal skills.

Speaking Skills

The successful speaker must be able to transmit the message by using the psychomotor skills suitable to the message's topic, its purpose, and its listeners. To achieve this goal, the student must be able to:

- Employ vocal variety in terms of rate, pitch, and intensity.

Common Speaking Strengths

- ◆ Am I friendly?
  - articulate?
  - sincere?
  - sympathetic?
  - open to others' ideas?
  - straightforward in my answers?
  - relaxed in strangers' presence?

- ◆ Do I speak clearly?
  - listen attentively?
  - help others relax?
  - employ proper grammar?
  - allow others speaking time?
  - understand what others say?

Common Speaking Weaknesses

- ◆ Am I too formal?
  - rattled?
  - doubtful of others?
  - easily upset?
  - impulsive?
  - inattentive?
  - anxious?

- ◆ Do I dominate conversations?
  - shun others?
  - judge prematurely?
  - become aggressive?
  - become angry easily?
  - receive blame poorly?
  - find fault readily?
  - dodge problem situations?

- Articulate clearly.
- Use the level of American English appropriate to the listeners.
- Employ the nonverbal behavior that supports the verbal message.

Listening Competencies and Skills

Listening is the *process of receiving and assimilating ideas and information from verbal messages.* Successful listening entails both literal and critical comprehension of ideas and information transmitted in oral language.

Listening Competencies

To be a successful listener, a student must know how to listen with literal comprehension. To achieve this goal, the student must know how to:

- Recognize main ideas in a message.
- Identify supporting materials.

◆ Recognize explicit relationships among ideas.

◆ Recall basic ideas and details.

Listening Skills

The successful listener must be able to listen critically. To achieve this goal, the student must be able to:

◆ Attend to what is said with an open mind.

◆ Perceive the speaker's purpose and message organization.

◆ Discriminate between statements of fact and statements of opinion.

◆ Distinguish between emotional and logical arguments.

◆ Detect bias and prejudice.

◆ Identify the speaker's attitude.

◆ Synthesize and evaluate by drawing logical inferences and conclusions.

◆ Recall the message's implications and arguments.

◆ Recognize discrepancies between a speaker's verbal and nonverbal messages.

◆ Employ active listening techniques when appropriate.[16]

REASONS FOR IMPROVING

For college students, an answer to the question "Why improve?" could be a selfish one. Communication plays a large role in the average student's life. Therefore, communicating successfully should pay off in better classroom performance and higher grades. And being a successful communicator should bring an even bigger pay-off in the student's occupational career.[17] In school and on the job, the student needs to be prepared to speak with competence and skill in person-to-person, small-group, and public speaking situations — the types of oral communication that occur constantly in academic and work settings. Even students who plan careers in skilled or unskilled occupations, working principally with tools and things, have to communicate successfully if they have visions of moving beyond the bottom rung.

Although becoming successful oral communicators will pay off for us in school and later at work, there are better reasons for achieving competence and skill as communicators. The three that follow are advanced as vital by prominent communication authorities.[18]

Personal Growth

One reason for improving communication is primal: personal growth. Only through communication do we become who we are, and we are more than skin and bones. The mental and emotional characteristics of our being make us who we are.

As children, through communication we learned the names and meanings of things, developed language and became symbol users, and developed and expressed our personalities. Moreover, our personal growth did not stop when we left high school or, say, at age eighteen. It continues. Our mental and emotional development is ongoing and always changing.

Most important, our continuing personal growth is directly related to our ability to communicate. It is related to our ability to think and express our thoughts clearly, to be open and trustful, to be confident, fearless, and proud. Communication and personality are refined together, and that is one reason we study communication.

Social Growth

A second reason we should continue to improve our speaking capabilities is for social growth. We live surrounded by other people. Actually, it is almost impossible for us not to be in the company of other people. Most likely, few of us would want to be devoid of human companionship. We are social creatures with strong interpersonal needs, and those needs are fulfilled through oral communication.[19]

When we consider the times when our relationships with others have been satisfying and enjoyable, we probably can recognize that they have been successful because of competent and skillful communication. When we consider the times when our relationships have been less than satisfying, clouded by anger, frustration, or anxiety, we probably can realize that our communication was faulty. We failed to express ourselves to the satisfaction of those with whom we talked. As social beings, therefore, we have cause to communicate successfully with others.

Cooperative Action

Yet a third reason merits attention for improving our speaking capabilities. Through communication we cooperate with others to do the things we cannot do alone. Without cooperative action we would have little control over our environment and a less full and satisfying life. Without schools, local/state/federal governments, factories, corporations, businesses, clubs, associations, and religious groups, life with others would be chaotic. By working together in these organizations, we solve problems, produce goods and services, worship, are entertained, and perform a host of other tasks we could not accomplish alone.

At the heart of cooperative action is communication. We share knowledge, information, and feelings through speech. We persuade others, make decisions, and take action through speech. Sharing information and points of view is essential to cooperative action, and cooperative action is a requisite for a more fruitful life.[20]

SUMMARY

Communication is ubiquitous; everyone communicates everywhere. In virtually every part of our lives communication is predominant; it governs our interaction with others.

The principal form of communication, oral (speaking and listening), consumes the greatest share of the time we devote each day to communicating, talking with others in person-to-person, small-group, and public speaking settings. Oral communication is so vital to our personal well-being that we have to speak with reasonable success. We should be *competent* speakers, knowing and understanding the communication process, and we should be *skillful* speakers, mastering the expressive behaviors required to communicate orally. Nowadays this extends to communicating with an increasingly diverse population.

Successful oral communication requires that we be able to conceive messages of any length and deliver them in English appropriate to the listeners, demonstrating proper articulation, vocal variety, and nonverbal behavior. Successful oral communication also includes the critical and literal comprehension of ideas and information as we listen to others speak.

Benefits accrue from becoming successful oral communicators. Students' academic performance should improve and, upon entering the working world, the potential for upward mobility should increase. Furthermore, our lives should be enhanced by becoming more successful as communicators. We should grow personally and socially while interacting more cooperatively with others.

2

The Nature of Speech Communication

An old adage claims we must perform two acts in life: pay taxes and die. We can't avoid doing either. This adage, however, requires revision; it is not complete enough. We really are compelled to perform three acts. Communication should be added. Like paying taxes and dying, we must communicate. Living is largely a matter of communicating. It is a fact of life. *We cannot not communicate.*[1]

Communicating is such a vital part of life that we ought to be as successful at it as we can. Being successful means we need to be competent and skillful communicators. We need to possess knowledge and understanding of the communication process, and we need to attain skill in the psychomotor behaviors related to speaking and listening.

This book presents the necessary information for understanding the communication process. The class in which the book is being used should provide some training in these skills. The bulk of the training, however, will come through experience after the class is over, in the working world that lies ahead.

In this chapter we begin our explanation of the communication process by describing the general nature of speech communication. We offer a definition of oral communication, differentiate its various elements and portray them in model form, and analyze its outcomes and functions.

ORAL COMMUNICATION DEFINED

The word communication is abstract and, like all words, carries different meanings for different people.[2] One compilation has a dozen applications of the term,[3] and another contains 126 different definitions of communication.[4] Communication, however, is used generally in only two different ways:

1. *To transfer messages from place to place* — for example, by telephone, radio, or satellite. When

Communications:

Exchanging messages by telephone, radio, satellite, and other mechanical means

Communication:

Stimulating meaning in others

the word is used in this way, it usually is pluralized: communications. It emphasizes the exchange of messages through some mechanical device or means.

2. *To stimulate meaning in the mind of another person.* The stress is on meaning, not on message.[5] This second general usage is the topic of this book.

Communication can stimulate meaning through writing, reading, speaking, and nonverbal ways. Our interest is in speaking and the nonverbal messages that accompany or substitute for speech. Listening is a simultaneous communicative behavior occurring when one person speaks to another. It, too, concerns us. Thus, we are interested in oral communication — a term used interchangeably with *speech, oral interaction, verbal messages, and speech communication.* These terms all carry the same meaning:

> Oral communication is the process by which persons share information, meanings, and feelings through the exchange of verbal and nonverbal messages.[6]

THE ORAL COMMUNICATION PROCESS

Oral communication is a process. By examining the implications of *process,* we can obtain a better understanding of what oral communication entails. By process, we mean a series of happenings that does not have a beginning, an end, or a fixed chain of events. Hence, speaking is an ongoing, ever-changing activity in which all of its elements interact with each other to produce meaning.[7] A process is dynamic, systemic, adaptive, continuous, transactional, and irreversible.

Dynamic

Dynamics and change characterize process. Dynamic things are constantly changing, and anything that is a process is dynamic rather than static. *Oral communication is dynamic.* It deals with change.[8]

Take, for example, the oral communication between two friends, Heidi and Lisa, passing in the hall on the way to their first class. Relaxed after a refreshing night's sleep, Heidi cheerfully greets her friend with a hearty, "Hi, Lisa! How are things?" Lisa, up late studying for a first-hour exam, seems tense and anxious as she replies gloomily, "Okay, I guess," and dejectedly moves away. Heidi, expecting to talk for a few minutes as they normally do each morning, looks after her departing friend, puzzled by her odd behavior.

Oral communication is:

Dynamic

Systematic

Adaptive

Continuous

Transactional

Irreversible

This exchange between Heidi and Lisa could be analyzed in a fixed, static way. We could say that the speech act began when Heidi saw Lisa in the hall. The end of the act could be set at the time Heidi watched her friend leave. Within those time boundaries, we could identify certain fixed elements of the act: an originating communicator, speaker, or source (Heidi); a listener or receiver and responding communicator (Lisa); messages (the words exchanged); and a setting (the hall). Each of these elements in the act could be studied in and of itself without considering its effects on the other elements. Lisa's behavior, for instance, could be examined without considering its effects on Heidi.

That type of analysis, however, would not give us a complete picture of the happenings. For one thing, Lisa's behavior *did* affect Heidi. It caused her to change her own cheery approach to one of confusion, at least toward Lisa. In addition, we have to ask ourselves, "Can the end of this speech act be clearly identified?" Probably not, because Heidi's friendliness toward Lisa may have been altered somewhat, and the next time they meet, Heidi may be a little less friendly and a bit more reserved until the cause of Lisa's anxiety somehow becomes known to Heidi. By the same token, we have to ask, "Can the beginning of the act be clearly stated?" The two girls had established a friendship over time and undoubtedly enjoyed many good times together.

To paint a more complete picture of the happenings in their encounter in the hall, at least we would have to study their relationship together from the first time they met. Even then, however, our picture would be incomplete. We still would know little about Heidi and Lisa as persons. What do they believe in? Where do they live? What sort of schooling have they had? What are their interests? These and similar questions about their backgrounds would have to be answered. And still the picture would not be complete.

Systemic

Oral communication is systemic. Its elements are interrelated and work together to produce meaningful interaction.[9] Each element affects every other element, and each effects the outcome of communication. In the illustration above, Lisa's behavior affected Heidi. Heidi was puzzled; she didn't know exactly what to say or do. The next time they meet, chances are that Heidi will have slightly altered her behavior toward her friend Lisa, not knowing quite how to react until Heidi somehow finds out what caused Lisa's unusual coldness.

Adaptive

The idea that Heidi probably will change her behavior toward Lisa, albeit ever so slightly, suggests another quality of process. A process is adaptive; it adjusts to cope with change.[10] Heidi will adjust and adapt to Lisa's changed behavior. *Oral communication is adaptive.* Good communicators are flexible, adjusting and adapting to changing situations.

Continuous

The simple exchange between Heidi and Lisa illustrates another point about oral communication as a process. *Oral communication is continuous.* It has no clearly identifiable beginning and no determinable end.[11] The beginning of the two friends' communication really was not when they first saw each other in the hall, nor did it end as they moved away from each other. Their talk was based on past experiences, and it will have future implications affecting subsequent oral communication between the two. The communication process is ongoing; it has no beginning or end.

Transactional

Although the communication process is continuous, no communication encounter is exactly the same as some previous encounter. The next time Heidi and Lisa meet, they will do so under different circumstances. Heidi's behavior toward Lisa will have changed. The day or time, and probably the surroundings and circumstances also, will be different. This implies that *oral communication is transactional.* Each speech act is a unique combination of people, events, and messages, and consequently unlike any prior act.[12] The successful speaker, realizing communication's transactional nature, will approach each act not with a set of rules to follow rigidly but, instead, with an openness and willingness to adapt to the specifics of each act.

Irreversible

Once we say something, we cannot erase it or take it back. A promise we did not mean, an insult we wish we had not said, a hostile glance we regret making — these cannot be reversed. They become part of the shared experience of both parties. Often, when we say something we recognize too late that we should not have said, we try to reverse ourselves. We try to expunge what we said by denying that we meant what we said, by claiming we were misinterpreted, or by giving other explanations. Our attempts to blot out the record, however, do little except to provide new information for our listeners to consider. They do not erase the past. Thus, *oral communication is an irreversible process.* It moves ever forward as time itself.[13]

In understanding the process implications of oral communication, we should recognize that completely isolating for study the elements that make up communication is probably impossible. As part of a process, these elements dynamically interact with each other in a continuously changing fashion without fixed boundaries or stated time limits.

Our understanding of the oral communication process will be furthered by learning about several communication models. The four we present next provide differing viewpoints of the process.

MODELS OF THE COMMUNICATION PROCESS

If we think of models at all, we are apt to consider them to be small replicas of larger objects, like miniature cars. Another sort of model, however, is not used to represent concrete things. This sort of model helps us understand complex actions or occurrences. To analyze the parts of any process, be it basketball or nuclear fusion, we abstract them. We focus on the essential features and ignore the unessential ones. The coach diagrams plays, and the nuclear physicist portrays invisible chain reactions through mathematical symbols. Models of the oral communication process work the same way. Through them, we depict the forms and variables of human interaction so we are able to see more clearly how they operate.[14]

Models serve three purposes. They help *organize* the essential features or elements of communication and show how these relate to each other. Not every element may be included, but the essential ones are. Models also *predict* or help forecast what probably will happen in our conversation with others. Speaking to friends, from our knowledge of models, we recognize that noise, one of the elements of the communication process is a factor in our conversation; knowing the implications of noise, we can adjust our conversation accordingly. Finally, models help us *measure* the amount of speaking a person or channel can accommodate.[15]

The Aristotelian Model

Aristotle examined and labeled several basic elements of the communication process, which others later expanded. The model became a classic, one of the first depictions of the communication process. The key elements in Aristotle's process were simply the speaker, the speech, and the audience, as depicted in Figure 2.1. He focused on rhetorical communication, or the art of public speaking, a necessary skill in his day. According to Aristotle, public speaking involves persuasion, with the following

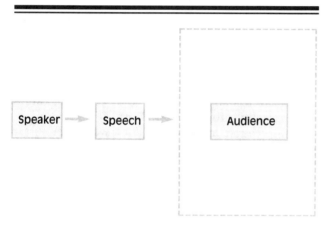

FIGURE 2.1. Aristotle's view of the communication process.

factors vital to determine the persuasiveness of a speech: the contents of the speech, their arrangement, the manner in which the speech is delivered, the role of the audience, the character of the speaker, and the speaker's arguments.

Aristotle's notion of communication was linear, a one-way event, speaker to audience. For that reason, the model is faulty. From our previous description of the communication process, we realize that speech is a complex activity in which the respective parties are mutually dependent. They send and receive messages simultaneously, not in a linear way. Even though the model is not totally accurate, it does represent one of the first attempts to explain what transpires when one person talks to another.[16]

The Shannon and Weaver Model

A Bell Telephone Company employee, Claude Shannon, conceived the most influential of all early communication models. The model, presented in Figure 2.2, sketched a communication system of functions necessary in transmitting electrical signals from one location to another. Behavioral scientists took it as an approximation of the process of human communication — hence its interest to us.

As the model illustrates, a source generates one signal (from a number of alternative possibilities). The signal moves from a transmitter through a channel to a receiver, where the signal is reconverted into its original form for its destination. The message is any input into the transmitter, and noise is any distracting disturbance that might occur at any point in the channel. In the case of a telephone conversation, one person's spoken message is encoded, or transformed into electrical pulses by the

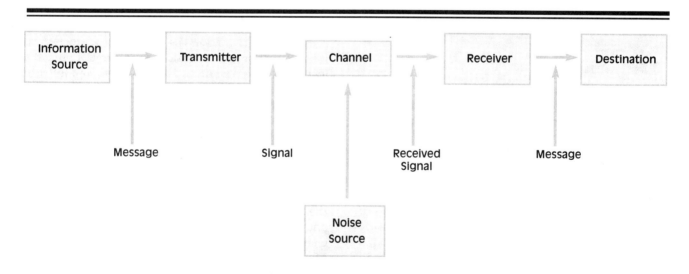

FIGURE 2.2. The Shannon-Weaver model of communication.

transmitter. Then the encoded message is sent through the telephone lines or channel to a receiver. In the receiver it is decoded into the spoken message for the listener.

Later Shannon introduced a mechanism that corrected for differences between the transmitted and the received signal. This mechanism was the forerunner of the currently widely used concept of feedback.[17]

Schramm's Model of Communication

Yet another model was conceived by Wilbur Schramm, a professor of communication at Stanford University and at the East-West Center. He was one of the first to alter the Shannon-Weaver model and account for the circular quality of speech, thus providing an alternative to the linear models characteristic of the past.

As Figure 2.3 shows, Schramm viewed encoding and decoding as simultaneous activities of both sender and receiver. He included "interpreter" as part of the process. The interpreter provides meaning to the message, in both encoding and decoding. Although it is not shown in the model, Schramm added the idea of a "field of experience," the type of orientation and attitudes the communicators hold toward each other.[18]

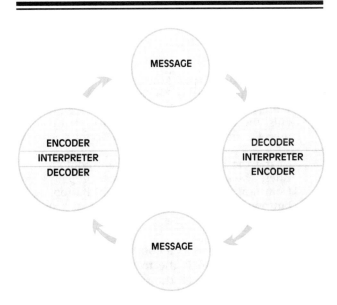

FIGURE 2.3 Schramm's model of communication.

The SMCR Model

The final model was developed by David K. Berlo, a professor of speech communication at Michigan State University. It is called the SMCR model because of its four major elements: source, message, channel, and receiver.

The source is the creator of the message — a person or group with a reason for engaging in communication. The message is the translation of ideas into a symbolic code such as language and gestures. The channel is the medium through which the message is carried. The receiver is the person who is the target of the communication. Noise is implied in the process, but Berlo ignores feedback.[19] The SMCR model is depicted in Figure 2.4.

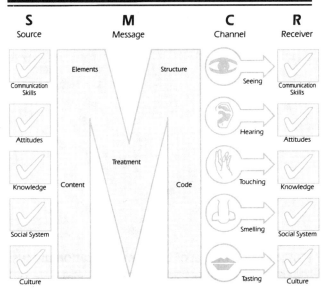

FIGURE 2.4 Berlo's SMCR model of communication.

ESSENTIAL ELEMENTS OF ORAL COMMUNICATION

The elements essential to understanding the speech process are given in Figure 2.5, the model to which we will refer throughout this book. It represents an interpersonal encounter between two persons, A and B. Called *dyadic* because two persons form a dyad, the encounter is the simplest form of human interaction.

Persons A and B serve as both senders and receivers, with the sender and receiver roles alternating. In the model, Person A initiates the interaction and assumes the sender's role. Person B is the receiver. Then the roles reverse as Person B replies to A's message; B becomes the sender and A the receiver. In this manner, the talk flows back and forth between the two with the roles alternating until they terminate the encounter.

If more than two persons are involved, the roles are shared among the people. First there is one

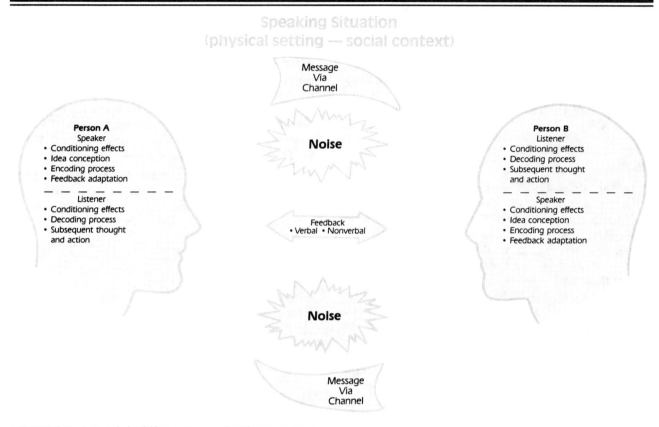

FIGURE 2.5. A model of the communication process.

sender and the others are receivers. When the sender stops talking, a receiver takes on the sending role while the original sender becomes a listener. As the speaking continues, the roles alternate among those present. In the following explanation of the elements of communication, *speaker* stands for the sender or source and listener designates the receiver.

Speaker

The speaker is the person who does the talking at a given moment. Under normal circumstances, the speaker is the person who conceives the message before delivering it. Occasionally the speaker may not be the actual conceiver of the message but instead may be orally transmitting the message of the real source — another person, a group, or an organization. The speaker acts as the mouthpiece for the real source.[20]

In this illustration, the sergeant functions as the captain's spokesperson:

The squadron's noncommissioned officer, Sgt. Smith, is meeting with the squadron commander, Capt. Jones, regarding the enlisted men's attire. The captain orders: "I want your men to dress properly — shirt tails tucked in, buttons buttoned, pants pressed, shoes shined. They look sloppy."

Facing the squadron, the sergeant admonishes: "Men! I want you to dress properly from now on. Shirt tails tucked in! Buttons buttoned! Pants pressed! Shoes shined! You look sloppy!"

The sergeant serves as a conduit for the captain's message. The captain is the real source of the message. Normally, however, the speaker is the source of messages.

Conditioning Effects

Our messages are conditioned by many factors. Our *culture* is the principal one. Culture is a part of everyone's life and in that sense is a unifying factor. Although we all are governed by similar aspects of culture, the diversity of human behavior is attributed largely to the fact that the people of the world do not belong to the same culture. If we desire to talk effectively with people from other cultures, we have to understand the cultural world they inhabit. We must perceive the world as they see it.

Our *knowledge* of the subject about which we speak is a factor that may limit our success. If we are extremely conversant on the subject, having done our homework and learned the facts, we should prove successful. If we failed to prepare, our messages are apt to be unconvincing.

Our command of the *speaking skills* is a conditioning factor. If our level of American English is not appropriate for the listeners, our message may not be well received. If we fail to use vocal variety as we speak, or are inarticulate, we probably will be unsuccessful.

Our *attitude* toward ourselves, our listeners, and our subject affects what we say and how we say it. If we are positive, our messages will come across that way. Full of enthusiasm, we convey our eagerness to our listeners. If we are pessimistic, our cynicism may be contagious.

Success in achieving our purpose as a speaker depends also upon the *listener's estimate* of our worth and competence as a speaker. If the listener considers us unbelievable, our message will fall on deaf ears. If the listener believes us to be credible, our message will receive a better reception.

Message Formulation

Before uttering a message, we must accomplish three things:

1. *Conceive the idea* to be communicated.

2. *Decide on our intent* toward the listener — our purpose in speaking. Do we want to inform the listener, persuade, exchange friendly greetings? Whatever the purpose, we must have it in mind.

3. *Determine the meaning* we wish to convey to the listener.

Encoding

After the message has been formulated, the encoding process takes over. Encoding is the *process of translating an already conceived idea into a message appropriate for transmission to the listeners.*[21] The speaker creates a message that represents the meaning to be communicated, one that will stimulate similar meaning in the listener's mind.

The encoding process involves selecting symbols that will make up the message. Symbols stand for or represent something. In the communicative process, symbols most likely are the words or nonverbal signals that stand for the idea being talked about.

The symbols chosen must be selected with the listener in mind. If the speaker expects to share meanings, he or she has to adapt the message to the interests and desires of the intended listener. Careful encoding is vital to successful speaking. If the messages we create do not represent our meaning or if they stimulate different meanings in the listener, the interaction will not result in the outcome we desire.

Feedback Adaptation

As the speaker talks, he or she must adjust to the listener's overt responses, whatever these responses may be. If the listener indicates verbally or nonverbally that the message is not being understood, the speaker must take the feedback into account and make adjustments to clarify what is not being understood.

Message

A message is *the information, meanings, and feelings we desire to transmit to our listeners.* A message could be of any length. An hour-long lecture, a fifteen-minute speech, a two-minute statement, or a simple "hello" in greeting can be messages. A message can be *intentional,* delivered purposefully, or *unintentional,* transmitted without the speaker being aware of the communication. A message can be delivered both verbally and nonverbally — *verbally* through the words and language we choose to symbolize our thoughts and *nonverbally* through our physical behavior. A message also can be entirely nonverbal, with our actions speaking for us. Even though we do not speak, we still send messages; our nonverbal behavior transmits them.

We Cannot Not Communicate

The fact that nonverbal behavior can carry messages raises an important principle in communication: We cannot not communicate in the physical presence of someone else. Even though we may not utter a word, we will be communicating. All observable behavior is communication and can be considered a message. No word, manner, or gesture is neutral. Even when we try to act inconspicuously, we are communicating. Choosing to be anonymous by being inconspicuous says something about us. Realizing that we cannot *not* communicate should make us more sensitive to our behavior at all times. When we are with others, we probably reveal far more about ourselves than we appreciate.[22] Communication is inevitable when two or more people are together.

Defining Relationships

Messages do more than transmit information, meanings, and feelings. They also define relationships. Most of us have a wide variety of social affiliations. Included among them are relationships such as those between siblings, friends, fellow students, family, employer and employee, and dozens of others, if we are typical human beings.

We are interested here in two types of relationships because of their impact on communication: complementary and symmetrical relationships. *Complementary relationships* are those that involve high- and low-status persons. One person occupies the superior position, the other the subordinate. The lower-status person defers to the person in the superior position, and this deference appears in the subordinate's messages. We might overhear two people talking and note that one constantly refers to the other as "sir." In that instance, it is not difficult to tell who is superior and who is subordinate.

Symmetrical relationships are those involving people of equal status. We are likely to be more open and self-disclosing when we are conversing with people who are equal to us. With our friends, our messages reveal more of our personal feelings, and certainly we do not address each other as "madam" or "sir!"

Many of our messages are based on how we see our status. If we consider ourselves as equals in a given communication situation, our messages display a symmetrical relationship. If we consider ourselves to be better or inferior, however, our messages are complementary in nature.[23]

Channel

After we as speakers have encoded a message, we can send it to the listeners via a variety of channels. We can speak, write, wave flags, draw pictures, tap telegraph keys, flash lights, release smoke signals, employ sign language, and so on. Because we are interested primarily in oral communication here, the important channel is the one most often used, the voice. And the audible message, as we have said, is complemented by certain visual messages. A smile may accompany a cheery greeting, a frown may go along with an expression of puzzlement, a solemn face with a message of despair, a waving of arms with a football yell. The nonverbal messages of gesturing and physical action naturally accompany the spoken ones.

Noise

As the message moves via the channel to the listeners, it faces many hazards. Familiar to us is the classroom setting in which the teacher talks with the students. Frequently the teacher's spoken message competes with messages of teachers in the neighboring classrooms or with sounds from outside, such as the honking horns, squealing tires, and roaring motors of passing cars and trucks or the boom of low-flying jet airplanes. The teacher's visual message, created by gestures and bodily movements, may suffer a similar fate as poor lighting, overcrowded classrooms, and moving students hinder listeners' views. Such distracting and interfering messages, sounds, and movements are called noise. Noise often leads to message distortion, which prevents ideal meaning transfer from speaker to listeners.

The noise element in communication holds a broader meaning than that of most dictionary definitions. In a dictionary, noise usually is defined as loud shouting, clamor, din, and words to that effect. In communication, the term includes factors in the channel, speaker, and listener that can confuse the message's meaning. Noise is defined as *any factor that interferes with the intended meaning of the message being received by the listeners.*[24]

Channel Noise

We have noted examples of channel noise — the sights, sounds, and other stimuli that draw our attention away from the intended meaning. Loud noises or unusual sights may distract enough so the message is not received as transmitted.

Speaker Noise

Three types of noise occur in the speaker. The first comes from *foggy thinking* about the subject matter under discussion. Often it is caused by lack of knowledge on the subject. The speaker has not prepared and does not know what the subject is all about.

The second type of speaker noise is found in the *encoding process.* It occurs when the speaker knows little or nothing about speech organization, use of language, style of presentation, and forms of evidence and proof. In addition, encoding noise occurs when the speaker knows little about the audience and fails to adapt the message to the listeners' needs and interests.

Speaker noise can be caused also by *physical problems* or *psychological stress.* Physical problems include stuttering, neurogenic and neuromotor disorders, and articulation difficulties. These are best handled by a properly trained speech therapist. Psychological problems, too, require the attention of specialists trained to handle them. Fatigue, stress, and emotional disorders can benefit from expert consultation. All of these physical and psychological difficulties can hamper understanding of messages. They constitute noise.

Listener Noise

The physical and psychological noise that has an impact on the speaker obviously has an effect on the listener as well. The listener's reception of the speaker's intended meaning can be blocked by physical problems, stress, fatigue, and emotional disorders. Poor listening skills also influence message reception. We will deal with them later in this book, with suggested methods for improving listening. At this point, we should be aware that a lack of training in listening can interfere with reception of messages.

A final cause of listener noise is found in the decoding process, which we will take up shortly. The speaker's ideas can be misperceived, causing misinterpretation of what was meant.

The Speaking Situation

Every form of oral communication is conditioned by the situation in which it occurs. Both the physical setting and the social context determine, to a considerable degree, how a message will be received.

Physical Setting

In Chapter 9, "Communicating Nonverbally," we describe in more detail how the physical setting influences the communication process. In this chapter we only point out the setting's impact, and this can be done with several examples.

Reflect on a setting we know well, the classroom. Some seating arrangements facilitate instruction. When listening and note-taking are the techniques the teachers wishes the student to use, the traditional row-and-column seating typical of the lecture hall is appropriate. The students must sit facing the teacher and listen. Interacting orally with their neighbors is difficult. On the other hand, when the teacher would like the whole class to talk, a semicircular or horseshoe arrangement enables this. If

The physical setting influences communication.

small-group discussion is the preferred instructional mode, the seats should be arranged in small circles of five or six chairs. In these ways the teacher can arrange the physical setting to suit the teaching method.

Think about another school circumstance — a meeting between teacher and student. Places in which they would meet include the classroom, hall, or teacher's office. The classroom tends to be seen as neutral territory, not a threatening site for the meeting. The hall is less neutral, informal but a bit more threatening. The office, being the teacher's "territory," is the most threatening and most formal. The meeting's location, therefore, makes a difference. The teacher who talks to the student from behind a desk in a book-lined office gains an advantage not only because of the teacher's superior position but also because of the setting in which the meeting takes place.

Social Context

Perhaps more important in determining how a message will be received is the social context in which the message is presented. Custom and good manners largely determine how we talk to people under a given set of circumstances. At a football game, for example, the teacher should not chastise a recalcitrant student, because it would not be in good taste; this should be done in the privacy of the office. In respect to the bereaved, a funeral is not the time or the place to talk business, to socialize, or to joke.

How we react to a message likewise is influenced by the social context. We cheer and applaud political candidates speaking at a rally but respond with silence to a minister's sermon. At a lecture, even though we might disagree with the speaker, we politely clap, holding our displeasure until later, when we can discuss our reaction personally with the speaker.

Listener

The listener is the receiver of messages. As is the case with the speaker, the listener is conditioned by various factors. The listener receives and responds to the speaker's message conditioned by the knowledge and interest the listener has in the subject, the level of the listener's skills as a listener, and the listener's attitude toward self, the speaker, and the subject.

The listener's role is threefold: message reception, message decoding, and message response.[25] Decoding has implications that require clarification.

Decoding

As the destination of messages, the listener must decode what is heard and seen. Decoding means *translating the messages received into comprehensible information, meanings, and feelings.* Culture plays an essential role in decoding, and we will consider its importance in a later chapter.

The process of decoding has four steps:

1. *Hearing* and seeing the message.

2. *Interpreting* the message to determine what it means.

3. *Evaluating* the message from the listener's point of view. The listener decides whether he or she correctly understands the message, whether he or she agrees with it, and whether the message is good or bad.

4. *Responding* to the message overtly or covertly.

Though the listener may hear or see the message, he or she may not interpret it as the speaker intended. Noise in the channel, speaker, or listener may have distorted the message. This may have a negative influence. The speaker should be aware that messages are easily misinterpreted. Also, much of the decoding process is related to perception, a topic we will discuss at some length in Chapter 5.

Subsequent Thought and Action

Having heard the message and made some sort of response, the listener probably will reflect on what was heard and perhaps take action immediately or sometime in the future. Listening to a used car salesperson, the potential buyer will think about what was said and then purchase or not purchase the car. After listening to a candidate for election, the voter will reflect on what was said and later vote for the candidate or for the opponent.

Feedback

Feedback is a term known to virtually everyone in our society beyond the age of puberty. The average person does not consider "feedback" a highly technical term, and therefore uses it without restraint. The word probably originates from, and is the central process of, cybernetics, a mechanistic theory of self-regulation or control. The very popularity of the term, however, has caused an explosion of meanings and interpretations, and feedback now has a variety of definitions.[26] Our interest in feedback relates to interpersonal communication, so our definition is confined to this area of study.

For our purposes, feedback is *the listener's overt response to the speaker's message.* The response can be verbal or nonverbal. Examples of verbal responses are comments such as: What do you mean? Yes, I see! Could you rephrase that? Like the verbal signs, nonverbal responses such as those of acceptance

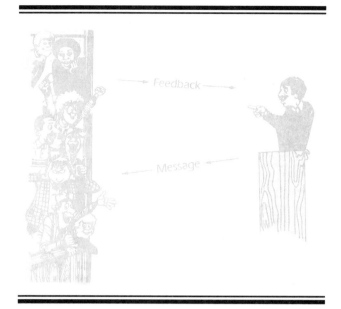

(nods of approval, smiles, applause) and rejection (frowns, inattention, puzzled looks) tell the speaker whether the message has been received and understood. If it has not, the speaker can modify the message to clarify what he or she meant.

When the speaker receives the feedback, he or she takes on dual functions, becoming both speaker and listener. The speaker must decode the listener's feedback just as the listener receives the speaker's message and must decode it. And, just like the listener, the speaker can misinterpret the feedback and respond inappropriately.

Feedback as Regulator

Feedback helps regulate, achieve, and maintain certain constant states that we desire. For example, a teacher provides feedback to students about exam results, to regulate their behavior and to achieve or maintain some desired level of achievement. Likewise, the students give feedback about how tough the exam was to try to keep the exams from becoming too difficult.

In the same way, an employee probably will not come right out and tell the employer that the employer's idea is worthless even though the employee is right. Instead, to achieve or maintain a constant state of goodwill with the boss, the employee is likely to be noncommittal, although he or she may go so far as to suggest something like, "The idea sounds good to me; let's try it out and see if it works." In the manner of the employee, we regulate desired states with others, wanting to achieve or maintain fidelity in our relationship.

Feedback as Reinforcer

Feedback has rewarding and punishing powers. When we reward people, we tend to stabilize the behavior being rewarded. When we punish, we are more likely to reduce or extinguish the behavior. If we are rewarded by positive feedback when we speak, we are apt to continue speaking. If we get negative feedback — being punished in effect — we probably will cut short what we are saying. When we receive no response in the way of feedback, this is called *zero feedback,* which is considered negative.

Effects of Feedback

Feedback has additional effects on our speaking behavior. For instance, negative feedback tends to increase the nonfluencies (ahs, ums, pauses) in most speakers, and positive feedback usually increases fluency. Positive feedback seems to increase the rate of delivery and volume, along with the length of speaking, as we just mentioned.

We respond more favorably to people who give us positive feedback than to those who react negatively to what we say. In a public speaking situation, we direct more talk to those in the audience who respond favorably and less to those who react negatively. As speakers, we feel more positive toward our subject matter when we get positive feedback, strengthening our attitudes and beliefs in what we are saying.[27]

OUTCOMES OF SPEAKING

When we communicate orally with other people, we do so in most cases for the purpose of influencing or changing their behavior in some way. We speak, therefore, to affect with intent. On occasion we speak serendipitously or accidentally. Our interest here, however, is with messages that are purposeful — those we desire to transmit. These sorts of messages have three general purposes or outcomes: utilitarian, aesthetic, and therapeutic.

Utilitarian Messages

The utilitarian outcome refers *to practical accomplishments that benefit us.* We want our listeners to do what we ask. The importance attached to speech communication comes largely from this practical emphasis. Speech is one of the primary tools at our disposal to manipulate, control, and understand our environment. For example the mealtime message "please pass the butter" is utilitarian. The message has a practical purpose: to get the butter. Moreover, it is of benefit to the speaker. The message will save that person the trouble of getting up to get the butter or of reaching for it. Through the message, the speaker manipulates the listener and obtains the listener's help in getting the butter.

Much of our daily talk is practical in nature. Our conversations with friends often deal with topics that we hope will lead to useful results. Other communication situations with practical purposes include the lawyer's defense of the client, the teacher's explanation of a class assignment, and the customer's discussion of an article's price with a storekeeper.

Most public speeches are utilitarian. Speakers attempt to influence their audience's behavior. Public speeches such as campaign talks, sermons, sales speeches, lectures, and presidential addresses have a utilitarian intent. The speakers seek to influence or change the opinions of their audiences. Political candidates making campaign speeches want to get elected to office. Ministers would like to strengthen the religious beliefs of their parishioners. Salespeople hope to sell their products and increase their income.

Aesthetic Messages

The aesthetic outcome *relates to the enjoyment, pleasure, or entertainment* that speakers may transmit to listeners by their messages. Reading aloud, storytelling, acting, and other forms of artistic expression use speech communication as a tool to create pleasure. Public speeches can entertain listeners as well.

Therapeutic Messages

The therapeutic outcome *relates to speech communication as a tool to treat inhibitions, diagnose problems, or re-establish communicative personalities.* Speech becomes therapy when it permits us to release our tensions, to explore personality problems that affect our ability to talk normally with others, and to rehabilitate the voice mechanism. This sort of communication is best carried on in the presence of a trained therapist — psychiatrist, social worker, physician, or speech clinician — who is prepared to handle the extremes in behavior that could occur when tensions are released or personal problems are discussed.[28]

FUNCTIONS OF ORAL COMMUNICATION

The major uses of oral communication in social life can be classified according to five functions: controlling, expressing feelings, informing, ritualizing, and imagining.

Controlling

Many occasions arise each day in which we attempt to control the behavior of others. We command, suggest, bargain, contract, persuade, and argue to get other people to believe or behave as we would have them believe or behave. Similarly, we receive numerous messages attempting to fulfill the same purpose.

A basic way of controlling other people's behavior is by using the *imperative* form of language. We make simple *commands or requests* of others: Sit down! Keep quiet! Open the door! Come here! *Invitations* also can be used to control: Please come in! Will you take the garbage out? *Offers* can be used to control: Have a doughnut? Care for a soda? *Suggestions* may serve to control as well: Let's go to the dance tonight! I suggest doing it this way.

The most complex way to control is through *argument*. In argument, the speaker uses evidence and reasoning to attempt to convince listeners to respond as the speaker desires. Note how evidence supports the reasonableness of this position:

> When asked why I don't buy American-made cars, I cite the facts. *Consumer Reports* has a monthly listing of recalls of cars for mechanical problems. Each month a half dozen recalls are given, involving thousands upon thousands of cars — all American-made. In the course of a year, almost every American car manufacturer has recalls. It is rare to find a foreign car listed. The local consumer protection association confirms these reports, as does the leading automobile association.

Expressing Feelings

Speech is used to share feelings of joy, surprise, anger, disappointment, love, respect, and concern. Speech can cause us to smile or to be sad. Through speech, we can express our sympathy to someone who is ill, our anxiety about our own health, and our concern for the health of others. We can tell when a friend or relative is cheerful, content, or happy by the way he or she speaks. A person in ill humor can communicate that feeling to others verbally and nonverbally.

Informing

Through the informing function, we communicate to share information in speech acts such as naming, defining, describing, and giving directions. Listeners ask questions, follow directions, summarize, clarify, and organize ideas as they seek to process the informative messages they encounter each day.

Informing involves providing others with information they would not know unless they were told. To be informing, something "new" must be said to the listener. The "I've got something to tell you" function is what teachers perform when they lecture, describe assignments, or lead discussions. Students employ the informing function when they ask or answer questions. Thus, informing encompasses both speaking and listening, as well as both seeking and delivering information.

Ritualizing

When we greet one another, we ritualize — take leave appropriately, banter, joke, take turns in conversation, and otherwise engage one another in socially appropriate and conventional ways. The ritualizing function has as its parameters those acts of speech that maintain social relationships and facilitate social interaction. In the morning upon arising, we greet those around us with "good morning." Passing friends and acquaintances, we extend a "hi!" or "hello — how are you?" We introduce ourselves to newcomers with a handshake and words of introduction. Departing, we acknowledge our leave-taking with "goodbye." Going to bed, we wish everyone around us a "good night."

Imagining

When we daydream outloud, fantasize, speculate, role-play, dramatize, and theorize about life as it is or might be, we are imagining. Imagining can help us see options.[29] We can speculate with others about how to do something:

> How might this work out?
>
> Given these notions, what might be expected to happen next?

◆ Or it can be used to help uncover relationships:

> What does this make you think of?
>
> What is it like?

◆ Or imagining can be used to gain insights through inferring and speculating:

> What might have caused it to happen? What could we predict will occur next, knowing what we know?
>
> Which suggestion do you think will be most promising?

◆ Or it can be used to take hypothetical leaps:

> Should this happen, what would you do?
>
> If that happened, what would you do?

SUMMARY

Speaker, encoding, message, channel, noise, situation, listener, decoding, and feedback are the fundamental elements of every speaking transaction, be it dyadic, small-group, or a form of public speaking. Oral communication as a process is an ongoing, ever-changing, continuous activity in which all of the elements interact with one another to produce meaning. To examine each essential element, in this chapter we "froze" the action, or stopped the process and analyzed each element as though it were a part of a static entity. But speech is not a static concept. Between and among the elements is continuous interplay — an influencing and a counter-influencing, a shaping and a reshaping.

The speaker's background, personality, and experience, together with the channel and the setting, influence the message's content, structure, and style. Whether the listeners understand and respond as the speaker desires depends upon their backgrounds, personalities and experiences, noise, and the setting. In turn, the listener's feedback influences the way subsequent portions of the speaker's message are presented. When a listener encodes a message in response to that of the speaker, the listener reverses the whole speech communication process. The originating speaker becomes the listener, and the responding listener becomes the new speaker. Thus, dynamic interaction is occurring when people talk together — interaction that is systemic, adaptive, continuous, transactional, and irreversible.

We communicate because communicating is a fundamental part of life. Living is largely a matter of communication, so we should be successful at it. Being skilled oral communicators should help us grow personally, develop socially, and act cooperatively as we go about the daily business of living.

LEARNING CHECK

The following statements relate to information presented in this book so far. The slash in each statement separates the possibilities. Circle the one that will make the statement correct. The answers are on page 243.

1. The speaker is always/usually a message's source.

2. Zero feedback is considered positive/negative.

3. Complementary/symmetrical relationships involve high- and low-status persons.

4. Intrapersonal/interpersonal talk involves two or more people.

5. Translating an already conceived idea into a message is decoding/encoding.

6. Therapeutic/aesthetic speaking relates to enjoyment.

7. Low-flying airplanes/foggy thinking is speaker noise.

8. Speech is irreversible/reversible.

9. The communication model of Aristotle/Schramm is linear.

10. Communications/communication refers to the exchange of messages via radio.

Types of
Oral Communication

Our focus in this book is on the process of communication, a process that permits people to initiate, establish, and maintain relationships with other people by sharing information, meanings, and feelings. When we want to interact with others, we use three types of oral communication, relational in nature: person-to-person, small-group, and public communication.[1] Accompanying each type are methods and a system of principles that we can learn and apply in the oral situations encountered in life.

Although these methods and principles are our major concern, at this juncture our interest centers on the three types of communication. Each has distinctive characteristics, which are explained in the following descriptions of the three types.

PERSON-TO-PERSON COMMUNICATION

Person-to-person, a form of interpersonal communication, involves two people (a dyad), each of whom accepts the other as the principal center of attention and responds to the other simultaneously to influence and be influenced. One person's communicative behavior is a direct consequence of the other person's behavior. Interpersonal communication is *focused interaction, implying concentrated mutual attention.* The messages that are exchanged may be either verbal or nonverbal.[2]

The person-to-person relationship is the smallest unit of oral communication, and it is indivisible. If

Types of Oral Communication

Person-to-person   Small Group   Public Speaking
(Interpersonal Speech)

one person drops out, the relationship no longer exists. Two people are necessary to maintain it.[3]

Figure 2.5, in the previous chapter, shows the dyadic, person-to-person relationship and the essential elements that constitute this type of oral communication. We already reviewed those elements, so let us now consider the three forms of person-to-person speaking: conversation, dialogue, and interview. Each varies in *seriousness, purposiveness, and intimacy*.[4]

Conversation

The talk of everyday, commonplace social experience, conversation fulfills important functions. Because it is the friendly and informal exchange of feelings, observations, opinions, and ideas, conversation serves to establish and maintain relationships with other people. It is a friendly recognition that the other person is present and helps to open or keep open the channels of communication. Although conversation is less serious, less purposive, and less intimate than the other two types, it is going on almost everywhere — home, school, work, and play. Conversations seem to be endless.

Phatic Communion

Much of our conversation tends to be mundane and simplistic, cliche sorts of talk. This shallow, superficial form of conversation is called phatic communion. It performs ritualistic functions, maintaining social relationships and facilitating social interaction. It seems to be necessary for the development of later, more intimate communication.[5]

Phatic communion usually is platitudinous. While walking to class, for instance, we run into a friend and greet the person with "Hi! How're you doing?" The friend replies, "Great! It's a nice day!" We then continue on our way to class, concluding the conversation. That conversation consisted of platitudes, an exchange of common pleasantries to communicate simple recognition rather than specific meaning. We do not expect the friend to stop and tell us what is happening. The friend recognizes this and does not stop.[6]

Phatic communion is a method for opening up conversations. Questions such as, "Where are you from?" "What are you majoring in?" "Where did you go to school?" and the answers to those questions serve as conversational openers. They "break the ice" and provide an entre to more substantive interaction.

Beyond Phatic

Moving on to the next level of conversation, we engage in fewer banalities and converse on a subject that is stimulating and perhaps provocative to us. We talk about our ideas and reveal something about our judgments and decisions. We share our reactions with our conversational partner, relating our thoughts and feelings about what the other person has said or done. The subject matter carries value and has substance even though the talk involves no specific purpose other than establishing or maintaining friendly relations.[7]

> Good conversation is characterized by an exchange of ideas and opinions about one or several subjects of significance to both parties. It is used as a means of creating or continuing an amicable association.[8]

Dialogue

In contrast to conversation, which is informal, friendly, and purposeless, dialogue is intimate, usually serious, and purposive. It *aims at achieving understanding and appreciation*. Persuasion is absent as the two people who participate share their feelings and emotions in the language of intimacy, talking about who they are, what they think, and how they feel. The self is entrusted to the other, in confidence and faith, as both explore deep, intimate, and personal relationships.[9] In dialogue, the partners want only to understand each other as completely as they can, to be able to say, without reservation: "I hear you; I share your feelings; I feel it with you." Empathizing in this manner requires each to move out of his or her own view and see things as the other person sees them. A willingness to be open, to listen, and to reveal themselves is necessary for the persons involved in dialogue.[10]

Trust and Understanding

Dialogue consists of an understanding and deep trust of oneself and of the other person. It also requires explicit message-sending and empathic listening — message-sending that is not ambiguous or based on ulterior motives and listening that captures the meanings and feelings the speaker intends.[11] In a dialogue, the participants have to understand their own thoughts and feelings so well that when they are in the company of each other, they can behave like they really are. Because they know and accept themselves, they are in a position to get to know the other as that person really is. The increased understanding of each other helps the two appreciate each other's joys, sorrows, attitudes, and values, and it results in a deep, meaningful relationship.

To make the relationship happen, the partners in dialogue say what they mean and mean what they say; they are explicit in their messages. When they trust themselves as persons, their defense mechanisms no longer hinder what they say and no longer prevent them from hearing what the other is really saying. Thus, they can listen with empathy. Whenever a person fails to be open, a crisis could develop. The ultimate test of dialogue is the ability of both parties to continue to listen and respond to each other when differences appear.[12]

Training or Therapeutic Uses

Dialogue as a form of communicative interaction plays a part occasionally in sensitivity training and therapeutic encounters.[13] The individual meets with a trainer or counselor in a "no exit"-type situation. The person cannot leave but must face himself or herself and the counselor without benefit of the masks behind which he or she ordinarily hides. The person is encouraged to express his or her true feelings to increase self-insight and self-knowledge. The result often is a highly emotional experience and, because this is so, the trainer or counselor has to be well-trained, skilled in the methodology, and possess a requisite understanding of human behavior.

Interview

Of the three types of person-to-person speaking, the interview is the most serious and purposive. The typical interview, however, does not carry the high level of intimacy characteristic of the dialogue, and it tends to be more formal and businesslike than both conversation and dialogue.

Whereas conversation and dialogue are freewheeling, with unstructured, back-and-forth talk, the interview is much more patterned. The interviewer determines the purpose, poses questions that may be partially or completely prepared in advance, and decides what answers achieve the purpose. The interviewee, on the other hand, may choose to accept the purpose and answer the question, or may not. The interviewee has the right not to be interviewed.[14]

Stated more formally, the interview is conceptualized as a dyadic communication system in which one of the participants, the interviewer, has as the major objective to obtain information from the other participant, the interviewee.[15] Our definition capsulizes the interview's nature. For us, an interview is *a dynamic interaction between two parties, interviewer and interviewee, who meet to fulfill a predetermined purpose of one or both parties, using questions and answers as the means of achieving the purpose.*[16]

Types of Interviewing

Employment interviews probably rank as the most significant in people's lives. Yet, in an average person's lifetime, these interviews are rare. Other types are more common and, for some people, interviewing is a routine part of the day.

Among the types of interviews are information-gathering interviews (surveys, polls, police investigations), medical interviews, research interviews, journalistic interviews, and insurance investigations. Information-giving interviews include orientation, training, and instructional interviews. Other interviews deal with problems of the interviewee's behavior: appraisal, discipline, counseling, and reprimand interviews. Still other types of interviews involve complaints and grievances. And there are sales interviews, in which products and services are sold.[17]

Components of Interviewing

Each of the types of interviewing has four components. The interaction is *purposeful, two parties are involved, questioning is used, and status differences occur.*

Purposeful Interaction. Interviews have a common feature: At least one of the parties has a reason for meeting with the other. Thus, the meeting has a purpose. And talk taking place is directed to achieving the purpose.

An interview is not an isolated act of communication. It usually is part of a larger process or a stage in a sequence of events. As examples: the medical interview is part of the process of diagnosis and treatment; the news interview is a stage in gathering and disseminating information; the employment interview is a step in the process of hiring employees; a courtroom interrogation is a phase of the process of accusation or defense. The interview always is related to some purpose, and its function is to serve that purpose.[18]

Two-Party Participation. Another characteristic of interviewing is that more than two people can be present, although only two parties, *interviewer* and *interviewee*, participate. For instance, husband and wife might interview their child's teacher about the child's progress. In that case, the husband and wife dyad is the interviewing party and the teacher is the interviewee. Or several detectives interrogate a suspect, in which case the detectives comprise the interviewer and the suspect is the interviewee. Or a faculty committee interviews a candidate for graduate school, in which case the committee is the interviewer. In each example, more than two people are present, but the only two parties are the interviewer and the interviewee.[19]

Questioning. The primary means of interaction between the two parties is asking and answering questions. Questions are important tools to get the answers required in many decision-making situations. Questions are used to get information, obtain involvement, stimulate thought and creativity, redirect thinking, clarify, amplify, establish rapport, criticize, identify needs, persuade, and obtain truth, among a host of others.[20]

Questions are of various types, each of which has a specific purpose. We describe the types when discussing how to conduct interviews, in Chapter 13.

Differences in Status. Despite the interactional character of the interview process, status or power differences typically appear as the two parties fulfill their roles. An example of this interviewing characteristic is when a teacher interviews a student. The power and status in this superior/subordinate relationship favors the teacher. Often intimidated by the relationship, a student tends to be guarded. Comments the student would make without reservation to friends become tentative, distorted, or withheld entirely in the teacher's presence. Perhaps the student fears teacher reprisal or punitive action and holds back accordingly.

In many other interviewing situations, too, the role barriers between interviewer and interviewee can result in guarded replies and distorted information. Consequently, the interviewer must recognize his or her authority and its effect on the interviewee and take action to minimize the imbalance.[21]

SMALL-GROUP COMMUNICATION

Much of our interpersonal social interaction takes place in small groups, that are casual gatherings of friends and acquaintances. Here we are interested in groups that come together for more serious reasons. Members are drawn to these groups to accomplish a common purpose or to reach a mutually acceptable goal. The members work together on a joint activity or project. Our interest centers, therefore, on learning, problem-solving, and action types of groups.

Because these groups are made up of three or more people, by our definition, the communication process takes on added complexity. Figure 3.1 presents a model of communication with a group of three. The interaction shown is more intricate than that depicted in the interpersonal communication model shown in Chapter 2 (Figure 2.5). Adding more people increases the interaction's complexity. In Figure 3.2 two more people are added and, in doing so, the number of feedback loops (the arrows between the members) doubles, suggesting a more complicated process of communication.

In examining the two figures, we have to recognize their lack of detail. Missing from the figures are

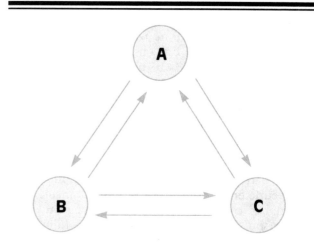

FIGURE 3.1   Model of communication for group of three.

the essential elements of the communication process found in the Chapter 2 interpersonal model. If we had provided those details in Figures 3.1 and 3.2, they would have become unmanageable for reproduction purposes. Keep in mind, therefore, that each exchange between a group's members involves the same elements and interrelationships shown in the Chapter 2 model. These elements are part of the small-group process just as they are part of the interpersonal process.

Figure 3.2, the model of communication for a group of five, has a series of broken arrows pointing toward the center of the group. These arrows signify that in small groups the members generally speak to

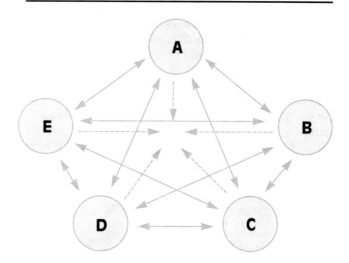

FIGURE 3.2   Model of communication for group of five.

the group at large. They direct their talk to all of the members, sharing their ideas with each other. Individual members can speak to each other, of course. We often see this in small-group interaction, depicted by the many feedback loops in Figure 3.2. The better course of action, however, is to talk to all of the members during group deliberations.

Nature of the Small Group

What is a small group? It has literally dozens of definitions. The psychologist, sociologist, social psychologist, and communication theorist define the small group from their respective frames of reference, making all the definitions slightly different. Each has its merits, and each meets the needs of the specific field of study. Our definition best suits our purposes. For us, *the small group consists of three or more people in physical proximity who dynamically interact orally about a common concern.*[22] By breaking up the definition into its major components and examining each, we can obtain a better understanding of the nature of the small group.

Three or More People

The minimum number of members is three. With two individuals, we have a dyadic relationship to which the principles of interpersonal communication apply. The maximum number is hard to establish because groups of as many as twenty people have functioned effectively. As the membership increases, fruitful interaction becomes increasingly difficult, however. Communication channels multiply as the group size becomes larger, and communication grows in complexity. The power structure changes, and cliques tend to form. With more people, face-to-face talk diminishes and the members have trouble seeing and hearing each other. The ideal small group is around five people, because groups of that size allow for direct face-to-face communication. Also, they provide fewer occasions for the formation of cliques, which tend to hinder productivity and member satisfaction.[23]

Physical Proximity

Members of a group have to be physically near each other. This physical closeness eliminates from consideration the sort of communication in which a mechanical device is used, because that prevents members from freely interacting with each other. Conference calls on the telephone or via a television hook-up allow a number of people to converse. They can hear and, in the video arrangements, see each other. But these devices restrict the unlimited interaction that characterizes a group of people meeting face-to-face.

Oral Interaction

Figure 3.1 illustrates the give-and-take communication typical of group deliberation. Group members play the dual roles of speaker and listener. One speaks and the others listen. Then someone else talks. And so it goes, back and forth, with the roles shifting among members. The interaction is primarily oral, but our use of the term "speech" or "oral communication" includes not only the vocalization of sounds patterned as words but also the nonverbal actions that support the oral message and the actions that may stand for an oral message. That interpretation should be kept in mind at this point, as our use of "oral" in relation to the small group carries the same meaning.

Common Concern

Our final point about the definition ought to be clear by now: To be a small group as we define it, three or more people have to be interested in a common problem, subject, or task. They are united in their desire to arrive at a satisfactory solution to the problem, to learn, or to complete the task. They have a common reason for meeting.[24]

Contrast that purposeful interaction with the talk of a small number of students waiting for a class to begin. They utter banalities about the weather, an assignment, the instructor, or whatever. The talk tends to be aimless; there is little reciprocal exchange over mutual problems. This is not a group, just a collection of a few students killing time until the instructor arrives.

Lest we have created a false impression about small groups, we emphasize that small groups do not result solely from bringing together a few individuals who are given a problem to solve or a task to do. There are many kinds of groups, and they vary in terms of their purpose or goals. The typical small group goes through a series of stages of phases of development that could involve considerable time. Small groups don't just happen. So we need to learn more about small groups and, to do so, we review what kinds of groups exist and then how groups develop.

Kinds of Groups

Our society has countless kinds of groups: athletic, business, educational, military, professional, political, religious, and scientific, among others. For purposes of study and analysis, these groups have been classified in many ways. One of the ways, *group goals*, is most useful for our purposes.

According to the group goal way of classifying groups, they are categorized into casual, learning, therapeutic, problem-solving and action groups.[25]

When we gather to develop, maintain, and expand friendships — for example, at parties, coffee breaks, and social engagements — we are in a *casual or social group*. When we meet to acquire, explain, or share information, we are part of a *learning group*. Those of us who are unable to handle personal problems such as alcoholism, drug addiction, marital difficulties, and a host of similar difficulties can turn to a *therapy group* organized to help people through these crises. In school, at work, and in community associations, we often are called upon to solve problems. When we meet with others to do so, we are part of a *problem-solving group*. An *action group* carries out the policies or decision made by a problem-solving group.

Many groups have a combination of goals. A committee, for instance, may have been organized primarily to solve a problem of some sort. In the process of doing so, the members might have to learn about the problem. Thus, for a time they are a learning group. At the beginning of their meetings, they likely function as a casual kind of group, chatting about matters unrelated to the problem they are trying to solve. Permanent groups such as service clubs, church groups, and fraternities, to name just three, usually combine goals, serving the members in a variety of ways as they socialize, learn, and work together.

In school the learning group is a major force, although all five group types function in the school setting. Learning groups meet regularly as parts of classes or laboratories, and informally when groups of students get together on their own to prepare for examinations or to complete class projects. Of course, the learning group is not restricted to schools. Learning groups meet in a variety of settings and affect people of any age.

In all phases of life, the problem-solving group assumes a large role. Whenever people gather to seek solutions to problems, or to make decisions about common concerns, the group problem-solving process can be utilized. In actuality, most people work in institutions or organizations that use problem-solving groups. Because the learning group and the problem-solving group play such major roles in life, we would do well to learn more about them. Later, in Chapter 15, we will do just that as we examine both kinds of groups in detail.

The five kinds of groups classified by group goal can be categorized further as either temporary or permanent and as either private or public. *Temporary* groups meet to accomplish a specific task. After the job is done, they disband. *Permanent* groups remain in existence for many years, or indefinitely. The membership changes, but the groups continue. *Private* groups meet without the presence of outsiders. Nobody except the members themselves attend the meetings. *Public* groups meet in the presence of other people. Members' interactions are on public display at they are observed and heard by the other people in the meeting place.[26]

Group Development

What happens when a collection of individuals first meets? For the typical group to come into existence, it must go through a series of phases or stages of development, which move through time in a definite order. The group must pass through the first phase before it reaches the second, the second before reaching the third, and so forth. The phases, however, are not distinct. Rather, the progression from phase to phase reflects a continuous and gradual change of behavior in the group. Also, the progression may be blocked from time to time, and the group may get stalled in a particular phase. Or regression might occur and the group has to go back and cover old ground again. Nevertheless, the phases consistently appear in most groups — especially the learning and problem-solving ones. We have labeled these phases orientation, emotional-response, discussion, and solution-emergence.

Orientation Phase

When people meet for the first time, they have not yet become a group. Relationships have not been formed, and channels of communication have not been established. The potential members wonder about the group's purpose, what will be required, and how this will affect them. Hence, most people enter a new group situation with a sense of bewilderment, confusion, tension, and anxiety about what will happen. Probably many people also enter the group with feelings of enthusiasm, interest, and desire to meet and do what is to be done. They anticipate making new acquaintances or renewing old friendships and gaining new knowledge.

In the first phase of the group's development, orientation, the members discover what they have to do, who the other members are, and what kinds of behavior are permitted. They begin to adjust to the new situation. Typically, the members have two major concerns: (a) *task*, related to the job they are undertaking, and (b) *maintenance*, related to maintaining group harmony and group behavior. The *task* concerns the members have at this stage are along these lines:

◆ What is the group's purpose?

◆ How do the members communicate? Should the members address only the leader, or can they talk freely among themselves?

◆ How are decisions reached? By majority vote? By concensus? By the leader?

◆ Under what rules and procedures do the members operate?

◆ Will the group atmosphere be democratic or autocratic?

◆ Will a few members dominate the discussion, or will all have a chance to talk?

The members' *maintenance* concerns are likely to be much like these:

◆ How will I be accepted in the group? Will the others listen to me? Will the power be shared?

◆ Will I be perceived as effective or ineffective, knowledgeable or not?

◆ What sort of behavior is expected? Can I have fun and enjoy myself, or am I supposed to be serious and concentrate entirely on the job?

◆ How do the members feel about attending the meetings? With anticipation or reluctance?

◆ What feelings should I have toward the others? Should I be warm and friendly or cold and businesslike?

During this phase the members tend to rely heavily on the chairperson or convener for direction and guidance as they try to find out what to do.

Emotional-Response Phase

The second phase begins when the members have clarified what they are to do. Usually they react emotionally to the task demands; hence, this is called the emotional-response phase. Their reactions may be positive if the task is comparatively simple or it could be negative if the task is difficult, requiring much time and energy.

Tension and hostility appear frequently in this stage, as ego-centered behavior is prevalent. Arguments may develop over minor points. Group morale often sags as differences appear between and among members. Personal feelings surface as the members jockey for power and fight for their way.

Discussion Phase

In the third phase, discussion, the group begins to regain its composure and deal with the task more sensibly. Members gain relevant information and share this with the others, assessing it in terms of adequacy and practicality for the task at hand. Total membership participation is encouraged, and the members start to become group-centered as the self-centeredness of the previous stages starts to disappear. The members want to become more cohesive, so they promote harmony. They discuss following an orderly, intellectual process and engage in active, cooperative participation.

Solution-Emergence Phase

In the final, solution-emergence phase, the task is completed, the problem is solved, or the goal is reached. The members have laid aside their differences, and unity prevails. For the most part, members exhibit favorable attitudes toward each other and are pleased with the results of their deliberation.

At this time, a temporary group usually disbands because the task the members were called together to do is done. With a permanent group the situation is different. Because a permanent group is ongoing, the members seem to go through the phases again and again as the group confronts new challenges or has different jobs to do. Each time the permanent group's members do face a new challenge, they should be able to handle it with greater efficiency and effectiveness, but this is not always the case. Even though the group continues, the membership changes periodically as older members drop out and new members replace them. And the members themselves change. Their personal expectations are altered over time. They may no longer desire what they wanted previously. The result is that the typical permanent group is a dynamic entity, ongoing yet ever-changing.

Phases of Group Development

Orientation		Emotional-Response		Discussion		Solution-Emergence
What are we supposed to do?	→	Tension and hostility may surface	→	Talk about problem and become group-centered	→	Solve problem

Prevalence in Society

The trend toward small-group interaction continues. Business and professions are holding more and more staff and committee meetings. Increasing numbers of conferences and workshops are taking up a significant amount of time. Family, neighborhood, church, school, club, and social groups are still growing in numbers. Some agencies, such as those found in city, county, state, and federal governments, are turning to citizen committees for counsel and guidance.

Interest in group activities is increasing because of:

— the trend toward a more socially interacting school and work climate;

— the trend in business and industry toward more employee participation in matters pertaining to employees;

— the growing practice of governmental agencies' consulting with citizens who are affected by governmental decisions;

— increased reliance on group decision making by those who supervise others;

— a greater focus on democratic management in many social, political, and industrial organizations.[28]

Undoubtedly federal regulations aimed at protecting the environment and people's health and welfare constitute no small factor in the escalating numbers and types of meetings and conferences. Whatever the reasons, meetings requiring small-group interaction of all kinds are on the rise.

PUBLIC SPEAKING

In public speaking, a single speaker, using a comparatively formal tone and manner, presents a continuous discourse on a subject supposedly of interest to a sizable number of other people.[29] This definition suggests that public speaking flows in a fixed pattern from speaker to listeners, as Figure 3.3 depicts. It is a linear, "I-talk-to-you" approach to communicative interaction in which one person talks to many.

Distinctive Features

Certain features of public speaking (public communication or public address) show how it differs from the interpersonal types.[30]

Physical Separation

In public speaking the *speaker and the listeners are physically separated.* The speaker normally stands in front of the listeners some feet away from the first row. On occasion he or she may be positioned behind a speaker's stand or a table, which serves as a barrier between the speaker and the listeners. Usually the room or auditorium is arranged in row-and-column seating, an arrangement that forces the listeners to face the speaker and also restricts the ability of the listeners to look at or interact with each other. Interpersonal settings offer no such barriers or restrictions.

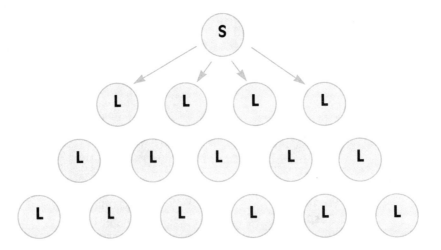

S = SPEAKER   L = LISTENER

FIGURE 3.3 Public speaking.

Psychological Distance

In public speaking a *psychological distance often develops between the speaker and the listeners*. Because of the speaker's special knowledge of the subject, he or she may be seen as an expert, a bit better than the listeners. Or the listeners may perceive the speaker as a person of authority, power, prestige, or fame. That perception also creates psychological distance.

Defined Speaking Time

In interpersonal small-group situations few restrictions are imposed on a speaker's speaking time. A speaker can talk as long as he or she wants — albeit the speeches ordinarily are brief. The public speaker, in contrast, usually is *allotted a specific amount of time* and is expected to stay within the imposed limit. In any case, it is long in comparison to the time speakers consume in dyadic and small-group situations. Public speeches might range from five to ten minutes for a brief report to an hour for a lecture.

Prestructured Message

Typically, the *public speech is tailored to fit the audience* and the occasion and is carefully planned and developed beforehand. The speaker comes with speech in hand and delivers it pretty much as planned. He or she has a definite purpose for speaking and a specific subject. The content, language, and organization are built around the purpose and subject.[31]

Fixed Roles

In public speaking the *speaker and listener roles are fixed* and remain stable throughout the talk. The speaker speaks, and the listeners listen. Yet, limited interaction does occur. The listeners can have an impact on the speaker through their feedback. Their grins, grimaces, puzzled faces, applause, cheers, groans, or boos convey their feelings, and this non-verbal feedback can affect the way the speaker presents subsequent portions of the speech. Therefore, the relationship between speaker and listeners is rarely static. It is dynamic, hardly one-dimensional or one-sided in the speaker's favor. Although it usually is reciprocal and multidirectional, it is not to the extent found in interpersonal interaction. In public speaking the opportunities are few for speaker and listeners to share knowledge and explore ideas together.[32]

Formal Atmosphere

A formal atmosphere characterizes the public speaking situation. With physical and psychological distances between speaker and listeners, specific time limits, prestructured message, and fixed roles, the intimacy and informality of interpersonal interaction is absent in public speaking.[33]

Sizable Audience

The number of listeners is another reason why channel sharing between speaker and listeners is not possible, and this adds to the situation's formality. The public speech is designed to influence many people, and the typical audience is sizable. The exact number varies, depending upon factors such as who speaks, where and when the speech is given, and who is expected. A political rally in a large auditorium might attract thousands, whereas a teacher's lecture will draw only the students enrolled in the class. In any case, the public speech does not lend itself to mutual exploration of ideas between speaker and listeners.[34]

Purposes of Speeches

We have said that public communication presents opportunities to influence a goodly number of people at one time. So it is a significant activity even though the average person does not spend as much time at it as he or she spends interacting orally in dyads or groups. Nonetheless, public presentations are by no means unimportant or uncommon. Within and between business, governmental, industrial, and professional organizations and groups, public speaking abounds. Speeches are made at meetings of fellow workers or colleagues at conventions and community meetings for informational, persuasive, or public relations purposes. Because these speeches often are presented to people who have control over speakers' destinies, the stakes are high more frequently than not. An idea accepted or rejected, a product sold or not, could mean the difference between success and failure for the speaker.

Kinds of Speeches

Selling ideas and products is a prominent reason for public speaking, but many other kinds of speeches exist. These include specialized ones such as speeches of introduction, welcome, commemoration, acceptance, tribute, after-dinner, memorial, farewell, and nomination — which the average member of a business, professional, social, political, or religious group will give once or twice in a lifetime. More often we hear, and perhaps deliver, briefings, oral reports, training talks, lectures, sermons, legislative addresses, and political speeches.

Speech Classifications

Regardless of the kind of speech, each has an overall purpose: to influence listeners' behavior by sharing information, meaning, and feeling. A speaker can go about fulfilling this purpose in a variety of ways. Perhaps the speaker wants the listeners to understand his or her ideas, or to take action and carry out the ideas, or to have a good time by being entertained. Speeches can have many possible ends or goals. The purpose remains constant; the ends differ.

In attempts to classify the ends or goals logically, scholars have judged many, many speeches over the years. Numerous systems have resulted. We elaborate on one that categorizes speeches by three general classes: to inform, to persuade, and to actuate.[35]

Speaking to Inform

Rarely does a school day go by when students are not exposed to informative speaking. The teacher's lectures are designed to dispense information, to broaden the student's understanding of a subject, be it mathematics, history, or speech. The central purpose is to provide students with information needed to understand an idea or concept. The teacher supplies the necessary data, examples, and other details to make the message clear and comprehensible.

Of course, teachers are not the only disseminators of information. Anyone who attempts to *widen the listener's range of knowledge* speaks to inform. The sales manager briefing the sales staff on the features of a new product is informing, as is the researcher acquainting doctors with a new medicine, the agricultural agent explaining to farmers how to gain maximum production, and the consumer affairs specialist advising people how to judge the value of products they buy.[36]

Speaking to Persuade

Speeches classified as persuasive have as their general goal a desire *to alter the direction, intensity, or salience of listeners' attitudes toward the speaker's subject.*[37] Many speeches have this general goal. Spokespersons for the Republican and Democratic parties urge the people to believe in their respective platform and the party's achievements; ministers ask their parishioners to dedicate their lives to a particular faith; salespeople try to develop interest in their products; philosophers debate the pros and cons of the world's great issues. In each case, the speakers are attempting to gain the listener's agreement or acceptance of their point of view. In speaking to persuade, the speaker is asking the listeners to take some sort of overt action (go to the polls and vote, buy product Q, join fraternity XYZ).

The definition's phrase, "alter the direction, intensity, or salience of listeners' attitudes toward the speaker's subject," deserves further explanation because the terms have technical meanings.[38] An *attitude* is a person's predisposition to behave in a certain way in response to something in the surrounding world. We have attitudes toward virtually everything we know about in the world and, when we perceive something new, we are likely to form an attitude about it. Persuasive speakers may want to change an attitude's *direction, intensity,* or *salience* in the listener's mind.

An attitude's *direction* will be favorable, unfavorable, or neutral. If the listener's attitude is unfavorable toward the subject, the speaker attempts to move it in a neutral or favorable direction; if it is neutral, the speaker tries for a more favorable direction.

An attitude's *intensity* refers to strength, and strength is thought of in terms of degree on a strong-to-weak continuum. If the listener's attitude is weak, the speaker attempts to strengthen it.

Salience refers to the perceived importance of an attitude toward a listener. It, too, ranges along a continuum — in this case, from very important to unimportant. The speaker tries to increase the importance in the listener's mind through the speech.

Speaking to Actuate

When the speaker wants the listeners *to perform a definite overt act,* the speaker is aiming to actuate.[39] The action may be to buy a product, vote for a candidate, take a vacation at a specified resort, contribute money, buy bonds, or whatever sort of physical action the speaker calls for. Thus, the actuation speech goes beyond the persuasive one because the speaker requests the listeners to perform some specific act at a stated time and place. The speech to actuate may have to include the persuasive elements when the listeners are not convinced they need to act. Thus, persuasion may be a necessary step

The Three General Aims of Public Speaking

General Aim	Response Desired
1. To inform	Widen listener's range of knowledge
2. To persuade	Change direction, salience, intensity of attitudes
3. To actuate	Perform a definite act

toward action. We treat speeches to persuade and actuate as one, calling both persuasive speeches.

SUMMARY

We use speech to initiate, establish, and maintain relationships with others, and, in doing so, we engage in person-to-person, small-group, and public communication. Each has characterizing qualities and conditions that determine its use.

Person-to-person communication involves two people, alternating in the speaker and listener roles, who participate in face-to-face talk because of their shared desire to converse, conduct a dialogue, or enter into an interview. Intimacy, purposiveness, and seriousness differentiate each kind. Conversation tends to be less intimate, purposeful, and serious than the other two, and dialogue is more intimate but less purposeful and serious than interviewing — the process in which two parties, interviewer and interviewee, dynamically interact using questions and answers to accomplish a predetermined purpose — is discussed in depth in Chapter 13.

Small-group communication involves as few as three and as many as fifteen to twenty people who engage in face-to-face deliberation about a common concern. The five kinds of groups — casual, learning, therapeutic, problem-solving, and action — have different purposes. The casual type, emphasizing socialization, and the therapeutic type, stressing the treatment of personal problems, are not covered in this book. Attention is directed later to the learning group because of the methods it offers for learning with others, and to problem-solving/action groups because of the techniques we can learn to solve group problems.

Public speaking involves a speaker and a sizable number of listeners. The speaker discourses continuously on a specific subject, with listener interaction restricted largely to feedback, and that often is nonverbal. The speaker may speak to inform, persuade, or actuate and, in doing so, the speaker draws on methods and principles that can be learned, mastered, and applied to the many aspects of speech preparation. In forthcoming chapters we describe the techniques and principles.

The Communicators

Principal among the elements common to oral communication are the individuals who communicate with each other, the communicators. Unfortunately, communicators are not all alike. Each has needs, interests, desires, attitudes, beliefs, and values somewhat different from those of other communicators, and typically these change in each person from time to time. In communicative interaction, one person's characteristics may complement those of another to help achieve fruitful talk. Yet those same characteristics could clash with the characteristics of another communicator and create disharmony, blocking successful communication. As a consequence, oral communication is dynamic and ever-changing, as it ebbs and flows with the moods and feelings of the individual communicators.

Innumerable personal characteristics influence speaking. In this chapter we consider the more significant ones, categorized into five classes: personality variables, personal orientation systems, credibility, attraction, and similarity.

A study of communication must take into account the nature of the individuals involved in the process. We should be aware of which personal characteristics help achieve successful communication and which ones block it. This chapter undertakes a study of the characteristics that impinge on the communication process and affect how people talk with each other.

PERSONALITY VARIABLES

Our personality represents our total psychological makeup and is a reflection of our experiences, motivations, attitudes, beliefs, values, and behaviors as these elements interact with our external environment. *Personality refers to the sum total of our individual characteristics that make us unique.*[1] Personality differences account for the variance we exhibit in communicative behavior with our fellow human beings.

More than 100 personality variables have been identified. Most of these, however, have not been studied in terms of their impact on communication. Little is known about how they affect our interactions with others. The variables described here are the ones known to have influence on communication. They should be viewed as *an individual's predispositions to respond in a certain way to various situations*. They are the consistent and usual behaviors in which the individual engages. Even though they tend to be consistent, they are not constant. By that, we mean that their strength and direction can change occasionally, depending upon the situation and circumstance.[2]

Authoritarianism

Authoritarian people tend to be exacting, directive, and controlling in their relations with those who are less powerful than themselves. They believe that some people are naturally more powerful, and they think these differences in power are right and proper. Hence, authoritarian persons tend to use their power whenever they can. In less powerful positions, however, they are submissive and accept their subordinate roles as part of the order of things.[3]

Authoritarians tend to control.

Dogmatism

Often equated with authoritarian personalities, dogmatics respect authority and usually are dominated by it. They are rigid in their thinking and can best be described as closed-minded. Insecure, they are inflexible and intolerant of others and not easily persuaded unless the persuader is a person of authority. The television character Archie Bunker, of "All in the Family," epitomizes dogmatism.[4]

Machiavellianism

Some people enjoy manipulating others for their own purposes, controlling them through guile, deceit, and opportunism. They believe that the end justifies the means. They are called Machiavellians after Niccolo Machiavelli, the sixteenth-century author of *The Prince*. The book's principal character was a manipulator who resorted to cunning to attain his goals. J. R. Ewing of the television show "Dallas" is a classic example of the "high Mach" type of personality, displaying a low regard for others and treating them as objects. High Machs usually are successful persuaders, seeing others as susceptible to manipulation. But they are not easily influenced, tending to distrust others and having little faith in human nature.[5]

Equalitarianism

Equalitarians contrast sharply with those of authoritarian personalities. They believe that all people are equal; power and status differences should not exist. Therefore, they reject the notion that some people should be more powerful than others. In interpersonal interactions they treat people as equals and are not submissive and complying, nor are they demanding, directive, or conforming.[6]

Approach/Avoidance Orientation

Individuals with approach predispositions are extroverted in nature. Positively oriented toward people, they like, esteem, and trust others. They prefer communicating with others and are seen as cooperative and adaptable. Individuals with avoidance tendencies are the opposite. They avoid interaction with others, preferring to deal with inanimate objects at work. They are introverted, often disliking or distrusting other people.[7]

Social Sensitivity

Socially sensitive people readily empathize with the needs, feelings, and preferences of others. They interact well and are personally effective in communicative situations. In contrast are the socially insensitive individuals, who are independent and resolute, unconcerned about others.[8]

Emotional Stability

This variable covers a wide range of personality types. Well-adjusted, stable persons tend to be calm, well-balanced, and flexible in their communication with others. Those who are less emotionally stable are changeable, dissatisfied, and easily annoyed. They often are oriented toward irrelevant social talk in their interactions with others. They are likely to be anxious or concerned about matters over which they have no control.[9]

Apprehensiveness

Apprehension is a form of anxiety or fear that negatively affects communication. About 20 percent of the American population suffers from communication apprehension to the extent that it interferes with the ability to function normally in human encounters.[10] Because it is so widespread, Chapter 7 examines communication anxiety in detail.

Self-Esteem

Self-esteem is the view people have of themselves in terms of overall worth. People with high self-esteem are prone to be active communicatively. They are confident, expect to succeed, and speak well. Those with low self-esteem, on the other hand, often lack confidence in their ability to communicate and, for that matter, in almost everything they do. Low self-esteem is related to communication apprehension; hence, those with low self-esteem tend to be followers in speaking situations.[11] Because a person's perception and self-esteem influence communication, we devote Chapters 5 and 6, respectively, to those concepts.

Although more than 100 personality characteristics or variables have been identified, we examined only the ones that seem most important in oral communication. By understanding these personality variables, we can become more adept at adjusting our communication skills in interpersonal interaction.

PERSONAL ORIENTATION SYSTEMS

We are oriented to behave in certain ways that help us determine how we perceive people and their ideas. These ways circumscribe the extent to which our communication will be successful. How we are conditioned to behave is directed largely by our needs, values, beliefs, and attitudes. These constitute our personal system of orientation, the system that governs our lives. Our needs, values, beliefs, and attitudes activate and regulate our behavior, telling us what is good or bad, right or wrong, and more or less control our conduct in society.

The focus in this section is on our personal orientation system and its constituent parts. Because needs tend to activate our communicative behavior, we attend to them first. Values guide or direct that behavior, and they are reviewed next. Beliefs — judgments about what is true or probable — help us evaluate what we confront at a given time in our environment. We consider beliefs before examining attitudes, the part of our orientation system that helps us decide what is favorable or unfavorable.

Needs

Needs are *the physical and psychological feelings that give rise to tensions and hence motivate people to act in a way so as to overcome the tensions.*[12] This definition suggests that a physical or psychological force within us causes tension and the tension drives us in some way to relieve the tension. Needs, therefore, are inner-striving conditions that energize, activate, and move us toward the goals we seek.

We seek, we want, and we fear. We seek safety, want happiness, and fear illness. We are motivated to reach those goals. Needs represent the motivating force, and their satisfaction is the aim of motivation.[13] Table 4.1 presents some of our important psychological needs.

Need Satisfaction and Communication

People's needs and communication are fundamentally interdependent. People communicate

because talking to someone is as vital to a person's psychological well-being as eating and drinking are to a person's physical well-being. People communicate because communication is the medium through which many human needs are satisfied. The ability to recognize people's needs becomes a factor in explaining much of the content and manner of communication.[14]

TABLE 4.1
IMPORTANT PSYCHOLOGICAL NEEDS

Acquisition	Conservation	Organization
Money	Collecting	Arranging
Goods	Repairing	Neatness
Property	Cleaning	Precision
	Preservation	
Retention	Protection	**Achievement**
Hoarding		Power
Frugality	**Construction**	Superiority
Economical	Building	Success
	Creating	
Recognition		**Self-**
Prestige	**Exhibition**	**Preservation**
Status	Attention	Pride
Respect	Praise	Protection
Praise	Amusement	Defense
Boasting	Shock	
High Office	Excitement	**Domination**
	Dramatization	Influencing
Deference		Controlling
Following	**Similarity**	Leading
Admiring	Empathy	Directing
Cooperation	Emulating	Persuading
Service	Agreement	Dictating
Autonomy	**Aggression**	**Abasement**
Independence	Belittling	Surrender
Freedom	Harming	Compliance
Defying	Blaming	Apologies
Authority	Accusing	Confession
	Punishing	Atonement
Affiliation		
Joining	**Rejection**	**Nurturance**
Socializing	Snubbing	Nourishment
Associating	Ignoring	Aid
Cooperating	Excluding	Protection
	Discriminating	Sympathy
Succor		
Dependency	**Play**	**Exploration**
Seeking Aid	Relaxation	Asking
Adhering	Amusement	Studying
	Laughing	Learning
Exposition	Joking	Reading
Demonstrating		Inspecting
Lecturing		
Informing		
Explaining		

Types of Needs

Our definition of needs implies two major classes — physical and psychological. Our physical needs are most primary. Life itself depends upon their satisfaction, as they are inborn, universal, and un-irradicable. Psychological needs consist of hundreds of needs learned or acquired as a result of our social development and the culture in which we were reared.[15]

Physical Needs

Physiological needs arise from the stuff of which we are made. These needs get dissipated and require replenishment from time to time. Therefore, we must eat and drink and eliminate accumulated waste products. To survive as intact organisms, we must avoid anything that will injure us. To perpetuate our kind, we must engage in sexual activity. To overcome fatigue, we need to rest from time to time.[16]

The primary needs are for oxygen, food, water, rest, waste elimination, exercise, and sexual activity. For most of us, these needs are satisfied regularly and pose no problem. We eat and drink in adequate amounts and get our proper rest without undue concern. If one, or several, of these needs is not properly satisfied, however, it becomes tension-provoking and may override all of our other concerns until it is satisfied. When we go without food or drink for a long time, we realize this.

Psychological Needs

Our psychological needs are secondary. They achieve importance when our primary needs are adequately satisfied. Dozens of secondary needs exist for the average person. For instance, we need to gain possessions and property, to collect, repair, clean, and preserve things, to arrange, organize, and put things away, to hoard or retain possession of things, to achieve and be recognized for achieving, to attract attention to ourselves, to control others or be controlled, to join groups, form friendships, and live with others, among other secondary needs.[17]

The Needs Hierarchy

So many needs have been identified that ways of classifying them have been created. Two classification plans can give us a better understanding of the importance of these needs in motivating our behavior and in oral communication. The first was developed by Abraham Maslow.

Figure 4.1 shows Maslow's hierarchy of needs, in which needs are classified into five major categories. Consisting of many individual needs, each category is part of a hierarchical order. The most basic or primary need category comes first, followed in order by the important secondary need groups.

Note how Figure 4.1 is ordered. The most basic need group is shown at the bottom. The physiological needs have to be fulfilled before the safety, love, esteem, and self-actualization needs come into play. What the figure shows, in terms of priority, is that the primary needs (oxygen, food, rest, etc.) have to be satisfied first. When they are fulfilled, our desire for a safe environment, free from personal harm, violence, and disease, attains importance. Our safety needs usually are not dominant except in emergency situations. If a threatening situation develops, protecting ourselves becomes a priority.

We need to feel wanted and accepted by others and, in turn, we need to want and accept others. Sharing our love with family and friends normally satisfies this category of needs. If we are denied this, we alter our behavior to obtain it.

When our more basic psychological, safety, and love needs are met, the desire for respect, attention,

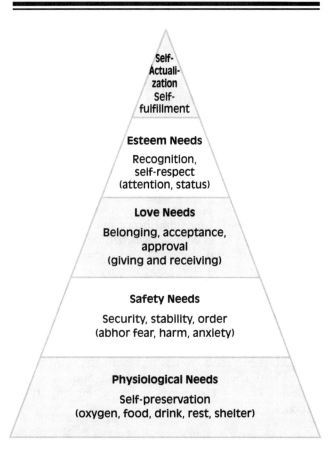

FIGURE 4.1 Maslow's hierarchy of needs.

and recognition become more important. We seek to be strong and adequate so we can face the world confidently with a sense of freedom and independence. As our other needs are fulfilled, our desire to reach the height of our personal abilities increases. To attain peace with ourselves, we want to achieve what we are best suited for.[18]

Maslow's priorities fit cultures motivated by personal, individual success in the form of wealth, recognition, and self-actualization, such as the dominant American culture. Few other cultures worldwide, however, place self-actualization as life's ultimate goal. People reared in Oriental cultures are more likely to rank belonging, acceptance, and approval at the top, deeming the favor and respect of their peers more important than self-actualization. The group ranks above the individual, and collective success is more important than individual prominence. For Latin Americans security is uppermost, in the form of freedom from personal harm and disease and a steady income to meet family needs. Many European cultures measure success as the quality of living of the collective society. A pleasant human environment tops their hierarchy.

Communicators who want to tap the needs of their listeners through their messages have to be aware that people's motivating forces vary. In the presence of people from different cultures, messages appealing to personal needs will have to take into account possible cultural variations.

Interpersonal Needs

Whereas Maslow's hierarchy covers the gamut of need categories, Schutz is concerned solely with interpersonal needs — ones that can be fulfilled only through interaction with other persons. Every individual has three interpersonal needs that must be satisfied, Schutz postulates. These are *inclusion, control,* and *affection.* Schutz's scheme does not deal with the primary needs, nor are the three Schutz needs stated in a priority order, as in the case with the Maslow hierarchy. Yet they represent significant human motivating forces and encompass a number of similar, more specific needs.

Inclusion has to do with interacting with people. It concerns establishing and maintaining satisfying relationships with others. Most of us have a need to be with others — to be in their company and to talk with them. We often seek out individuals with whom we can talk and share our hopes and dreams. We need to belong or feel part of some group. Lacking such relationships, we tend to feel excluded, lonely, or isolated.

Control is the need to be influenced by people and occasionally to have power over them. In communicative relationships we try to establish and maintain a satisfying degree of influence over others —

sometimes to dominate, to rule, or to lead, and sometimes to resist the control and domination of others. We attempt to control by winning arguments, by making suggestions that others will adopt, by dominating conversations, and sometimes by rebelling against the desires of other individuals.

Affection relates to being liked or loved. We need to establish close emotional ties with other people and to obtain affection through love and intimacy. Interestingly, we can fulfill this need on occasion through hate and hostility.[19]

The strength of the three needs varies among individuals. For some the affection need may be relatively weak, and for others the need for affection may be strong. Likewise, the inclusion and control needs vary from person to person.

Based on studies across cultures, differences appear in the strength of the three needs. Americans have much stronger inclusion needs than the Japanese, Koreans, Chinese, Micronesians, and Australians studied. Americans desire to join groups more so than the other cultures mentioned. The desire seems to surface in American teenagers as they are constantly joining groups.

A reason for cultural differences in need strength may relate to family life. The Orientals, Micronesians, and Australians studied maintain strong family bonds. Loyalty to the family is high and family relationships are close, satisfying the inclusion, control, and affection needs. Americans are taught to become more independent of the family and encouraged to assume larger roles in the society. American children are readied to leave home as they grow older, and family ties are weaker than those of the other cultures. The consequence is stronger interpersonal needs, and Americans are looking for groups to fulfill these needs.

To sum up, needs are the activators of our communicative behavior, the physiological and psychological desires that bring about the tensions we have to satisfy. Our physiological needs are few in number when compared to the psychological ones, but they are significant to our well-being and have priority over the psychological ones, as the Maslow hierarchy shows. If our physiological needs are satisfied, the psychological ones assume more prominent roles in our behavior. If Schutz's analysis is correct, our interpersonal needs are especially important in interpersonal interactions.

Values

Values are the evaluative aspect of our personal orientation system. They serve as the governing framework of our needs, and they guide and direct our behavior.[20] They tell us what is good or bad, right or wrong, true or false, positive or negative, and they prescribe how we should act. Thus, needs supply the motivation to act, and values provide the direction.[21]

Values usually originate with the larger principles or laws that govern a society. These principles make known to the society's members what should and should not be done. *Values are the standards or guidelines that determine proper behavior.*

Typical Values

Everyone possesses a complex set of values. These are learned, and they stem from the person's background, training, and culture. Although each person has a specific set of values, as a whole they tend to be much like those of other family members and those of the society in which the person lives. Some values are:

independence	frankness
patriotism	punctuality
education	sexual equality
hospitality	informality
cooperation	respect for environment
materialism	modesty
doing	efficiency
religion	competition
authoritarianism	sincerity
loyalty	openness
human dignity	honesty
self-reliance	practicality
money	freedom
democracy	group-centeredness
perfectionism	dependency
privacy	obligation
peace	aggressiveness
respect of elders	progress
individuality	skin color
"firstness"	property
fair play	affection
optimism	equality
pessimism	conformity
logic	rationality
harmony	directness

Types of Values

To illustrate the types of values that help guide people's behavior, we have selected "universal" values — those common to almost all cultures. Although they differ in *salience* (perceived importance), *direction* (positive, negative, neutral), and *degree* (strength with which held) from culture to culture, they have universal application.

Individuality is important to Americans but not so in all cultures. This value implies that the individual is significant, should be heard, and should stand up

for his or her beliefs. *Peace,* or the absence of war, is important to Hindus and Moslems but not as much so to Americans. *Punctuality* is considered important by most Americans, but being on time is not regarded as highly everywhere. *Respect for elders* is a value of importance to most cultures, although Americans tend to favor the young over the old. *Equality,* or equal treatment of both genders, is emphasized more in America than in many other cultures. Among other universal values are honesty, fair play, patriotism, modesty, efficiency, perfectionism, hospitality to guests, frankness, kindness, sincerity, obligation, and human dignity. All carry some salience among the world's cultures.[22]

To obtain a better understanding of how a universal value differs in salience, direction, and degree across cultures, we might compare gender equality in Korea with that in the United States. In Korea it is taboo for men and women to walk side by side in public; a woman's place is a few paces behind the man by Korean tradition. The United States traditionally indicates "ladies first," and men help women with their coats, hold doors open, and help them be seated. In fact, according to some Koreans, American men fill female roles — washing dishes, cooking, and doing the laundry — causing a few Korean males and females to view American males as "henpecked."[23]

Beliefs

The third aspect of our personal orientation system, beliefs, are *judgments about what is true or probable.*[24] Beliefs are the thousands and thousands of statements, usually inferences, that we make about ourselves and the world around us. Beliefs may be about the *past* (It was cold yesterday), about the *present* (It is raining today), or about the *future* (It surely will rain tomorrow). Beliefs may be expressions of a *conceptual nature* ($3 \times 3 = 9$) or *descriptions of the real world* (Hawaii is a series of islands). They may be *causal inferences* (The poor quality is why we don't buy American) or statements about *environmental elements* (Gardenias bloom only in the spring). They may be about *people* (Kerry likes Eric) or about *ourselves* (I like London in June).

Types of Beliefs

Three types of beliefs — experiential, informational, and inferential — are recognized.[25] *Experiential* beliefs are derived from direct experience. Through firsthand contact, we learn and, hence, believe that an object we perceive has certain characteristics. By standing next to a fire, we learn that it gives off heat. Because of our direct experience, an experiential belief holds a great deal of probability for us.

Informational beliefs come from sources other than ourselves. Newspapers, magazines, books, radio, television, all sorts of periodicals, teachers, preachers, and other people we trust supply the information from which we derive informational beliefs. For example, if *Newsweek* says the Russians have a huge fleet of submarines plying the Pacific, we are prone to believe the statement, provided *Newsweek* is a credible source in our mind. The information making up this type of belief comes to us secondhand, through a source. The magazine *Newsweek* provides us with the information about the Russians. Unless we have been sailing the Pacific frequently, we do not have firsthand knowledge as is the case with experiential beliefs. Therefore, informational beliefs, because of their reliance on secondary sources, do not hold as much probability as experiential beliefs do.

Inferential beliefs are formed by going beyond experience and information from reliable sources to draw inferences from our perceptions. We experience something and then guess, infer, or draw conclusions. For example, a student may be absent from class one day and believe there will be no penalty for the absence. The student has no basis for the judgment, no previous experience or data upon which to draw. The inference is based solely on a personal perception. Maybe the student thinks the instructor looks like a nice guy who would not penalize anyone. Or a student may get a "90" on a test and infer that the final grade in the course will be an "A." That inference is based on only perception.

Because we are guessing when we infer, inferential beliefs often are faulty. Our guesses may well be erroneous because of their lack of substantiation. Hence, they have a low degree of probability.

Personal Beliefs

At the center of an individual's belief system is a core of beliefs that are well-established and relatively unchangeable. A part of this core contains beliefs about the nature of the universe and its effects on the environment, our *world view*. The world view deals with ontological matters such as God, humankind, lower forms of life, inanimate objects, supernatural beings, nature, and other matters concerning the relations of humans to one another and the world. Our view of the world serves to explain to us how and why things got to be as they are and why they continue that way.

By answering questions such as these, we gain knowledge about our world view: Do we believe in the existence of a Supreme Being? Is the Supreme Being God? Does the Supreme Being control our destiny, or do we have ultimate control over our own fate? Does our society try to dominate nature? Control it? Blend in harmoniously with it? Submit itself to nature? What is the origin of people? Are Adam and Eve responsible? Evolution? Is there an afterlife? Heaven and hell? Do we believe in reincarnation? Are thunder, lightning, earthquakes, and other natural calamities caused by a God who is punishing us for our transgressions?

Do we believe that inanimate objects such as rocks, plants, rivers, and other forms of inanimate reality have being? Do certain persons carry the power of curing, divining, or serving as mediums with the spirit world? Do we believe in the supernatural?[26] Our answers to this sort of questions should give us insight into our own conception of the world around us, what we believe about world reality.

Cultures are distinguished by their world view. By structuring reality, members of a culture have a frame of reference for their thoughts, feelings, and behaviors. Most cultures do not share the same world view. Variations abound. Major differences in world views are found in the dichotomous perspectives of the East and the West.

The Eastern perspective was born out of the major Eastern religions of Buddhism, Taoism, Confucianism, and Hinduism. An overriding characteristic of these is *monism,* a tendency to seek a life of oneness and wholeness. The Western perspective was derived from Judeo-Christian traditions, which promote duality and choosing between opposites. Table 4.2 contrasts the two perspectives.

Attitudes

Attitudes, the final component of our personal orientation system, are defined as *learned tendencies to respond favorably or unfavorably toward a given object of orientation.*[27] Attitudes are responses to something — a proposal, an event, people, things, or places. We hold attitudes toward ourselves, toward others, toward policies, toward things. They are founded on our beliefs and values, and they help create our system of direction toward the perceptual world that our needs set in motion.

We are not born with attitudes, but we begin to form them shortly after birth. Almost everyone has an attitude toward truth, for example. As children we were encouraged to speak the truth. Our parents and relatives taught us that speaking the truth was good, proper, and right. When we spoke the truth at an early age, we may have been praised. If we told a lie, we may have been punished. In a similar fashion we learn the many attitudes that we hold about people, things, and ideas.

Characteristics

Attitudes vary in terms of *direction,* being favorable or unfavorable. We may favor apples and not

---

TABLE 4.2

CONTRASTING BELIEFS OF THE EAST AND WEST

The Eastern Perspective	The Western Perspective
1. Humans are one with nature.	1. Humans have characteristics that distinguish them from nature and the spiritual.
2. Humans perceive the spiritual and physical as one.	2. Humans are overshadowed by the existence of a personal God.
3. Humans perceive the mind and body as one.	3. Humans consist of body, mind, and spirit.
4. Humans should accept the basic oneness with nature rather than try to control it.	4. Humans must manipulate and control nature to survive.
5. Humans should feel comfortable with anyone, because they are one with all existence.	5. Humans must think rationally and analytically.
6. Science and technology create an illusion of progress at best.	6. The good life and hope for the future are found in science and technology.
7. Enlightenment, a state in which all differences disappear, means to achieve oneness with the universe. Enlightenment is achieved through meditation.	7. Humans should reward action and the competitive spirit.

Based on Albert R. Gilgen and Jae Hyung Cho, "Questionnaire to Measure Eastern and Western Thought." Psychological Reports, 44, (1979): 835-841.

---

oranges, pizza and not tacos, rock and not jazz. In addition, attitudes vary in terms of *degree* — strong, moderate, mild, or weak. We may have a strong, favorable attitude toward rock and an unfavorable, weak attitude about jazz. Figure 4.1 graphically shows one person's degree of attitude toward three issues.

Attitudes tend to be *relatively enduring*. They last unless something occurs to change them. If we feel strongly favorable toward rock music, we probably will keep that attitude, barring an unforeseen circumstance that could change it.

Attitudes are *responses to something*. We hold attitudes about almost everything in our perceptual world.[28]

Communicative Importance

Through oral interaction we discover how similar our attitudes are to those of other people. It is a way

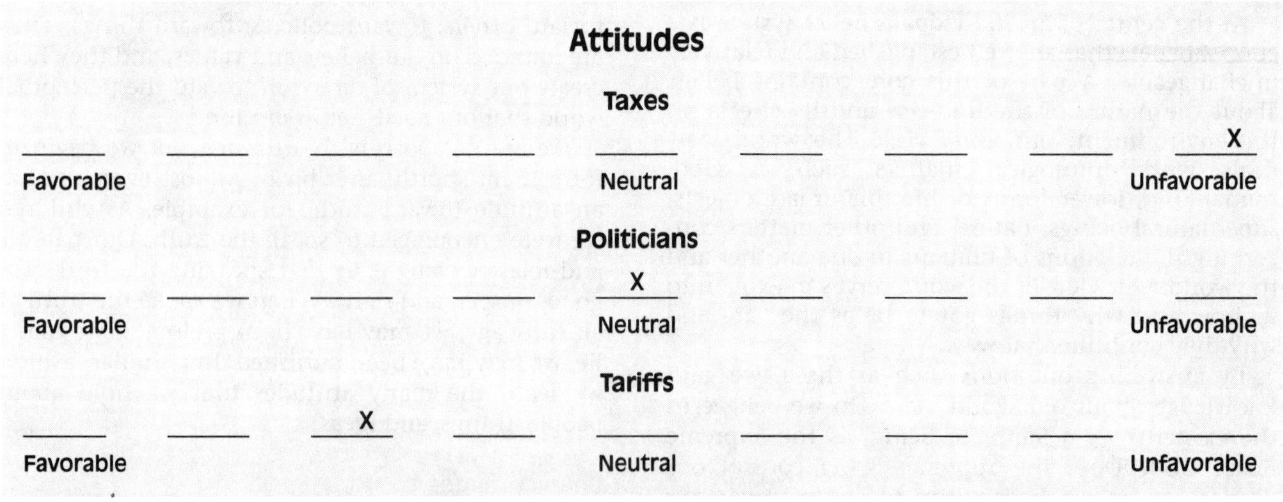

Attitudes

Taxes

Favorable — Neutral — Unfavorable X

Politicians

Favorable — X Neutral — Unfavorable

Tariffs

Favorable — X — Neutral — Unfavorable

FIGURE 4.1 Degree of attitude on a continuum.

of establishing relationships with others. If our attitude toward rock is similar to that of a new acquaintance, we are more likely to accept that individual as a friend than someone whose attitude is different from ours. Likewise, if our attitude about mathematics is similar to that of the math teacher, we are more prone to accept the teacher's instruction than is someone whose attitude differs considerably from the teacher's. Talking with people, therefore, helps us discover what they are like. If we are attitudinally similar, the possibilities of establishing and maintaining a relationship increase.[29]

COMMUNICATOR CREDIBILITY

A significant personal quality important to communicators is credibility. *Credibility is the listener's attitude about the speaker at a given time.*[30] It is the dominant factor in determining a communicator's ability to influence the listeners, and the most potent means of persuasion available to a speaker. We have learned, through experience, to value the words of our elders, the wise, subject-matter experts, and persons of goodwill. We come to trust and rely on what they say. They are credible in our perception of things. In the same fashion, we place our trust in any speaker we consider credible. What the speaker says, therefore, becomes persuasive to us.

Although credibility is an attribute of speakers, it must be attributed to speakers by the listeners. No speaker is credible unless those listening to the speaker think the speaker is credible. Moreover, a speaker talking to a group of people may be viewed as credible by one listener but not by the others.

Credibility is attributed to the speaker by the listener.

Listening to our instructor, some of us might conclude that we are listening to the new "Messiah," and others might leave class feeling skeptical. Speaker credibility, therefore, is not some quality that speakers carry around with them. It is a quality the listener perceives. Nonetheless, a listener's impressions of a speaker's credibility are accurate as far as that listener is concerned. Thus, the listener's impressions go a long way in helping the speaker convince that listener.

Phases of Credibility

Credibility is a changeable factor. That statement perhaps is best understood in terms of communicators who are public speakers. The conclusions we draw, however, are applicable to any speaker, whether that person is engaged in an interview, a group discussion, or a public speaking situation.

Listeners hold three images of speakers. The first is called the *initial* image, the image the listeners have about speakers before they speak. The *derived* image is produced as the speakers speak. And the *terminal* image is what the listeners carry away about the speakers after listening to their speeches. These three images might remain identical throughout the speeches, or they might change, depending upon what is said or done.

Initial Image

Before the speaker speaks for the first time, his or her image with the listeners could be favorable, unfavorable, or neutral. The initial image relates to what the listeners know about the speaker. This knowledge includes information about the speaker's education, experience, and reputation earned in previous speeches, passed on by former listeners. Listeners tend to react favorably to speakers they consider competent and trustworthy, unfavorably to speakers not so considered, and neutral to ones unknown to them.

The speaker's appearance also affects the initial image. Appropriate dress, neat grooming, and overall attractiveness cause favorable responses from listeners who are viewing the speaker for the first time. Appropriate dress for one audience may not be so for another, though. Speakers who come to Hawaii from outside the state wearing a shirt, tie, and coat, as is the custom elsewhere, often are considered overdressed by listeners accustomed to seeing "aloha" shirts — multicolored sports shirts usually worn loose, not tucked in the pants. Speakers from Hawaii may experience a similar lack of initial credibility as they walk in to speak, aloha-shirt-clad, at a place where the standard attire is shirt, tie, and coat.

During the speech the speaker's initial image can be reinforced or changed depending upon what the speaker says and does and how he or she says or does it. Speakers with high initial credibility have to maintain it; speakers with low credibility have to enhance it. The speaker's image can be modified by the content and presentation of the subject material and by a sincere manner, demonstration of goodwill, and respect for the listeners.

The terminal image results from the interaction of initial and derived images. As such, the terminal image may be higher, lower, or equivalent to the initial image. The speaker, or course, wants to end the speech with an image that is higher than when the talk began. The terminal image becomes the initial image for the next speech to the same listeners.

Dimensions of Credibility

Speaker credibility stems from a number of sources. We have mentioned competence, goodwill, trustworthiness, appearance, sincere manner, and respect for the listener. Among other possibilities are intention (Is the speaker truly concerned about the listener's well-being or merely going through the motions?) and character. We have categorized the sources into expertness, trustworthiness, and forcefulness.

Competence and intelligence fall under the label of expertness, which deals with having much training and knowledge in the subject matter. Does the speaker know what he or she is talking about? Is he or she well-informed and intelligent? The answers to these questions convey perceptions of the speaker's expertness. Expertness is an important credibility dimension. Speakers are expected to know their stuff and be a cut above everyone else in knowledge about the subject.

Is the speaker fair? Just? Sincere? A conveyer of goodwill? Ethical? Concerned personally about the listeners? Answers to questions such as these offer perceptions of the speaker's basic character. We can judge a speaker to be an expert on the subject matter, but if we cannot trust the person to be honest about what he or she says, we are not likely to perceive the speaker as credible. We are not sure whether the person is speaking the truth.

This dimension is shown in a lively, vivid, enthusiastic, and energetic platform presence. The manner in which speakers conduct themselves has a significant impact on the listeners. A speaker in our experience ran hot and cold. In one speech he was dynamic and vital; his forcefulness won over the listeners. In another he stuttered and stammered, searching for words, seemingly unfamiliar with his topic although he knew it well. He lost listener interest quickly through his lack of intensity.[31]

The three dimensions of credibility do not always operate together. Sometimes they do function together, but at other times they do not. They function independently. If we are approached by two speakers we consider to be equally expert, we are more likely to believe the speaker we consider most trustworthy. If we are confronted by two speakers we consider to be equally trustworthy, we probably will accept the views of the person we consider to be more expert. If we are approached by two speakers, one who is expert but not trustworthy and one who is trustworthy but not expert, both speaking on the same subject, it is difficult to predict whose views we will accept. If we are approached by only one speaker, whom we perceive to be high on one of the dimensions but not on the others, it is difficult to predict what effect that will have on our evaluation of the person. Usually, of course, the three dimensions of a speaker's credibility are perceived to be qualitatively comparable.[32]

INTERPERSONAL ATTRACTIVENESS

Another set of personal characteristics that influences oral communication is related to interpersonal attractiveness. Attractiveness is the power of drawing people to us. People see qualities in us that appeal to them, making communication easier. People judge us on the basis of physical, social, and task attractiveness.

Physical Attractiveness

How we perceive someone's physical appearance determines whether we will interact with that person for any length of time. In our initial contact, if we perceive the person as physically attractive, we probably will want to interact more often.

Attraction, obviously, is a matter of personal judgment. What we consider to be attractive in a person may seem plain to someone else. Someone we believe is handsome may be perceived as homely by someone else. We may consider blond, blue-eyed, tall, well-proportioned men or women as beautiful people. An acquaintance may see little beauty in those individuals, preferring short, stocky, brown-eyed, black-haired people. Beauty, the adage goes, is in the eyes of the beholder.

Regardless, if a person is not physically appealing to us, the possibility of our developing a liking for the person is reduced. But if we are thrown together with a person we think is unattractive physically and spend some time with that person, we tend to discount the physical qualities that are unappealing to us and become more interested in the person's social and task attractiveness.

Social Attractiveness

People whose company we enjoy usually are those we think are socially attractive. Even though they may not be physically pleasing, we think of them as attractive because they are friendly and likable. We find them to be interesting individuals, good companions, and loyal friends.

Usually social attractiveness develops following initial contacts. We might sit next to someone in class and begin to see the person regularly. After exchanging small talk with the person for a time, we get to know him or her better and become attracted by the person's social graces. As a result, we might establish a long-term relationship.

Social attractiveness, too, is a matter of individual choice. Like physical beauty, the social qualities one person finds desirable may be undesirable in another person's view.

Task Attractiveness

When we like to work with a given individual, we perceive that person as task-attractive. We judge this person to be easy to work with, productive, and motivated to perform up to capacity irrespective of the task to be completed. The person is competent, in our estimation, and we are drawn to the individual.

The three dimensions of attractiveness are independent. A person we enjoy working with may not be physically attractive or even socially attractive, but if we perceive the person as a good worker, that dimension may be all that is necessary to draw the individual to us. On the other hand, we may be attracted to an individual socially, yet know that we would not want to work with that person. Then, too, an individual might be exceedingly handsome in our eyes, and we are drawn to him or her because of the beauty. But the person could be someone we would not want to socially interact or work with.[33]

SIMILARITY

The last personality characteristic bearing on oral communication is similarity — *how much the people we interact with are like we are.* The more similar to ourselves we see another person, the more attracted to that person we are apt to be. Further, the more the person is like ourselves, the more influence the person will have over us, and the more likely we will learn from that person.[34] Similarity is of three types: demographic, background, and attitude.

Demographic Similarity

Demographics consist of actual characteristics such as gender, age, height, socioeconomic status, educational level, religion, and ethnicity. They are observable and knowable to us; they exist concretely. If both authors of this text were Caucasian, forty years of age, male, married university professors, we would have demographic similarities. Such is not the case; we are not similar in several demographic areas.

Knowing the extent of demographic similarities between two communicators, we can make predictions about the probable outcomes of communication between the two. For example, we can predict that a woman born, reared, and educated in Hawaii will be more successful teaching in Hawaii schools than a woman born, reared, and educated in Milwaukee. Why? The Hawaii-born teacher can relate better to the students in Hawaii. Her demographic characteristics are more like the children she will be teaching than those of the Milwaukeean.

Background Similarity

We perceive people who have backgrounds similar to our own as more like us than people with different backgrounds. Two people born in San Francisco probably are going to perceive each other as similar in background. Americans traveling abroad are inclined to think they have more in common with each other than with the natives in the country they are visiting. Perceptions of background similarity, however, are not the same as demographic similarity because background similarity need not be real. Two Americans visiting Paris may have little in common with each other except for their American citizenship. Yet they will perceive some background similarity with each other.

The greater the perceived similarity, the greater is the likelihood for wanting to communicate. The greater the desire to communicate the more frequent communication becomes. The more frequent the communication, the more successful the communication becomes.

Attitude Similarity

A third dimension of similarity that causes us to like people is similarity in attitudes, beliefs, and values. If we perceive that certain people think and act as we do, we will consider them to be similar to us. Realizing this, we probably will be more inclined to communicate interpersonally with them.

Ordinarily, however, learning about an individual's attitudes, beliefs, and values takes time. Therefore, attitude similarity tends to develop after the communicators have become acquainted and have interacted with one another. Too, attitude similarity can fluctuate over time. Rather than continuing a relationship, the communicators may break off the relationship, as in divorce, realizing that they disagree strongly on crucial issues.

To sum up: similarity is significant in oral communication to the extent that, as we perceive ourselves to be similar to one another, we are likely to interact with each other.[35]

SUMMARY

Personality variables that influence speaking include authoritarianism, dogmatism, Machiavellianism, equalitarianism, approach/avoidance tendencies, social sensitivity, emotional stability, apprehensiveness, and self-esteem. Our interpersonal communication is directed or governed by a system of personal orientation. Need satisfaction is the motivating factor in our communication with others, but how we interact depends upon our values, beliefs, and attitudes. These attributes are culturally related.

Whether we are successful communicators depends in part upon our credibility as perceived by the listeners. Whether we actually get to speak with someone for a time, and perhaps establish a relationship, is dependent upon attractiveness and similarity.

VOCABULARY CHECK

The following terms were defined or explained in the first four chapters. Match the term with the proper definition or explanation. The answers are on page 243.

_____ 1. People who manipulate others for their own gain.

_____ 2. Inclusion, control and affection.

_____ 3. A desire to alter the intensity or salience of listeners' attitudes toward the speaker's subject.

_____ 4. Three or more people in physical proximity who dynamically interact orally about a common concern.

_____ 5. Shallow, mundane, simplistic talk.

_____ 6. The listener's overt response to a speaker's message.

_____ 7. Relationships involving people of equal status.

_____ 8. A transactional process.

_____ 9. The result of knowledge and understanding.

_____ 10. The listener's attitude about a speaker at a given time.

A. Credibility

B. Machiavellians

C. Persuasion

D. Interpersonal needs

E. Competence

F. Phatic communion

G. Symmetrical

H. Small-group communication

I. Feedback

J. Oral communication

5

Perception

The "frosh fifteen" affects many first-year students living in the dormitories. The "fifteen" are the fifteen pounds the student gains from eating the high-calorie dorm cafeteria food. Brenda heard about the frosh fifteen, but she was determined not to put on those pounds. By midterm, however, her clothes no longer fit, and the dreaded fifteen were showing. She decided to diet and subsisted on salads and fruits for a week. She lost a few pounds, but she was hungry all the time for "real" food. The diet was torturous, and she began to perceive food everywhere. On television she saw only food commercials. Looking at a magazine, the food ads caught her eye. Campus posters pointed out local restaurants, and the smell of food was everywhere. Her friends, she thought, talked only of food. Food pervaded her thoughts.

Brenda's experience is a common one for dieters. Hungry, their attention turns to food. They perceive only the food stimuli, ignoring the others that bombard them. The commercials, ads, posters, and smells were always present, but Brenda paid them little heed when she was eating well. On her diet her need for sustenance caused her to attend to every sign of food. Brenda selectively attended to what motivated her at the time: food.[1]

Selective attention is part of the perception process, a process we concentrate on in this chapter. Perception is a vital process in communication, influencing how we act toward ourselves and others. Our perception of ourself affects our communication. If we think we are shy, for example, we are apt to avoid talking. If we think we are great speakers, we might be prone to dominate conversations, perhaps being loud and boisterous as well.

Our perception of others also influences how we communicate. In the presence of a person we consider an expert, we may come across as meek and humble. With people we like, we try to respond in a likeable fashion. Meeting someone for the first time, we size up the person, making judgments about that individual. Our perception of the newcomer will largely determine how we interact with him or her. We communicate what we perceive. Thus, perception is the key to recognizing what is happening, how, and why.

THE NATURE OF PERCEPTION

Perception is the *process by which people select, organize, and interpret sensory stimulation into a meaningful and coherent picture of the world*.[2] It is the process of assigning meaning to sensory data. Through our senses we become aware of objects and events in the external world and then interpret what we sense.

The senses affecting perception fall into three classes. The major *distance* senses are seeing and hearing. The *skin* senses involve touch, warmth, cold, pain, and the closely related chemical senses of taste and smell. The *deep* senses are the position and motion of the muscles and joints (kinesthesis), the senses of equilibrium, and the senses of the internal organs.[3]

Under the normal conditions of everyday life, several senses, or receptors, as they are sometimes called, are activated simultaneously by a stimulus. We not only see the stimulus object, but we hear and maybe even smell it at the same time. As we toss a handful of sliced potatoes into the pan to fry, we hear them sizzle in the oil and we smell the aroma from cooking simultaneously as we watch them fry.

Although we may employ only one of the senses at a given time, there is more to the process of sensing. Viewing a stimulus, for example, sets off a complicated pattern of neural events that recall former stimulation. The sight of potatoes frying may remind us of the sizzle and the smell even though we cannot hear or smell them frying. We recollect the sound and odor despite their absence.[4]

Characteristics of Perception

By describing six characteristics[5] of perception, we should better know why we can recall the sound and odor despite their absence.

1. Perception is generally *knowledge-based*. If we learned that frying potatoes give off a sizzling sound and a special smell, this knowledge will help us remember the sound and smell when we see potatoes frying.

2. Perception is *inferential*. We do not always have complete sensory information at hand, but our perceptual system uses what knowledge we have to make inferences about what we may not be able to see, hear, or feel. Thus, if we know that frying food sizzles and emits an aroma, we infer that potatoes will sizzle and give off an aroma when fried. We generate a mental image of the frying potatoes even though we have no idea of its exact properties.

3. Perception is *categorical*. It allows us to place apparently different sensations in the same category based on common features. We may not know exactly what kind of food is frying, but it has the characteristics of frying foods, so we place it in the fried-food category. We hear sounds and can put them in the category called "fried foods" even if the sounds are not entirely like any other frying sound we ever heard.

4. Perception is *relational*. We perceive a stimulus pattern as a frying food and we are able to identify it as a frying food because the stove, pan, food, and oil are related to one another in a coherent and consistent way. The pan is on the stove, and the food is in the pan in the oil — all fitting together in a logical manner, which to us means food frying.

5. Perception is *adaptive*. It allows us to focus on the most important information for handling a given situation. For example, our peripheral vision is sensitive to moving stimuli. It is adaptive because it allows us to react quickly to threatening motions across a wide range of space. Suppose we are frying potatoes and, while waiting for them to get done, we read at the kitchen table. Our peripheral vision picks up a flickering on the stove. Our perceptual process decides whether it is a fire or sputtering oil. If it is a fire, we act fast to put it out. If it is sputtering oil and not dangerous, we may merely reduce the heat. Our perceptive process caused us to take action; we adapted to the situation.

6. Most perceptual processes *operate automatically*. We do not have to stop and consciously ask what is frying. The question is asked and answered quickly — so quickly we are unaware of doing it.

Differing Perceptions

We perceive, and we tend to believe that what we perceive is reality. Yet several of us reporting about the same event may report it differently, and we all will swear to the truth of what we are reporting. This point is well-illustrated in a classic study conducted more than forty years ago and frequently repeated with much the same results.[6]

The scene is a university classroom in which a carefully staged incident takes place involving the instructor and four students named Al, Bill, Carl, and Dick. None of the other twenty students is aware of the stunt. At a given signal, Al hits Bill with his fist and Bill retaliates by striking Al with a book. At the same time, Carl throws two coins on the floor and scrambles after them as they roll away. The instructor then orders Al, Bill, and Carl from the room and, as he does so, Dick slowly walks out also. The instructor tells the remaining students that a police investigation may result and asks them to write out reports of what they observed.

The following answers represent the students' eyewitness accounts. *What did Al do?* Only two students accurately reported that Al hit Bill with his fist. Some claimed Bill struck Al. Others said Al hit Bill with the book. *What did Carl do?* Most believed Carl scrambled after money that Al and Bill dropped. No one gave an accurate account of what Carl did. *What did Dick do?* Some students reported that Dick was ejected along with the others. A few said he rushed from the room. He saw blood, it was reported, and, at the sight of the blood, he ran out (in spite of the fact that no blood appeared). Several believed Dick was sick.

None of the students reported the incident accurately, and no two reports were the same. The students reported what they perceived, what they interpreted from the data their senses received. What happened in this situation is what typically occurs when we see, feel, taste, hear, or smell something. Normally the sensory data we take in do not directly correspond to our perception of them. Sensory data and perception of the data are not likely to be the same because sensory data interact with certain predispositions and states we already hold. What we see, hear, feel, smell, or taste depends upon these predispositions and states. They determine our perceptions of what we sense.

Limiting Predispositions

Predispositions that restrict our perceptions might be considered in two major classes: physiological and psychological.[7]

Physiological Limitations

Problems of health are major causes of perceptual restrictions. We may have difficulties with hearing or seeing, which limit our ability to report adequately. The sense of smell is virtually nonexistent in some people. Others are unable to taste certain kinds of food. Three additional physiologically related problems can limit perception: illusions, neurological inhibitions, and innate characteristics.

Illusions

People sometimes accurately detect a stimulus but improperly decode it. The sensation is normal, but the interpretation is faulty, and erroneous perception results.[8] The Muller-Lyer illusion in Figure 5.1 (A) offers an example. Unsophisticated viewers often see line A as being shorter than line B. The lines, of course, are equal in length and are registered accurately on the retina of the eye but inaccurately interpreted. The fins on A make it seem shorter than B. B's fins draw out the line, making it look longer. The two figures in (B) are the same size, as are the three cats (E). The lines in (C) are all parallel, and the lines forming the square (D) are all straight. The moon presents a similar illusion. It appears to be much larger near the horizon than when it is directly overhead. The eye detects it accurately; our interpretation is in error.[9]

Neurological Inhibitions

The body's neural networks, composed of many nerve cells that transmit messages to the higher centers of the nervous system, can become overloaded. When too many messages are received, inhibitory impulses from special nerve fibers stop the incoming messages from reaching the brain.

Innate Characteristics

Traits that have been in us from birth also govern our perceptions.[10] For instance, our ability to discriminate between nonvocal or vocal tones is determined largely by the structure of our ears, an innate

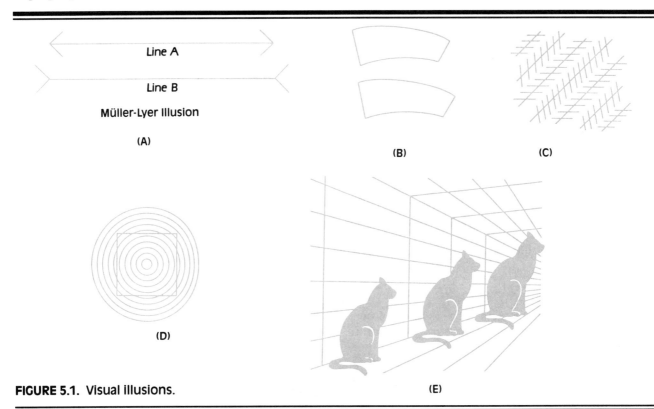

FIGURE 5.1. Visual illusions.

characteristic. We hear only the tones our ear structure will allow us to hear. We are born with this limitation, and little can be done about it.

Psychological Limitations

Our perceptions also are limited by various psychological factors including our attitudes, values, beliefs, and needs. We covered these in detail in Chapter 4. Here we consider our *experience* and *emotional states* and touch on the phenomenon of *selective perception*, part of the first step in the perception process.[11]

Experience

Experience is the general tendency to perceive an object or event on the basis of what happened in the past — termed the *habit factor*.[12] This factor encompasses more than simply a memory of facts, figures, and solid objects. It includes previous interpretations of the stimuli and the outcomes of those interpretations and subsequent behavior.[13] Objects and events we sense as adults have a history of meaning attached to them because of our associations with similar objects and events in the past.

As an example, consider the apple. It can be perceived in a number of ways, principally by its taste, color, shape, smell, and feel. Any one of these perceptions is likely to arouse symbolic processes that represent previous experiences we have had with apples. When we see an apple today, our perception depends a great deal upon our past experience. The perception is colored by our previous experiences with apples.

Emotional State

Emotional state can color our perception of what we sense. An example is the emotional state called "love," which one pundit believes is a form of discomfort in some people and a grave mental disease in others, for it is the triumph of imagination over intelligence. Love is said to be blind, and that "blindness" can discolor the lover's perceptions toward the object of the love. Fear is another example of an emotional state. It is said that fear casts out intelligence, casts out goodness, casts out beauty and truth and, most likely, in the process distorts what is perceived.

Selective Perception

Certain predispositions screen the richness of perceptual experience around us in the physical world. Because of this screening, we pay attention to only a few of the stimuli that bombard us. Selective perception is part of the first stage in the perception process, so we will deal with it more completely in the next section.

THE PERCEPTION PROCESS

Our sensory world consists of an almost infinite number of discrete impulses in constantly changing patterns. Vision alone confronts us with 7,500,000 distinguishable colors. When we add the other dimensions of seeing, such as the perception of form, lightness, and space, our perceptual world becomes an array of bewildering stimuli. Though sight may be the richest of our senses, hearing has been estimated to provide approximately 340,000 discriminable tones. Add to seeing and hearing the senses of smell, touch, kinesthesis, pain, taste, and others, and we have a wealth of perceptual experience beyond our wildest imagination.[14]

Unfortunately, the specific stimuli in the external environment usually do not correspond to our perceptions of them. The stimuli interact with certain predispositions and states we already hold, to form our perceptions, as the previous section indicated. The nature of our perceptions, therefore, depends upon the physical stimuli from the environment and upon our learned reactions. This sets in motion the perceptual process, which consists of three stages or steps: attention, organization, and interpretation. These stages are not distinct or discrete, as the explanation that follows might imply. They are continuous and blend into one another, making it difficult to separate one from the others.[15]

Attention

Imagine that we are spectators at a football game. We are watching the players move back and forth across the field. At the same time, friends sitting next to us are conversing, and we eavesdrop, sometimes joining in the talk. The band plays, and it intrudes on our thoughts. Hungry and thirsty, we watch for the vendors selling soda and food. Our team scores, so we stand and cheer. We wave to classmates we see several rows in front of us. We eat and drink, check the scoreboard, look at the program, and join in when the "wave" reaches our section. All of these actions represent attention, *that part of the perceptual process in which we focus our consciousness on a particular stimulus or event*.[16] We cannot attend to all of the stimuli around us at one time so we zero-in on certain ones in the perceptual array. Our attention focuses on one or several stimuli at a given time.

Selective Attention

The "cocktail party phenomenon" illustrates our ability to focus on certain stimuli while ignoring others around us. In a crowded room, talking with

The Perception Process

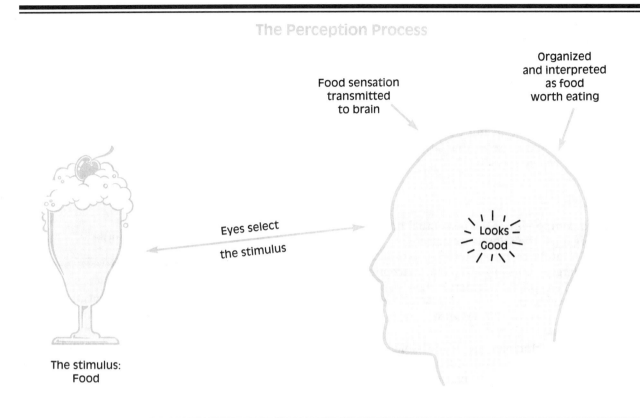

Food sensation
transmitted
to brain

Organized
and interpreted
as food
worth eating

Eyes select
the stimulus

Looks
Good

The stimulus:
Food

one or two friends, we know other small groups also are conversing. We can attend to our friends and converse with them, or we can shift our attention to other conversations going on around us. We might be so engrossed in our own conversation that we may hear nothing of what someone is saying immediately adjacent to our group. Then we could become so bored with our group that we attend to what the others are saying. This ability of ours is indicative of selective attention. We *eliminate interfering messages at the level of the senses.*[17]

Our attention in the crowded room can be *divided.* We might be deeply engaged in a conversation with our friends, yet monitor the conversation of another group or two, although later we may not recall the content of any of the conversations. We more successfully recall when several senses are involved. Sitting in the stands watching the football game, we see the action and hear our friends talk. We see our team score a touchdown and feel the person next to us jubilantly pound us on the back. We can read and listen to the radio, dividing our attention between the two.[18]

Usually divided attention produces meager results. If we want to pass the exam covering the textbook, we likely will do better if we study by giving the text our undivided attention. A student reports: "My roommate brags about how she can watch TV and study at the same time. Me — I have to concentrate on the book. She earns C's and D's. My fraternity named me scholar of the year. I got all A's."

We do not use all of the sensory information available to us. Normally we are bombarded with sensory data from which we select. *We choose from all of the public, private, and behavioral stimuli available to us those to which we will attend.* We may select consciously, knowing we are doing so, or unconsciously, totally unaware of what is attracting our attention. Selection is necessary because we cannot possibly respond to every event we sense. If we did, we would have a sensory overload, accumulating more data than our nervous system could handle. Therefore, we do not process all we hear, see, smell, feel, or touch in a given moment. Nor does our sensory system respond to all of the sensations that take place around us.[19]

What We Select

Sometimes the nature of the sensory stimuli attracts us. A loud noise may wake us from a deep sleep. Flashing lights on the streets at night gain our attention and warn us of construction work.

Sometimes our selection is physiological. If we are hungry or thirsty, we seek food or drink, ignoring almost everything else around us.

In the last part of this book, we suggest ways of capturing our listeners' attention when we speak. When we do speak, we should keep in mind that all sorts of stimuli will be competing with our utterances for the listeners' attention. If we want their attention, if we want to transmit our messages successfully, we will have to seize that attention and maintain it while we are speaking.

Organization

As a second component of the perceptual process, we have to organize the stimuli we selectively take in. The smaller units of our perceptual world are grouped into larger units, making our perception more efficient. Perceptual judgments then can be made more accurately in a shorter time. We try to form meaningful patterns of what we hear, see, smell, feel, and taste.

Two organizing principles are identifiable. One involves perceiving a figure embedded in a perceptual background. The other is to perceive the world in the simplest way possible.

Figure/Ground

Watching a basketball game, we see a complex visual scene. Ten players are running back and forth, each performing actions vital to the game. Referees join the flow of movement as they adjudicate the play. Coaches and players on the sidelines add to the complexity as they move about, urging their team on. Looking at this complex scene, our perceptual abilities automatically pick out certain persons or objects as *figures* (the features to be emphasized) and relegate the rest as the *ground* (the background). With the example of the basketball game, our tendency is to watch the ball and the player who has it at the moment. That player and the ball become the figure, the other players and officials the ground. The figure is the part of the visual field that has meaning, is prominent (at least to us), and includes the contours or borders separating it from the background, meaningless to some degree.[20]

Usually the relationship between the figure and ground is definite, but not always, as Figure 5.2 demonstrates. What can be seen in the figure? Something black on a white ground? Or white shapes on a black ground? At first we probably will see either the goblet or the famous twins. We will never see them both at exactly the same time. Upon looking at the figure repeatedly, we will notice that each comes in and out of focus. We may think we see both at once. In reality we focus briefly on one, then the other.

FIGURE 5.2. Figure and ground example.

Our emphasis thus far has been on visual scenes. Our other senses also can come into play in the figure/ground relationship. In a noisy environment we may automatically pick out certain sounds to be figures. Loud voices will become figures over the hum of other, softer voices. "Flicking through a batch of fabrics," a professor said, "my wife will settle on one that feels good to her." That fabric became the figure; the other fabrics she touched were the ground.

How do we decide what will be figure and what will be ground? Various features help us determine what will be the figure:

1. *Size.* Smaller areas are more likely than larger areas to be seen as figures. In basketball we focus on the ball, not on the players running around.

2. *Familiarity.* Familiar shapes and forms, familiar sounds and voices, things that feel familiar are more often perceived as figures.

3. *Brightness.* Brighter objects tend to become figures.

4. *Motion.* Moving persons or things will probably stand out as figures.

5. *Interest.* When everything is moving, as in a basketball game, our focus will be directed to that of interest to us.

6. *Unusual features.* Unusual sights and sounds can become figures. Listening to a student give a speech as a class assignment, the class noted her tendency to interject ahs, uhms, and you-knows frequently into her remarks. They concentrated on these and did not pay attention to the rest of her message. These vocalized pauses became the figure; the words of the message the ground.

The point is that we can focus on only one part of the total before us in any given instance. When two actions are simultaneous, we can see only one of them. When two individuals speak to us at the same time, we can listen to only one of them. We can switch our focus rapidly sometimes and then believe we are seeing or listening to both, but it is not so. We can focus on only one at a time.

Realizing that we can focus on only one part of the total at a given moment, and that part becomes the figure for us while the rest of the total is the ground, we can understand more readily why two people looking at the identical total scene may see entirely different parts of it. Two friends watching a football game on television may have different perceptions about what is happening. If they do, they likely are focusing on different parts of the action before them. Ten people watching the same game may well come up with ten different perceptions of what took place. *The focal point is always the figure; the rest is the ground.*[21]

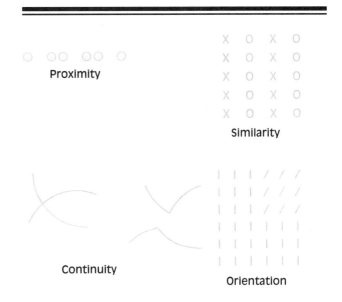

FIGURE 5.3. Grouping of stimuli.

Simplicity

We have a tendency to see things in the simplest form possible. Elements of the perceptual world seem to belong together because they provide better continuity of the stimulus. We perceive sights and sounds as organized wholes.[22] We put together elements that are near each other, are alike, and form an unbroken, continuous whole. We *group,* and we *close.*

Grouping. Certain features of stimuli cause us to group them together, more or less automatically, into coherent objects or sounds. We group objects or sounds that are near each other, are similar, appear to have a continuous form, and have the same orientation. In Figure 5.3 the stimuli are arranged according to proximity, similarity, continuity, and orientation.

Most people probably perceive the dots in the *proximity* example in Figure 5.3 as consisting of two groups of two dots plus two single dots rather than three groups of two dots or some other arrangement. In the *similarity* example, a person typically sees two rows of X's and two rows of O's rather than five rows of X O X O. In the *continuity* example, the lefthand form is seen as two continuous curved lines, not as two separate forms as the righthand forms suggest. In the *orientation* example, the different orientation of the lines in the upper right quadrant makes that quadrant stand out.

Our tendency is to group people according to proximity, similarity, continuity, and orientation. If we see several people standing close to each other, we are likely to consider them as a group of friends

or associates. If several people look alike, we are apt to group them together. If we see several people engaged in a continuous activity at work or play, our tendency will be to group them together. Five carpenters building a house will be perceived as members of the same work group. If we see several people standing up and several lying down, we will group them as their orientation suggests — a group of upright persons and a group of recliners.

GROUPING CHECK

Match the proper form of grouping with its appropriate example. Answers on page 243.

_____ 1. The action unfolding on a television screen.

_____ 2. Three Caucasians walking along the Ginza in Tokyo.

_____ 3. The driver of the approaching bus sees Tom, Dick, and Harry clustered around the bus stop sign, so he expects them to get aboard.

_____ 4. The ambulance driver sees two people lying on the ground near a wrecked car.

A. Proximity   B. Similarity
C. Continuity   D. Orientation

Closure. Another way we simplify is to make what we perceive into wholes. If a stimulus pattern is incomplete, we fill in the missing parts to make it a whole, as in Figure 5.4. Parts are missing in the figure, and we tend to complete or close the patterns represented by the drawings. We make a triangle, circle, and straight line out of what we see.[23]

Some people are "outloud closers." When they are conversing with someone and the partner pauses longer than appropriate, "closers" supply the rest of the sentence, outloud or in their heads.[24] They may err in the process, saying or thinking something that the speaker may not have intended. Note what happens in these examples:

Jim: Hmm! The weather . . .
Ginny: [. . . sure looks like it's gonna be lousy. I'm going.]
Jim: The weatherman says it's going to clear up and be perfect all day.

Matt: Well, I suppose I should be going. . .
Christine: [Hurrah! His talk is driving me crazy!]
Matt: But I'll stay for another hour or so. You're very hospitable.

To themselves, in the above examples, Ginny and Christine complete the thoughts of Jim and Matt and, in the process, come up with inaccurate interpretations of what Jim and Matt meant. Of course, we also can complete someone's message accurately.

Interpretation

The third stage in the perceptual process is interpretation, *the attribution of meaning to what we perceive.* Interpretation is a subjective process involving evaluations on the part of the perceiver.

Interpretation of what we perceive is not based solely on the stimulus itself but, rather, is influenced greatly by our past experiences, needs, wants, values, beliefs, physical and emotional states at the time we sense the stimulus, expectations, and so on. With all of these influences coming to bear, the chances of our interpreting the stimulus the same as someone else who is subject to the same stimulus is highly unlikely. Although we are exposed to the same stimulus, the way it is interpreted differs for each person and, from one time to another, for the same person.[25]

An experiment was conducted to illustrate how past experiences affect interpretation. American and foreign students were asked to identify the contents of a glass jar. The liquid inside was white. Most Americans perceived the liquid to be milk. To them the liquid seemed familiar, having a consistency and color they had learned to associate with milk, a fluid they drank daily as children. Actually the liquid was colored water. Nevertheless, the students recalled the past and interpreted the jar's contents as milk. Of the foreign students who participated in the experiment, those who were not fed milk from bottles as babies or who had not often seen milk in bottles more often identified the liquid as something other than milk, some sort of white fluid they had seen or learned about previously.

The knowledge and experience individuals gain over a lifetime are among the most significant determiners of their actions in any situation. Because most of us are products of a single culture, our experiences for the most part are representative of that culture. Our self-concept is largely bound to that culture. Throughout our lives we learn from family, from peers, from other people, and from more remote sources such as books, newspapers, and television. We learn facts, patterns of action, habits, stereotypes, and prejudices, all of which we apply in

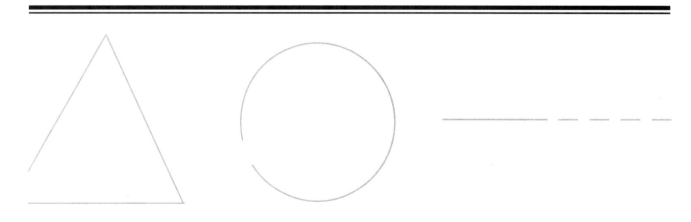

FIGURE 5.4. Closure.

the communication situations in which we become involved. Likewise, our self-concept is developed in this manner. We acquire this concept largely in terms of the expectations that we think others have of us.

Our present needs and the intensity of the stimulus likewise influence our perception. One woman tells how she misinterpreted the name "Ford" on the back of a rapidly moving truck as "food." She had not eaten for a long time, so food was foremost in her mind. Hunger represents a single illustration of a need. When we are hungry, we feel tension and discomfort. Our irritability grows until we eat, and then the tension subsides. In the woman's case, hunger so overcame her that it affected her comprehension and she mentally substituted "food" for "Ford."

When we interact with people, our perceptions about them are influenced by certain psychological events. Six that bear upon our interpretations of people are described next.[26]

1. *Self-fulfilling prophecy.* Simply stated, the self-fulfilling prophecy operates when we make a forecast and then go about fulfilling it. If we look at the cover of a book and prophesize that it will be dull, it will turn out to be dull if the self-fulfilling prophecy is operationalized. We define it as dull, and thus we make it dull when it may be anything but dull. Similarly, when we meet a person for the first time and prophesize that we will dislike the person, chances are that we will. We probably will act in a way to encourage negative responses. The old adage, "A man can't ride your back unless it is bent," applies here. *We act in a manner so as to fulfill our prophecies.*[27]

2. *Primacy/recency.* In people's perception, primary/recency suggests that the first impressions we have of a person provide us with a general idea of what the person is like (primacy information). As we acquire more information (recency information) about the person, the later information makes the general idea more specific. If we meet someone for the first time and get the impression that this person is a nerd (primacy information), whatever later information (recency information) we obtain, we perceive as supporting our original impression. No doubt about it, the person is a nerd — even though our information may be inaccurate.

3. *Perceptual accentuation.* Known also as the *halo effect*, this factor in perceiving people implies that we will see what we expect to see and what we want to see. If we like someone, we will see that person as better looking or more intelligent than someone we do not like. Some of us may want or like to be in the company of smart people, so we will perceive those

around us that way. Some of us may want or like to be around good-looking people; thus, we will perceive those around us as good looking. *We heighten the effect of that which satisfies our wants or desires.*[28]

4. *Consistency.* We tend to maintain balance or consistency among our perceptions. We expect a person we like to like us, a person we dislike to dislike us, and a friend to like our friend and dislike our enemy. We expect the people we like to have the qualities we like, and our enemies not to have them. Our enemies have the qualities we dislike in people.

5. *Implicit personality theory.* According to this theory, we have a set of rules that tells us what personality characteristics go with what other characteristics. Certain characteristics seem to fit with certain other ones. If Paul is bright, lively, and intelligent, chances are that we will characterize him also as attractive rather than unattractive, even though no law says he could not be unattractive. If he is stupid, fat, and introverted, chances are that we will characterize him as unlikeable rather than likeable, even though there is no reason why he could not be likeable.

Our implicit theory holds that good characteristics go together with other good characteristics, and that bad go with bad. This suggests that when we meet someone for the first time and perceive that person in a certain way, we will begin to assign him or her other characteristics that fit our system. For example, if we perceive the person to be attractive and likeable, we might then decide that the person is also bright and lively, even though we have no reason to know if the person is or not.

6. *Stereotyping.* A stereotype is defined as *a generalized attitude, notion, or idea held by an individual or the members of one group about the members of another group and treated as though it were universally true about all members of the other group.* Even though members of the other group undoubtedly possess individual differences, these are not taken into account. The notion is considered to apply to everyone in the group.[29] For instance, in a large group of Japanese females, the stereotype of the American male is that he is big, tall, white, active, daring, quick, kind, cheerful, and frank. Only three females in this group had ever visited the United States, so the image of the American male was contrived largely from the media.[30] Of course, it is inaccurate. Although many American males fit the stereotype, many more do not.

Stereotyping is widely practiced. Judging an individual on the basis of assumed group characteristics not only is common but is actually unavoidable. Because dealing with every individual in a group as a unique individual is impossible, stereotyping is inevitable.

SUMMARY

Perception is the process whereby we select, organize, and interpret sensory stimulation into a meaningful and coherent picture of the world. The senses stimulated are the distance senses (seeing and hearing), the skin senses (touch, taste, and smell), and the deep senses (kinesthesis, equilibrium, and internal organ senses). Perception has six major characteristics. It is based on knowledge, is inferential and categorical, is relational and adaptive, and is operationally automatic.

People's perceptions differ, and they do so because of physiological and psychological differences. Physiologically our perceptions are limited by illusions, neurological inhibitions, and innate characteristics. Psychologically our perceptions are limited by experience, emotional state, and selection, a part of the attention step in the perceptual process.

The perceptual process consists of three stages: attention, organization, and interpretation. We sense a stimulus, organize it in some fashion, and seek meaning in what we sensed and organized.

Of the many stimuli in our sensory field at any one time, we attend to only a few. We select those that are of interest to us, are novel or moving, and are colorful or repeated. Selection is influenced also by our predispositions and culture. What we select we tend to organize into meaningful patterns. We organize by figure and ground or in some simple fashion through grouping or closure. What we sense and organize, we interpret; we look for meaning in it. In our perceptions of people, we tend to be affected by psychological phenomena such as the self-fulfilling prophecy, primacy/recency, perceptual accentuation, consistency, implicit personality theory, and stereotyping.

6

The Concept of Self

Oral communication begins with *self*.[1] Skill in interpersonal, small-group, and public communication is closely associated with a useful and realistic perception of self. Indeed, how we handle ourselves in speaking situations is often thought to depend not only on how capable we actually are as speakers but also on how capable we think we are. In fact, success in school and in life may depend less upon the qualities we inherit or acquire than how we feel about those qualities.[2]

A world-famous speaker and author, Norman Vincent Peale, is a case in point. In an account of his life, he told how he had some negative self-images as a youngster. His father and mother were able and successful, and he thought he would never measure up to their achievements. His self-concept greatly affected his behavior; he felt inadequate and performed miserably. He had inherited the qualities essential to success, but he felt inferior, and his feelings outweighed his naturally acquired brilliance. One day a college professor took him aside and demanded, "How long are you going to be bashful like this, a scared rabbit afraid of the sound of your own voice?" After that admonishment, Peale began to change and became the person his natural talents allowed him to be.

Like Peale's manner of speaking as a college student, our speech is apt to reveal what we think of ourselves. Our idea of who we think we are — our self-concept — is indicative of how we behave as speakers. As a youth, Peale was unsure of himself, and his speech betrayed him. So it is with us. If we are confident and self-assured, our speech reflects this assurance. If we are kind, modest, and truthful, our speech reveals these qualities. If we lack confidence in ourselves, our speech conveys this feeling.

In this chapter, we examine the concept of the self. Successful speaking requires understanding of how we perceive our self and how others perceive their self; hence its importance in personal and public speaking. In considering the self, we define it and discuss its general nature. We look at its formation and its relationship to speech. Some people need to enhance the self, to increase their self-esteem, and we include suggestions for upgrading the self-concept.

THE NATURE OF SELF-CONCEPT

The self-concept is the *total collection of attitudes, beliefs, and values that an individual holds with respect to the individual's behavior, ability, body, and worth as a person* — in short, how the individual perceives and evaluates his or her self.[3] Although we refer to it as a single entity here, the definition of self-concept implies that we have a number of perceptions of our self. Our self-concept is not a single, all-encompassing identity. We have perceptions of our physical self, our attractiveness to others, how we act, our personality, our background and experience, our talents and shortcomings, and our value as human beings. We have many selves, or images of who and what we are.

In our world the most important aspect is that portion consisting of the perceptions of "I" or "me" — the self. A basic motive we have is the inherent tendency to develop all of our capacities in ways that serve to maintain or enhance our lives. We have a need for positive regard, a desire to be loved and respected. Satisfying this need, however, is

The Self-Concept

The way one thinks of oneself:

How I feel about ME

dependent on others, specifically in the way we perceive that others regard us. We are influenced more by our perceptions of how others think of us than by our actual actions.[4] Norman Vincent Peale was affected by his perception of the college professor's thoughts and did something about them. The professor, we recall, thought poorly, in Peale's perception, of Peale's bashful behavior. Peale did little to help himself until the professor offered his admonishment. People's perceptions of our behavior, thus, are more important to us than the actual results of that behavior.

The self has dimensions or levels, according to various theories. One theory specifies a *private* self and a *public* self. The private self is one we do not share with others, and the public self is one we do display publicly. Another theory states that we have a *superego*, an *ego*, and an *id*, each of which plays a different role in behavior. Still another theory, one discussed more fully later in the chapter, suggests that the self has four levels — *open, blind, hidden,* and *unknown.*

Which one of our selves appears at a given moment depends upon the circumstances, the people we are with, the time, and what we are talking about. At home we may be quiet, agreeable, and polite. In the company of friends we may be just the opposite — loud and aggressive, but friendly. In school we might be studious, alert, and vocal. Thus, as we move from situation to situation, we change our image and project the one we think is appropriate for that specific situation.

Formation of Self-Concept

Our concept of self begins to take shape in early childhood. Through interaction with *significant*

others — parents, relatives, and peers — we derive our self-concept by judging the satisfaction we get from these interactions. If the significant others show us love and respect, our self-evaluation probably will develop positively. If we are ignored or neglected, our self-evaluation may become negative. If we are better athletes than our peers, we might conclude that we have the makings of stardom. If we are more inclined academically than our peers, we might conclude that we are studious. We learn about who we are from the way people who are significant in our lives act toward us and by comparing ourselves to them.

Group memberships likewise influence our perception of self, and our self-concept reflects the society in which we live. Church, school, and neighborhood groups have a great impact, as does the culture of which we are a part.

The *roles* we play in groups also influence the development of self-concept. Roles are positions we assume in relation to someone or something else. They may be assigned, or they may be a stance we take in a particular situation. For instance, at school we are assigned the student role; at home, the son or daughter role; at work, the employee role; at church, the parishioner's role. These are assigned roles; we do not have much choice about them if we want to attend school, church, work, or be a family member. Our gender role is another role over which we have little control. Among friends we might take roles upon ourselves, but with the friends' concurrence.[5]

Whatever role we play in a particular situation, it affects our expectations, beliefs, needs, and attitudes about that situation, and it restricts how we perceive that situation. This, in turn, affects our self-concept. If our role as a son or daughter is that of an obedient child, for instance, that characteristic affects the development of our self-concept.

Self-concept, therefore is formed through experience and interactions with others. We adopt or internalize this need to be thought worthwhile. We see ourselves and evaluate ourselves as others do. We come to evaluate our own experiences in terms of the values we acquire from others. Self-concept is a picture we hold of ourselves at a given moment in a specific situation, based on our hopes and fears, successes and failures, attractiveness to others, and good and bad points.

Culture and the Self-Concept

The American self-concept is an integral part of our culture.[6] We naturally assume that each person is not only a separate biological entity but also a unique psychological being and a singular member of our society. The self is deeply ingrained in our culture, and we seldom question its importance. Our dominant self, visible in the form of individualism, pervades our relationships and is part of all of our activities. It is as though we have a wall around our self that differentiates our self from other people. The wall makes all or parts of our self inaccessible to outsiders. Our self is distinct from others. Typically, as Americans, we are interested in our self-image, self-esteem, self-reliance, self-awareness, self-actualization, and self-determination. The self is a unifying concept, providing a direction in thinking, a perspective for activity, a source of motivation, and a focus for decision making. Communication with typical Americans hinges on the ability to evoke their self-interests.

Other cultures do not share our concern for the self. In other cultures people may not think their own selves are much different from other selves. In India, for example, the tendency is not to erect a wall between one's self and others. Another self is not independent from one's own self.

In other cultures the uniqueness of perception characterizing Americans does not exist. Personal preference does not carry the same priority as Americans give it. The emphasis in other cultures is not so much on the "I" and "me," as in America, as on the "we" and "us." The Japanese stress understanding and sharing the general attitudes of others. The Chinese self-concept has deep roots in the social structure of the society. Identities of individuals are inclined to form around the lineal family, including ancestors and future offspring. This Chinese concept of self implies that anything that has been done, is done, or will be done by family members is an action of the self. The Chinese self, thus, can span centuries, including a wide range of family experiences.[7]

In many cultures, especially the non-Western ones, the group, not the individual member's self, is the vital entity. The group might be the family, clan, or state, but it is the essential unit. Individual group members are more interested in the group's fate than their own. The group's image, esteem, and achievement are primary. The individual self is subservient to the group. Upgrading the individual's self-esteem does not merit the attention that Americans direct to this activity. The counseling, workshops, courses, and other types of instruction Americans give to self-development are virtually nonexistent.

An illustration of how different cultures treat the self is shown in the way addresses are written. In America we address an envelope like this: Ms. Brenda I. Wear, 130 Armstrong Avenue, Morgantown, West Virginia, U.S.A. The most important part, the self, comes first, followed in order by the family, the neighborhood, the city, and the country, the least important. In Japan and Korea, addresses are written in this manner: Japan, Chiba-ken, Mobara, 130 Takashi, Kanetake, Yoko. The country is named first, because it is the most important feature. Then we see the prefecture, city, neighborhood, family name, and finally the addressee, the least important aspect.[8]

In multicultural United States, where people from many cultures are welcome to live, we should anticipate variations in the conception of self. People originally from collectivistic cultures where the group or state is supreme do not share the same beliefs about the self as those of the more individualistic climate in the United States.

With respect to culture, we can conclude, differing attitudes prevail about the self. The concept of self is strong in people whose culture is largely Western. Typical Americans, for instance, carry with them a sense of who they are, what they should be, and what they want to be. Their behavior is determined largely by their perceptions of self. This attitude is a phenomenon of the predominantly Western-influenced culture in America and is not shared universally by all cultures.

Our self-concept indicates how we will behave as speakers.

Relationship to Speech

We are interested in the nature of the self-concept because of its influence on the communication process. Speech begins with the self, and skill in speaking is closely related to a useful and realistic perception of the self. A person's image of self affects the person's speaking in several ways. One way is in *facilitating communication with others.* Our self-concept helps us to communicate by allowing us to provide information about ourselves to others. When we converse with strangers, for instance, we spend a lot of time initially trying to learn about those individuals, and they do likewise, trying to learn about us. We want to know who and what they are, and they ask for similar sorts of information from us. Because we possess concepts of self, we can satisfy those requests.

In addition, the self-concept *influences our verbal and nonverbal communicative behavior and the meanings we assign to the communicative behavior of others.* We tend to behave in a manner consistent with our self-concept and act like the person we think we are. In the classroom, for example, our concept of school shows in our behavior. If we feel negative about school, most likely we will behave negatively, being unfriendly, uncooperative, and unwilling to learn. If we feel positive about school, we undoubtedly will behave positively, being friendly, cooperative, and eager to learn. If we think of ourselves in certain ways, we will behave in those ways.

As we just said, our self-concept also influences the meaning we assign to the behavior of others. If we dislike ourselves, we are apt to seek confirming behavior from others and project negative implications into their verbal or nonverbal behavior toward us. Following this thinking in the case of teacher-student relationships, as students we might be prone to believe that the teacher dislikes us as much as we dislike ourselves. Then, whatever the teacher says or does, we will tend to read negatively. As a consequence, we could end up not doing well in class, partially because we do not feel positive about ourselves as students and partially because we might think the teacher feels the same way, so why bother; we don't stand a chance. Thus, if we think of ourselves in certain ways, we look for cues that confirm our self-view. The self-fulfilling prophecy, discussed previously, is at work.

Effect on Academic Performance

From what we said about the influence of the self-image on communication, we can surmise that the self-concept affects academic performance as well. It does. Those who do well in school typically have a high regard for themselves, are optimistic about their chances of future success, believe they are competent, and tend to be hard workers. Those who are low academic achievers are virtually the opposite, holding unfavorable attitudes toward school and their teachers, assuming little responsibility for learning, displaying low morale, low motivation, and low class participation, creating discipline problems, and having high dropout rates.[9]

Changing the Self

By now we should be aware that we hold many concepts of self and that the concepts we do hold vary from situation to situation. In some situations we think highly of ourselves; in others we carry a

low self-esteem. In addition, we usually hold a generalized concept of self. We total up our many selves and obtain a general or broad concept of self. It could be good, bad, so-so, fair-to-good, great, or whatever.

When in our minds the situational or general self is not the highest, we usually can do something about making changes. Remember Norman Vincent Peale, whom we mentioned earlier? He changed his general concept of self through a program of positive thinking. Bespectacled former President Harry S. Truman, taunted as a boy because of his "four eyes," overcame the inferior feelings the taunts evoked in him. He did so by being above the name calling and by doing more work than the name callers. "You've got to fight for everything you do," he advised, believing everything then will turn out all right.

Though Truman's advice deserves consideration, more than advice is needed. Throughout this book we offer ways to enhance the self-concept. Communication apprehension, for instance, is a major cause of low self-esteem.[10] In the next chapter we describe its nature and suggest ways to reduce its impact. Forthcoming chapters indicate methods for interacting more effectively in interpersonal, small-group, and public speaking situations. Being a more successful speaker should help. Self-revelation also is important to becoming a more successful speaker. In the next section we tell what to reveal.

DISCLOSING THE SELF

Self-disclosure — *voluntarily telling others information about ourselves that they are unlikely to learn from other sources* — occurs when we are our real selves in the presence of others.[11] That intellectual and emotional honesty comes when we refuse to veil our inner self from other people. Willingness to reveal the inner self is the key to self-disclosure.

The Inner Self

What is the inner self? The Johari window, represented in Figure 6.1, was created by Joseph Luft and Harry Ingham to illustrate relationships in terms of awareness.[12] The window is a square divided into four quadrants, each of which contains a different depiction of self.

The *open* quadrant refers to the feelings and behaviors known to ourselves and to others. Here we might find information such as our name, nickname, gender, age, year in school, religion, political affiliation, marital status, and so on.

The *blind* quadrant contains the feelings and behaviors known to others but not to us. This is information about ourself others know but we are

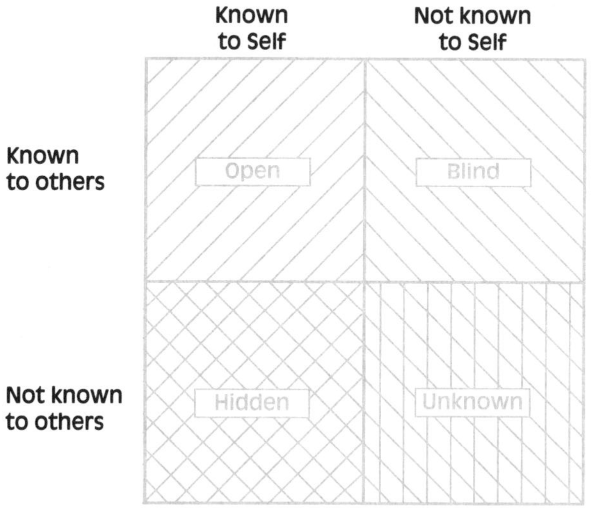

FIGURE 6.1. Johari window.

unaware of. When communicating, for instance, we may constantly interrupt others, be critical of our instructors, and reveal friends' secrets.

The *hidden* quadrant — the inner self — is the part known to us but not revealed to others. For example, Ron, Jim, and Virginia have no idea that Don coached basketball and won a half dozen championships but coached football and finished last in the league each year he coached. Don has not shared this information with his friends.

The fourth quadrant, the *unknown* self, holds the feelings and behaviors unknown both to us and to others. For whatever reason, we tend to submerge part of our self, letting no one including ourself know that part. During psychological counseling some of this information might come out. Secrets kept from our self emerge in some instances after years of psychotherapy, helping us to better understand our motivations.

More effective oral interaction results from self-disclosure or increasing the size of the open quadrant — revealing more of the hidden part. We enlarge the open quadrant when we share with others the feelings and behaviors we have kept hidden from them. Our inner self is opened to the others.

Chances are that we will self-disclose or tell more of our hidden feelings in a dyadic relationship than in small-group or public speaking situations. The more people who are present as we talk, the harder it becomes for us to judge how accepting people are of us. When we cannot monitor the reactions of those who hear us, we are reluctant to self-disclose too much. We are more inclined to bare our souls to

one person than many, and we certainly will not do so with strangers. The better we know someone, the more willing we are to self-disclose.

Self-disclosure increases with people we know well — close friends, mates, family members — and when the disclosure is rewarded, we receive positive responses for what we disclose. We also self-disclose more when a need to reduce uncertainty occurs in a relationship. Peggy and Beth meet frequently to study together. Once in a while Peggy fails to show up at the appointed hour. This discourtesy upsets Beth. Peggy tries to ameliorate the situation by disclosing the reason for her absences. "My boyfriend drops over just when I'm about to leave," Peggy reveals, "and there's no way I can call you." Beth had not been aware of Peggy's boyfriend — a secret other students were not in on either.

Women tend to be higher self-disclosers than men, and they disclose more with people they like. Men tend to disclose more with individuals they trust. Both men and women disclose negative information about themselves more often in highly intimate settings, yet they disclose positive information more readily in nonintimate surroundings.[13]

Self: oneself

Self-actualization: achieving one's potential

Self-assurance: having or showing confidence or sureness

Self-awareness: cognizant of one's own personality or individual qualities

Self-concept: the way one thinks of oneself

Self-conscious: discomfort with or embarrassment about one's own appearance or manner; ill-at-ease socially

Self-disclosure: voluntarily revealing information about the self to others

Self-doubt: lack of confidence in self

Self-efficacy: modesty, shyness, not calling attention to self

Self-esteem: pride in one's self, self-respect

Self-examination: careful introspection of one's own thoughts, feelings

Self-fulfilling prophecy: predicting a result that then happens

Self-fulfillment: measuring up to self-expectations

Self-image: one's mental concept of one's self; how one sees oneself in relationship to others

Self-knowledge: understanding of one's own abilities, nature, and limitations

Self-respect: valuing of one's own personal worth

When we self-disclose, hidden information moves from the hidden part to the open, and another event usually occurs when the communication becomes more open: feedback. Other people respond to what we self-disclose, and this often reveals feelings and behaviors in the blind part — feelings and behaviors unknown to us but apparent to the other person. After the other person exposes these feelings and behaviors to us, they move from the blind to the open part, and so we learn more about ourselves.[14]

To sum up, how we represent ourselves to others shows what happens when we disclose more of what is hidden in the inner self. When we reveal more of the hidden part, we tend to be more open in our communication. We then show more of our real self to others. In addition, because of the other's feedback, we should become more aware of what lies in the blind part, causing what is there to open itself up to us.

What to Disclose

A problem arises in self-disclosing: what to disclose? When we are called upon to self-disclose, we tend to become defensive. Classroom exercises in self-disclosure often are less than successful and more often are failures because the students taking part are reluctant to share their true self with others. Instead, they try to identify those parts they want to share and those they want to keep hidden. They actually end up revealing little. This reaction is normal. We allow some people to know certain things about ourselves and others to see other things. We do not share everything with everyone.

Underlying the self-disclosure process is a key principle: Our communication with another person will be more effective and efficient when we know more about the other person and the other person knows more about us. Therefore, as we consider what to reveal, we should realize that we need to reveal information that will enhance the communication, information that the other person does not already know, information that he or she is unlikely to learn from others.

What sort of information would such disclosure include? Some items we might share with others include our attitudes, opinions, tastes, interests, feelings about people, work and money, likes, dislikes, loves, hates, fears, anxieties, and self-perceptions. Before self-disclosing on personal topics such as these, we should be in a proper setting. We speak most effectively in non-threatening situations, those that do not pose possibilities for acceptance or rejection, approval or disapproval. The key to effective oral communication is: *We speak best in situations wherein mutual self-disclosure is possible.* Those situations usually are nonevaluative and nonthreatening, settings of goodwill.

Self-disclosure requires courage, and it also requires discretion so it does not become "emotional nudity," baring oneself to the world. We should self-disclose only in certain circumstances. Self-disclosure seems best when it is (a) to the right person, one who is capable of understanding; (b) to the right degree, disclosing all or part of the experience; (c) for the right reasons, not to burden others or show off; (d) at the right time, when the listener is not burdened with his or her own needs; and (e) in the right place, a quiet, private location.[15]

Although we may inhibit our talk if we follow these guidelines too closely, to ignore them totally — to bare our soul to the world — would be foolish. At times we should refrain from expressing our true feelings. Being polite or diplomatic is necessary in some circumstances. Self-disclosure does not necessarily produce liking, and inappropriate disclosure actually can result in negative impressions. In some cases, with persons we like, self-disclosure may not always be the best course of action, because it has the potential of damaging the relationship. In the long run and in most circumstances, a healthier relationship will develop if we practice thoughtful disclosure, not unconditional openness.

SUMMARY

To understand the self, we must be familiar with the concept of perception, the topic of the last chapter. The self is largely what we perceive it to be; thus, perception and self-identity are linked inseparably.

The self-concept is a collection of perceptions that relate to every aspect of a person's being. Formed by views of self and experience and also by the reactions of significant others, the self influences the way we communicate with others.

Some people need to enhance the self. Suggestions for improving speech effectiveness, and thereby the self, appear throughout the remaining chapters. Self-disclosure is one way to develop a better self-image. Revealing ourselves to others should provide information that will allow them to more rapidly interpret our words and actions as we intended them, but this also requires discretion.

7

Communication Anxiety

Closely related to the communicator's self-concept is the fear of speaking, affecting the oral communication abilities of millions. In 1973, speaking before a group was the number one American fear, ranking well above other fears such as fear of heights, insects, financial problems, deep water, sickness, and death. In 1988, it still ranked high, exceeded only by the fear of snakes in the minds of representative Americans.[1]

Although the fear of speaking is common, it is more than ordinary for some Americans. An estimated 20 percent of the nation's school population — elementary, secondary, and college students — experience unacceptably high levels of oral communication apprehension. For those who have this fear, it is handicapping; the fear is of sufficient magnitude to seriously interfere with their functioning in normal social situations.[2]

Even the people who are not among the fear-handicapped, 20 percent usually have felt "butterflies in the stomach" at one time or another. The "butterflies" may happen in any one of many speaking situations — public speaking, interviewing, discussing — and this, more common pre-speaking anxiety tends to appear in many people prior to important speaking engagements. Stage fright can affect even the most experienced speakers.

In this chapter, we describe the fear of speaking, from the common stage fright to the more debilitating forms. By understanding the nature of communication apprehension, we should be better prepared to deal with it if we have reason to be so affected.

THE NATURE OF SPEAKING FEARS

Called by a variety of names — apprehension, stage fright, tenseness, speaking anxiety, reticence, and shyness — the fear of speaking is *a person's level of fear or anxiety associated with either real or anticipated talk with one or more persons.*[3] Almost everyone

What scares Americans:

In 1973*
1. speaking before a group
2. height
3. insects and bugs
4. financial problems
5. deep water

In 1988**
1. snakes
2. public speaking
3. heights
4. flying
5. mice and rats

* According to the Bruskin Report
** According to the Roper Survey

has a degree of anxiety in some, but not all, speaking situations. Those with a high degree of anxiety, however, are different. They experience fear in almost every communication encounter or expected encounter. Not only do they suffer from the stage fright most people experience, but they are almost always fearful or anxious in all speaking situations.

Their fear or anxiety surpasses any rewards they think they will get by talking and, therefore, they either do not speak at all or avoid speaking unless they are obligated to do so. When they do speak, they appear shy, nonassertive, nervous, embarrassed, uncomfortable, and reticent. They respond negatively to all communication situations and are not perceived positively at school, on the job, or in social interactions.[4]

Symptoms of Speaking Anxiety

Speech anxiety has many symptoms. Anxious individuals may experience one or several of the following prevalent symptoms at any given speaking encounter:

- Feel nervous when talking to a new acquaintance
- Feel shy or self-conscious in the presence of others
- Are afraid to express opinions in a group
- Feel strained or unnatural when speaking
- Tense up or feel nervous in group discussion
- Are at a loss for words in the presence of others
- Have trembling hands when speaking before others
- Desire to avoid public speaking
- Have confused and jumbled thoughts when speaking
- Do not like to use the voice and body expressively
- Feel self-conscious when expected to answer questions
- Perspire, experience headaches, have a dry mouth

This list gives a general idea of the signs of anxiety.

Another way of ascertaining speaking apprehension is to look at the observable behavior patterns of individuals who are supposedly frightened by speaking. Three categories of these patterns are fidgetiness, inhibition, and autonomia. *Fidgetiness* patterns include shuffling feet, swaying, swinging the arms, stiffening the arms, making little eye contact, and pacing. *Inhibition* patterns include behaviors such as

having a "deadpan" look, trembling knees, hands in pockets, a pale face, trembling hands, and returning to seat before uttering the closing remarks. *Autonomic* behaviors include moistening the lips frequently, playing with objects while speaking, blushing, breathing heavily, and swallowing repeatedly.

Linda and Susan, two college students questioned about their symptoms, express their feelings in the following sets of comments. Linda says:

> My whole problem is that I hate to talk in front of people whether it is impromptu or planned. It isn't necessarily just people I don't know, but a lot of times it's a group of friends or even a group of relatives. Whenever I get embarrassed or am put on the spot for a question or comment, or have to talk in front of a group, my face turns red.

She goes on to talk about her feeling in class:

> I'm very easily swayed, so almost immediately I'm agreeing with the opposite view, and then it makes me look like a fool because I change my mind so rapidly. I never ask questions in class for two reasons. First, when you raise your hand, everyone turns their attention to you, and then I start to blush. Then, when I ask the questions, to me, all of a sudden they sound dumb. So I don't bother.

Linda feels foolish and thinks she comes across as dumb-sounding. Susan's fears in contrast, center on informal situations, whereas she does better with public speeches. She says:

> I have a lot of difficulty talking to people informally. I can usually handle any discourse which has a formal basis with only nervousness and stuttering. But group meetings or casual conversations are very hard for me, and I usually don't say anything in these situations. Meeting people always strains me. I usually respond to them very bluntly and mispronounce my words.

> The hardest people for me to talk to are guys my age. I also find it difficult to talk with anyone at meals, parties, dorm raps, or in class. When I'm approached at a party, even though I might want to get to know the person, I can never seem to convey my interests.[5]

Even the man called the "great communicator," former American President Ronald Reagan, admitted that he gets nervous in certain circumstances. When he addressed the British Parliament and when he gave the State of the Union Address before Congress, he felt nervous: "You recognize that you face a professional audience that is aware of all the same problems you are going to discuss," he said, "There was a group sitting there kind of saying 'show me.' "

Types of Apprehension

Linda, Susan, and Ronald Reagan seem to be talking about different types of fear. Linda appears to be apprehensive in just about all speaking situations. Susan's comments imply a general feeling of apprehension, which becomes more pronounced in informal encounters. Reagan's nervousness comes only in specific situations. Each represents a different type of fear.

Speaking fears in people have been categorized into four major types. Figure 6.1 places them equidistant on a scale. The traitlike and the situational types are at opposite ends; audience-based and context-based fears fall in between.

Traitlike Apprehension

A trait is something that is constant; it cannot be changed. Eye color is an example; true eye color is permanent and unchangeable. A traitlike quality is highly resistant to change and, because this is so, it seems like a trait. A traitlike quality can be changed, however — albeit only with considerable effort. *Traitlike apprehension is highly resistant to change.* Through a carefully administered treatment program, however, alterations can be made to alleviate the fears.[6]

Traitlike apprehension is characterized by fear of communication in many different contexts. People who have this type of fear tend to be apprehensive in just about all speaking situations. The fear is relatively enduring and will not change without some type of intervention program. Hence, if a person has traitlike apprehension on Monday, the person will be like that every other day of the week and, for that matter, every day of the person's life unless he or she undertakes treatment to reduce the fear. The person with traitlike apprehension is fearful in virtually all speaking situations, with the possible exception of speaking with family or friends.[7]

Context-Based Apprehension

People who have context-based apprehension are fearful or anxious about communicating in only one type of context. They have no fear or anxiety in other contexts. Susan did well in public speaking contexts but was fearful in informal situations, as she mentioned in her remarks, quoted earlier. Usually it is the other way around; the fear of public speaking, or stage fright, is most common.

Context-based apprehension is also relatively enduring. It becomes apparent whenever the person is in the fear-producing context, whatever that context may be — job interview, public speaking, group discussion, or informal talk with friends.[8]

Audience-Based Apprehension

Audience-based apprehension refers to the reactions of an individual to communicating with a given individual or group of people across time. Certain individuals or groups cause people with this type of apprehension to be highly anxious, whereas other people or groups do not. Some of us may be more apprehensive in the company of our peers. Others might become apprehensive in the presence of unfamiliar individuals or groups. A student may be highly apprehensive when talking to the teacher but have no apprehension when talking to a classmate.

Thus, *audience-based apprehension is a response to situational constraints generated by a specific person or group.* Relatively enduring, it is a normal sort of behavior most people experience, particularly in situations involving superior-subordinate relationships. In the teacher's office, the student is likely to exhibit this type of apprehension.[9]

Situational Apprehension

The mildest type, situational apprehension, occurs with a given person or group at one time but not at another time. For example, a student may have little or no apprehension when questioning the teacher about an assignment, but if the teacher calls the student into the office for a conference about suspected cheating, the student is fearful. In the same vein, if the boss calls in an employee to

Figure 6.1. Types of speaking fears.

discuss the possibility that the employee took company property, or if the boss directs the employee to give a speech on a topic the employee knows little about, or if a person is called into court to testify, these situations may cause the individuals involved to become apprehensive. The apprehension is transitory, however, lasting only until the specific situation is finished.[10]

CONSEQUENCES OF APPREHENSION

Speech is extremely important in the development of interpersonal relationships. In the American culture the more a person talks — unless the talk is overly negative or offensive — the more positively that person usually is perceived. Speech also is essential in school and in certain sorts of employment. The school fosters oral communication; it is an oral environment. In business and the professions millions of oral transactions take place every day. Hardly a business or profession could operate without some sort of oral communication. For those who are highly apprehensive, therefore, negative *academic, economic,* and *social* consequences may ensue. Some implications worthy of consideration are noted next.

Academic Implications

In the academic area, research reveals the characterizing behavior of highly apprehensive students. In school, they tend to drop speech classes early in the semester, if they enroll at all.[11] They prefer large lecture classes over small classes that encourage extensive student participation.[12] In the large classes, they choose seats in the back or on the classroom's periphery. The seats front and center are most accessible to the teacher; students in those seats are more likely to be called upon.[13] If a class offers tutoring help or advising of any sort, highly apprehensive students are not likely to seek it.[14] Because they avoid talking, their fellow students ignore them, having learned to do so from trying to draw them into class discussions.[15] When highly apprehensive individuals do participate, their comments often are irrelevant to the ongoing discussion, or their verbalizations differ from the others.[16] They are low producers of original ideas in group discussion.[17]

More devastating than their speech behavior is the feeling the others in the classroom — students and teacher — have of them. The others perceive them as nonassertive, risk-avoiders, cooperative, nondirective, go-along persons, uncommunicative, hard-to-know.[18] Highly apprehensive individuals also are seen as less socially attractive, less sexually attractive, less sociable, less competent, less task-attractive, and less composed than other students.[19] They are rarely turned to for opinion leadership.[20]

Teachers expect students who are highly apprehensive to have a lower overall academic achievement, less satisfactory relationships with others, and lower probability of educational success than their less apprehensive peers.[21] Within the academic environment, the results of negativism toward the high apprehensives have been established. The high apprehensives have lower overall college grade-point averages,[22] lower grades in small classes,[23] and lower achievement on standardized tests than those who are less apprehensive — this in spite of their intelligence level, which in many cases is high.[24]

The research seems overwhelming. Highly apprehensive persons are impacted negatively in their academic life.

Economic Implications

In the employment arena, research reveals negative economic implications. Job applicants who have excellent credentials but are highly apprehensive are seen as less task- and socially attractive than those with low apprehension. They are predicted to be less satisfied in their jobs, to have poorer relationships with their work peers, supervisors, and subordinates, to be less productive, and to be less likely to advance. In addition, highly apprehensive applicants are less likely to be offered an interview and, even if they are interviewed, they are less likely to be hired than low apprehensives.[25]

High apprehensives prefer positions with lower pay and status to jobs with higher pay and status and that involve higher communication requirements,[26] as state and federal government employees actually demonstrated.[27] Of course, highly apprehensive people work, but they do not often find a job that is pleasing to them,[28] nor do they stay on the job as long as low apprehensives.[29]

Although much more study has to be done on the economic implications, the evidence accumulated so far seems to clearly support the proposition that highly apprehensive people are affected negatively on the job.

Social Implications

The effect of high apprehension on a person's social life follows the patterns already described. High apprehensives interact less with peer strangers, engage in more exclusive dating,[30] marry more quickly after graduating from college,[31] prefer housing remote from others,[32] and register and vote less than their peers with low apprehension.[33]

Highly apprehensive people:

Academically earn

  lower grade point averages
  lower class grades
  lower test scores

Economically are perceived as

  less task-attractive
  less satisfied on job
  less productive
  less likely to get promoted
  having poorer relationships with peers on job

Socially

  interact less with peer strangers
  engage in more exclusive dating
  marry more quickly after graduation
  prefer remote housing
  register and vote less often

Communication apprehension has been correlated with a variety of socially undesirable personality characteristics. Self-esteem and communication apprehension are negatively correlated for college students, elementary and secondary school teachers, and federal employees.[34] High communication apprehension is associated with negative self-image. Also, communication apprehension is positively correlated with general anxiety and negatively correlated with emotional maturity, dominance, surgency, character, adventurousness, confidence, self-control, and trustfulness.[35]

Thus, communication apprehension is closely linked to socially maladaptive individuals, although these people are not necessarily less intelligent than others. Communication apprehensives may have a low image of themselves, but they are not different intellectually from people with little apprehension.[36]

CAUSES OF APPREHENSION

What causes apprehension about speaking? No primary cause has been identified. Although research supports five theoretical explanations of what causes apprehension, none has been chosen as the principal cause. The theories are: heredity, modeling, reinforcement, skill acquisition, and expectancy learning.

Heredity

The theory of hereditary, that certain traits are passed on genetically, suggests that some people were born to be highly talkative, whereas others were not,[37] and major differences in the sociability of infants have been recorded. Sociability is the antecedent of verbal behavior patterns that develop as the infant grows older. Some infants exhibit much more sociability than others. As they grow older, the sociable ones become more talkative than those showing less sociability as infants.

Inherited predispositions, however, can be modified by the environment, and they often are. In the proper environment, infants who display little sociability can nevertheless develop into a talkative people. Thus, not too much credibility is attached to the heredity theory, although it is conceded that heredity does have an influence.[38]

Modeling

Modeling is a *form of learning based on observing and then imitating others' behavior.* Young children watch their parents, older brothers and sisters, teachers and peers, and from the observations the children learn how they are supposed to act as older boys and girls. Their play often is patterned on their perceptions of adolescent or adult behavior.[39] Modeling seems to be a reasonable explanation as to why Hawaii's children in the past grew up speaking "pidgin" and why Southern children grow up with a Southern accent.

Modeling also is advanced as a possible cause for apprehension. If a child is reared in an environment where "silence is golden," the child may be quiet. Children who are reared in an environment where talk is valued may become talkative. Children who are taught by educators known to be low verbalizers are more likely to become low verbalizers like their teachers.[40]

Although modeling has been suggested as a cause of apprehension, it probably is not the sole cause — merely a contributor. Not every child reared in a quiet household turns out to be apprehensive in communication situations.[41]

Reinforcement

The most popular current explanation for communication apprehension is offered by reinforcement theory. It says that a child learns to repeat behaviors that are rewarded and does not repeat, and tends to eliminate, over time, behaviors that are not rewarded. When the child is positively reinforced for speaking, the child probably will not become highly apprehensive. With positive reinforcement, the child learns to value speech both as a tool and as an intrinsically desirable experience.

A child who is not reinforced for speaking, or is punished, fails to develop appreciation for oral communication. This child does not find intrinsic reward in communication itself, nor does he or she learn the instrumental functions of communication. For this child, communication is not a tool; rather, it results in negative experiences. Such a child is likely to develop a high level of communication apprehension.[42]

Usually high communication apprehension develops in the preschool years or does not develop at all. In some instances, however, it develops later, or it develops early but is eliminated during the early school years. Each of these effects can be attributed to the impact of the school environment — teachers and peers.

Children who have experienced negative reinforcement in the preschool years and enter school with high communication apprehension can overcome the problem with extensive positive reinforcement from teachers and, later, from peers. Schools and peers, however, do not always provide positive reinforcement. Similarly, a child may enter school with moderate communication apprehension, but negative reinforcement from teachers and peers may cause the level of communication apprehension to increase.

Neither of these effects occurs quickly, and the change in the child may be hardly noticeable, even to a trained observer. Patterns that develop over several years prior to entering school are seldom reversed in a single year.[43]

Furthermore, reinforcement theory provides a reason why children in the same family can be almost opposite from each other in speaking behavior — why one is talkative, one shy. Because parents reinforce each child in a different fashion, one can be reinforced for talking and another reinforced for being quiet.

Many procedures for reducing apprehension that are based on reinforcement theory seem to be successful. This may be a reason to favor this theory.

Lack of Skill

Akin to the reinforcement explanation, the skill acquisition theory suggests that children become apprehensive because they fail to learn the skills necessary for effective speaking. Following the reasoning of this theory, we expect that a person will feel awkward in initiating conversations with strangers because the person never had acquired the skills to do so, or that a person has difficulty in interview situations because he or she had not been taught the skills vital to effective interviewing, or that a public speaker's ideas are embarrassingly disorganized because the speaker never had learned how to organize properly.[44]

In many cases of apprehension, especially those typed as situational apprehension, this theory probably has import. It certainly gives reason to advocate speech training at all educational levels, and it forms the basis for at least one method of reducing apprehension.

Expectancy Learning

As a theory, expectancy learning lacks the quantity of research support the other theories have. Nonetheless, it is a reasonable theory and, therefore, worth noting. This theory concerns the outcomes of people's communicative behavior — what the results of that behavior will be. People wish to know what will happen, what to expect, if they communicate in particular ways. When they find out the results, they will adjust their future communicative behavior so as to increase the likelihood of rewards for communicating and to decrease the likelihood of punishment. Hence, if their speaking ability results in positive responses, the more likely they are to speak. On the other hand, if their speaking brings punishment, they are likely to change their communicative approach.

Through expectancy learning we learn what to say in a given situation or in the presence of a certain type of person. We learn what to expect under a variety of conditions. We learn what to expect if we fail to talk in certain situations or to specific people. For example, in class discussion, if we do not participate and for that reason earn a low grade, we know what to expect during the next class discussion and we adjust to that circumstance. Likewise, we learn what to expect if we do speak in certain situations or to specific people. When the teacher calls upon us to report and then we receive a good grade for doing so, we know what to expect the next time we are called upon.

Some people, however, are unable to predict how others will react to them in speaking situations. This happens because one time they are rewarded for communicating as they did and another time they are punished for communicating in the same fashion. If children are rewarded for sitting quietly, they may not want to speak when the time comes because they were rewarded for not speaking. Now they are punished for not speaking. They cannot sort out the differences in situations and consequently, become helpless and withdrawn.

The expectancy learning theory builds upon reinforcement. When expectancies become habitual behaviors, this is because of consistent patterns of reinforcement. When the patterns are perceived as inconsistent, varying from similar situation to similar situation in the communicator's perception, the patterns become unpredictable. The communicator does not know what to expect, and apprehension results.[45]

QUIET PEOPLE

On occasion we meet people who appear to be apprehensive, but as we get to know them better, we discover they are not apprehensive at all, just quiet. They do not speak as often and as frequently as we think they should — like average people do. They are quiet people, and they may be quiet for any of a number of reasons. They may be *skills-deficient, socially introverted, socially alienated, or culturally divergent.*

Skills-Deficient

We have described people who are apprehensive because of deficiencies in speaking skills. Some quiet people may not be apprehensive, but they still might possess inadequate skills in speaking. They avoid oral interaction because they do not know quite how to go about it.

Some skills-deficient people have speech problems, such as stuttering, articulation disorders, or voice difficulties. Others cannot speak English as a second language very well. Most, however, simply have substandard skills. Once their skills improve, their speaking attempts will increase.

Socially Introverted

Social introverts constitute another group of low verbalizers who may not be termed apprehensive. These people do not have a very high need to be with others, preferring to be alone most of the time. They tend to be quiet not because they are apprehensive but simply because they have little desire to interact orally.

Socially Alienated

Some people become alienated from the people around them, rejecting the norms and behavior patterns of their society. They make no attempt to conform and see little value in speaking because they are not interested in the goals and values of others. They are not apprehensive, but merely uninterested in their peers' activities.

Culturally Divergent

Not all cultures prize verbalizing as the North American culture apparently does. Some cultures reward silence. Many of the Oriental cultures, for instance, downplay oral skills, placing a greater emphasis on nonverbal communication. In their own cultures, this behavior serves these people well. When in a different culture, however, their communication behavior may not be appropriate and their quietness may not serve them well.[46]

REDUCING SPEECH ANXIETY

What can be done to reduce speech anxiety? More than a dozen ways have been tested and proven useful. Among them are biofeedback, cognitive behavior modification, group counseling, hypnosis, implosion/flooding, modeling, rational restructuring, rational emotive therapy, reciprocal inhibition, self-efficacy, stress inoculation, systematic desensitization, assertiveness training, reality therapy/goal setting, rhetoritherapy, social/conversational skills training, oral role playing, and treatment via the basic speech course.

We first describe three methods that are most helpful to people with more than an ordinary amount of fear. These are followed by a section on how to reduce the more normal anxieties symptomatic of stage fright.

Systematic Desensitization

A popular and successful method for reducing apprehension, systematic desensitization is a behavior therapy derived from learning theory. Its rationale is that *apprehension is learned and anything that is learned can be unlearned.* The desensitization process involves two steps: (a) learning to relax, and (b) learning to respond with relaxation in the presence of tension-producing situations.

In the first step, the person being desensitized is taught how to recognize tension in the body and how to relax that tension. This can be accomplished through a series of relaxation exercises requiring the student to tense various muscles and then relax them. The learning can be directed by an instructor who is trained in these techniques or privately, by listening to a tape- recorded program, of which there are dozens. The programs expect the listeners to perform essentially the same exercises as a teacher would use in the classroom setting.

The second step involves conditioning apprehensive persons to respond in a relaxed manner to stimuli that create tension in them. They imagine a series of speaking situations, from those that produce little tension to those that instigate much tension. Beginning with the least tension-producing situations, they practice relaxing while thinking of those situations. Then, as they learn to relax in those situations, they progress to ones that produce more tension, relaxing while imagining those situations. Again, the teacher can direct the program, or the student can use one of the available commercial programs.[47]

The whole desensitization process, which takes about six hours, apparently is successful. A high percentage of those treated claim to have eliminated apprehension about speaking.[48] The training can be repeated periodically to reinforce the learning.

Cognitive Behavior Modification

The underlying rationale for cognitive behavior modification also is based on learning theory. It implies that some people have learned to think negatively about how they communicate and that they can be taught to think positively. The process has four steps:

1. The trainer or the teacher (if done in the classroom) helps those being treated recognize that their fear is learned and they have adapted behaviors that impair their speaking ability.

2. The apprehensive individuals identify their negative behaviors, with help from the teacher or trainer. Negative behaviors are identifiable in self-degrading statements such as, "I hate to talk to others," "I feel awkward in opening conversations," and "I can't call someone to make a date."

3. The apprehensive individuals learn positive statements to replace the negative ones. Again, the trainer provides assistance in developing the list. Statements such as "There's nothing to fear but fear itself," "All she can say is 'no,'" and "This is easier than I thought" make up the list.

4. The apprehensive trainees practice substituting the positive statements for the negative ones, both in training sessions and in actual speaking situations.

As in the case of systematic desensitization, the effectiveness of cognitive behavior modification reportedly is high, but not as high as the desensitization method. Combined, the two have proven exceedingly successful.[49]

Skills Training

Skills training is most useful for people who are apprehensive as a result of not having learned the skills necessary for effective speaking. If a person feels fearful in public speaking situations because he or she does not know how to prepare and present a speech, the person is trained in the know-how to give a speech.

Properly conducted, skills training is useful if skill deficiency is the only reason for the apprehension. If the apprehension has additional causes, the other causes must be treated before the skills improve.

To remedy the skill deficiencies, they first must be identified. This could become a complex task because most oral communication situations involve multiple skills. Public speaking, for instance, requires a half dozen major skills: subject analysis, research, organization, use of support, choice of language, and delivery, plus many minor skills. Taking a public speaking class may be the best way, therefore, to overcome the deficiencies, but that type of class can be time-consuming and might require more learning than the apprehensive person needs.

Minimally, in the public speaking class a student with public speaking deficiencies will accomplish the other steps in the training process: identifying and learning appropriate ways to overcome the deficiencies and practicing what is learned. The results of this type of training are usually excellent. Apprehensive people usually master the skills and thereby reduce their anxiety.

People who have skill deficiencies in more than one form of communication — for example, public speaking and interviewing — should augment the training in public speaking with training in interviewing. Learning one of those skills will not generalize to the other because the two activities call for different sets of skills. Therefore, two courses or training programs are needed. Most colleges have a variety of speech courses that provide skills training. If the apprehensive individuals are college students, they can easily obtain the training. Business and professional people can enroll in college courses through continuing education courses or receive the requisite training through one of the many private speech classes found in most cities.[50]

REDUCING ORDINARY TENSION

To many conscientious people, tenseness is a normal, natural condition. Tension arises in almost anyone who is confronted with a situation in which the speaking performance is important and the outcome uncertain. As speakers in a situation where we have something at stake, we realize that our success depends largely upon our speaking abilities. We fear failure and desire success, and we know that speaking to others constitutes a vital activity. We want to measure up to the speaking assignment, but we may have doubts about how well we will do. Capable people experience these feelings as a normal form of anxiety.

Actually, some tenseness is desirable. It serves as a stimulant to produce our best efforts. It is nature's way of causing us to be alert. Relieving tenseness entirely would deprive us of an essential prod to action; we should want to feel nervous before important speaking engagements. The tension sharpens our minds and gives our whole body more focus. Hence, we should welcome tension but should learn to control it so that the tension helps rather than hinders our efforts. As we contemplate ways to control tension, we should keep in mind that we are dealing with the natural, normal tenseness that virtually everyone feels when facing an important speaking situation. We previously suggested ways of treating serious apprehension problems, and the recommendations that follow will not alleviate those problems.

The Physiology of Emotions

Controlling stage fright must start with understanding the emotions involved. We tend to be afraid of what we do not understand. Tension, anxiety, and apprehension are emotional reactions and, if we know what emotion is, we should be better prepared to control it.

When we are faced with a threatening situation such as making a speech, our body reacts physically, almost automatically, to prepare us for it. Our muscles tense to make us more agile; our heartbeat and breathing quicken to supply more fuel; and our glands secrete fluids to sharpen our senses — all in a flash. Then we become cognizant of these physical reactions, and this awareness is what frightens us. The awareness is the emotional reaction or a reinforcement of the emotion — the fear we are discussing.

Our arms and hands tremble because the antagonistic flexor and extensor muscles of the arm, in highly emotional situations such as speaking, contract at the same time, causing the trembling. The emotion, acting as it normally does, increases the tension of the two opposing sets of muscles, which leads to the trembling.

The "butterflies in the stomach" feeling, like the trembling, is a natural physiological reaction to threatening situations. The body secretes glandular fluids, especially adrenalin, for additional energy when under duress. The secretions interfere with, and virtually stop, the digestive functions. The stomach contracts, producing a sinking feeling. At the same time, the heartbeat increases and breathing becomes heavier as the body prepares for survival.

Interestingly, it is believed that several antagonistic emotions cannot exist together. They can follow each other closely, but they cannot mix. We cannot be fearful and angry, love and hate, be sorrowful and joyful at the same time. Thus, as speakers, when we are enthusiastic or angry about our topic, we most likely will not be as afraid. According to what we just said, enthusiasm or anger cannot occur along with fear. Being keenly interested in our topic, therefore, can help control our fright.[51]

Relaxation Methods

Besides finding a topic we can become enthusiastic or angry about, other means of controlling stage fright are available. One of these is to reduce the tension by relaxing before speaking. Moderate physical exercise is helpful, as is a long walk. Relaxation exercises can be done just prior to the threatening occasion; they are effective tension reducers.

The two exercises[52] that follow are proven relaxers when done seriously and with concentration, shutting out environmental distractions. They take only a few minutes.

1. Sit comfortably in your seat, feet flat on the floor, back against the chair. Close your eyes. Take a few moments to sense your body breathing. After thirty seconds exhale through your nose; blow all the air out with a final puff or two. Let your shoulders slump forward as you exhale. Now inhale through your mouth with an audible sound, filling up every corner of your lungs, and

slowly pull your shoulders up. Continue breathing in this fashion for several minutes, alternately exhaling and inhaling every fifteen to twenty seconds.

Tense the muscles of your toes in the right foot as hard as you can. After a second or two, relax the toes. Then wiggle them for ten to fifteen seconds. Now do the same with your left foot, tensing the muscles, then relaxing them and wiggling your toes. Repeat with the calf, and follow with the thigh. Now move to the right leg and follow the same procedure. Finally, shake each arm vigorously, letting the shaking slowly subside.

Repeat this routine with the back muscles, facial muscles, eye muscles, and shoulder muscles.

After you have tensed and relaxed all of the muscles, return to the breathing pattern you began this exercise with. This time as you exhale, go limp; feel relaxed.

2. Imagine you are a doll, a stiff, ordinary doll. Tense your body like that of the stiff doll. Now imagine you are a rag doll, limp and floppy, as you quietly and calmly recite this verse:

   I'm a limp rag doll. (Let your body go limp.)

   I have no bones.

   My arms are limp. (Swing arms loosely.)

   My legs are limp. (Swing legs loosely.)

   My neck is limp. (Let your neck flop around.)

   I'm a limp rag doll.

Another way to control tension is to be well prepared to speak. Realizing that we know the speech topic well increases our feeling of confidence. Knowing that we can give the listeners factual information and mature judgments about that information creates confidence.

A great deal of this book relates to preparing to speak properly in interviewing, small-group, and public speaking situations. At this point we need not labor over how to prepare. Remember, however, that preparation is a key to reducing anxiety.

Using notes can help overcome fear. By placing the key ideas, statistics, and other details on a note card, we will have a means of refreshing our memory about what we plan to cover. In public speaking, notes are a must, as we explain later.

Practice is a useful pre-speaking activity to reduce fear. While practicing, we can try to visualize the speaking situation, thereby dealing with potential environmental concerns. Suggestions for appropriate practice are found in subsequent chapters.

SUMMARY

Up to 20 percent of the nation's population experiences levels of oral communication apprehension that are unacceptably high and can even be handicapping. At lesser levels, almost everyone has a degree of apprehension, or stage fright, in oral situations.

The effects of apprehension have costly implications for us because they impact negatively on our academic, economic, and social lives. The causes are tied closely to the learning process, and what happens in the home and school affects that personal learning process. Symptoms of oral communication apprehension are numerous, from stomach contractions to body trembling. Being quiet also is considered a symptom sometimes, but often quietness is a characteristic of people who may possess little fear and are quiet for other reasons.

Many methods have been tested to reduce fear in people who are highly apprehensive about speaking. Systematic desensitization, cognitive modification, and skills training are three that have met with success. In addition, ways of reducing "normal" tension include relaxation techniques and speech preparation skills.

8

Verbal Communication

"Dear, I have a confession to make," the instructor told his bride. "I'm a golf nut. You'll never see me on weekends when the weather is good."

"Well, honey," she cooed, "I've a confession to make too. I'm a hooker."

"That's no problem," replied the groom, "Just keep your head down and your left arm straight."

This anecdote is told to make a point. A speaker's words may carry different meaning for different people. Being understood is a luxury, as a well-known saying emphasizes: "I know you believe you understand what you think I said, but I'm not sure you realize that what you heard is not what I meant." A sign in a store window underscores the point: "Any faulty merchandise will be cheerfully replaced with merchandise of equal quality."

What happens when we talk with others that causes some of our listeners to understand what we say and others to miscomprehend? Why are some of our messages successful and others failures? Messages succeed and fail for many reasons. One principal reason stems from our use of language.

Language is used to express and elicit meanings. In fact, a language function is to give and get meanings. Meaning is inherent in the concept of language. Meaning, moreover, is the cause of much message distortion and misinterpretation.

This chapter discusses language and its component, meaning. We begin by concentrating on language characteristics. Then we consider meaning and its implications in oral communication.

THE NATURE OF LANGUAGE

What is language? Linguists, semanticists, grammarians, lexicographers, and writers all have their own definitions of language. For that matter, so does the average person.[1]

For us, language is *the faculty of verbal expression.* It includes a set of significant symbols, known as *words*, which constitute a *vocabulary*. To be part of a language, the words must be put into a sequence; they must be ordered in a way that makes sense. This is the *syntax* of language. The rules and procedures followed in structuring the words form the *grammar* of language. To be a language, words and structure both must be used in a manner that produces similar responses from a group of people. When a group uses words that are mutually important to them and combines the words similarly, the group has a language.[2]

Language is uniquely human. Animals are able to communicate, but they do so through movements, gestures, grunts, and other sounds. Humans can use not only these nonverbal means, but they also can verbalize symbolically about the reality around them and conceptualize broadly about that reality, its past, and its future.[3]

From comparisons between human and animal systems of communication,[4] we can draw the distinguishing characteristics of language. If we think of language as a specialized, productive system capable of displacement and composed of rapidly fading, arbitrary, culturally transmitted symbols, we can break down the term *language* into its important characteristics. At the same time, we can pinpoint qualities that differentiate human and animal communication.[5]

1. *Specialized.* Language is a specialized system of communication. By specialized we mean that language serves no function except to communicate. It has no other purpose. With animals, the communication system serves several functions. A dog panting with its tongue hanging out is making a sound that other dogs understand and is performing a biologically essential activity, cooling off.[6]

2. *Productive.* Language is a productive system. Through language, humans have the ability to produce messages on thousands of different topics and say them in thousands of different ways. Further, humans can listen to thousands of different messages and understand them if they know the meaning of the words, even though they might not have heard the specific message before. Animals do not have this capability.[7]

3. *Capable of displacement.* Language is capable of displacement, the capacity to relate to things that are remote in space or time, or both.[8] Humans can talk about the past, present, or future, about events, people, and objects that they may never have seen and perhaps never will see, about the real and the imaginary — all with equal ease. Animals can learn to respond to simple commands only after sound and action have been paired many times. No animal can comply with, "Come here in two minutes" or "From now on, don't move when I say 'stay.'"

4. *Rapidly fading symbols.* When employed as speech, language fades away rapidly. If a message is not heard when it is uttered, it will not be heard at all. It can be recorded, but recording is an extralinguistic means of reception, not a human characteristic.

5. *Arbitrary symbols.* The selection of words to fit particular meanings is arbitrary, having been determined by will or caprice. Words are symbols used for, or regarded as representing, something else. They are chosen for communication purposes and not because the words and their referents have any real associations.[9]

   The term "floppy disk" is an example of arbitrary selection. It stands for a flexible, round magnetic recording medium and storage device. The device could have been called anything. "Floppy disk" was assigned to the device so its users could talk about it without having to point to it, but almost any name could have been attached to it. Words do not possess any of the physical qualities they refer to.

6. *Culturally transmitted.* The form and substance of any language are culturally transmitted through learning and teaching. A child is not born knowing a language; the child learns the language in the culture in which he or she is reared. A Russian-born child brought up in the United States by English speakers will learn English as a native speaker. The child is not born with an ability to learn only Russian.[10]

   The United States, being multicultural, is a country where numerous languages are spoken. In the Los Angeles public schools, for example, 82 different languages are spoken. *Bilingualism,* the ability to use two different languages, such as the mother tongue and English, is common. Nativelike fluency in English often is lacking in American bilinguals, especially recent immigrants. In our classes we can expect to hear accents, dialects, and even bidialectism from student speakers who are trying to master English. Understanding and assistance, not ridicule and punishment, will aid their progress. Learning to speak a second language is difficult past our formative years.

MEANING

Meaning is an essential part of language.[11] Language is used to express and elicit meanings, which makes language and meaning inseparable. The study of meaning is called *semantics,* and scholars in linguistics, philosophy, psychology, language teaching, and communication have contributed to the study.

Meaning is the correlation between language and experience, of which humans bring a wealth to any communication event.[12] Experience and meaning are incorporated in the definition of meaning we employ. For us, meaning is *the association we make with a given behavior, object, event, person, or idea.*[13]

Three factors are involved in this definition: referent, experience, and purpose.[14]

1. *Referent* concerns the relational aspect of meaning. Language symbols — words — represent objects, ideas, states, and conditions. A symbol stands for something but bears no relationship to it. "Floppy disk" stands for a recording medium and storage device; the term is a referent, representing the object, as we have already learned.

2. The *experiential* factor connects meaning with experience. The meanings we have for words are shaped largely by the experiences we have while learning the words. This concept is significant

enough for us to consider it at length in the next section.

3. *Purpose* links meaning with our reasons for interacting with people. People's intentions when talking with others constitute an important aspect of meaning. We fulfill purposes in using language, and our intentions shape the way symbols are understood.[15] "When I use a word," Humpty Dumpty said in a rather scornful tone, "it means just what I choose it to mean — nothing more nor less."

Meanings Are Learned

Meanings are learned in much the same fashion as we learn anything.[16] When we were born, we did not have meanings. Objects or symbols meant nothing to us. Before long, as normal children, we learned to organize the world. We organized the things we saw into shapes and objects. We organized the things we heard into sounds. Soon we produced sounds on our own, much like the sounds produced by children everywhere. By the time we were almost a year old, we made sounds like the sounds our parents made and unlike the sounds of infants whose parents spoke different languages. As children, we learned to structure our perceptions, to produce sounds in combination, and to mean something by our sounds.[17]

How do we learn? How do we get meanings from the world around us? Recognizing that views about this learning process are constantly undergoing modification, our conception of learning is based on the classical conditioning model of learning.

Learning, a relatively permanent change in our behavior, results from reinforced practice. Three elements are essential: the learner, a stimulus, and a response. The *learner* — the person who is to learn — brings to the process his or her previous experience. This experience represents the entering behavior in the learning situation. For example, a small child who is about to learn the meaning of "cow" brings to that situation what he or she has learned previously about animals and objects in general. The *stimulus* represents the event in the environment we are about to learn. For the child in the example, a cow (or perhaps a photo of one) serves as the stimulus. The *response* represents the behavior internal or external to the stimulus.[18]

When a stimulus is first presented, there is no external response. When it is presented the next time, there *is* a response. A mother gives a child ice cream and asks the child to name it. There may be no external response. She tells the child that it is "ice cream" and thus presents the stimulus. When she serves it a second time, the child responds "ice cream." This response indicates a change in performance from the time prior to the stimulus situation to the time subsequent to the situation. From this change in behavior, we infer the occurrence of learning. An association has been created in the mind between the product, ice cream, and the words used to symbolize that foodstuff. As time passes and the child continues to hear the word associated with a product, the word develops a meaning for the person.

In this manner we learn the meanings of words. If a stimulus is presented to us a few times, we learn to respond to it, thereby giving it meaning. Meanings are learned.[19]

A Russian immigrant apparently did not learn his English in class or from his mother. When his English teacher asked him what the word "straight" means, he replied, "It means without ginger ale."

The meanings we do learn are always subject to change. The meanings for objects and events we first learn are not static; they can be altered in light of new experiences and learning.

Meanings Are In People

A prevailing delusion about language is that words and structure carry meaning. Most people seem to believe that when they arrange a number of words in an orderly pattern, this arrangement will carry the meaning they intended. They think the listener should understand the message. Is this so? Do words have meaning? Semanticists — those who study the relationships between words and meaning — say, "No, people mean, not words. Meanings are in people, not in words." They claim that words are only pencil or ink marks on paper and that speech is only a set of airborne sounds. Words do not mean anything at all because people, not words, mean.

If the semanticists are correct — and the evidence is heavily in their favor — what about dictionaries? Don't they contain "meanings" for words? Most semanticists agree that words have common or public meanings, and these are found in dictionaries. Nonetheless, they argue that dictionaries cannot and do not provide meanings that are useful in every circumstance, because meanings are in people. Meanings are covert responses within us. They are our property, personal to us, and are learned. We cannot find meanings. Fortunately, most people have similar meanings for the same words, making communication possible. If these similarities were not present, we could not communicate. Thus, words and structure do not in themselves have meaning, but they function as cues that cause our own meanings to come into play.

Meanings, therefore, are not transmittable or transferable. Only messages are transmittable, and

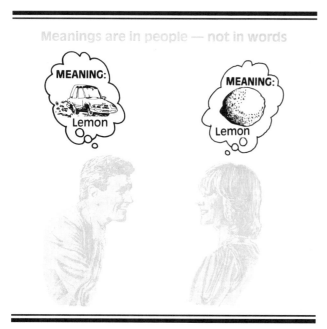

Meanings are in people — not in words

meanings are not in the message. Meanings reside in speakers and listeners. The messages merely trigger meanings in the speakers or listeners.[20]

TYPES OF MEANING

The meanings we learn become our personal property because of the very personal way in which we learn them. Hence, our meanings for certain words probably are not going to be the same meanings that another person will have for those words. In addition, words acquire several different meanings for different people because of the types of meanings words can have. Dictionary meanings, however, help provide uniformity in thought. Without some uniformity, communication would not be possible.

In examining the common meanings of words, we find several dimensions or types of meaning. These are described here as if they are not the personal property of people, to gain a better understanding of the whole concept of meaning. This understanding should help us to better communicate our own ideas and understand others' ideas. Four types of meaning are: denotative, connotative, contextual, and figurative.

Denotative Meaning

The first words most of us learn are the names of persons, places, and things, such as "mother," "father," "home," "store," "ball," "rice," and so on. We also learn words that refer to processes or

actions, such as "talk," "run," "sleep," "play," and "eat." When we learn one of these words, someone says the word and the thing itself is before us or we can see the action taking place. Mother points to the ball and says "ball." She says "walk" when someone is walking and as she points to the walker. From the earlier example of how the term "ice cream" takes on meaning, we see how the relationships between the name and the corresponding object becomes meaningful. This meaning is called *denotative* because the name or word used denotes or refers to the object. The word "ball" denotes the actual object, ball, and the word "walk" refers to the actual process of walking. Denotative meaning is defined as *the relationship between the word symbol and the object or action referred to.*[21]

Denotation is relatively fixed and stable. Meanings of words are imprinted on our brains with the recurrent association of the word with the thing. Words formed in this manner have set meanings, and these meanings tend to be independent of the context of talk in which they are used. Words and the things the words symbolize acquire an organic relationship and become properties of each other.

We must be careful, however, not to push this line of reasoning too far lest we start to believe that words themselves have meanings rather than being symbolic of objects, processes, or actions. We could look at words erroneously as containers of meaning — that words mean, not people. This reasoning represents a barrier to understanding.

Important to communicators is the recognition that what a word denotes for one person may not be the same for another. The relationship that one mother might make between the word "run" and the process of running could be different from that made by another mother who might call the process "jogging," "racing," or whatever. We should be aware, therefore, that denotative meanings are people-centered. Denotative meanings reside in people as a consequence of the way they learned the relationships between words and the objects, actions, or processes they symbolize.

Just as essential, we must realize that single words may have multiple meanings. The word "go," for instance, has eighty-one meanings, according to our dictionary; "come" has twenty-four, "low" sixteen, and "love" seventeen. "Love" means, among other things, a strong affection for, or attachment or devotion to, a person or persons, a strong liking for something, a strong liking for a person of the opposite sex, the person who is the object of such affection, sexual passion or gratification, a score of zero, God's benevolent concern for humankind, and the brotherhood that people should have for each other. Almost all words listed in the better dictionaries similarly have multiple meanings. The context in which the word is being used usually helps in determining the meaning intended. A forthcoming section explains the significance of context.

Connotative Meaning

Words have an evaluative, emotional, or affective meaning that comes from the way the denotative meaning was learned. "Ball" denotes the object, ball, and in addition the word undoubtedly holds a feeling for its user based upon his or her experiences in learning the word. "Ball" can *connote* feelings about the object. The feelings might be pleasurable, derived from joyous experiences when playing with a ball as a child. The feelings also could be painful because of unhappy experiences associated with ball playing. Connotative meanings *relate to the internal feelings a word calls up for its speaker and for the person hearing the word.*[22]

Connotative meanings are based on personal feelings. These feelings belong to the individuals who hold them and usually are not the same as the feelings others hold. Like denotative meanings, connotative meanings are people-centered. Yet, many words may stimulate approximately the same connotation for most people living in the same environment who hear the connotative meanings being used in roughly the same contexts. Some words are associated with a positive feeling; others have a negative connotation. For most of us, words such as "mother," "home," "freedom," "love," and "friend" carry a positive connotation. Words such as "thief," "killer," "war," and "sickness" evoke a negative feeling.

Frequently connotative meanings are far stronger than denotative meanings. The emotional aspects associated with words carry more weight in people's minds than the direct, explicit meanings. As a result, we can generate highly intense listener reactions by using words with negative emotive meanings. Calling a friend "uneducated" probably will make him or her mildly upset. Calling the friend "stupid" may make him or her quite angry because of the stronger negative feelings attached to "stupid."

When we converse with people of other cultures or ethnic groups, we should be particularly aware of connotative meanings. In these conversations, the connotative meanings of words take on special significance. In all cultures certain words have unique meanings. In some cases the meaning of a word might be different in different cultures. In Hindu cultures the word "cow" carries a connotative meaning different from that ascribed to in other cultures. To Hindus the cow is a sacred animal to be protected and revered. To people in other cultures, the cow connotes a food producing animal to be milked or eaten. The word "propaganda" in America connotes

deception or distortion, but this is not the case in other cultures, some of which use the term to mean propagating the faith, a valued activity.[23] Hence, in the intercultural or interethnic communication setting, the connotative meaning, more so than the denotative meaning, can bring about either understanding or misunderstanding.

Contextual Meaning

The meanings of words can change depending upon the contexts in which they are used. Note how "love" expresses different shades of thought and feeling in these two contexts: "Mary, I love you!" "Mary, I would love to go!" In the first context the speaker is expressing a strong and passionate affection. In the second the speaker is conveying a desire to go where Mary suggests, for the pleasure the act will bring. Obviously the two different contexts alter the meaning attached to "love." Two types of context concern us: *linguistic and nonlinguistic.*[24]

Linguistic Context

The linguistic context deals with the grammatical orders to which words belong. In written speech this could be a sentence, a paragraph, or a chapter. Of

---

Words have multiple meanings; the speaker chooses the meaning to use.

SEE (sē) vt., to observe, show, see, tell; to get knowledge or an awareness through the eyes; perceive visually; look at; view; to visualize as though present; picture; to get a clear mental impression of; grasp by thinking; understand; to accept as right, proper, or suitable; to consider to be; judge; to learn, discover; find out; to have personal knowledge of; experience; witness; to look over; inspect; examine; to take care, make sure; to escort, accompany, attend; to keep company with; to encounter, meet, come in contact with; to recognize by sight; to call on, to visit, to consult; to have an interview with; receive; to be a spectator at; to meet a bet — vi. to have the power of sight; to be able to see far; to investigate; inquire; to comprehend; understand; reflect.

SIGHT (sīt) n. something seen, view; spectacle; a thing worth seeing; the act of seeing; perception by the eyes; any device to help the eyes line up a gun, optical instrument on its objective; aim; vision; eyesight; mental vision; perception; opinion; judgment; any person or thing of an unusual appearance; vt. to observe or examine; to see; to catch sight of; aim at; to look carefully in a specific direction; adj. read, done, understood quickly; due or payable when presented.

Based on *Webster's Collegiate Dictionary*, 1948, 5th edition, (Springfield, MA: G. & C. Merriam Co., Publishers).

Language can be tricky.
Answer the following:

_____ There is three errers in this sentence. What are they?

_____ You have thirty-five cents in two coins. One is not a quarter. What are they?

_____ Can a man living in Chapel Hill, NC, be buried west of the Mississippi?

_____ Is it legal in South Dakota for a man to marry his widow's sister?

_____ Do they have a Fourth of July in England?

_____ If a plane crashes directly on the line between two states, where are the survivors buried?

_____ Some months have 30 days. Some have 31. How many have 28?

_____ How many animals of each species did Moses take on the ark with him?

_____ An electric train moves north at 90 miles an hour. An east wind is blowing at 30 miles an hour. Which way is the engine smoke blowing?

the two types of context, the linguistic context tends to be more readily understood. Words interact with each other in specific sentences and paragraphs, where they shape and focus each other until a comprehensive meaning comes forth. For instance, the phrase, "They are racing horses," could be interpreted in at least two ways. The context in which the phrase appears should make the meaning clearer, as in: "John's horses are valuable. *They are racing horses.* Tomorrow he will enter them in a race." "See all the people going to the stadium? *They are racing horses* there today, and the people are going to watch."

Thus, the meaning of a word depends upon the way the word functions within a particular context. "Stone" is a noun in, "John threw the *stone*; a verb in, "The mob will *stone* him to death; and an adjective in, "He is *stone* deaf."

Nonlinguistic Context

Nonlinguistic context refers to the conditions of utterance that may influence interpretation — for example, vocal inflection, emotional intensity, rate, and speaker credibility. By stressing the different words in "I love you," three different nonlinguistic interpretations can be given that sentence when spoken in English. "*I* love you" means "I really do love you." "I *love* you" means "I don't just like you; I *love* you." "I love *you*," means "I don't love Patti,

Sharon, or Diane; I love *you*." The stress offers cues to how words can be interpreted. The nonlinguistic context can be easily misunderstood if careful attention is not paid to the emphasis, especially in English.

Whenever we deal with meaning in terms of words isolated from discourse, difficulties can arise. Only in the context of discourse are possible ambiguities actually resolved.

Figurative Meaning

When words are used in an unusual or nonliteral sense, they become figurative and are employed to give beauty or vividness.[25] Their meaning changes because the words are used in seemingly odd ways. Some examples are: "A machine gun *spits* bullets." "The revolver *barked* in the night." "The volcano *vomits* fire." "He's got *tons* of money." "I'm so tired I'm simply *dead*." Each example contains a word that is used figuratively. Ordinarily people *spit*, guns *fire*, dogs *bark*, revolvers *shoot*, people *vomit*, and volcanoes *spew*. A person has a lot of money rather than *tons* of it. And a person is so tired that she is *exhausted* rather than dead. The examples are nonsensical if they are interpreted literally, but they nevertheless do make sense when taken figuratively. Spitting bullets, barking revolvers, and vomiting volcanoes enhance the expressions by making them more graphic and dramatic.

Figurative meanings carry affective connotations and help bring the speaker's feelings to the listener. The speaker who exclaims, "I've been waiting ages for you — you're an hour late" lets the listener know the speaker's feelings — how angry the speaker is because of the hour's wait. "Waiting ages" is inaccurate, but this expression does intensify the feeling that the wait was unnecessarily long and the speaker feels put upon. It makes its point indirectly by stating the speaker's feelings vividly in terms of something other than the actual waiting time. Of course, it is not literally meant or interpreted.

Idiom, used in the sense of an accepted phrase, construction, or expression having a meaning different from the literal, bears discussion here. In oral communication the use of idioms can be irritating and frustrating. Speakers of idiom use one or several hundreds of word combinations whose meaning carries little or no relationship to the individual words making them up.

A foreign visitor to America recounts his experiences with American idioms, telling of the hard time he had trying to understand idioms such as "talking through your hat" (talking nonsense), "talking shop" (discussing business matters at social events), "breaking up" (disturbing, being upset over bad

Examples of Informal Language

We sometimes use language in highly informal ways, causing misunderstandings and possible communication breakdowns. In addition to figurative language and idiom, here are a few forms of informal language:

Cliche: overused words or phrases; trite expressions. Examples: crack of dawn, picture of health, as old as the hills, reign supreme.

Colloquialism: words or phrases characteristic of informal speaking; not formal English. Examples: Howzit? Take it easy! See ya' later!

Euphemism: words that are less direct but less offensive or distasteful. Examples: pass away for die, illegitimate child for bastard, expectorate for spit, separate from college for flunk out.

Jargon: the specialized vocabulary and idioms of those in the same group. Examples: house, crib, casa — a prisoner's assigned cell. *Newsweek* publishes a weekly list for various professions.

Regionalism: words or phrases unique to a specific section of the country. Examples: sweet roll, bun, and danish mean the same thing in various parts of the country.

Slang: newly coined words or phrases, established terms given new meanings shared by a subcultural group wanting fresh, vigorous, colorful, humorous expressions for old ideas. Examples: stupid (cool), stupid fresh (really cool), peace out (goodbye), roped (going steady), dap (lots of compliments).

language can be misinterpreted by members of the same culture, albeit of different subcultures. The blind man said to his sighted friend: "Tell me, what is white like?"

Replied the friend with perfect vision: "It's like newly fallen snow."

"Oh, it's light in weight and damp?"

"No, not really. I guess it's more like paper."

"Now I understand — it rustles."

"No, no — it's like an albino rabbit."

"Aha!" said the blind man, "it's soft and furry."[27]

The sighted man's use of figurative language created for his friend an erroneous image of white.

Many subcultures exist, each of which has a figurative language. We can be left out of many conversations for the simple reason that we don't "dig" (understand) the "gee" (guy) who is talking. When we are in the company of doctors, we have to know their "inside" language — medicalese — to be able to understand what they are saying. With lawyers, we had better know legalese. In talking to athletes, "basic jock" has to be part of our vocabulary. In the culture of computers and computer users, a "barf" is when a computer ceases to work or becomes erratic; a "glitch" is the source of a malfunction; a "dump" is a printout of all the information the computer contains. The motion picture industry likewise has its own language. "Between projects" means out of work; "on spec" means work but no pay; "bankable" means an actor, producer, or director will make money; a "blue" movie is also known as a "nudie," "porno," or "skin flick." Television, too, claims its share of idioms. "Kidvid" is TV for children. A

news), "pulling your leg" (teasing or fooling someone), "barking up the wrong tree" (attacking the wrong thing), and so forth. He found idioms unpredictable and patternless. They are derived not from language but, rather, from cultural factors, folklore, proverbs, and current events.[26]

Idiomatic expressions are found in many languages, and in each language they provide color, informality, charm, and exactness in daily speech. An American expression such as "breaking the ice" (promoting informality) states exactly what the speaker means, and "cutting down" (reducing) carries more emphasis than the proper term, "reducing." Yet if they are translated literally, idioms make little sense because of their peculiar meanings.

Even though a single culture attributes a common meaning to specific figures, each individual within that culture will have a slightly different meaning for a figure because of his or her unique past experience. The following story illustrates how figurative

Mountain Talk

Match the lefthand column of mountain terms with the general-language counterparts in the righthand column.

Answers are on page 243.

_____ 1. Peaked	A. Look
_____ 2. Askeered of	B. Heat up, upset
_____ 3. Doin's	C. Eaten
_____ 4. Dast	D. Breezy
_____ 5. Et	E. Pale
_____ 6. Shed of	F. Frightened
_____ 7. Kivver	G. Dare
_____ 8. Het	H. A function
_____ 9. Airish	I. Get rid of
_____ 10. Gander	J. Cover

Donald Klopf, *Workbook for Intercultural Encounters* (Englewood, CO: Morton, 1987)

"tease" is an announcement of a future show. "Pass" means to reject a show. A "gofer" goes for coffee. And so on. And the government seems to have refined Americanese to the incomprehensible. "Endusers" are those who are ultimate recipients of government largesse; "phase zero" is the starting stage of a project; "optimization of procurement" means to get as much as you can; "monitoring function" is to keep track of something.

Our discussion of the four types of meaning should support the point that the semantic component of a language is complex and intricate. By far, meaning is the most unstable element in any language. Much difficulty is involved in carrying over from one person to another the variety of logotactic, contextual, and empirical meanings rendered through an infinitude of language structures. Oral communication does not consist of the transmission of meanings. Meanings aren't transmitted, nor are they transferable. Only messages are transmittable, and meanings are not in the message; they are in the message-user.

BARRIERS TO MEANING

Communication barriers can develop at any point in the transmission of messages from speaker to listener. An obvious point for barriers to occur is in the message itself. In this section, five barriers in verbal communication are considered:

1. Confusing fact and inference: the tendency to react to inferences as though they are facts.

2. The container myth: the tendency to believe words have meanings.

3. Allness: the tendency to assume we know all there is to know about a subject.

4. Polarization: the tendency to think in unrealistic extremes.

5. Indiscrimination: the tendency to neglect differences and emphasize similarities.

Confusing Fact and Inference

We can make two kinds of statements about what we perceive: statements of fact and statements of inference. A *statement of fact* is one that can be or has been confirmed by observation and that can be termed true or false. A *statement of inference* is a sentence that concerns unknown events based on other events that are known. It is a guess, a deduction, a judgment of what we think occurred or will occur.[28]

We can look at a girl wearing a yellow blouse and say, "That girl is wearing a yellow blouse." The

statement is factual; it corresponds directly to what we see. We also might say, "The girl bought that yellow blouse." Unless we actually had seen the girl buy the blouse or if she had told us she bought it, the statement would be an inference. We inferred or guessed that she bought the blouse. She could have stolen, borrowed, or received the blouse as a gift.

If we had jumped to the conclusion that she bought the blouse, we would have been basing our conclusion about the unknown event (whether she bought it) on other events that we know. We look at her and decide she didn't steal it because she looks honest, and honest girls don't steal (known event). Or we decide that she bought it because she is wearing it and most people buy the clothes they wear (known event). In any case, we would have been guessing because we did not see her buy it, nor did she tell us she bought it.

Sentences of fact and inference are difficult to differentiate. Our language is void of clues to help us make the distinction. As a result, we frequently confuse fact and inference and behave as though the inferences we make are facts. Misunderstandings are the consequences.[29]

Misunderstandings caused by fact-inference confusion comes about more or less in this fashion:

1. We perceive an event;

2. We could make either a factual or an inferential statement about what we perceived;

3. We infer but fail to realize we did infer;

4. We act on the inference as though it were a fact;

5. We end up taking a calculated risk. That risk could prove to be embarrassing, costly, or fatal.

How can we avoid inferring? At times isn't inference inevitable, necessary, or important? The answer is that life is impossible to live without making certain assumptions. We assume that the food we eat is not poisoned, that our car is safe to drive, that the classroom chairs will support our weight. Without making some assumptions, we probably could not act at all.

Those who know their car's performance is based on inference, however, will not be quite so disturbed when it develops engine problems. If we expect our date to show up on time and he or she does not, we should ask why before jumping to conclusions about the date's behavior. If we fail a test, we should check our own preparation for the test to see if we were at fault before assuming the teacher created a tricky, unfair, or stupid test.

This checklist may help us distinguish fact from inference:

☐ 1. Did I personally observe what I'm talking about, or am I repeating what someone else said?

2. Do my statements stay with what I saw rather than go beyond the facts?

3. When I infer, do I ask myself if my inference is right or wrong?

4. When I talk with others, do I label my inferences as such?[30]

The Container Myth

A second misuse of language stems from the belief that words have meanings, a belief we noted earlier. People who harbor this belief act as though words and meanings are somehow bundled together, that words are containers that hold meanings.[31]

Speakers who believe words contain meanings are apt to assume that when they talk, they are handing their listeners "containers of meanings." The listeners, they seem to think, should have no problem comprehending what was said. As we know, however, words are not containers of meaning. British author Samuel Butler makes the point in these words: "We want words to do more than they can. . . . We expect them to help us grip and dissect that which in ultimate essence is as ungrippable as shadow. . . . What we should read is not the words but the man whom we feel is behind the words."

Words are just pointers people use to represent or stand for the things around them. People manipulate the words, juggle them around to form sentences, and speak to each other using the sentences to visualize the meanings contained in their minds. Words provide the means for people to express their thoughts and feelings.

Although there is no panacea for overcoming this misuse of language, a few techniques can help to decrease its seriousness or prevent ill effects:[32]

1. Be person-minded, not word-minded.

2. Query when unsure.

3. Paraphrase what the other person said to check the meaning.

4. Use the context and the surrounding words to help determine what the speaker meant.

Allness

When listening to some people talk, we notice a tone of finality and completeness. When they speak, they seem to be saying, "What I'm saying is all there is to say about the subject. There is no more." Radio and television commentators often speak as if they know all the answers about what is happening in the world. Their talk takes on a note of assurance or "know-it-allness" that implies they know all there is

to know about their topic. Can they, or any other person, know all there is to know about a topic? Obviously not; knowledge of everything about anything is an impossibility.[33]

The word *allness* refers to the erroneous belief that someone can possibly know all there is to know about something. Allness constitutes a barrier to communication, and our language is largely at fault for its occurrence.

When we speak about something, we abstract. We focus on some details of the something we are talking about and neglect others. Under ordinary circumstances we cannot cover all the details. Abstracting is a necessary part of communication. We cannot possibly say all there is to say about something. We are forced to be selective and to speak about some aspects and ignore others. We have to abstract.

John Saxe's poem, "The Parable of the Blind Men and the Elephant," illustrates how abstracting works; it is a good example of the allness barrier. The parable deals with the problems six blind and learned men of Indostan had upon examining an elephant, an animal they had heard about but never had perceived in any fashion. The first blind man, after encountering the elephant's broad and sturdy side, concluded that the elephant was like a wall. The second man felt only the tusk, and its smooth, sharp surface led him to believe the elephant was like a spear. The third took the squirming trunk in his hands and concluded that the elephant was like a snake. The hands of the fourth blind man touched the elephant's knee, and he believed he had hold of a tree. The fifth man concluded that the elephant was like a fan, because he touched the ear. Grasping the tail, the sixth blind man said the elephant was like a rope.

Each of the six learned men in this story came to his own conclusion about what the elephant was, and each argued loud and long that his perception of the elephant was the correct one. Each was partly right, but all were wrong! The point of Saxe's poem is that we are much like the blind men of Indostan. We never perceive all of something, never experience anything fully. We perceive part of an event, an object, a person, or an idea and, on the basis of our limited experience, conclude what the whole is like.[34]

The barrier in communication arises when we are unaware that we are abstracting and assume that what we know or what we say is all we really need to know or say. We behave on the basis of the few details we know about. We judge the whole by the parts we perceive, and we become intolerant of the viewpoints of those who disagree with our judgments. Our messages come across to others with a tone of finality and completeness that says, "What I am saying is all there is to say about the topic; there is nothing more."

The allness barrier is hard to break down. When we think we know all there is to know, we fail to recognize the details we have left out. We believe there is no more to be said, or at least no more that is worthwhile. As our allness increases, our learnability decreases. We close ourselves to new or different information. We think we know it all.

Being open to new and different ideas is essential to learning, and by decreasing allness, our learnability increases. Teachability — being open to new ideas and adaptable rather than dogmatic, rigid, and narrow — is necessary to allness. What can keep us teachable? We can begin by developing a sincere humility that we can never know or say everything about anything, by remembering that whatever we know, there is always more. There is always an *et cetera*. Semanticists say we should add an *etc.* to what we say to remind ourselves that we can never finish saying all there is to say. The *etc.* is to remind us of our ignorance; there always is more that we do not know.[35]

Polarization

Polarization comes about when we *divide the world around us into opposites*.[36] Things are good or bad, positive or negative, hot or cold; people are honest or dishonest, beautiful or ugly, rich or poor, successes or failures. Polarization is either-or or black-and-white thinking. We see the two poles but ignore the middle ground. Hitler argued: "Everyone in Germany is a Nationalist Socialist or an idiot or lunatic." A child questions: "What are you going to buy me, Mom, a VCR or a compact disc player?" A mother asks: "What do you want to do first, Jimmy, take a bath or brush your teeth?"

When we polarize, we disregard or avoid the shadings and gradations between the extremes; we neglect the middle ground. Certainly a few people are extremely rich and some are extremely poor, but most people fall in between these two poles. Most of us exist somewhere in between the extremes of good or bad, beautiful or ugly, honest or dishonest, success or failure. Yet we have a strong tendency to see only the extremes and to classify people, objects, and events in terms of the two poles. To think of a fellow student as either smart or dumb is much easier than to rate the student more precisely along a continuum of mental ability. Rating the student along the range of A-B-C-D-F takes a little more doing. We have to investigate and analyze, and that takes time.

Then, too, the middle ground usually is a vast area covering many cases, probably the majority. If a person is not rich or poor, what is he or she? Slightly rich, fairly rich, slightly poor, fairly poor? Our language fails to include many terms that describe the middle ground. We have to use relatively long phrases, but using them requires extra thought and effort, so we are prone to ignore them. We use the extremes instead.

To diminish polarization, we can specify the degree between the extremes. We can avoid the either-or poles and talk about how much. One national magazine often uses specific details to avoid polarizing. "The yacht was large (110 feet) for its cost ($75,000), and its owner is rich (annual income: $500,000)." . . . "The school has the largest number of football players (ten) earning degrees in the nation." . . . "He's a fast miler (best time: 1: 59)."

When the extremes cannot be quantified, substantive middle terms are helpful, when available. To describe a person as 75 percent beautiful sounds foolish, but we can use terms such as "pretty" or "pleasing" to specify approximate degrees between the beautiful-ugly poles.

Qualifying terms can be used also. Words such as "very," "often," "frequently," "seldom," "approximately," "generally," and "most" are not as specific as quantitative details. Even so, they are better than the absence of quantification. Note what happens to the following statement if we take out the qualifier "some": "Some people go to the cinema or the ballet." The statement becomes an either-or type without the "some."[37]

Indiscrimination

Indiscrimination is defined as *neglecting differences while overemphasizing similarities*.[38] It reflects a human tendency to group like things together and attach the same label to them, failing to recognize variations, nuances, or differences between them in doing so. Stereotyping is another term for treating people indiscriminately, but the problem is not confined to people. We can lump together ideas, events, and objects that seem similar, being unaware or unwilling to admit that each is unique.

Everything is unique; everything is unlike everything else. In the world around us, nowhere can two things be found that are identical. We can pick two gardenias off the same bush and easily note the similarities. They are white, have petals, and give off a strong fragrance. Yet the differences are just as apparent — in size, number of petals, strength of scent, and so on.

When we do fail to discriminate, our language can be a cause. It leads us to focus on similarities. Certain common nouns allow us to group things: doctors, teachers, Southerners, Yankees, Democrats,

Republicans, professors, artists, teenagers, politicians, Orientals. Nouns like these help us classify people and things. Meeting a person for the first time, we are uneasy until we can classify him or her. What is the person? A teacher, student, lawyer, Catholic, Protestant, Jew, atheist? We want to pigeonhole the person, and our language helps us do so.

Categorizing, as such, is not undesirable. It is essential in dealing with complexity, helping us to order the world around us. It is extremely useful in making sense out of complicated matters. The problem arises not from classifying per se. The problem comes about when we classify and then attach an evaluative label to what we classify. The label we attach to the class becomes the basis on which we judge each member of the class, overlooking the unique qualities in doing so.

A student reports: "Rolling into class the first day was this six foot guy — small head, no neck, grotesque upper torso, slim hips, bulging thighs. We knew he was a jock. No competition here, we figure — just another dumb football player. We were wrong. He earns the class's highest average, is articulate and friendly, and everyone likes him." The student had judged the individual on the basis of the label he had attached to athletes, overlooking the person's uniqueness, and erred in the process.

SUMMARY

Language is the principal ingredient of verbal communication. Language consists of a vocabulary of words or significant symbols ordered in a way so as to make sense to a group of people — a culture.

Language is a specialized, productive system capable of displacement and is composed of rapidly fading, culturally transmitted symbols. It is a uniquely human phenomenon, one that separates humans and animals.

An essential part of language is meaning, the association attached to a given behavior, object, event, or idea. Meanings are learned and, although there are various theories of learning, we considered only one, akin to the classical conditioning model of learning. It stresses the point that meanings are in people, not in words.

Four types of meaning influence verbal communication. Denotation is the relationship between the word and the object or action referred to. Connotation concerns the evaluative, emotional, affective meaning of words, derived from the way words are learned. Contextual meaning is the type of meaning given to words by the words that surround it. Figurative meanings come from words used in a nonliteral manner to express beauty or vividness.

Five barriers or misunderstandings that can develop in verbal communication and have roots in the language are fact versus inference confusion, the container myth, allness, polarization, and indiscrimination.

LEARNING CHECK

The statements below, based on the discussions in Chapters 7 and 8, are either true or false. In the space provided, place a "T" for true, an "F" for false. The answers are on page 243.

_____ 1. About 20% of the nation's school population suffers from communication apprehension.

_____ 2. Speaking fears are similar in character.

_____ 3. When we neglect differences and overemphasize similarities, we stereotype.

_____ 4. People mean, not words.

_____ 5. Some cultures reward silence; America does not.

_____ 6. Meaning is the association we make with a given behavior, object, event, person, or idea.

_____ 7. A cliche is a newly coined word or phrase.

_____ 8. Allness refers to the erroneous belief that we can know all there is to know about something.

_____ 9. High communication apprehension is associated with a negative self-image.

_____ 10. Connotative meaning is the relationship between the word symbol or action referred to.

9

Communicating Nonverbally

Too often the process of oral communication is thought to consist solely of speaking and listening, with words the only raw materials for speaking. But a clenched fist, a nod, a smile, a bow, and a frown are powerful communicators as well, and each communicates without the benefit of words. In fact, surrounding us are dozens of sources of nonverbal communication, or *communication that does not use oral or written language to carry its message.* Things such as uniforms, bells, horns, traffic lights, paintings, and photographs all communicate without words, although we might not think of them as sources of communication. Even silence is a form of communication, as, for example, when a girlfriend asks: "Do you love me?" and the young man fails to respond, or looks down or away. The silence figuratively speaks louder than the words he might say, "No, I don't."

To discover how commonplace nonverbal communication is, observe people's behavior for a few moments. Watch for signs of nonverbal communication. Their body movements, their facial expressions, and their posture function as sources of nonverbal communication. Look at people's body shape, weight, height, hair, and skin. Check their breath or body odors. Note how their laughs, silences, yawns, coughs, cries, belches, whispers, yells, and moans transmit messages. Watch how they walk, sit, and stand, and you will observe nonverbal messages. Two people hurrying down the street send a different message than a man and woman sauntering arm-in-arm. A person slouched in a chair conveys a different message than one who is sitting up straight, alert to what is happening.

Sometimes people are aware of their nonverbal behavior and try to control it. Sometimes they are not aware of it at all. Regardless, they are always communicating nonverbally even if they don't realize it.

This chapter covers the ways people communicate nonverbally after analyzing how nonverbal behaviors function in communication. The functions of space, time, eyes, face, body, voice, objects, and appearances are considered.

COMMUNICATIVE FUNCTIONS OF NONVERBAL BEHAVIOR

What we do nonverbally is important in communication, and it influences the communication process. Nonverbal messages are always present; in normal human interaction they constitute about 55 percent of the message and the verbal components make up about 35 percent.[1] When speaking to others, the impact of nonverbal messages should not be ignored.

Even in written communication the nonverbal impact is present. For instance, the length of a written piece communicates. A long letter could reflect time, effort, and a great deal of attention on the writer's part. A short letter might suggest that the writer has an interest in the receiver, but it also may reflect a lack of time or of something to say. A nicely typed letter could represent the written desire to make a favorable impression. A sloppily written

How We Communicate Nonverbally

Repeating

She: Where do I catch the "15" bus?

He: (pointing) Over there, by the drugstore.

Substituting

She: Where?

He: (only pointing)

Emphasizing

She: I still don't see where.

He: (Turning her around) There!

Contradicting

He: (Smiling and patting her on the back) Gee, you're dumb!

She: (Smiling back) You're not so smart either.

Regulating

She: (Walking away) Thanks!

She: (Hesitating, looking back)

He: (Starting to follow) Miss . . .

student term paper could indicate a poorly motivated person.

Nonverbal communication supports verbal communication, transmits emotions, conveys immediacy, is not universal, and is culturally learned. Each of these factors is explained next.

Supports Verbal Communication

Nonverbal behavior supports speech in a number of ways.[2]

1. Nonverbal communication can simply repeat what we say orally. For example, if one of us were

to tell a friend that she has a spot on her dress and then point to it, the act of pointing would be the nonverbal act of repeating. The same message is carried verbally and nonverbally.

2. A nonverbal message can substitute for an oral message. If the person were to merely point to the spot on the friend's dress instead of telling her, the pointing would substitute for the oral message and, in this case, would be just as effective.

3. Nonverbal communication can emphasize verbal messages. If you were to grab someone by his shirt, scowl, and say, "Look, buster, don't fool with me," both the grip on the shirt and the scowl emphasize the point being made and stress the importance of what is being said.

4. Nonverbal communication can contradict verbal behavior. If someone says "Look, buster, don't fool with me," while smiling and giving him a friendly pat on the back, the nonverbal and verbal messages are contradicting each other. The nonverbal message suggests, "I'm just kidding; don't take me seriously."

5. Nonverbal messages can regulate verbal ones. An eye movement, a shift in position, or a nod of the head can tell the other person to continue talking, or these movements can say "stop" because it is someone else's turn to speak. In this instance, the nonverbal message acts as a traffic cop and regulates the flow of talk.

Transmits Emotions

Nonverbal behavior also conveys emotions. We can partially determine how people feel by watching their nonverbal behavior. Research reveals that our nonverbal behavior has more bearing than the words we utter in communicating our feelings or attitudes toward others. About 7 percent of the total emotional expression of an oral message is verbal, 38 percent is vocal expressiveness, and the remaining 55 percent consists of facial and bodily motion, as depicted in Figure 9.1.[3] Face, body, and vocal expressions of feeling, therefore, carry more weight than the words used to orally express the feelings.[4]

Three independent dimensions are said to encompass all nonverbal emotional displays: pleasure/displeasure, arousal/nonarousal, and dominance/submissiveness.[5]

Pleasure/Displeasure

Smiles, laughter, and generally happy facial expressions convey pleasure, as do jovial and happy voice qualities. Watching a group of people from a distance, we know they are enjoying themselves

when we see smiles and happy faces and hear laughter. If, instead, we observe frowning, angry, glaring, fearful, crying, disgusted looks or hear unhappy, sad, sneering, or angry voices, our inference that displeasure abounds probably is accurate.

Arousal/Nonarousal

A group of mentally alert and physically active people suggest that they are aroused or stirred up about something. They might be talking in loud, rapid, animated speech and, if not actually moving about, exhibit a somewhat tense, forward-leaning, attentive posture.

On the other hand, a quiet and calm group indicates nonarousal or tranquility. Their speech is quieter, slower, and less animated, perhaps even monosyllabic. They are stationary and relaxed.

Dominance/Submissiveness

By watching nonverbal behavior, we can readily determine in a pair who is in control, who is the more influential and important, and who is the more dominant. The dominant one conveys a feeling of strength, fearlessness, comfort, and relaxation. The behavior of the other, the submissive person — the one being controlled, influenced, awed, or guided — transmits weakness, smallness, discomfort, tension, and fearfulness.

This behavior often is apparent in an employer-employee dyad. The employer's dominance is reflected in behaviors suggesting greater energy, such as an assertive voice, fewer pauses or hesitations in speech, and louder volume, as well as

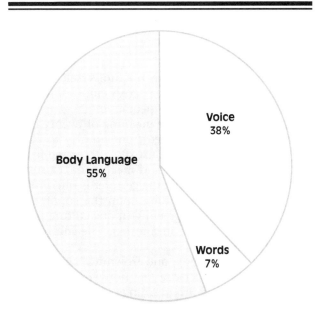

FIGURE 9.1. Relative contributions to messages.

control over the territory the two occupy. A relaxed, confident demeanor often accompanies such behavior. If the two are seated, the dominating employer may lean backward slightly with a relaxed posture, while the employee might lean forward, appearing tense. Or if the employee is defiant, he or she might slouch, showing disrespect for authority. The submissive employee, on the other hand, might display halting, tremulous speech and other signs of fear, head nodding, and even perhaps much smiling, because smiling in situations of this nature usually indicates submissiveness.

Conveys Immediacy

A third communicative function of nonverbal behavior is to convey immediacy. Immediacy means *closeness, physical and mental.* Nonverbal behaviors displaying immediacy send *approach messages* rather than avoidance ones. Immediacy behaviors such as a wave of the hand, a pat on the back, and a smile indicate that the person can be approached. They are "you can talk to me" sorts of behaviors. Immediacy forms of nonverbal behavior similarly can signal *availability* for talking. Behaviors that signify availability include moving close to someone, facing the person, and making eye contact. Further, immediacy behaviors increase *sensory stimulation.* Reducing distance, maintaining eye contact, and touching stimulate physiological and psychological processes that tend to increase interaction. And, finally, immediacy behaviors communicate *personal closeness and warmth.* Moving close, touching, maintaining eye contact suggest a willingness to listen and a desire to understand.[6]

Is Not Universal

Nonverbal behaviors are not universal; they do not carry the same meaning across cultures. A cross-cultural survey of 1,200 people in 25 European countries revealed that the meaning of twenty common hand gestures changed from country to country. The "thumbs up" sign, usually interpreted in the United States as "okay" could mean "one," a sexual insult, a direction, or that the gesturer is hitchhiking and wants a ride, depending upon the country the person is in. A sign of greeting in one culture might be an obscene gesture in another. The meaning is culturally dependent.

Only smiling, crying, and frowning have universal significance; otherwise few nonverbal behaviors have commonality in meanings. Even the smile, though, can be misinterpreted. In Japan the smile often is used to cover up sadness. Wanting to maintain harmony in social interactions, the Japanese will smile rather than express their feelings of unhappiness in sorrowful situations.

Is Culturally Learned

Our culture determines the meanings attached to nonverbal behaviors. We learn the behaviors, usually through observation and imitation rather than explicit verbal instruction or expression. The meanings are communicated implicitly, without awareness, by our family, friends, and teachers.

Although languages can be learned, nonverbal behavior learning is a subtle, multidimensional, and ordinarily spontaneous process. Usually we are not even aware of most of our nonverbal behavior. It is enacted mindlessly, spontaneously, and unconsciously. If we are unaware of our own nonverbal behavior, we will have extreme difficulty mastering the nonverbal behavior of another culture or even guessing what it means. When we meet people from foreign cultures, we are likely to interpret their nonverbal behavior as we would our own, resulting in misunderstanding.

FORMS OF NONVERBAL BEHAVIOR

Few of us are aware of the nonverbal messages we continuously transmit when talking with others. Fewer still are able to consciously control these messages so they assist rather than hamper successful oral communication. The first step to controlling nonverbal communication is to understand the various forms that nonverbal messages typically take. To help us understand, we next explain the impact of space, time, the eyes, the face, touch, bodily movements, artifacts, paralanguage, and appearance on communications.[7]

Spatial Communication

Proxemics concerns our use and perceptions of social and personal space.[8] It covers a variety of subjects.

1. Proxemics deals with how people use and respond to spatial arrangements in formal and informal group settings, a subject area called small-group ecology.

2. Proxemics concerns the influence that architecture has on residential living and on community life.

3. Proxemics relates to spatial relationships in crowds and densely populated areas.

4. Proxemics covers territoriality, the human tendency to stake out personal territory that we think of as our own.

5. Proxemics relates to conversational distance.

We will not discuss each of these five factors, here, but we can obtain a general understanding of how space communicates by briefly considering two of them, conversational distance and territoriality.

Distance

Distance tells a great deal about the nature of the message.[9] Note the effect of distance in this example: "She snuggled up and whispered words of tenderness; he moved away to the far corner of the car's front seat and spoke to her harshly." The girl had whispered a message of affection a few inches from her partner's ear, but the young man had moved away and spoken less pleasantly. He probably had other things on his mind besides feelings of tenderness.

This example relates space to the type of message uttered. The scale in Figure 9.2 suggests how we control voice volume in relation to the space between us and others indoors. Outdoors, the volume usually increases depending upon outside noises.

At the *intimate level* (0–18 inches), our voices are soft or barely audible as we share top-secret, confidential, or intimate information. Physical contact can be made easily, so we use this distance for an exchange of affection, physical comforting, and, for that matter, fighting.

At the *personal level* (1½ to 4 feet), we tend to discuss matters that are more or less confidential and mutually involving. At this distance we can touch each other if we want to, but not in an intimate way. It is the distance we typically use when talking to friends in the school corridor or at a party. At work several people might talk about work-related problems at this distance. Small-group discussions occur at this distance. When seated in a circle close enough to touch, the participants talk loud enough so each can hear the other but not so loud that they

"Leave me alone."

Communication at the personal level
can be positive or negative

interfere with the discourse of other groups that might be in their vicinity.

At the *social level* (4 to 12 feet), our talk usually concerns other than personal matters. At this level we speak at a normal volume while conversing with a small circle of friends or business associates about matters of common interest. The greater the physical distance between us, the more formal the talk is likely to be.

At the *public level* (12 feet and beyond), our talk is well outside the range of personal interaction with another individual. At this distance impersonal talk probably is required. One person most likely will not choose to speak about personal matters with someone 12 or more feet away, especially if others are present. The volume necessarily is loud, permitting anyone in the vicinity to hear. Thus, the range is more suitable for public speaking situations in which the talk is directed to a large group with little feedback expected.[10]

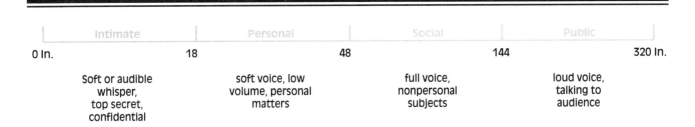

Intimate	Personal	Social	Public
0 In. 18	48	144	320 In.
Soft or audible whisper, top secret, confidential	soft voice, low volume, personal matters	full voice, nonpersonal subjects	loud voice, talking to audience

Figure 9.2. Volume control in relation to distance.

Physical distance also exerts a major impact on the communication between individuals when they are seated. If people are seated at a table, for example, they naturally tend to talk to the people seated either directly or diagonally across from them. These positions encourage communication. They are least likely to speak to the person seated directly at either elbow. Interestingly enough, the natural communication positions seem to change when people are seated in a living room at a party or social gathering. In circumstances like these, people seem to engage in conversation more effortlessly with the people seated next to them, and conversation across the room is much less frequent.

The traditional row-and-column classroom seating has an effect on student involvement. In the typical class a zone of participation is easily identifiable, as Figure 9.3 shows. Students sitting in the center of the room participate most. Those on the extremities and the rear rarely take part.[11]

Territoriality

The space we select for communication communicates something in itself. A teacher, for example, might talk to a student in the classroom, the hall, or the faculty office. The classroom is rather neutral territory, and the student usually does not view it as a threatening site for conversation. The hall is a little less neutral and slightly more threatening. The faculty office is clearly "teacher territory." If summoned there, a student usually views it as a threatening site. The very location of the talk predictably increases the student's anxiety and puts him or her on the defensive.

Each of us has spaces we consider our own — a bedroom, a desk, a favorite chair, a seat at the dining table, or a parking place, for instance. When someone "invades" our space or territory, we may become quite anxious and upset. One student reported: "When Dad comes home from work and finds one of us sitting in *his* chair reading *his* paper, he doesn't say much, yet we know he's put out. Mom yells if I sit in front of *her* mirror and touch *her* things. And my brother — if we'd so much as breathe in his room, he'd have fits!"[12]

Chronemic Communication

The *use of time in communication is called chronemics.* It concerns how people respond to matters such as time between statements, arrival/waiting/ departure times, and the hour at which a person chooses to communicate.[13]

In the United States, time talks, and what it says is crucial in our relations with others.[14] Promises to meet deadlines or keep appointments are taken seriously. Being late or not keeping a promise to complete a task by a given time evokes penalties. A student's repeatedly being late for a class could lead to suspension from school. Some teachers deduct 10 percent for late papers. Others give a failing grade. Almost all bestow some sort of penalty.

How we use time in communication situations suggests a great deal about ourselves to other people. Many of our feelings about those who attempt to communicate with us are based upon how they use time. Americans, for example, habitually leave little

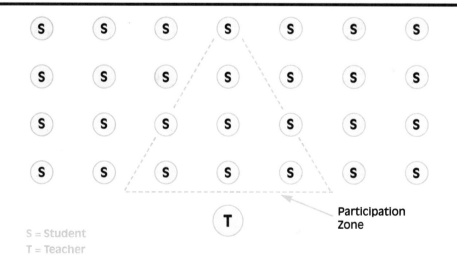

Figure 9.3. Student participation in class.

time between statements in face-to-face communication. An unusual pause in a conversation generally signifies that it is the other person's turn to talk. In some other cultures the length of pauses in conversation tends to be much longer. When communicating with individuals from cultures such as those, Americans usually interject comments more often and more quickly than is customary in the other culture. This is because Americans feel strained and uncomfortable if pauses between contributions are longer than two or three seconds. Americans are uncomfortable with silence.

Also, waiting time exerts considerable impact upon our communication behavior. Most people become uneasy, for instance, if they are kept waiting more than five minutes for an appointment. They assume the person who is making them wait is unconcerned with their well-being and holds them in fairly low regard. Anxiety or anger builds in the person who is kept waiting. These emotions frequently affect whatever communication follows. If John has to cool his heels in Mary's living room for 45 minutes while she dresses, chances are that he is going to express his anxiety in some manner once she appears.

The length of time we spend with someone also has its impact, as in the length of appointments. Consider the impact of a baseball player's remark: "He spent over an hour with the coach." Everyone knows that the discussion must have been important. Or reflect on these words from the team captain: "The coach had only 10 minutes to spare, so we didn't talk about much." The 10 minutes suggest that the coach had more important things to do than talk with his captain.

The more time we spend with a person, the closer is the connection between us. Lovers, for instance, are together a great deal of the time. On the other hand, the less time we spend with someone, the weaker is the connection. Absence does not make the heart grow fonder.

Some of us are representative of the type of people who like a lot of social contact with others. Our date books are filled weeks in advance. In contrast, others of us, who prefer individual freedom and privacy over much socializing, often do not know whether we are going to go someplace until it is time to go.

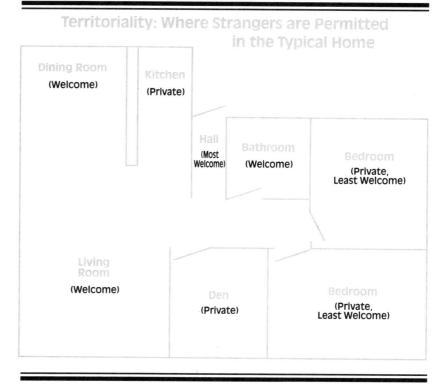

Being early, as to baseball practice, a club meeting, or a game, also communicates something. It projects an eagerness to participate, that we have been looking forward to the event and are raring to go.

Time communicates in yet another way. The very time we choose for communication communicates a great deal. Whenever we receive a phone call after midnight, we become concerned. That time of day usually is reserved for calls that report emergencies of one kind or another. Similarly, most business calls

"She's late again. Doesn't she like me?"

Waiting time influences our communication ability.

are placed on weekdays between 9 and 5 o'clock. A business call on Saturday or Sunday is unusual, and the person who is called responds accordingly.

Most people learn at an early age about the importance of time in communication situations. No intelligent American child asks a father for an increase in allowance when the father first wakes up in the morning. Experience teaches that another time would be more appropriate. American teenagers do not ask to borrow the car immediately after being taken to task for some sort of misbehavior. Even though people usually learn about proper timing for communication at an early age, most of us occasionally run afoul of the timing expectations of others. When we do so, the effectiveness of our communication is sharply curtailed. Five minutes past four is tomorrow if the boat left at four.

Ocular Communication

Oculesics refers to the use of eyes in communication.[15] A variety of behavior is associated with the eyes. Eye movements cover an extensive range of expression. Modesty is revealed by downward glances; frankness, wonder, or terror with wide open eyes; coldness by staring eyes and immobile facial muscles; displeasure by raised upper eyelids and contracted orbs; anxiety by excessive blinking; concentration by decreased blinking; fatigue by eyes rolled upward.

For centuries, authors have described people and their behavior by referring to their eyes, through statements like these: "At the end, his little eyes shining, George got a plaque." "Ellen's blameless blue eyes had a look of almost suffocating innocence." "Harrison was a beefy man with a tawny complexion and soft, sad eyes." "His chilling stare, set off by his ice cold eyes, froze the killer in his tracks." Eyes, we read, can be knowing, warm, mean, mocking, wise, loving, caressing, and spiteful. One's glance is burning, hurt, melting, freezing, hate-filled, and so on. Eyes, the old adage states, are the mirrors of the soul, and through the eyes we transmit our innermost feelings.

In American culture, the fiction has persisted through the ages that dishonest people — the liars, the cheats — and weak-willed individuals can't look us in the eye. Experienced liars use this bit of fiction to their advantage and never let their glance waver when they are knowingly telling a lie. Their invented honesty is hard to detect except by the most experienced observer. Other cultures have different outlooks, however. In Puerto Rico, children are taught, as a sign of respect and obedience, not to meet the eyes of adults. In Asian cultures, to show respect, one does not look the speaker straight in the eye. Men do not stare at women, and vice versa. But

women of loose character are supposed to look straight at men's faces. In France, an accepted cultural norm permits men to stare at women.[16]

In the American culture, direct eye contact with another also communicates interest and attention. The absence of direct eye contact, on the other hand, indicates a lack of interest and attention. Eye contact is such a powerful communicator that it can even be used to control communication. For example, when we do not want to be interrupted while talking we can avert our gaze from the person to whom we are speaking. By doing so, we can continue to speak without interference. When we are through talking, we look at the other, signaling that we are finished for the time being and the other can now speak. We learn this sort of nonverbal behavior although we may not be aware of it. When necessary, we tend to use it automatically.

A "taboo" we learn early in life is not to stare at another person.[17] Stares are reserved for things. We stare at art, scenery, zoo animals. But, according to the "rules," we don't stare at people unless we deliberately mean to transmit a feeling of contempt for the other. Or we employ the blank stare as a protective device. We do not want to get personally involved with the one we are dealing with; we desire the person's services only. We communicate on a non-person level through the stare. In a high-class restaurant, for example, we tend to place our order with a slightly unfocused look that does not really see the waiter. That type of stare helps waiters as well as us. They can go about their business efficiently, and we can do the same without going through the social formalities of introductions, small talk about the weather, and so forth. While shopping, especially in a strange store, we want to concentrate on the product, not on the salesperson, so the blank stare helps.

In the United States, eye contact is an important form of nonverbal communication in the initial stages of courtship. The male establishes what might be called a "courtship stare" with the female. This somewhat prolonged eye contact communicates strong interest on the male's part. It says to the female, "I'm interested in you," and it asks, "Are you interested in me?" If the girl turns away, the answer is usually no. If she smiles or in some way indicates approval, the answer is probably yes. At this point verbal communication often begins.

A problem can arise when either the boy or the girl is unaware of this cultural practice. A girl who complains about the number of unattractive men who seem to want to engage her in conversation is probably flashing the wrong signals. The girl most likely responds positively to courtship stares without being aware that she is doing so. A boy, on the other hand, might fail to recognize the conventional "turn-off" signals. As in the case with most non-verbal communication behavior, the courtship stare is not something normally taught to children. Nevertheless most people seem to learn it at a rather early age.

Eye contact is essential in establishing immediacy, and positive effects usually result from eye contact.[18] Visual interaction communicates warmth and a desire to be involved. If a magazine poll can be believed, it apparently also implies interest. When asked what physical characteristics women consider most attractive in men, women ranked eyes as a male's sexiest part. One woman reported: "One look in a man's eyes, and I know if I'm interested." Another said: "If his eyes dart around nervously, he's not self-confident. A man who can't sustain eye contact is a washout — at least with me."

Facial Communication

The face communicates affective states mostly through facial configurations. Love, fear, anger, pleasure, and sadness are among the many emotions the face communicates. Sometimes our attitudes toward another person's ideas are expressed facially. We send feelings of approval, disapproval, neutrality, and lack of understanding through facial movements. The face gives clues about our reactions to other people's remarks, causing some experts to claim that, except for speech, the face is the primary means of communication. When we talk with others we rely heavily on facial cues to obtain feedback about how well our ideas are being received. Our facial expressions change constantly as we talk, however, and these changes often are hard to keep up with. To assess facially expressed emotions accurately is not easy.[19]

The face communicates more than affective states. Parts of the face are used to open and close communication. We can open communication channels with a smile, a wink, or an open mouth, signifying that we are ready to talk. We close the channels by closing the mouth or looking away.

In addition, the face is used to complement or qualify verbal and nonverbal responses. Through the face we can emphasize, magnify, minimize, or support messages. A smile, for instance, can temper what otherwise might be considered a negative message. Lowered eyebrows can be used to stress the sadness conveyed by a verbal message.

The face can replace spoken messages. When one's jaw drops and the mouth hangs open, the surprise this expression communicates does not require a verbal message to indicate how flabbergasted a person feels.[20]

The smile is a powerful immediacy cue. It can quickly establish a feeling of warmth and personal closeness and also can communicate willingness to associate. It promotes reciprocal feelings of warmth. Persons who smile frequently express immediacy in an easy and influential way.[21]

These qualities of the smile point up another characteristic of facial expressions: We often mask our real feelings by facially expressing an opposite or neutral feeling. The "poker face" displays no emotion whatsoever; we sometimes use it when we do not want to reveal our true feelings. A professional wrestler contorts his face into expressions of pain and agony although his opponent is not hurting him at all. The sales clerk's mechanical smile usually hides his or her real feelings toward the customer.[22] The Japanese so-called inscrutable smile might be misunderstood when it is used to conceal anguish or enmity.

The face is a commanding, complicated, and occasionally confusing source of information. It is commanding because of its visibility and its presence, making it an important element in nonverbal communication. It is complicated and confusing because the face often blends several emotions and its expressions change rapidly. The face is a multimessage system, conveying a variety of information.[23]

Tactile Communication

Haptics is the term referring to the use of touch to communicate feelings and emotions.[24] Touch is an important factor in the psychological development of children, and it seems to be equally important in the lives of elderly and sick people. Actually, everyone benefits from the security and satisfaction that touch brings.[25] Touch plays a role in giving encouragement, expressing tenderness, and showing emotional support.

Those of us who have blind acquaintances know that touch is a vital form of communication, and a moment's thought will tell us that for those who are both blind and deaf, touch is the principal means of communication. Even without these handicaps the average person relies heavily on touch. We understand the language of hot and cold, a pin prick, a warm embrace, the dentist's drill, the helping hand. We know that a slap on the back can mean a touch of friendship or a sign of encouragement and that stroking a dog or cat conveys affection.

Touch may be the most basic or primitive form of communication. One of our first contacts with life itself came through the doctor's hands and, as newborn children, the touching that came with diaper changing, feeding, bathing, rocking and comforting constituted the earliest form of affection and tenderness we learned.

Touch remains a crucial aspect of human relationships throughout our lives. As we said, it has a part in expressing tenderness, giving encouragement, and showing emotional support. Through touch we also can communicate anger (a punch in the nose), strength (a healthy shove), and fear (trembling hands).

As with other forms of nonverbal communication, the use of touch to communicate feelings and emotions varies considerably from one culture to another. For example, American males are not inclined to touch one another, except for a handshake or an occasional slap on the back. Females do not use the handshake as much. In other parts of the world, touch tends to be more widespread. African, Arab, and Southeast Asian males commonly hold hands as a sign of friendship. European females shake hands universally.[26]

In the American culture various ethnic groups show significant and interesting deviations in touching behavior. Black Americans and Italian-Americans — to offer two examples — use touch rather widely to communicate closeness and affection. Anglo-Americans, on the other hand, normally are restrained as far as touching goes. When people from different ethnic backgrounds talk with one another, they naturally engage in the "normal" touching behavior for their particular culture. What is normal for one group, however, is not necessarily normal for another. As a result, serious misunderstandings can occur. An Anglo-American can be perceived as reserved and distant. A Black American, an Italian-American, or a Greek-American might be judged as too assertive and pushy.

Touch is an important factor in interpersonal interaction because it helps communicate immedi-

acy. At the same time, touch is one of the most intimate forms of nonverbal communication. Therefore, it should be used with care. Touching in interpersonal interaction varies with the age, gender, situation, and relationship of those involved, and it is likely to be taboo in certain social situations, except for the commonplace handshake, pat on the back, and other nonthreatening or nonsexual forms.[27] Nevertheless, touch does convey feelings of immediacy and thus promotes friendship and warmth.

Kinesic Communication

Kinesics refers to body movements, such as movements of the head, arms, legs and torso, in communication. It includes facial expressions, eye behavior, gestures, and posture. Some authorities include tactile, or touching, behavior as a kinesic form.[28] Body movement is the most common nonverbal form of communication. An estimated 700,000-plus possible signals can be transmitted through bodily movement. Most are automatic and difficult for us to completely control.[29]

We learn to communicate through body movement at an early age — in fact, in infancy, when we start to smile and to extend our hands for something we want. In early childhood we began to master other common movements and gestures, learning to wave our hands in greeting and leaving and to shake our head to signify agreement or disagreement.

The body communicates a variety of messages. It can reveal, for example, the intensity of an emotion. Angry talk might be reinforced with a clenched fist, a tense or rigid body, or a forward leaning, ready-to-fight posture. The body also can signal readiness to communicate. We interpret turning or moving toward someone as a communication attempt. Bodily action, moreover, can show how genuine a person feels toward those in the communicative interaction. Posture can reveal warmth, status, inconclusiveness, and deception.

In addition, body movements can communicate immediacy, agreement or disagreement, and the relative power we have. Open arm and leg positions convey positiveness. Folding one's arms and holding one's legs tightly together signify defensiveness and coldness. Bodily relaxation communicates immediacy; it demonstrates freedom from stress and anxiety. Conversely, bodily tension suggests anxiety and possible aggressive behavior.

Gestures — movements of hands, feet, legs, and other parts of the body — are closely coordinated with speech/verbal behavior. Most gestures are not innate. Because they are learned communicative behavior, they vary considerably from culture to culture. Hand gestures, used with great frequency,

"You're great!"

Touch is a vital form of communication.

Gestures play a key role in communication

"Stop!"   "Peace."   "Okay."

A ring is an example of artifactual communication

"You're engaged!"

play a key role in interpersonal talk. They sometimes take the place of words, as when we motion to another person to sit or stand and where to move. Usually hand gestures reinforce our verbal messages — for instance, when we shake our head while we say no.

For deaf people gestures are a primary form of communication. Sign language, which takes the place of spoken language, involves a complex set of hand gestures capable of conveying fine subtleties of meaning. Although those whose hearing is not impaired do not have to rely on hand gestures, they do rely on the hands as a communicative tool.[30]

Artifactual Communication

An *artifact is any object made by human effort.* Artifacts communicate just by their presence or through their manipulation. Interior decoration, coats-of-arms, and clothes play significant roles in communication. The types and numbers of cars, books, TV sets, and stereos we own may indicate our interests, status in life, and the amount of money we earn. The number of rings on the hand, the type of watch on the wrist, the make of pen and pencil, suggest power and position.

In Roman times the people believed that diamonds protected them from their enemies, emeralds made them rich, rubies gave them peace of mind, sapphires bestowed happiness, and amethysts were responsible for good digestion. A rich man might wear them all to make sure he would have honor, happiness, safety, and health. In the Middle Ages when knights put on helmets and chain mail to go into battle, nobody could tell them apart, so each one wore a colored flag on his spear and painted his shield the same color. Off the battlefield these colors were called "coats of arms" and were painted or engraved on all the warrior's possessions.[31]

People are always surrounded by objects. When we communicate, these objects often are brought into play. Even if the object is not used directly in the communication situation, its very presence may say something of considerable importance in the communication situation. A person who constantly clicks a ballpoint pen while talking, for example, is probably extremely nervous or bored. The object communicates his or her internal feelings. Similarly, the furniture, colors, and fabrics that decorate a home or office communicate a great deal about the individuals who live or work there. The color and style of the clothing we wear tells much about us as persons. Blue clothing, for instance, supposedly conveys peace and contentment, but those who are motivated by a need for security choose dark blue. Yellow suggests modernity, achievement, and the future. Red clothing conjures up power, an urge to win, and vitality; it is a color often chosen for football uniforms.

Objects often are used to encourage or discourage communication. Furniture arranged in a circular fashion in a living room usually stimulates conversation among guests. If an office desk is situated so that it clearly becomes a barrier between the person behind it and the person who comes into the office, the communication that takes place is prone to be formal, reserved, and rather brief.

Attached to some objects are traditional associations that serve as powerful communicators. The mere presence of a gun or a knife suggests violence. A uniform communicates that the wearer belongs to a structured organization. Medals are signs of valor or bravery. A statue or wall decoration of a blindfolded woman holding two scales communicates something about justice. A red light signifies stop or danger. *Objects, or artifacts, communicate all kinds of messages.*

Paralanguage as Communication

Paralanguage is *concerned with how something is said, not with what is said.* It covers the range of

Nonverbal Behaviors Communicating Positiveness

Warm, inviting smile
Good eye contact
Proper dress, good grooming
Slight forward lean of body
Facing the other squarely
Relaxed posture
Observing a *personal* distance
Natural voice, warm, interesting
Proper volume and pitch
Proper rate
Fluency in delivery
Enthusiasm
Firm handshake
Welcoming wave or outstretched arm
Concentrating on other

Nonverbal Behaviors Communicating Negativeness

Cold, frowning, neutral face
Unkept appearance, improper dress
Downcast eyes, staring, peering, darting
Rigid posture
Constant shifting and moving of body
Observing an *intimate* or a *public* distance
Voice too loud or quiet
Mumbling
Speaking too fast, too abrupt, too terse
Low voice pitch
Overly enthusiastic
Cold, impersonal greeting
Weak handshake, or too strong
Concentrating on other things

nonverbal vocal cues surrounding common speech behavior, including *qualities* such a pitch range and control, rhythm control, rate, articulation control, glottis control, and lip control. It also includes *vocal characteristics* such as laughing, crying, sighing, moaning, groaning, yawning, belching, coughing, throat clearing, whining, yelling, whispering, and swallowing, *vocal qualifiers* such as volume and pitch height and extent, and *vocal segregates* such as "uh-huh," "um," "ah," and "uh."[32]

Vocal cues often help us recognize the person we speak to. When we get a telephone call, if it is someone we know well, we usually can tell who it is by the vocal quality. He or she does not have to say who is calling.

Based upon their voices, we frequently form conclusions about people's personalities, but these conclusions are not necessarily accurate. Over the years the qualities of various voices actually have led us to certain stereotypes about people. A female with a breathy voice, for example, frequently is considered to be prettier and more feminine than her counterpart without the breathy voice. A male with a deep voice often is considered more virile and solid than one with a higher voice. Both males and females who speak rapidly tend to be considered animated and outgoing.

The conclusions reached about people from their vocal qualities are uninformed and born of pure chance.[33] Nevertheless, people do form conclusions based upon qualities of voice. As often as not, however, the girl with the breathy voice turns out to be rather plain and unpleasant. The man with the high voice turns out to be a war hero.

Some personality traits can be accurately understood by listening to the voice. The voice can indicate the speaker's gender, age, and race. The voice also indicates the region of origin within a country. Furthermore, the voice can disclose the speaker's social status and level of education. The voice also sheds some light upon the speaker's emotional state while he or she is speaking. The voice often says more about us than we want another person to know — and it sometimes suggests things about us that simply are not true.[34]

Vocal expression communicates emotional meanings. Affection, for example, is communicated in a soft, low, resonant voice at a slow tempo with a regular rhythm. Anger is expressed in a loud, high, blaring voice at a fast rate with irregular rhythm and clipped enunciation. Joy is transmitted in a loud, high, moderately blaring voice at a fast tempo with regular rhythm and upward inflection. Sadness is conveyed in a soft, low, resonant voice at a slow tempo with a downward inflection and irregular and pause-filled rhythm.[35]

When speaking for informing or persuasive purposes, vocal cues have an impact on what listeners comprehend and retain, as well as how effective a person is as a persuader. Vocal variety — large variations in rate, volume, pitch, and quality — increases comprehension and persuasiveness. A mono-pitch decreases both, although this may be because listeners judge the speaker as less credible or believable when the speaker talks in a monotone.[36]

Vocal cues also play a role in managing the oral interaction when several people talk together. The cues govern who speaks to whom, when, and for how long. We request a turn to speak through devices such as a stuttering start ("I-I-I"; "Let's-let's-let's") and the increasingly rapid use of vocalizations ("uh-uh-uh"). We maintain the floor by increasing our volume and rate or by reducing the number of pauses when we sense someone wants a turn. We yield to another speaker by asking a question or letting our voice drop away.[37]

Pauses are common in ordinary speech. Spontaneous speech is highly fragmented and discontinuous. Two-thirds of the most fluent speech comes in chunks of fewer than six words. Pauses of milliseconds to minutes may interrupt such talk, depending upon the situational pressures, the speaker, and the task at hand. Decision-making situations tend to be pressure-filled and we are more apt to be careful of what we say, causing us to pause more. Apprehensive speakers typically use more pauses. Some tasks may cause us to think and, as we are doing so, pause frequently, trying to work out answers in our brain. Excessive pausing, however, often is viewed as impairing performance. Speakers who pause a lot are thought not to speak well, to be fearful, to lack knowledge on the subject, or to be disinterested in the conversation.[38]

Appearance as Communication

A speech class that observed television commercials for one week found that roughly 50 percent advertised products designed to advance one's personal appearance in some way. Among the products advertised were soaps and deodorants to decrease body odors; women's perfumes and men's colognes to enhance body scents; mouth washes, breath mints, and toothpastes to mask mouth odors; creams, lotions, sprays, shampoos, rinses, and tints to make one's hair more attractive; creams and lotions to soften the skin; cosmetics of many varieties to heighten the beauty of the mouth, eyes, face, and fingernails; wigs to add hair and depilatories to remove unwanted hair; shaving creams, razors, blades, and lotions to make whisker removing more enjoyable and give closer shaves; a multitude of laundry products to make clothes cleaner, neater, and fresher smelling; and many more. Making and selling products to enhance one's personal appearance is a multibillion-dollar industry.[39]

Why are people so turned-on about physical appearance? The importance of appearance as a nonverbal communicator leaves no doubt. Our physical appearance appears to be highly influential in determining how successful we are in persuading others and in deciding whom we seek out as companions, date, and eventually marry. This seems to be so because we tend to respond in a stereotyped manner to specific features such as body shape, hair, and overall appearance.

Body shapes supposedly communicate a great deal about people's temperament. Soft, round, fat people are supposed to be calm, relaxed, leisurely, sluggish, cooperative, warm, forgiving, soft-hearted, soft-tempered, sociable, in some combination. Bony, muscular, athletic types are considered confident, competitive, energetic, assertive, active, talkative, courageous, optimistic, adventurous, hot-tempered, reckless. Tall, thin, fragile individuals are thought to be the opposite of the soft, round, and fat ones — tense, anxious, shy, thoughtful, suspicious, serious, cautious, self- conscious, precise.

Naturally, most people's bodies do not exactly fit one or another of these three classifications. Nor do the traits of their temperaments correspond perfectly. Some extra-tall people are round and fat; some fat people are competitive; many tall, thin people are warm, calm, and leisurely. Nevertheless, people often are judged in terms of their body shape. For example, insurance companies judge fat people to be poor health risks, so they have more difficulty buying life insurance than individuals who are not fat. Fat and sloppy people may have trouble obtaining jobs and getting dates. Many women prefer tall men, and men prefer average-sized women over those who are extremely tall or very short.[40]

Hair always has played a major role in structuring interpersonal communication. The ladies of ancient Rome liked blond hair so much that they sometimes wore bright yellow wigs. Those with dark hair were not a part of the "in" group. Desirable Roman men cut their hair short, and slaves and barbarians were long-haired. The European barbarians who eventually conquered Rome wore long hair and thought those with short hair were slaves. Under Charlemagne (800 A.D.) the nobles' hair was short. Japanese men at about the same time shaved the tops of their heads. Egyptians shaved off all their hair. In every age, those whose hair did not correspond to the style of the time often were ridiculed or abused.

General appearance similarly affects communication. Sloppy, smelly, dirty-looking people do not generate as much confidence as neat, clean people. In the school cafeteria, service from workers with dirty hands, soiled garments, and objectionable hair might result in loss of appetite. A foul-smelling, filthily-dressed dentist would have no business working on our teeth. A girl on a date with an auto mechanic who didn't bathe or change his greasy clothes probably would not enjoy the experience.

EVALUATING NONVERBAL MESSAGES

As we become sensitive to, and judge the nonverbal behavior of, others, we should keep three points in mind.[41] First, nonverbal behavior always occurs in a context, and it should be assessed in terms of that context. An employee who slouches in his chair and seems uninterested as the employer talks might be demonstrating defiance. In the company cafeteria with fellow workers, the employee who displays the same signs may simply be expressing boredom.

Second, nonverbal cues cannot be viewed as isolated parts of a person's behavior. Rather, the person's total behavior must be considered when making judgments. We cannot conclude, based solely on the employee's posture and disinterest in the employer's presence, that the employee was defiant. We should consider all aspects of that person's behavior — what the employee says and what else that person does — before passing judgment.

Finally, our conclusions about what we perceive should remain tentative. The possibility could exist that what we think a nonverbal event represents is actually not that at all. Meaning is in us, not in that which we perceive, and the meaning we perceive may not be what was intended.

SUMMARY

Nonverbal communication supports verbal communication, conveys emotion, enhances immediacy, is not universal, and is culturally learned. It is characterized by repeating, substituting for, emphasizing, contradicting, and regulating verbal messages. Nonverbal behavior plays a larger role in communicating emotions than verbal behavior does. Its emotional impact is viewed on three dimensions: pleasure/displeasure, arousal/nonarousal, and dominance/submissiveness.

Immediacy or closeness can be established nonverbally. To help do this, people use space, time, the eyes, the face, touch, bodily movement, objects, the voice, and appearance. Each of these aspects further communicates in ways communicators are not always conscious of. Nonverbal behavior communicates subtly and usually so automatically that we are not aware that our face, bodily movement, voice, appearance, and other factors are sending messages.

As we judge nonverbal communication, we must recognize an act of nonverbal behavior as context-bound, observable only in combination with other behaviors, and as tentative because its meaning resides in our interpretation. Our meaning may not be the meaning the user intended.

Vocabulary Check

These terms were defined in this chapter. Match the correct definition with its appropriate term. Answers are on page 243.

_____ 1. Immediacy

_____ 2. Chronemics

_____ 3. Territoriality

_____ 4. Oculesics

_____ 5. Kinesics

_____ 6. Proxemics

_____ 7. Tactile communication

_____ 8. Artifacts

_____ 9. Paralanguage

_____ 10. Nonverbal communication

A. Perceptions of social and personal space.

B. Closeness, physical and mental.

C. Touch in communication.

D. Our own personal space.

E. Manmade objects.

F. The study of time.

G. Use of eyes in communication.

H. How something is said.

I. Communication not using oral or written language.

J. Body movements.

10

Listening

Of the time people spend communicating each day, listening accounts for roughly 45 percent. Yet many people conduct this communication activity poorly.[1]

We ignore or, worse, misunderstand and often forget about 75 percent of what we hear. Rarely do we listen for the deepest feelings that people frequently include in their messages. We are poor listeners probably because we do not know *how* to listen. We may *hear* well, but not too many of us have acquired the necessary skills to *listen* well. All too frequently what we hear goes in one ear and out the other, and normally we remember no more than half of what we hear no matter how carefully we thought we were listening. Within as little as eight hours, we tend to forget as much as a third more of what we hear.[2]

Hearing and listening are dissimilar processes, and this chapter explains the differences between the two. After discussing the two processes, we describe the forms of listening and then consider the variables that affect listening. The chapter closes with suggestions on how to be more successful as a listener.

HEARING

Hearing refers to the *physiological sensory process by which the ear receives auditory sensations and transmits them to the brain*.[3] Next to sight, it is our most important sense in terms of being essential in the development of our language ability and crucial in communication. Like sight, hearing is a "distance sense." It informs us about things not actually in contact with the body and warns us of approaching danger. Like sight, hearing functions as a medium for artistic and aesthetic enjoyment.

The Hearing Process

The hearing process involves a series of steps or events that occur almost instantaneously when a sound is heard, and continuously as many sounds are perceived. The sequence begins with the sound waves traveling down the *auditory canal* to the *eardrum*, which vibrates. As it does so, three small bones, the *hammer*, *anvil*, and *stirrup*, also vibrate. The shape and geometry of the connections between the three bones serve to magnify the vibrations about twenty-five-fold. This causes the *oval window*, the beginning of the inner ear, to vibrate.

Within the inner ear, what has been mechanical to this point now becomes electrical as the vibrations convert to electrical impulses. The cochlea, the primary structure related to hearing in the inner ear, comes into play at this time; it is a spiral-shaped chamber filled with fluid and divided into three chambers by two membranes. Resting on the *basilar membrane*, one of the two, is the *organ of Corti*, which contains the nerve cells for hearing. These cells or *neurons* form a bundle called the *auditory nerve*, which carries information about sound to the brain. In the brain, the sounds are interpreted as the listening process takes over.[4]

Hearing Limitations

Contemporary life, with its labor-saving conveniences, is filled with noise pollution. Machinery of all sorts makes household chores easier. Lawn mowers, snow blowers, vacuum cleaners, washing machines, dishwashers, automatic tools, and other electrical appliances cut down on time and labor around the house, but they do increase the noise level. Add to those labor-saving devices noise makers such as air conditioners, radios, TVs, and stereos, and mix in heavy traffic, low-flying airplanes and helicopters, and screaming children, and we have many of the ingredients for noise pollution. Hearing loss is a result.

As people grow older, a degree of hearing loss is expected in normal circumstances. In recent years more and more younger people are experiencing hearing loss, and a much larger proportion of the population can expect restricted hearing because of noise pollution.

Hearing loss imposes one limitation on the ability to hear people speak with unrestricted intelligibility. Two additional limitations — masking and auditory fatigue — bear mention. *Masking* occurs when one sound covers another, making the other inaudible. Any sort of noise entering the ear in the same frequency as the speech we may be listening to could mask the speech sounds, preventing us from hearing the speaker clearly.

Auditory fatigue is the result of hearing sounds of the same frequency for long periods. A temporary hearing loss can be the consequence. Rock concert listeners often have this experience. Music played continuously at a high intensity level can cause auditory fatigue.[5]

THE LISTENING PROCESS

Whereas hearing is a physiological process, listening is a psychological one. It is a perceptual activity that involves making sense out of what we hear, as the definition of listening implies: *Listening is a complex psychological process that deals with interpreting and understanding the significance of auditory sensations.*[6] We can hear what another person is saying without really listening to that person. As one student said, "My friends listen to what I say, but my parents only hear me talk."

The distinction between merely hearing and really listening is deeply embedded in our language. The word "listen" is derived from two Anglo-Saxon words. One is *hlystan*, which means "hearing." The other is *hlosnian*, which means "to wait in suspense." Listening, then, is the combination of

The Importance of Listening

The most important factor for successful communication is not only the ability to use language well or to speak well or to present one's own point of view; it is rather the ability to listen well to the other person's point of view.

> — J. D. Winrauch and J. R. Swanda, Jr.
> *Journal of Business Communication*, 13,
> Feb. 1975

Listening is used more frequently than any other form of verbal communication, particularly in the classroom.

> — Larry L. Barker
> *Listening Behavior.* (Englewood Cliffs, NJ:
> Prentice Hall. 1971).

You ain't learning nothing when you're talking.

> — Sign in President Lyndon B. Johnson's office

Listening is viewed as a critical factor in job success.

> — James J. Floyd
> *Listening: A Practical Approach.* (Glenview, IL:
> Scott, Foresman, 1985).

hearing what the other person says and a suspenseful waiting, an intense psychological involvement with the other.[7]

Listening is a four-stage process — the first of which is hearing. The other stages are attention, understanding, and remembering.[8]

Attention

Our senses are bombarded constantly by countless stimuli. An athletic contest offers a vivid example of what our senses confront all day long. The total environment of cheering people, hawkers of food, flashing scoreboard lights, cheerleaders, bands, and the players themselves could overload our senses. The brain, however, screens these stimuli and allows us to focus on a select few — the ones we want to pay attention to, the game itself perhaps. Similarly, as we go about our daily activities, our senses are barraged with stimuli, but we attend to only those that interest us at the moment.

Attending is a motivational process. We do not respond indiscriminately to every stimulus bombarding us. We react selectively, in terms of our interests and attitudes. The doctor who hears the telephone during the night but fails to hear his baby cry is listening for the telephone. He attends to the telephone most likely because it is part of his work. His wife, on the other hand, may not hear the telephone but hears the baby. Her interests are different;

she is more concerned with the baby's well-being than the health of her husband's patients.

We may be so preoccupied with studying that we fail to hear what is being said on a nearby radio. At the moment, we are interested in studying, not in the radio. The studying interferes with listening to the radio. The ventriloquist, through manipulations of the doll, gets us to attend to the doll and its mouth movements. We become so attentive to the doll that we fail to see the ventriloquist's lips move, which they invariably do.

Understanding

The next stage in the listening process is understanding. Hearing and attending are not enough for listening. We must understand what we hear, and this requires us to attach meaning to the stimuli we hear. The stimuli are not only words but other sounds as well. The sounds of slamming doors, air raid sirens, typewriters, car horns can have symbolic meanings for us. We learn these meanings just as we learn the meanings of words. For successful listening, we must understand the intended meaning.

Remembering

The final stage is to store the sounds in our memory bank for later recall and recognition. Listening, in a sense, is known by its outcome — the listener's performance or response to what was heard. Hearing a lecture, we will have been listening if we can recall later what we heard. Listening cannot be said to have happened without the occurrence of remembering also.

During relatively short times, under circumstances in which no extreme distractions have been introduced, virtually perfect remembering of a short message is to be expected. These conditions for remembering, however, rarely are present in the typical listening situation. The presence of noise caused by distracting or interfering sounds impedes recall. The passing of time likewise affects remembering. Hearing loss, auditory fatigue, and lack of motivation, among other factors, also affect what is remembered.[9]

TYPES OF LISTENING

Scholars who are interested in the subject have categorized listening in a number of different systems.[10] The categories differ because of the diverse backgrounds and interests of those who study listening. To provide a broad spectrum of listening types,

we introduce several of these systems of classifying listening.

The first system — deliberative/empathic — is essentially bipolar. It places the two major styles on opposite ends on a listening continuum, recognizing that an individual's listening style may vary from time to time depending upon the situation.

The Listening Process

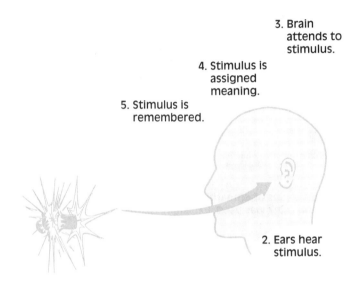

3. Brain attends to stimulus.

4. Stimulus is assigned meaning.

5. Stimulus is remembered.

2. Ears hear stimulus.

1. Stimulus, catching our attention.

The second system — active/passive — can be viewed similarly. Here, too, the types represent extremes on a listening continuum. Two more systems — social and serious — are included. Under each of these classification systems are a number of types that do not fall on any sort of continuum.

Deliberative/Empathic

Our analysis of this classification of listening types considers the two opposite ends without discussing gradations between them. As listeners, the type of listening in which we engage can vary along the continuum, depending upon the circumstances.

Both deliberative and empathic listeners have much the same objective in mind as they listen — to accurately understand the speaker's messages — but they listen with a different attitude toward what they hear.[11] The deliberative listener functions as a critic; the empathic listener listens with an open mind.

Listening as a critic, the deliberative listener filters what is heard through a set of predispositions, which are evaluative in nature. The deliberative listener is predisposed to criticize what is heard, agreeing or disagreeing and drawing conclusions from the speaker's remarks. While listening, the deliberative listener is pronouncing judgments upon the speaker's message. The result is that the deliberative listener obtains minimum understanding of the speaker's comments from the speaker's point of view.

In contrast, the empathic[12] listener, listening with an open mind, attempts to understand the speaker's message before making judgments about it. The empathic listener tries to achieve maximum understanding of the speaker's comments from the speaker's point of view. Empathic listeners question, seek clarification, and request elaboration if they don't understand the message. Once they understand the message, empathic listeners offer critical responses if any are necessary.

In summary, the deliberative listener judges the message as it is being heard, and the empathic listener tries to understand the message from the speaker's frame of reference before judging it. Deliberative listening is comparatively easy; most of us listen that way. Empathic listening is more difficult, requiring desire and practice.[13] Suggestions for being more empathic are given later in the chapter.

Active/Passive

A second system of classifying listening behavior is also bipolar; the two styles represent opposite ends on a listening continuum. In *active* listening the individual listens with his or her total self — the person's attitudes, beliefs, values, feelings, and intuitions. The purpose fulfilled through active listening is to enjoy, comprehend, evaluate.

Listening Types

Examples of empathic and deliberative listening are given below. For each response, indicate which of the two types you think was used. Explain why. Answers are on page 243.

1. Speaker: I got a "C" on today's exam.

   Response A: A "C!" You're smart enough to get an "A." You've got to study more!

   _____

   Response B: A "C." Are you pleased or displeased?

   _____

2. Speaker: Tom and I are breaking up. He says I shouldn't come around any more.

   Response A: You mean he doesn't want to see you again?

   _____

   Response B: He's a fink! And all you've done for him. You're lucky to get rid of him.

   _____

3. Speaker: My dad says I can't use the car Saturday.

   Response A: He's mean! How will we get to the party?

   _____

   Response B: You can't use the car? Is he using it? Is something wrong? What happened?

   _____

4. Speaker: I just lost my part-time job. I don't know what to do. I needed the money for school.

   Response A: You're out of work and you need the income? You've got no other funds? How much do you need?

   _____

   Response B: What a lousy break! You'll have to quit school!

   _____

In active listening, the whole person is involved.

In *passive* listening the listener becomes mainly an organ for the passive reception of sound, with little personal involvement. The listener just happens to be present when someone else is talking, and the listening is barely more than hearing. Passive listening simply requires receiving the sound stimuli and letting the stimuli evoke conscious thoughts sporadically but not consistently.[14]

Social Listening

Among the types of listening that are part of this category are those employed in informal, nonstructured communication settings — social settings. Conversation and entertainment are the aims in social settings.

Appreciative Listening

We engage in appreciative listening when we attend a concert or a play, listen to musical or dramatic programs on radio or television, and go to the movies to be entertained. We receive satisfaction or gratification from listening to rhythm in speech and music, visualizing images from a story line or a musical passage, recognizing tone and mood and interpreting character from a dialogue.

Conversational Listening

Phatic communion is a term for conversational listening. Face-to-face communication, with the roles of speaker and listener switching back and forth, requires conversational listening. Occurring in informal settings, the talk can be about a variety of subjects, mostly entailing an exchange of pleasantries and the maintenance of relationships.

Courteous Listening

The courteous listener is primarily that — a listener. He or she listens with an open mind, giving positive feedback and reinforcement to the speaker, who is most likely a friend. The speaker is talking about his or her troubles and needs someone who will listen with courtesy.

Respectful Listening

This type of social listening occurs in merely showing attention to the speaker, which is rewarding to that person. A mother listening to her child may not be overly interested in the child's topic, but she recognizes that, for the child, the topic is important. Listening respectfully to the child indicates an interest in the child as a person.[15]

Serious Listening

Serious listening deals with important and weighty situations — at school, at work, in community activities. A class lecture, a business meeting, a discussion among community leaders are examples of situations in which the listening style may be crucial to success or failure of some endeavor.

Critical Listening

In critical listening the message receiver attempts to analyze the speaker's evidence and ideas and then to render a judgment about their validity or quality. To perform ably, the listener has to possess certain evaluative skills. He or she has to know how to distinguish between fact and opinion, between logical and emotional arguments. The critical listener has to be able to detect bias and prejudice, recognize propaganda, and evaluate sales gimmicks.

Discriminative Listening

Discriminative listening requires the listener to understand and remember, as in a classroom lecture situation. The listener has to know how to relate details to main points, follow steps when given directions, follow the organization of a message, listen for details, recognize the speaker's purpose, take notes for outlining purposes, and be able to repeat what was said.

Our aim in presenting these various systems of listening is to enhance understanding about the listening process. This does not imply that a given listening event represents only one type of listening.

That is rarely the case. In the typical listening setting listeners usually engage in a variety of listening types. In a class session we probably practice several types. During the moments before class begins, we may listen socially to our classmates, engaging in phatic communion before the instructor arrives. During this time we may alternate between active and passive listening. If a fellow student asks a question concerning a class assignment, we probably will switch to critical listening, or to courteous listening if the student has a gripe to air. When the instructor arrives and begins to lecture, we switch again, this time to discriminative listening — drinking in the lecture data with the best of our attention.[16]

VARIABLES INFLUENCING LISTENING

Our listening ability is influenced by a number of variables.[17] We have mentioned several already, particularly those related to hearing: hearing loss, masking, and auditory fatigue. Deliberative listening undoubtedly has an affect on how well we understand a speaker, as do other variables.

Listener Characteristics

Certain listener characteristics, experiences, and abilities affect an individual's ability to listen successfully. Some of these are:

1. *Anxiety.* When we are worried or apprehensive, our listening is affected. When we are anxious, we do not pay attention as well to the speaker.

2. *Bias.* When we are biased for or against what we hear, our prejudices can get in the way of clear interpretation, especially if our prejudices run contrary to the speaker's message.

3. *Boredom.* When a speaker's subject is perceived as dull or tedious and has little interest to us, we likely will pay little attention to what is said.

4. *Lack of concentration.* Our minds wander, perhaps out of boredom, but often because other, more pressing concerns than the speaker's subject weigh heavily on our minds.

5. *Inner conflicts.* Internal turmoil produces lost concentration and poor listening.

6. *Fatigue.*

7. *Intense emotions.* These might include fright, anger, and intense joy.

Moreover, listening is influenced by the skills we possess.

8. *Lack of note-taking ability.* We concentrate on the facts being presented and miss the speaker's main points. The end result is that we gain much data but little knowledge of its value.

9. *Excessive note-taking.* We are so busy writing that we have a hard time listening. Most speakers talk faster than we can write, and if we try to transcribe everything that is said, we soon fall behind.

10. *Inadequate vocabulary.* If we do not understand the meanings of the words being uttered, we give up and stop listening.

11. *Prematurely dismissing the subject as not worth our time.* Sometimes when listening to a speaker's opening remarks, we decide that what we are hearing is not going to be important to us, so we stop listening.[18]

Speaker Characteristics

A second set of variables having an impact on listening relates to the speaker. Perhaps the most significant variable has to do with a speaker's perceived *credibility.* The more credibility a speaker possesses, the more respect the speaker will command and the more people will listen. Being liked is a feature of credibility; the more a listener likes a speaker, the more the listener will pay attention to the speaker.

Certain nonverbal qualities of a speaker also influence listening. For short periods of time, *rapid speech* captures a listener's attention, but for longer time periods, a *speech rate* approximating 135–175 words per minute seems ideal. The more *fluent* a speaker is, the more "listenable" is the message. *Vocalized pauses* (uhs, ahs) tend to distract listeners. *Gestures* play a role; the more gesturing a speaker does, the more information listeners comprehend.

Of course, to enhance listening, the speaker must be *seen* and *heard.* Speaking to large audiences gives rise to danger because the people who cannot see the speaker well enough to view his or her nonverbal behavior will miss much of the message. And, obviously, if audience members cannot hear the speaker, the message will be virtually worthless.[19]

Message Influences

Messages that are novel and significant in the listener's perception capture a listener's attention more readily than those that are drab and ordinary. A listener who is strongly opposed to a given appeal will listen more intently than a listener who does not feel strongly about it. An individual will listen more carefully to material that he or she regards highly, and less carefully to information considered of low quality.[20]

Defensive Behavior

Defensiveness is defined as *behavior that occurs when a person perceives a threat or anticipates a threat when conversing with others*.[21] Individuals who behave defensively, even though displaying interest in what is being said, devote an appreciable amount of time to defending themselves. Defensive individuals think about how they are seen by others, how to win, dominate, impress, or control others, how to escape punishment, or how to prevent a possible attack. Individuals who are preoccupied with defense are not able to concentrate on the messages heard.

Defensiveness is aroused in a number of ways. Some of them are:[22]

- Ordering, directing, commanding.
- Warning, admonishing, threatening.
- Exhorting, moralizing, preaching.
- Judging, criticizing, disagreeing, blaming.
- Name-calling, ridiculing, shaming.
- Withdrawing, distracting, humoring, diverting.

The counterparts of these defense-provoking behaviors are:[23]

- Advising, giving solutions or suggestions.
- Teaching, giving logical arguments.
- Praising, agreeing.
- Interpreting, diagnosing, analyzing.
- Reassuring, sympathizing, consoling, supporting.
- Questioning.

Another list of categories of behavior that create defensiveness contains six groupings: evaluation, control, strategy, neutrality, superiority, and certainty.[24] When a speaker appears *evaluative*, listener defensiveness increases. If, by expression, manner, tone of voice, or verbal content, the speaker seems to be judging the receiver, the receiver is likely to go on guard. Speakers who blame or accuse, judge others as good or bad, and make moral judgments are prone to create defensiveness.

Speakers who attempt to *control* their receivers evoke defensiveness. Controlling-type talk suggests that the receiver's behavior is inadequate or inferior. Manipulative talk involving *strategy* and hidden motives leads to defensiveness also. After a time the receiver becomes wary and starts listening for tricks and gimmicks from the speaker rather than listening to understand.

Speech that seems *neutral* and indicates a lack of interest in the receiver as a person can create defensiveness. Neutral messages such as "You can do it if you want; I don't care" convey a sense of detachment or rejection, giving an impression of unconcern and not caring.

When a person communicates a *feeling of superiority* in position, power, wealth, intelligence, or other ways, he or she arouses defensiveness. Feelings of inadequacy can be awakened, causing the receiver to feel inferior. The receiver reacts by not listening, by competing with the speaker, or by being jealous of the speaker.

Dogmatic speakers also provoke defensiveness. They come across sounding like they know all there is to know, thereby putting their receivers on guard. Speakers like these convey a high degree of *certainty*, making listeners feel inferior.[25]

Environmental Influences

Noise in the environment can influence listening. Passing trucks, cars, motorcycles, and airplanes can give rise to a level of din that hinders our listening ability. Poor acoustics in a meeting hall, rooms that are too hot or cold, crowded meeting space, and poorly arranged seating also create listening problems.

IMPROVING LISTENING

The suggestions in this section, culled from various sources, tend to emphasize common sense. Applied in our own listening experiences and practiced diligently, they can become habitual behaviors, enhancing our listening skills.

Active Listening

Successful listening involves more than staying awake, paying attention, and being courteous to the speaker. It also includes active, empathic, and supportive behaviors that inform the speaker, "I understand — please continue." The active listener tries to create an encouraging atmosphere in which the speaker can express himself or herself. Active listeners attempt to feed back to the speaker neutral summaries of what they heard so the speaker will know that understanding has occurred and he or she can continue.[26]

Defensive Behavior

The text contains a list of defense-arousing behaviors and a list of behaviors that are not. Examples of defense-arousing behaviors are given below. For each, select from the defense-arousing list the behavior you think is being illustrated. Then choose a behavior from the other list as a better alternative and give an example of it.

Example: "You're a naughty girl, Jill!"
Name-calling, shaming, ridiculing.
Reassuring, sympathizing, consoling, supporting.
That's too bad, Jill! Here's a better way to drink your milk.

1. You're a slime ball! A lazy bum!

   _____

   _____

   _____

2. If you don't turn in your paper on time, you'll flunk!

   _____

   _____

   _____

3. Come here! Pick up that garbage!

   _____

   _____

   _____

4. It's your fault! That's not the way to do it!

   _____

   _____

   _____

5. In my twenty-five years of teaching, I found that students who don't attend class rarely earn good grades. After all, why attend school if you're not going to go to class?

   _____

   _____

   _____

Active listening has four characteristics: empathy, acceptance, congruence, and concreteness. *Empathy* is the quality of trying to understand the speaker from the speaker's frame of reference, rather than the listener's. *Acceptance* denotes deep concern for the speaker's welfare, as well as for the speaker's individuality and worth as a person. *Congruence* involves openness and frankness, which should encourage the same sort of reaction from the speaker. *Concreteness* is the quality of focusing on specifics and avoiding vagueness by helping the speaker to concentrate on real problems and to avoid generalities such as "they say" or "everyone knows." Active listeners try to foster these characteristics.[27]

Decreasing Defensiveness

Defensive behavior obstructs listening. When a speaker, by expression, manner of speech, tone of voice, or verbal content, arouses defensiveness, listeners devote unnecessary energy to resisting the speaker, preventing him or her from concentrating on the message. The result is poor listening.

Speakers can decrease defensiveness in their listeners — and thereby help them to become better listeners — by creating a supportive climate, an open and trusting atmosphere. We can develop such a climate by being descriptive, problem-oriented, equal, and tentative or provisional in our remarks.[28]

Descriptive Speech

Descriptive speech usually arouses a minimum of uneasiness because it comes across as being neutral; it does not imply that the listener should change his or her behavior. Genuine requests for information and straightforward expressions of feelings are minimally defense-producing. Here is an example:

Student:	I'm sorry I'm late again for class. Something always happens to delay me.
Instructor: (being judgmental)	Being tardy frequently doesn't help your grade any. Look for a way to get to class on time.
Instructor: (being descriptive)	You sound put out for being late again.

Problem-Oriented Speech

In problem-oriented speech the speaker communicates a desire to collaborate with the listener in seeking a solution to a common problem. The speaker implies that he or she has no predetermined solution, that speaker and listener will work together to find one. The speaker does not try to persuade the listener to accept a solution the speaker conceived. In responding to the student's plight in the dialogue above, the instructor could respond in a persuasive fashion, trying to control the student, or in a problem-oriented fashion, suggesting that they work together to find a solution, as in the following:

Instructor: (being persuasive)	It looks like if you want to pass this class, you'll have to buy an alarm clock to get you up in time.
Instructor: (being problem-oriented)	You have trouble getting up in the morning? Do you study late or work late? Let's figure out what the problem is, and then maybe we can find solution.

Equality in Speaking

Equality in speaking suggests that the speaker is much like the listener, even though differences in talent, ability, worth, appearance, status, and power exist between speaker and listener. The speaker should create the feeling that the listener and the speaker are on equal levels, attaching little importance to the differences that might be present. Defenses thus are reduced, and the listener and

speaker can enter into participative planning with mutual trust. Here is an example:

Instructor: (being superior)	I've been teaching this subject for twenty-five years and have written ten books about it. The way you should do the project is: . . .
Instructor: (being equal)	Each of us has ways of doing things that are best for us. I'm not sure how you do your best work, but you probably know. Let's sit down and try to work out the best way of completing the project, using your talents to advantage.

Tentative Speech

Instead of being dogmatic and sounding as though he or she knows all the answers, the tentative speaker adopts a less certain attitude and becomes more provisional. The speaker sounds as though he or she is not positive about what to do but is willing to investigate it with the listener and try to find the best solution.[29] An example is:

Student: (speaking to another student, being dogmatic)	This is the best way to do it. I've done it this way before and always got an "A." So we'll do it my way.
Student: (being tentative)	I've found this way to be best, but I'm not sure how my way will work for you. Maybe we should talk about it and figure out what may work the best for both of us.

Being Open-Minded

An inhibiting factor in listening is *closed-mindedness*. We shut off our minds to new information and ideas, unwilling to listen to views that do not coincide with our personal biases. We do not listen to voices that contradict our own, screening out data with which we do not identify.

In contrast, open-mindedness calls for us to be receptive to others' ideas to the point that we understand fully what they are saying. We do not have to agree with their point of view or even accept it, but we should try to understand it. We should give the speaker a full hearing.[30]

To test for *open-mindedness*, a checklist was devised, consisting of eight questions, most relating to personal biases. By answering the questions in view of a speech we heard, discussion we participated in, or meeting we attended, we can obtain a somewhat better understanding of how open-minded we are. Here are the questions:

- Do I immediately reject what has been said merely because it is *different* from what I believe?

- Am I accepting or rejecting the idea on the basis of my reaction to the speaker? Or because of his or her reputation?

- Am I casting aside this proposal, which affects the welfare of others, because of my self-interest?

- What is my own attitude? Do I *want* to believe this statement is true, or do I *want* to believe it is false?

- Do I welcome the speaker's ideas as warmly as if they were my own?

- Does personal, family, or group loyalty blind me to the truth?

- When I see the truth, do I cling to my loyalties?

- Do I have such an exaggerated opinion of my own knowledge that I listen with half an ear, shutting my mind to accepting what someone else says?[31]

Being open-minded means being tolerant of the other person's viewpoint. It does not mean we must give up our own views, if we hold them for good reasons, a long as we remember that some other, contradictory views may have merit.

Evaluating What Is Received

In the discussion of empathic listening, we noted that the listener tries to understand what the speaker is saying before evaluating it. The listener attempts to capture the speaker's meaning. Knowing the meaning, the listener then can assess what is being said.

Now we move to the evaluation step, in which we try to discover the value of the information we are receiving. To function as a judge of what is being said, several skills are required. We must be able to discern facts from opinions and fiction. We also must be able to determine whether the arguments we may be hearing are based on logic or on emotion. Is the speaker presenting a reasoned discourse based on factual material? Or is the discourse highly emotional, appealing to our baser instincts and needs? Finally, we must maintain an objective attitude toward the speaker and the message. We must listen with an open mind. If we possess these skills, we are better able to evaluate what we hear.

Our ability to criticize what we hear can be sharpened by following three guidelines: overcome speaker-related obstacles, verify our interpretations, and observe evaluation guidelines.

Overcoming Obstacles

We can increase our effectiveness as critics by trying to break through speaker-related obstacles. If our criticism is to be worthwhile, these barriers, stemming from the speaker or from the message, have to be dealt with.

A major obstacle for some of us arises in the speaker's *manner of presentation.* If a speaker comes across as charming, glib, and believable, we may be swept off our feet because of the speaker's manner, not the ideas (which we fail to clearly understand). The message may be mostly sound and little substance. We are literally conned into believing the speaker.

Another potential barrier to effective evaluation is the speaker's *superior position* in life. We may fail to listen critically because the speaker out-ranks us, has more power or authority, is wealthier or better educated, is an expert in the subject area, or is older and we respect age. The speaker might be lying outright, but we accept what is said because we are in awe of the person or intimidated by the person's status.

A third obstacle might be the message's *subject matter.* It may be way beyond our comprehension and we accept what we hear simply because it is too difficult for us to deal with. If we desire to purchase a home, for example, and we are not versed on matters such as short-term mortgages, convertible mortgages, reduction options, rate improvement loans, fixed-rate interest, variable-rate interest, and so on, we are in trouble and may end up with a more costly purchase because we did not understand the salesperson's message. Many elderly people have trouble comprehending bureaucratic officials of the federal government who explain provisions of benefits such as social security and Medicare. Because the issues are complex, the message may be incomprehensible and they might lose out on their rightful benefits.

Verifying Interpretations

To be effective critics, we must verify our understanding of what was said. This is what we do first as empathic listeners. As we receive new information or explanations in response to the questions we ask about data already received, we must keep the spirit of inquiry alive in our minds. The new data or the explanation may be unclear, and we have to continue to check our interpretations with the speaker.

As we listen to what a speaker says, we should ask ourselves a set of questions. We should know the speaker's motivation for what he or she is saying. Does the speaker have a personal motive, such as personal gain? Does the speaker represent an organization, the aims of which we do not approve? Does what is being said have a factual basis? Here is a more complete list of questions that could be profitably asked:[32]

- What is the speaker's motive? Has the speaker a personal ax to grind?
- Is the speaker's message based on reasoning or on feeling?
- As the listener, am I separating fact from opinion?
- In a discussion, are the speaker's statements relevant to the issues being discussed?
- Do the speaker's data support the arguments being advanced?
- Is there evidence of the speaker's credibility? Does the speaker distort facts? Gloss over items to which honest answers would be damaging? Lay claim to false authority? Is the speaker guilty of specious reasoning?
- What about me as a listener? Am I prejudiced? Does my desire to believe or disbelieve affect my judgment? Am I guilty of discrediting an idea because it is new or different?

If you are conversing with a friend, he or she may not appreciate your checking the message against these guidelines. In a more serious listening situation, though, applying these guidelines should prove helpful in evaluating what is heard.

Developing Empathy

Reducing defensiveness, being open-minded, and listening with a critical ear are steps toward becoming an empathic listener, *one who projects his or her own personality into the personality of the speaker to*

Listen with empathy:

by paraphrasing
by reflecting meanings
by reflecting feelings
by summarizing

understand the speaker better. Empathy is the ability to share in the other person's emotions and feelings, to reach beyond the words the person utters, or to see through the words, to find the real emotions and feelings the words are trying to convey.

In the following illustration, the husband would have been served better by an empathic wife.

The supervisor of a small department in a large business called the workers in and proceeded to verbally chastise one of them. "But," the chastised employee countered, "you told me to do it that way."

"I told you nothing of the kind," he replied. "Don't do it again."

Later, at dinner, the still-agitated employee started to tell his wife what had happened: "He said to do it that way, but it didn't work out, so he blamed me."

"Oh!" said the wife. "Did you hear about the Browns?"

"He blamed me in front of the others," the man excitedly continued.

"They bought a new car," his wife rambled on.

The wife's seeming unconcern with her husband's difficulty upset him, and he left the table to vent his anger elsewhere. Because her husband had a problem, the wife's role should have been that of a listener. Unfortunately, however, she interrupted and tried to divert the talk to the latest neighborhood gossip. She did what so many of us do when we should be listening: We try to take over the conversation, to lead and direct it rather than listen.

When people are burdened or excited about something, they send out nonverbal clues — through tone of voice, body posture, energy level — that express their feelings. Some start talking about what is bothersome. Others do not, and they may need an invitation to talk. "What's up?" is a common way to invite a person to talk, especially if it comes from friends or people who trust us. With others, a more formal invitation may be in order ("Looks like the conversation with the boss didn't go well, Joe. Do you want to talk about it?")

The wife in our story could have encouraged her husband to continue by asking something like, "Go on — tell me about it." Or she could have used other encouragers. "Mmm" is a *minimal encourager*, as is "Oh?" "I see" "Then?" Or she could have remained silent, waiting for him to continue and demonstrating her interest and concern through eye contact and an attentive listening posture.

Listening with empathy calls for the listener to project his or her own personality into the speaker's personality so as to understand the speaker better. When we do this we listen more to the meanings than to the words, reaching behind the words or seeing through them to find the person who is being revealed. This can be done in several ways. Four of them are: paraphrasing, reflecting feelings, reflecting meanings, and summarizing.

Paraphrasing

Paraphrasing is *rewording the thought or meaning in something said before.* The listener concisely states in his or her own words what the speaker said. For example, Dave says: "I'm agitated. I spent a good hour preparing that assignment and the teacher said it was all wrong." Paraphrasing, Mike replies: "You're upset because your work was discounted." Mike's paraphrase has the characteristics of being effective. It is briefer than Dave's message, and to the point, focusing on the content of Dave's message but using Mike's own words, not Dave's. The effective paraphrase restates the content or feeling of the speaker's message in a way that conveys understanding and acceptance; it is nonjudgmental.[33]

Reflecting Feelings

Reflection of feelings means giving back to the speaker, in a concise manner, the feelings being communicated. An instructor says: "The class did well on the test. No one scored below 90." Reflecting the instructor's feelings, a colleague responds: "You're proud of them." The purpose for reflecting the speaker's emotions is to encourage disclosure of feelings. This is useful for several reasons. First, the listener can share with the speaker the speaker's reaction to the events being described and empathize with the speaker in this fashion. Second, if the speaker is talking about a problem, reflecting feelings helps the speaker understand personal feelings about the problem and perhaps deal with them more ably.[34]

Reflecting Meanings

Although the empathic listener has to be attuned to feelings, he or she also must be aware of the factual content of the message. Then the listener can reflect the true meaning more ably. Mary says: "It's high time I got a raise. I've worked for five years without one." Sue, reflecting the meaning, replies: "You feel angry because you haven't gotten a raise." In her reply, Sue links Mary's feeling with the fact that Mary has not received a raise. The formula for doing this is: "You feel (insert the appropriate feeling word) because (insert the event)."[35]

Summarizing

The summary is a brief restatement of the principal themes and feelings a speaker expresses over a long period of talk. Through summarizing, the listener can tie together bits and pieces of the speaker's talk by concisely recapitulating them. This recapping can help the speaker sort out his or her own feelings and ideas.

General Suggestions

Up to this point, our suggestions for listening improvement have been directed to specific areas. Our final suggestions are more general, covering a wide range of communicative experiences.[36] If incorporated into our listening behavior, the following should result in noticeable improvement.

1. *Be in shape mentally and physically to listen.* Our attention span is directly related to our mental and physical well-being. If we are healthy and alert, our capacity to listen actively and effectively increases.

2. *Prepare for the listening assignment.* When we know we will be participating in some sort of communicative situation that requires serious and active listening on our part, we will be better able to gain from it if we prepare. Before going to class to listen to the instructor lecture, for instance, we can get ready by reading the text assignment and giving it some conscious thought. We can prepare similarly before attending a public lecture, a discussion, or a meeting. We can read up on the topic of discussion to obtain an understanding of what it entails.

3. *Estimate what is in it for the listeners.* This suggestion is selfish. It implies that we try to determine what value we will secure from the information we hear in a public speaking or discussion situation. If we know that we can gain personally from what we hear, we will listen better. Therefore, we should look for personal benefits: economic gain, help in passing a course, aid in locating a job, personal satisfaction, or ways of developing new interests.

4. *Listen for the major points.* We probably are not going to remember every bit of information we hear in a lecture or discussion. Therefore, we should concentrate on learning the central theme and the main points. Ordinarily these will stand out from the body of the material. We should write those down to cue us as to what the rest of the message is all about.

5. *Build a vocabulary.* Many speakers use a specialized language to explain their concepts. Mastering the technical language of the subject matter can be half the battle in understanding what is being talked about. Comprehension is directly related to

the listener's gaining meaningful associations with the words used. To understand what is being said, the listener has to have a sufficiently developed vocabulary.

6. *Judge content, not delivery.* Many speakers are not very good transmitters of messages. Their oral presentation leaves much to be desired, which can hamper successful understanding of the message. Listeners should skip over delivery errors and attend to the content of the message.

7. *Capitalize on the fact that thought is faster than speech.* We can think much faster than we can speak. When listening to someone speak at a normal rate of delivery, we can race ahead of the speaker quite readily. If we are not careful, our thoughts will wander. We will daydream or think about other things. Rather than allowing our mind to roam to other subjects, we should challenge, anticipate, and mentally summarize what the speaker is driving at. We can weigh the evidence being presented, consider the merits of the speaker's ideas, and listen for bias on the speaker's part.

8. *Take notes.* Note-taking is a well-known classroom activity, but it also can be employed in most public speaking or discussion situations. Notes are not useful in all settings. Taking notes may be pointless sometimes. If the information is to be used in the future, however, taking notes probably will be valuable.

At least three types of note-taking are useful: key words, partial outline, and complete outline. The key word outline is useful for remembering specific points in a message. The key words are written down for later reference. The partial outline probably is most valuable when the goal is to remember selected portions or elements of a message, perhaps related to a specific interest of the listener or concerned with a forthcoming test. The complete outline contains a full record of what was said. Suggestions for outlining are considered in Chapter 17.

Whatever outline form is used, the notes should be clear and brief. By clear, we mean the statements written down should be understandable to the note-taker when they are used later. They also should be written so they can be read later — not scribbled unintelligibly. By brief, we mean that the note-taker should spend more time listening than writing; otherwise some of what the speaker says may be missed.

SUMMARY

We spend much time listening each day, but much of that time is wasted. We might hear well but listen poorly. Hearing and listening are different processes. Hearing is a physiological sensory process, and listening is a psychological process involving interpretation and understanding. Actually, hearing is only the first stage in listening. Attention, understanding, and remembering are the other steps.

Types of listening can be classified in a number of ways. Four different classification systems are: deliberative/empathic, active/ passive, social, and serious listening. In a given communication situation listening probably will involve several of the types, not just one, so we should be prepared to function well using all of the types.

A large number of variables influence listening. We grouped the variables into five categories: listener, speaker, message, environmental influences, and defensive behavior.

Four principal ways to improve listening are: decrease defensiveness, become open-minded, listen critically, and further empathy.

Interpersonal Relationships

Typical human beings have dozens of interpersonal relationships. If we are extremely active socially and involved with many people, we can have hundreds of relationships covering a wide variety of social affiliations. Many are brief and casual; others are intense and long-lasting. Relationships include those with friends, fellow students, teachers, parents, siblings, mate, opposite-sex partners, physician, dentist, favorite service station attendant, minister, relatives, and many others. Interpersonal relationships are important in our lives because they help satisfy our social needs.

In examining interpersonal relationships in depth, we will draw on the discussions of previous chapters. Knowledge about attraction, similarity, the self, self-disclosure, apprehension, and empathy is helpful in understanding the topics in the following pages.

A PERSPECTIVE ON RELATIONSHIPS

Before describing interpersonal relationships more fully, we must establish a common conception of the term *relationship* and gain a similar perspective on the concept of *interpersonal relationships*. Although various definitions exist, we choose *Webster's Collegiate Dictionary*, which defines *relationship* as *the state of being mutually or reciprocally interested*, as in social or business matters. That means the parties involved must realize they are parts of the relationship and have entered into it for social or practical gain. Their communication is *purposeful*.

In this interpretation of interpersonal relationships, the relationship does not have to develop with the feeling that it will grow into an intimate one. In fact, our intimate relationships most likely are few in number. From our perspective, relationships can be formed for various reasons and with varying degrees of personal intimacy.[1]

We can form a relationship for its own sake — because we desire to socially affiliate with someone. More often, we form relationships as an outgrowth of a joint task or activity. For example, we may need a mechanic to service our car or a dentist to look after our teeth. We may have to collaborate with a fellow student on a class project or work with specific individuals in our occupation. A relationship, thus, may be formed for reasons other than social.

In developing the relationship, our expectations shape the way it evolves. The demands of the situation govern its development. In dealing with our mechanic, for example, ordinarily we would not expect the relationship to develop into an intimate one. We want the person to service our car ably, and that is about all we expect. Even so, the relationship with the mechanic can be stable and enduring — albeit limited to the context of car care.

The degree of satisfaction obtained from a relationship is based on our implicit judgments about the others in the relationship. These judgments vary with the context and the path the relationship takes. In the case of a mechanic, we probably want the mechanic to be painstaking and vigorous in attending to our car. With a close friend, we may value different qualities. How painstaking the mechanic is will determine how satisfied we are with the relationship. With a friend, if the qualities we are seeking are present, we will be satisfied.[2]

CHARACTERISTICS OF RELATIONSHIPS

All relationships are characterized by one quality: communication. It is the foundation upon which relationships develop, and in reality communication is the relationship. Without it no relationship would develop or exist![3]

Most interpersonal relationships are characterized by several additional factors. Eight of these — variability, duration, frequency, revelation, meshing, support, anxiety reduction, and proximity — are considered next.[4] All of the factors do not have to be present in all relationships, and those that are present need not be present to the same degree. In any case, reviewing the eight factors clarifies the nature of interpersonal relationships.

Variability

Partners in a relationship engage in a number of different interactions. For example, two students who attend class together interact differently in social situations after class. Similarly, a friend who also is our car mechanic is likely to act in a more formal way when we are at the garage than outside of the garage. This characteristic is not necessarily present in every relationship, but, generally speaking, behavior in an interpersonal relationship is variable.

Duration

Interpersonal relationships require time to develop, and normally they last a long time. Ron and Don, for example, became acquainted years ago and, as they saw each other more and more, the relationship developed, but it took several years. The relationship has lasted, however, more than thirty years.

Frequency

Closely tied to duration is frequency of contact. For a relationship to develop, interaction between the communicators has to be regular and often. For example, years ago Beverly started to purchase gasoline from her mechanic, Bobby, every week. They had a chance to interact regularly. When her car required servicing, she also took it to Bobby. Their relationship is characterized by frequent contact. Frequency of contact is important in relationships because the more we interact with a person, the better we get to know that person, understanding the individual's needs and interests more completely.

Revelation

As an interpersonal relationship develops over time and through frequency of contact, it matures. The individuals involved reveal their beliefs and attitudes to each other; they begin to share their innermost feelings — to a point. Usually we have to know someone very well to divulge our financial status, for example. With Bobby, the mechanic, Beverly probably never will reveal all of the specifics about her financial condition.

Meshing

Meshing refers to the way a relationship fits together, how the behavior of one person meshes with the behavior of the other. Two types of meshing occur. The relationship can be *symmetrical*, with the two sharing similar behaviors or being alike in many ways, such as in age, gender, education, background, and attitudes. Or the relationship can be *complementary*, with the communicators being different in most respects. Chapter 2 elaborated on these two types of relationships.

Support

Support appears in a relationship when the partners look after each other, help one another in some way. The assistance can be physical, emotional, intellectual, or any combination of these. Beverly has a car problem; she seeks Bobby's help, and he provides it immediately. Or someone presents some sort of threat to a husband; the wife quickly comes to the husband's aid.

Anxiety Reduction

All people have fears, stresses, and anxieties. Many times these can be reduced or alleviated through an interpersonal relationship. Jeff fears he is going to fail a course in his major. He meets with his instructor, with whom he has established a relationship. The two talk through Jeff's fear, and the fear is greatly reduced.

Proximity

Nearness, being spatially close enough to a person to carry on a relationship, is necessary. Individuals who are physically separated by a long distance obviously do not have much opportunity to interact. We are more likely to initiate and maintain communication with those who are nearer spatially than with those who are far away.

Beverly decides to move from the large metropolitan city to a suburban neighborhood some distance from her former dwelling. As a result, her relationship with Bobby, the mechanic, probably will diminish in importance. Bobby's garage is just too far away for Beverly to buy gas and get her car serviced. Close relationships develop readily among students who attend the same classes or live in the same housing unit, but once they graduate and leave, the relationships are difficult to maintain unless the former students happen to live near each other. Proximity, thus, is vital in developing and maintaining a relationship.

The eight characteristics described do not necessarily characterize every relationship, nor does each always carry the same importance. They are interdependent, however, with a change in one characteristic leading to changes in the others. For example, while they were university students, Jack and Jill sat next to each other in a number of classes and developed a rewarding relationship. In addition to studying together, they frequently socialized. They saw each other often over a four-year period, and their relationship evolved into a supportive one, with both revealing their innermost thoughts to the other.

Then the two graduated and returned to their respective homes in different parts of the country. They no longer were in close proximity. Being far apart, they could not meet frequently, take part in various activities together, support each other in a face-to-face fashion, and share their feelings. Several of the characteristics no longer carried any weight in what remained of the relationship.[5]

DIMENSIONS OF RELATIONSHIPS

Relationships are characterized by an interdependence of various factors, as we just discovered. Communication is the underlying characteristic in all relationships and, to understand relationships, we should be aware of the sort of communication that can take place in a relationship. Relational communication has three distinct dimensions—immediacy, intimacy, and status—the variability of which accounts for much of the difference in our relationships with other individuals.[6]

Immediacy

Immediacy is the *degree of perceived physical or psychological distance between the persons in a relationship.*[7] The individuals involved in an immediate relationship see themselves as close to one another. In a nonimmediate relationship the communicators are not near each other often physically, nor are they psychologically close. By the absence of psychological closeness, we mean that they do not share the same

beliefs, attitudes, values, and behaviors. As they begin to get closer to each other psychologically, however, they start to think and act more like each other.

Immediacy is communicated both verbally and nonverbally. Verbally, we achieve immediacy through oral messages indicating responsiveness to the other person in the relationship. Messages indicating our willingness to be open and friendly, our personal concern for the welfare of the other, our desire to encourage and support the other's behavior, and our wish to empathize have the effect of creating immediacy. Nonverbally, we achieve immediacy through a variety of "you can talk to me" sorts of behaviors. A wave of the hand, a pat on the back, and a smile suggest that we can be approached.[8] Nonverbal behaviors can signal availability for talking, can increase sensory stimulation, and can communicate personal closeness, as stated in Chapter 9, on nonverbal communication.

Intimacy

Intimacy refers to the *perceived depth of a relationship between people.*[9] Individuals in an intimate relationship perceive themselves as closely linked to each other, their partner being almost an extension of themselves. Intimate people tend to consult each other before taking some sort of action that affects either.

Because intimate relationships demand much of the people involved, we ordinarily have only a few relationships of this kind in a lifetime. A spouse or a very close friend or two may share intimacy with us. The common ingredients of intimacy are the verbal quality of self-disclosure and the nonverbal qualities related, for the most part, to touching behaviors. These verbal and nonverbal behaviors can take place in less than intimate relationships, but they are vital in intimate ones.

Status

Status refers to *a person's position in some sort of hierarchy.*[10] In interpersonal interaction, the difference in the communicators' status is a significant element. The "status differential" impacts heavily on what is considered appropriate or inappropriate communication.

The person of higher status tends to control the communication in a relationship. The boss in the workplace, the teacher in the classroom, the father in the family, the coach on the athletic field all exemplify this control. The boss, teacher, father, and coach have higher status than the worker, student, other family members, and athletic team members. They tell the other what to do and control the communication between them.

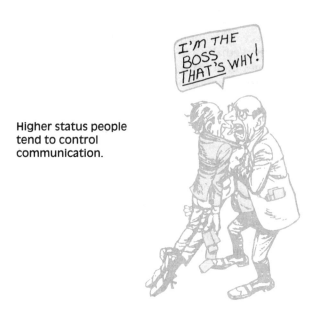

Higher status people tend to control communication.

Higher-status people have the freedom to initiate and terminate conversations. Their messages tend to be dominant, whereas those of lower-status persons are more apt to be submissive. Higher status people usually determine the subject to be discussed and decide how long the conversation will last. Higher-status people are likely to speak louder than lower-status persons and can interrupt lower-status individuals at will. Higher-status people control the distance between speakers, and the amount and type of touch; lower-status people may not be in a position to touch higher-status individuals at all.

Higher-status individuals can control the time allowable for communicating with lower-status ones, and higher-status people can arrive late, if they so choose. Lower-status people must be on time, or early. Higher-status people can dress much as they please. Lower-status individuals must dress as custom dictates for the particular communicative setting.[11]

Status is relative to the situation. In one situation a person may hold the higher status and in another situation may possess the lower status. At home the father may be the high-status person; at work he may be a lowly employee with no status. At home the family defers to him; at work he defers to his bosses. Different situations call for different hierarchical relationships.

Immediacy, intimacy, and status place boundaries on the communication that takes place in a relationship. They each contribute to determining what is appropriate and what is inappropriate.

DEVELOPING INTERPERSONAL RELATIONSHIPS

Of the possible goals that can be attained through interpersonal communication, none seems so central to our social survival as that of developing interpersonal relationships. Just as our survival depends upon the satisfaction of certain physiological and psychological needs, it also depends upon our fulfilling certain social needs (three of which were identified previously as inclusion, control, and affection). These needs can be satisfied only by interacting with other people, developing interpersonal relationships. The goal of developing relationships through interpersonal communication, therefore, is important in meeting our basic social needs.

Steps in Developing Relationships

Interpersonal relationships follow a general developmental pattern involving three separate but related processes: (a) coming together and building a relationship,[12] (b) staying together and maintaining the relationship,[13] and (c) moving apart and terminating the relationship.[14] Not all relationships terminate, of course, but that potential exists in any relationship.

In examining the three processes, we should be aware that relationships do not always follow the pattern exactly as we state it. They do not always proceed in the step-by-step sequence we describe, nor do they all require the same amount of time to develop.

Coming Together[15]

Initiating is the first step in coming together. When we see someone we consider attractive, we may attempt to initiate interaction with that person. We might say something like, "Hello! How are you?" or "Hi! What's up?" to initiate a conversation.

If we are successful in our initial attempt, the *experimenting* step follows. In this step we try to discover how much the person is like us. We are looking for a basis to continue developing the relationship and, if we discover similarities in background and experience, we probably will move to the next step. This may take considerable time, however, as we try to measure the other person's interests and desires. In fact, some developing relationships never get beyond this point.

When they do, the relationship moves to the *intensifying* step. We see more of the other person, spend more time with the person, reveal more of ourselves, reduce formality, and devise private ways of symbolizing our respect for the other person.

The *integrating* step comes as the relationship begins to mature. The individuals involved become partners on a psychological and social level. They begin to think and act as one. This stage is more commonly reached with an opposite-sex partner. It does occur, however, with same-sex friends and with teenagers.

Bonding, the final step, is formal and contractual. Usually occurring with opposite-sex partners, it is characterized by a formal, public announcement such as the engagement of a man and a woman, the first formal step to marriage.

Staying Together[16]

What is required to maintain a relationship? The answer is found in the characteristics of long-term relationships. Not every characteristic may be pertinent to the same degree in each relationship, but these suggest the necessary requirements for staying together:

1. *Amusement.* As a relationship begins, we expect to have fun. To make it last, the fun and enjoyment must continue.

2. *Affection.* The partners must provide ways of continually satisfying the need for affection.

3. *Commitment equity.* Both partners must have equal commitment to the relationship. Opposite-sex friends, for instance, expect each other to be similarly committed to the relationship and not date others.

Getting Together: Desirable Attributes of a Partner

What young women consider important in a male partner:

> record of achievement
> leadership qualities
> skill in his job
> potential for earning income
> sense of humor
> intellectual ability
> attentiveness
> common sense
> athletic ability
> good reasoning ability

What young men consider important in a female partner:

> physical attractiveness
> sexuality
> warmth and affection
> social skill
> home making ability
> sense of how to dress
> sensitivity to others' needs
> good taste
> moral perception
> artistic creativity

From *Eye to Eye: How People Interact* by Peter Marsh (Toppsfield, MA: Salem House Publishers, 1988).

4. *Fidelity equity.* This requires the faithfulness of both partners —sexual faithfulness with opposite-sex partners and interest fidelity with same-sex partners. A mutual level and expression of fidelity characterizes long-term relationships.

5. *Contracting.* We expect our partner to keep his or her part of the implicit arrangements made over time. Married couples, for instance, probably have a number of unspoken contracts. Even less intimate relationships have contracts. A contract typically exists, for instance, between teacher and student: If the student completes the assignments properly, attends class, and listens carefully, the teacher assigns an appropriate grade.

6. *Twosome.* The partners think in terms of "us" rather than "you" and "me." Each person depends upon the other. They express the feeling, "What happens to you happens to me."

7. *Recognition.* The partners want others to think of them as a pair, as an inseparable twosome. If they are opposite sex partners, they may go places together, share the same class schedule, and hold hands.

8. *Frankness.* Early in the relationship each partner may have hidden personal facts from the other. As the relationship matures, however, the two become more honest with each other and tell all there is to tell. They express their feelings more openly about each other's actions and general behavior and scold one another for behavior that falls below expectations.

9. *Averaging.* The partners recognize that any relationship has good and bad times. Over the long run the good and bad should average out. The partners realize that strife, conflict, and other problems will enter into the relationship, but there will be good times as well. If the good cannot outweigh the bad, at least they will equal each other. If the bad continually outweighs the good, the relationship probably will not work out.

Moving Apart[17]

A relationship can terminate at almost any point in its development, after the initiation stage or after the partners have been together for years. Typically, the relationship comes apart in a five-step sequence:

1. *Differentiation.* The individuals focus on their disagreements and differences. They begin to think more of "I" and "me" than "we" and "us." Conflicts most likely will arise.

2. *Circumscribing.* The amount of talk diminishes, with less revelation and fewer statements of commitment.

3. *Stagnation.* The relationship ceases to be alive and functional. Communication becomes difficult, narrow, and awkward as the parties start to move away from each other psychologically.

4. *Avoidance.* The partners either avoid seeing each other or ignore each other, sending nonverbal signs of avoidance.

5. *Termination.* The relationship ends; it has fallen apart. The partners no longer see each other; they have dissociated.

The Role of Attitude

What is required to achieve a successful relationship, one that remains solid and does not fall apart? Previously we mentioned the characteristics of long-term relationships. These certainly are essential in a successful relationship. Equally important, however, is *effective expression.* And the communicator must have a basic *attitude of wanting to succeed.* Communication depends on this basic attitude as well as on the skills of effective expression. Without the proper attitude on the communicator's part, the skills will be wasted, at least in achieving successful relationships. Important as they are, the communication skills by themselves are unable to forge successful relationships.[18]

The attitude that fosters communication and, thus, successful relationships is built around four key qualities. These are *genuineness, commitment, dialogue,* and *empathy.*

Conversational Skills for Staying Together

Do You:

Interrupt too often?
Talk too long?
Bore with too much detail?
Generalize too much?
Speak too formally?
Speak too intimately for the situation?
Disclose too much?
Disclose too little?
Cover a variety of topics?
Show humor? Too much? Too little?
Watch for feedback, interpret it, and react correctly?
React with appropriate timing?
Take turns? Hog the conversation? Stay too quiet?
Ask questions? Listen to answers?
Use appropriate body language?
Support the speaker?
Greet and part using the proper words?

From *Eye to Eye: How People Interact* by Peter Marsh (Toppsfield, MA: Salem House Publishers, 1988).

Genuineness

Genuineness means being *honest and open about feelings, needs, and interests* — being what we really are without front or facade. Genuine persons are authentic and, as such, express their feelings as they experience them. If we are genuine, we act spontaneously in the presence of our partners and, hence, they come to know us as we truly are. By contrast, inauthentic people conceal their true feelings; they are defensive and closed as persons.[19]

Three ingredients — self-awareness, self-acceptance, and self-expression — go into genuineness.[20] The discussion of self concept (Chapter 6) mentioned these elements, and a brief review should be helpful here.

Self-awareness means to understand oneself, to observe the Socratic injunction "Know thyself." *Self-acceptance* calls for us to accept our self as it is. Many people are ashamed of who they are and do not accept the full range of their feelings and thoughts, their angers, sex impulses, and fantasies. Although these are a part of every normal life, some people think these aspects of themselves are bad or sinful and they are not self-accepting. *Self-expression* means that, when appropriate, we share our innermost thoughts responsibly.

Genuineness does not mean expressing every feeling we have, just as it does not mean presenting ourselves in a phony manner. We avoid misrepresenting who we truly are, express feelings that we persistently experience, and do so responsibly.

Commitment

Commitment involves a *strong desire by the partners in a relationship for it to continue,* a willingness to share responsibility for the problems that occur. Wanting to continue the relationship is not enough, though. Both parties have to agree to make changes or compromises. Whether marriage, friendship, or business, the parties must work out their problems together for the relationship to continue. In good relationships the individuals involved are committed to each other. They may have disagreements, but their commitment is the foundation of the relationship.[21]

Dialogue

The third ingredient of a successful relationship, dialogue, was analyzed in Chapter 3. It is a *serious, purposive form of interpersonal communication that aims at achieving understanding and appreciation.* Dialogue calls for desire on the part of the communicators to be open, to listen, and to empathize. In a successful relationship, the partners are willing to discuss any problems they encounter, including points of conflict, personal expectations, and any other concerns.

They engage in dialogue to talk through their problems, whatever they may be.

Empathy

Empathy was discussed in Chapter 10, on listening. The word "empathy" is translated from the German *einfühlung*, which means "feeling into," *experiencing the speaker's feelings without losing one's own identity*. Empathy is the ability to understand other people pretty much as they understand themselves. The empathic person is able to figuratively "crawl into another's skin" and see the world through that person's eyes. Empathic listeners hear what the others have to say and note the special significance the speakers' messages have for them.[22]

CULTURAL DIFFERENCES

Our discussion so far has centered on the general qualities of relationships and their development among Americans indiscriminately. We are, however, a nation of many ethnic and racial groups representing various cultures, and not all cultures follow the pattern we have just outlined in precisely the same manner for similar purposes. In this section we sample relationships in other cultures, making the point that not all the people we come into contact with in our lives relate as most Americans do. We begin by being more specific about American relationships and then briefly analyzing those in selected cultures for comparative purposes.

Americans[23]

Our interpersonal relationships tend to be numerous and distinguished by friendliness and informality, but they are rarely deep and lasting. Prizing mobile, independent existences, Americans do not evoke the rights and duties of relationships found in other cultures we are about to review. Our relationships are more compartmentalized, revolving around an event, an activity, or shared history.

We have a friend or two we study with, another one or two we dine with, others we go out with. Our friendships are likely to be fragmented. Beverly, for example, goes to the symphony with one set of friends, exercises with another, socializes with still another group, and gossips with fellow workers. Formed around special interests and activities, the friendships are not all-encompassing and permanent. Friends are those whose company we enjoy, but we consider it poor form if they ask us for favors or for help beyond the ordinary.

Arabs[24]

Twenty countries comprise the Arab world, and millions of people live in these countries, which makes generalizing about Arab relationships risky, as is giving broad impressions of Americans and the other cultures we will cover. The individual differences characterizing any group of people are not taken in to account here. We must be aware, therefore, that the samples essentially are stereotypical. They are based on expert opinion, however, and are confirmable.

In the Arab world relations between people are personal, and friendships start and develop quickly. The Arab relationship, however, is different from that of Americans. Like Americans, friends are individuals whose company is enjoyable. Unlike Americans, Arabs expect the friend to give help and do favors to the best of one's ability. Fulfilling a friend's request may not always be possible, but an Arab will never deny the request. Saying "yes" to the request is proper etiquette. A positive response is an expression of goodwill and a declaration of intention. The result is another matter. The "yes" does not necessarily mean the request can or will be carried out. The verbalization itself indicates to the other that the person has done something. Translating the "yes" into action is up to God — "if God wills."

To the Arab the world consists of friends and strangers. An Arab treats a friend with politeness, being honest, generous, and helpful at all times. A stranger does not get the same kind of consideration and instead is liable to be pushed, shoved, treated aggressively, with no quarter given.

Australians[25]

The term "mate" reveals the importance of a relationship to an Australian. *Mate* is a masculine synonym for "friend," "buddy," or "pal." The mate could be a co-worker, teammate, or neighbor. A "true" mate is one who can be absolutely relied upon. Doing favors is part of mateship and so are obligations. Mateship embodies mutual support; a mate is someone who will lend a hand, whether the person is a lifelong intimate or recently met. An Australian's personal reputation for being "counted on" and carrying out his or her obligations is part of the mateship relationship.

Conversationally, Australians say little, understate, and are private about their feelings, in contrast to Americans, who say much, overstate, and freely express their feelings. Australians develop relationships slowly and hope they will last a long time. Americans are skilled at initiating new friendships, resulting most often in superficial acquaintanceships that are shortlived.

Chinese[26]

Chinese relationships tend to fall into three categories. *Affective* ties are deep, intimate relationships, which bind family members and close friends together. These are the most important relationships, and ongoing mutual dependency is the principal quality. These relationships are formed early in life and last a lifetime. *Instrumental* ties are formed for practical gain. They are temporary and usually anonymous, with equity; the rule is that each party tries to maintain a constant ratio between what each puts in and gets out of the relationship. A taxi driver and the fare have such a relationship. One wants to earn a living; the other wants to get someplace. *Mixed* ties are a combination of the other two. People who know each other well over a period of years are linked and have an emotional bond, which is not as strong as in the affective relationship. In a mixed tie people can attain practical ends. They give and receive over time, making sure the one balances out with the other. *Guanxi,* the term for this sort of relationship, connotes connection, obligation, and dependency. Those involved have a mutual dependency, which normally is ongoing, without the stability of an affective tie.

Filipinos[27]

Filipinos distinguish between "friend" and "acquaintance." "Friend" encompasses a great deal more intimacy and obligation than Americans give the term. Friendship takes time to develop and results from a process of commitment between those concerned. Friends share life's woes and joys, aspirations, needs, problems, and triumphs with complete trust and special caring. They give time to the well-being of each other, lending money when necessary, offering moral support, and helping in difficult situations. Dedication and unselfishness embody a permanent relationship.

Japanese[28]

The Japanese divide social relationships into three categories. The *first* consists of people within one's own group, the family, co-workers on the job, or close friends at school. Communication is informal, and little miscommunication occurs. Every one knows everyone else well, and their thoughts and feelings are shared. The *second* category includes people in the neighborhood, workers not in the immediate work group, and acquaintances at school. Communication is more restrained and formal, yet the people in this category are treated with politeness and warmth. The *third* category, "the general people," is made up of people who do not matter. They are strangers, and the Japanese world of relationships ends with the second category. Usually Japanese people do not speak to strangers and may even feel hostile toward them. Forced to sit next to them in a train or at a restaurant table, the Japanese will not interact. Foreigners are placed in the third category and not acknowledged.

Russians[29]

The Russian language has different words for friend (*drug,* pronounced droog) and acquaintance (*znakomy*), and they are separate kinds of relationship. A drug is more like the American "bosom buddy," a person to be trusted and confided in, like a family member. Though such friendships take a long time to develop, they normally last a lifetime and embrace the entire person. Friends are expected to give each other lots of time and to do favors for each other without question. Russians say of their friends, "What's yours is theirs, and what's theirs is yours, especially if it's in the refrigerator." When people are truly friends, they use each others' first name. Until reaching that stage — in the early phase of the relationship — the preferred form of address is the first name and patronymic (father's name) for both men and women. Informal talk comes with the true friendship.

INTERPERSONAL CONFLICT

Conflict is inevitable when two or more people are together for any length of time.[30] Often a conflict will start over simple matters, as in this conversation:

Nancy: Goodbye, Mom. I'm off to school!

Mother: Dear — it's raining. Wear your raincoat!

Nancy: Uh, I don't need it.

Mother: You do need it! You'll get wet — ruin your clothes and catch cold!

Nancy: It's not raining very hard.

Mother: It's pouring — and will be all morning!

Nancy: So? I don't want to wear a raincoat. Nobody wears them!

Mother: Dear, you'll be warmer and drier if you wear it. Please put it on!

Nancy: I hate that raincoat! I won't wear it!

Mother: You put that raincoat on immediately! I won't let you go to school without it!

Nancy: But — I don't like it. . . .

Mother: No "buts" about it! Put it on, or we'll have
            to ground you!

Nancy: (angrily) Okay, you win! I'll wear the stu-
            pid coat.[31]

A simple conversation between a mother and a daughter, isn't it? "Do this," says the mother. "No, I won't!" replies the daughter. And there is a conflict — not a serious one when we consider the number of interpersonal conflicts that have led to fights, divorces, and even homicides. But that mother/daughter incident is an example of what conflicts are all about and how commonplace they are.

Much of our interpersonal communication is filled with conflicts like this. To live with others and go about our daily affairs seems to bring about differences in opinions, which often result in conflicts. All relationships, even the most friendly ones, contain elements of conflict. A relationship without occasional conflict suggests the possibility of no relationship at all, or at least not a relationship that is successful.[32] In fact, the total, permanent absence of conflict (if such a possibility could exist) seems undesirable. When handled constructively, conflicts do have positive qualities.[33]

The Nature of Conflict

Interpersonal conflict is *an action that occurs when two or more people must deal with what are, or what seem to be, incompatible goals, values, relationships, or resources.*[34] Let us examine the definition more closely to understand its implications.

Two or more people suggests that conflicts are interpersonal in nature. The father wants his son to do his homework. The son wants to see his school's basketball team play. The two people are in opposition because of contradictory goals. Only one of the goals —either the father's or the son's — can be achieved in the time allotted. More than two people can be involved in interpersonal conflicts, however, and we must be aware that groups of people can be in conflict.

Incompatible goals suggests ends, aims, or purposes that are incapable of being met at the same time by the people involved. The example of the father and son illustrates incompatible goals. The father wants the son to study; the son wants to watch a basketball game. Both cannot be done at the same time.

When more than two people decide to do something together, goal compatibility becomes a stronger issue. For example, when a group of three or four starts on a job and the discussion centers on how to do it, several alternatives usually are possible. The struggle to decide on a way that is agreeable to all provides a possible source of conflict.

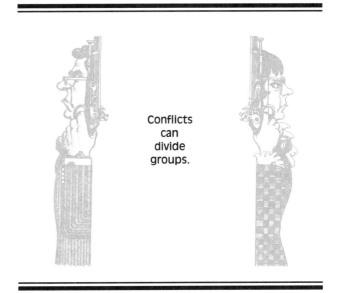

Conflicts can divide groups.

Incompatible values constitutes a second source of conflict. The husband values potatoes over rice; the wife values rice over potatoes. A source of conflict between the two is present.

Incompatible relationships make for conflict. Adolescent love affairs are potential sources of conflict when both parties do not precisely understand the obligations of the relationship. One of the partners may not practice commitment equity or fidelity equity, for example.

Incompatible resources suggests the possibility of conflict over control of things such as money, goods, property, and jobs, among others. Society has a limited supply of certain things, and most people want their full share. Conflict is possible, therefore, when things are scarce and people have to compete for them.[35]

In sum, a conflict is interpersonal in nature. It can occur when several people have to confront seemingly incompatible goals, values, relationships, or resources. They may be simple and readily managed or solved, or complex, requiring years to resolve.

The Conflict Process

Typical conflicts do not erupt suddenly. A person does not walk up to someone he or she meets on the street and punch the individual in the nose for no reason. Most conflicts are complex, involving a dynamic process consisting of six steps. By reviewing those steps, we should realize that conflicts just don't happen unexpectedly and then end. There is a lot more to a conflict than that.[36]

Antecedent Conditions

A newspaper story tells of a gunman who held another person hostage for three days, threatening to kill the person unless certain demands were met. The hostage was an employee of a finance company with which the gunman had experienced numerous misunderstandings. The gunman had brooded for months about his problems with the finance company. Finally he took action. Many communicative misunderstandings between the gunman and the finance company perpetrated the conflict. It was not without reason, even though the misunderstandings were relatively minor. They gained strength in the man's mind, however, until he had to act to relieve the pressure.

Typical conflicts do not occur spontaneously. In most of them the participants have been stewing over the antecedent conditions for some time before the overt conflict situation actually takes place. And the conditions themselves do not necessarily lead to some sort of overt action. For an overt action to occur, the perceptions and feelings of the people are contributing factors.

Perceptions of Antecedent Conditions

The second phase of the conflict process concerns the way participants view the antecedent conditions. In most cases, the participants do not perceive the conditions for potential conflict as sources of conflict at all. For example, in football the offensive and defensive tackles have the same goal: to take the opposing tackle out of the play. These conditions are ripe for conflict, but considering how often linemen knock heads, conflict is rare. To quote one tackle: "His job is to get me; my job is to get him. There's nothing personal in it. It's part of the game." This tackle perceives the physical contact in a positive manner; it is what he gets paid to do. It is not a reason for conflict.

Unfortunately, everyone does not view a potential source of conflict as this football player does. Frequently a person perceives the antecedent conditions inaccurately or illogically, and then trouble could be forthcoming. *Distorted perceptions ordinarily precede conflict.*

Emotional Responses

Tied closely to misperceptions of the antecedent conditions are the emotional responses the conditions evoke. Tension, anxiety, hostility, fear, and stress exacerbate the conditions in the mind of the person involved. The possibility of overt action thus is enhanced. The gunman who held the finance company employee hostage is a case in point. Apparently the gunman perceived his frequent misunderstandings with the finance company as attempts to thwart his business with the company. He became emotionally upset after each problem situation, and finally he grew tense and anxious, fearful that the company's

employees were trying to do him in. His emotional state was fuel for the fire, increasing the likelihood of overt action.

Manifest Conflict Behavior

Eventually the conflict shows itself in some form of overt behavior. The gunman takes a hostage and threatens the person's life. The conflict becomes visible at this point; finance company officials know there is a problem. Most conflicts show themselves in a similar fashion. After a period of development, the overt action is displayed. The person's frustrations and anxieties boil over, and the conflict behavior erupts. War is an excellent example of manifest conflict behavior.

Conflict Management or Resolution

In this step the visible act of conflict is terminated, or at least managed in a way that will keep it from erupting again. Ways of managing or resolving conflicts are discussed in the next section.

Conflict Aftermath

The typical conflict leaves a residue, a legacy, which affects the future relations of participants. Unless the conflict is resolved to everyone's satisfaction, the likelihood of another occurring is real. If there are losers, the seeds for future conflict are present. The residue is negative. When a conflict is resolved to everyone's gratification, the legacy is positive, perhaps leading to more productive relations in the future.[37]

In summary, then, conflicts don't just erupt; the visible symptoms are merely manifestations of deeper, underlying causes. The overt behavior is the only part of the process we usually see. In a sense, conflicts are like icebergs. A great deal is hidden below the surface.

Conflict Management and Resolution

Because conflict is inevitable, a necessary part of one's education is how to cope with it. Although conflicts are distressing, to experience them knowingly can be a valuable asset. The more we face up to our

The Conflict Process

1. Antecedent conditions
2. Perceptions of antecedent conditions
3. Emotional responses to antecedent conditions
4. Manifest conflict behavior
5. Conflict management or resolution
6. Conflict aftermath

conflicts and solve them ourselves, the more inner freedom and strength we will gain. Knowing how to solve our conflicts should help us run our own lives.[38]

Before explaining the methods of handling conflicts, the terms *management* and *resolution* should be made clear. When a conflict is managed, it is not resolved. Rather, it is drawn out, prolonged, or lengthened so as to diminish its intensity and increase its duration. A resolved conflict, in contrast, is solved and worked out to the satisfaction of all involved.[39]

The methods for handling conflicts are win/lose, negotiation/ mediation/arbitration, and withdrawal.[40]

Win-Lose

Under the win/lose method, problems can be solved in three ways: Win-lose, lose-lose, and win-win. In the *win-lose* method, one person wins and the other loses — and that is its fault. The loser is not going to attain his or her goal and most likely is going to be dissatisfied with the result. Examples of win-lose situations include those in which parents expect compliance from their children, the minority consistently loses to the majority, and games involving a winner and a loser.

In the *lose-lose* method, both parties lose; no one wins. Labor-management wage conflicts often end up being lose-lose situations. Labor does not receive what it wants, and management has to give up more than it wants to.

These two methods represent a "we-versus-they" orientation rather than a healthier "we-versus-the-problem" point of view. The communicators are trying to defeat each other instead of working toward a mutually rewarding solution. The conflicts involved are personalized, and they ought to be depersonalized — focusing on facts and issues instead of people. Few win-lose and lose-lose solutions are permanent. They are temporary at best.

A win-win way to resolve conflicts uses problem solving and a we-versus-the problem orientation.

Win-win methods are different. They lead to shared rewards. Both parties win. Instead of attempting to defeat each other as in the two previously mentioned methods, participants using win-win methods work together to arrive at solutions from which both sides will profit. They avoid solutions that favor only one side.

Of the win-win methods available, the most successful of these is the method described in Chapter 15 — the problem-solving method. It systematically orders the stages that are helpful in reaching a mutually beneficial solution. Cooperation is necessary, as well as a nonthreatening, accepting climate in which each side holds equal status (even though they may not outside of the meeting room). The causes and symptoms of the problem leading to the conflict — not the personalities of the participants — are attacked.

Negotiation/Mediation/Arbitration

These three common methods of handling conflicts have the negative qualities of win-lose and lose-lose. They often are identified in that manner, seen as either win-lose or lose-lose, but they are so popular that we consider them as possible methods to use in managing conflicts. Normally they fail to resolve conflicts.

In *negotiation*, each side gives a little until, after a number of concessions, the parties finally arrive at an agreement. *Mediation* involves the intervention of a third party, a mediator. The mediator works with the two parties to reach a settlement. *Arbitration* requires a third party to analyze the various issues of the conflict and award a decision to one side. The other side then has to abide by the decision.

The three methods leave much to be desired. Negotiation and mediation involve wringing concessions from participants until reaching a settlement. No one really wins unless the demands are inflated. In labor-management conflicts the tendency is to inflate the demands on both sides. After making the concessions, both sides might end up with what they actually wanted. Arbitration places the conflict in the hands of a neutral third party, and chances are that the arbitrator's decision will favor one side.

Withdrawal

A common practice for handling interpersonal conflicts is to withdraw from the situation, to leave the field.[41] By leaving the field, we mean stopping the communication that is stimulating the conflict. This can be done by leaving physically, breaking off talk and leaving. In doing so, the conflict may not actually be ended, but leaving probably will prevent the conflict from escalating.

We also can leave the field psychologically. We can stop talking about the subject. The other person can have his or her say; we just do not respond orally. We may continue to disagree privately, but we do not say so. Thus, the conflict is not permitted to escalate.

Finally, we can leave the field by changing the subject. We know there is no point in continuing the discussion, because the opinions of both sides are hard and fast. Hence, continuing to talk about the subject under contention serves no useful purpose.

Withdrawal obviously does not resolve conflicts. It helps to manage them by putting them out of sight for a time and permitting the ardor of the moment to cool. The conflicts, however, will still be present, albeit with less intensity.

SUMMARY

Of the possible kinds of interpersonal talk in which we can engage, that taking place in interpersonal relational situations consumes the greatest amount of our time and energy. We are part of dozens of relationships, all of which rely on oral communication for their existence. Therefore, we must understand interpersonal relationships and the role communication plays in them. Their characteristics include variability, duration, frequency, revelation, meshing, support, anxiety reduction, and proximity.

Relationships are built around communication, and three independent dimensions govern the kind of talk that transpires in interpersonal relationships. These are immediacy, intimacy, and status. Relationships develop, are maintained, and sometimes are terminated. Qualities that help maintain a relationship are genuineness, commitment, dialogue, and empathy.

Even the most successful relationships experience conflict. Conflict is inevitable, but so is our need to relate to others. Through our interpersonal relationships we satisfy our social needs, needs we have to meet if we want to live as normal human beings.

Intercultural Communication

A famous psychologist, Sidney M. Jourard, believes the crisis of our time is not the shortage of food, living space, and energy. The crisis we face is the failure to communicate, to engage in dialogue in which the listener not only hears but also understands what the speaker is saying and, then, in relevant response, also speaks the truth, honestly and sincerely. The heart of our dilemma on the shrinking planet we call Earth, Jourard thinks, is our inability to communicate in this fashion.[1]

Our planet is shrinking — not in size, of course, but in our sense of distance and time. Technological advances have made possible what seems to be a compression of time and space. We can travel faster and farther than ever before, and in less time than ever before. The consequence is an earth fast becoming a global village in which the many nations making it up are meeting increasing cultural, ethnic, and social diversity.

Millions of impoverished, unemployed, and politically persecuted people have left their homelands seeking refuge elsewhere. Few countries in the Western world have not been invaded by expatriates. The United States is no exception. Many have emigrated to our country, causing the nation's racial mix to change rapidly. From North to South and from East to West, the country's racial makeup is being altered, and along with this change have come modifications in the nation's cityscape and landscape, its taste in food and clothing, in its entire perception of itself and its way of life.

To students, racial diversification should be obvious. Fifteen years ago when many were enrolling in school for the first time, few classmates were non-White unless they lived in the heavily multicultural states of Hawaii, California, Florida, New York, and New Jersey. Today every third student is one viewed traditionally as a member of a cultural or ethnic minority. By the century's end roughly 40 percent of students in American schools will represent minority groups, mostly Asians and Latin Americans with a large population of Blacks.[2] Intercultural classrooms will soon be a reality in all but the most isolated parts of the country.

The classroom's cultural diversity is a mirror of society in general. If schools are becoming more multicultural, so, too, are our city streets and our country lanes. Residents of big cities and small towns encounter people speaking languages such as Thai, Hmong, Khmer, Lao, Chinese, Japanese, Vietnamese, Korean, Spanish, and a host of others. Culturally identical populations will soon be found only in the remotest regions of the nation. Figure 12.1 illustrates the growth in U.S. population from 1980 to 1990, by culture.

Americans are moving about the world also, not to escape political mistreatment necessarily, but for educational and job-related purposes, and to sightsee. Thousands of servicemen and women live abroad, stationed in all parts of the world. Students attend foreign universities, not in the large numbers of foreign students studying in the United States, yet enough to make their presence known. Business people travel to foreign countries to sell their wares. Too, a small number of Americans are employed in foreign lands, holding specialized jobs the natives cannot handle. And, of course, Americans travel, visiting all parts of the globe as tourists — for many, trips they dreamed about and saved money for years

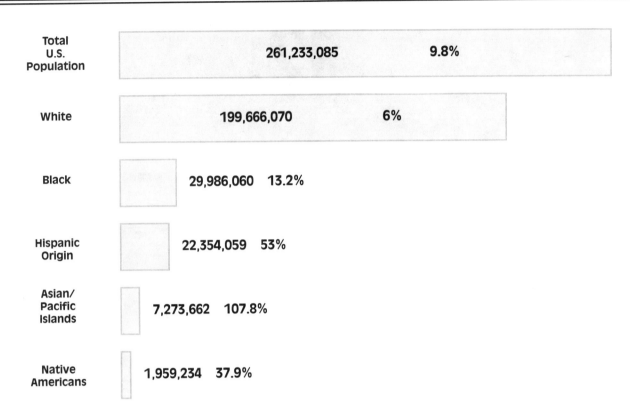

Population figures are estimates based on 1990 census and percents indicate growth since the 1980 census, as published in *USA Today.*

Hispanic origin includes Mexican, Puerto Rican, Cuban, and others.

Asian/Pacific Islands includes Chinese, Filipino, Japanese, Asian Indian, Korean, Vietnamese, Hawaiian, Samoan, Guamaian, and others. Vietnamese were the fastest growing group.

Native Americans includes American Indian, Eskimo, and Aleut.

Figure 12.1. Growth in U. S. population, 1980-1990.

to enjoy. Intercultural contact is a reality for Americans as it is for most people the world over.[3]

With this intermingling of cultures, problems arise. Most are minor misunderstandings, resulting from unfamiliarity with local customs, ethnocentric behavior, or stereotypical thinking. Americans visiting a Japanese home, for example, are apt to create a problem by failing to remove their shoes before entering. Other problems are of more import as people from different cultures intermingle. Violence can take place, and occasionally does, as foreign laborers, for example, working for cheaper wages, take jobs away from American workers. Prejudice is common, and the flames of racial hatred are easily fanned by disgruntled citizens.

Understanding the ramifications of intercultural communication assumes more importance in the United States with its growing mix of racial and ethnic minorities. Recognizing variations in behavior between people from various cultures can help reduce tensions and anxieties as individuals from varied backgrounds meet to communicate. In this chapter we examine the elements making up intercultural communication, recognizing that this topic is treated elsewhere in the book as part of the communication process. Some aspects, however, merit more attention, and we discuss them thoroughly here. Among them are ethnocentrism, stereotypes, prejudice, and differences in social institutions.

THE NATURE OF INTERCULTURAL COMMUNICATION

Jose Bulatao from Manila talks with Ichiro Nakamura from Tokyo. Sing Long Song from Beijing meets with Chong-hiok Park from Seoul. Aino Sallinen from Yvalskyla speaks with C. A. Steel of London. Warren Johnson of Minneapolis talks with Beth Cooke of Norwich, England. These conversations are occurring at a World Communication Association convention in Yvalskyla, Finland. All are examples of intercultural communication, the kind of communication involving people from different cultures. Intercultural communication is *communication between members of different cultures, and it takes place when a person (or persons) from one culture talks to a person (or persons) from another.*[4]

In each of the World Communication Association conversations, the speaker's message is bound to his or her culture, and the listener's understanding of the message is similarly bound to his or her culture. Culture is a major force in shaping each communicator, and it is largely responsible for the communicative behaviors and meanings each communicator possesses. The communicative behaviors and meanings members of different cultures hold are apt to be very different. Variations appear in values, beliefs, attitudes, religions, lifestyles, and political backgrounds, among others. These cultural dissimilarities are more understandable when we examine culture itself.

CULTURE

All humans are born with the same biological equipment and experience the same sort of life cycle: birth, youth, adulthood, old age, and death. How each person uses the biological equipment is culturally determined; the ways are almost limitless. The ways depend in part on the resources available and the climatic conditions in the region, and how the people adapt to them. The people of each culture have to eat to live, but what they eat is culturally determined based on what is available. Some cultures relish snails, grasshoppers, snakes, vermin, horses, dogs, and caterpillars. In America this is not true. Many Americans eat pork, but Muslims and Orthodox Jews do not. Hindus avoid beef, some Africans hate eggs, many Chinese do not drink milk — all foods common to American diets.

Although we have to eat, how, when and with whom we eat are culturally determined. We can use silverware, chopsticks, or our fingers to eat while we sit at tables or on the floor. Most Americans eat three meals a day, but the number of meals varies from culture to culture, as do the times they are eaten. We eat dissimilar foods at breakfast, lunch, and dinner, and most of us probably think people all over the world do the same. They do not. Our cultural ways are such a part of us that we frequently fail to realize people in other cultures may behave differently.

Culture Defined

Culture is all-encompassing, and we probably are rarely conscious of its presence in our lives and its control over our behavior. The scope of culture extends to every part of the environment made by humans. It refers to the nonbiological parts of human life and is composed of *artifacts* or things that surround us made by humans, *sociofacts* or social structures, relationships, languages, laws, and mores conceived by humans, and *mentifacts* or knowledge, beliefs, values, attitudes, and experiences each human possesses. Everything created by humans constitutes culture.[5]

Qualities of Culture

Four important qualities help explain its nature.[6]

1. *Culture is learned.* We are not born with culture, but soon after we are born, we start to learn it. What we do have at birth are certain human faculties, and the culture to which we belong teaches us how to use these faculties, and thus how we shall live. As we have said, a biological function is to eat, but our culture decides whether we shall eat rice or potatoes. A biological function is to sleep, but our culture teaches us how to sleep — on a hammock, on the ground, or in a bed.

2. *Culture is shared.* Members of an identifiable group share certain patterns and customs, and these bind them together, allowing them to function together more readily. Traffic laws make possible the sharing of highways without everybody ramming each other.

3. *Culture is adaptive.* Our culture came about to accommodate the environmental conditions existing in our part of the world and the available natural and technological resources. High winds sweep through the Pacific on occasion, so dwellings are made with longer and stronger nails, with roofs that can withstand gale forces, and without protuberances that can be blown off.

4. *Culture changes.* Cultures constantly undergo change, although the changes tend to be subtle.

Much of the time we are unaware that change has taken place. Many people were unmindful that last year the skirt style was short and this year it is long. Last year pizza was the number one take-out; this year it is tacos.

Universal Elements

Every culture has certain elements in common. These are termed cultural *universals* and are general classes of characteristics that help us ascertain the differences between cultures. The universals provide a basis for cultural comparison because they show areas of possible dissimilarity.[7]

Lists of universals have been constructed; seventy-three appear on one.[8] Age-grading, for example, is a characteristic of all cultures; it is a universal element. The actual way that a person's age is kept varies, although most cultures keep track the way Western nations do. From a person's birthdate, each passing year makes the person a year older. Bodily adornment is a universal, but not every culture wears Western-style dress. Women may wear dresses, cheongsam, grass skirts, muumuus, sarongs, or mantua, depending upon where they live. Cooking is universal, but not every culture cooks in the same manner. The possibilities are many: baking, toasting, roasting, frying, searing, simmering, stewing, broiling, boiling, braising, poaching, barbecuing, grilling, shirring, among others.

The universals imply that culture covers a wide range of human endeavor, including virtually everything that is nonbiological. Each universal, however, may have different applications in dissimilar cultures.

Cultural Universals

The following traits are common to all cultures and, because they are, they are called *universals*. The original list contained 73. This is a sampling from that list.

age grading	athletics
calendar	cleanliness
community groups	cooking
cosmology	dress
dancing	decorative art
education	ethics
ethnobotany	etiquette
faith healing	family
feasting	firemaking
folklore	food taboos
funeral rites	games
gift giving	government
greetings	hair styles
housing	hygiene
joking	kinship
language	laws
magic	marriage
modesty	mealtimes
medicine	mourning
music	numbers
obstetrics	postnatal care
puberty customs	religious ritual
sex restrictions	status
surgery	tool making
trade	visiting
weather control	

From George Murdock, "The Common Denominator of Cultures," in Ralph Linton, editor, *The Science of Man in World Crisis* (New York: Columbia World Press, 1945).

MACROCULTURE AND MICROCULTURES IN AMERICA

As a pluralistic nation, the United States comprises many cultures. Most of the country's citizens share a universal or national culture. We call this the nation's *macroculture,* a culture of the greatest size and with the largest number of people. In addition, many *microcultures* exist with distinct cultural patterns not common to all Americans. We use the term *microculture* to denote cultures smaller in size but parts of the macroculture.

The Macroculture

The macroculture has as its base the Anglo-Saxon political and social institutions influenced by Western European tradition, brought to the country by the early European settlers. These institutions, including government, schools, banks, social welfare groups, business, and laws affect many aspects of our lives. Members of the nation's largely middle class follow these fundamentally white, Anglo-Saxon, and mostly Protestant customs, and they provide the framework for most of the nation's culture.

Overshadowing the U.S. macroculture's traits is a dominant value: self-reliance. Most Americans subscribe to the right to control their own destiny, to advance or fall according to their own efforts. Most Americans believe they are their own master, being industrious, ambitious, competitive, individualistic, independent, and superior to the natural environmental forces. Of course, Americans practice other Anglo-Saxon traits, but self-reliance is most prominent.[9]

In this book, whenever we refer to Americans or citizens of the United States, we mean those who are a part of the dominant Anglo-Saxon macroculture. Other groups in the Western Hemisphere can rightfully call themselves Americans, and they do. For our purposes, we mean members of the macroculture, although we are mindful of other North and South Americans who are also Americans.

Microcultures

Existing within the macroculture are many microcultures. These are partners in the political and social institutions of the macroculture, yet they have distinctive characteristics of their own. Members of microculture share traits and values that bind them together and set them apart in specific ways from the macroculture. Thus, they are part of the macroculture but identifiable also because of their microculture membership.[10]

Many microcultures are found in the United States, and almost everyone is a member of several. Two of the largest are the male and female (gender) microcultures. Then there are the microcultures of the elderly, teenagers, Protestants, Catholics, Republicans, Democrats, federal workers, school teachers, ethnic groups, racial groups, geographical locations, socioeconomic groups, gangs, and so on. Hundreds can be named.

Each of these microcultures has distinct behavior patterns that members have in common. The socioeconomic group known as the poor, for example, perceive aspects of life differently than does the middle class. The poor are said to believe that today is to be lived fully for tomorrow may never come. The future is indefinite, so what is earned today should be spent before it disappears. The middle class sees a rosy horizon in the future, so money is to be spent cautiously and saved for the future. The poor person and the middle class person have identities that shape their lives, making each a bit different from the other.[11] Nonetheless, they endorse the macroculture's principles and are viable parts of it.

THE INTERCULTURAL COMMUNICATION PROCESS

Figure 12.2 depicts the intercultural communication process.[12] The model is much like the one in Chapter 2, with several variations. Primarily, Figure 12.2 portrays two persons from different cultures;

Example of a Macroculture and Microcultures

Within the United States (and every culture) are many microcultures. These share the political and social institutions of the macroculture. Within the microculture the members follow distinctive behavioral patterns of their own. Eight general microcultures are identifiable: age, gender/sex, ethnic or national origin, religion, class, geographic region, urban/suburban/rural location, and exceptionality (handicaps, special abilities). Most people are part of several microcultures, and these influence their lives — some to a greater extent than others.

In the example below, a twenty-year old student, female, middle-class Catholic of German-American parentage, lives in Seattle. She is a member of these microcultures but is largely influenced by one, as the larger segment implies. She is active in women's rights groups and considers her membership in them most important in her life.

In the other circle, determine for yourself the importance of the microcultures in your life. Decide which ones you are a part of, and then divide the circle according to their importance to you.

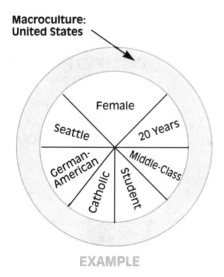

EXAMPLE

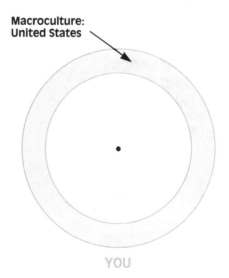

YOU

Based on Donna M. Gollnick and Philip C. Chinn, *Multicultural Education in a Pluralistic Society*, 3d ed. (New York: Merrill, 1990), 16.

Person A is shaded to suggest that this individual represents a culture different from Person B.

When Person A speaks, A's message is based on A's cultural background. The shaded arrow implies that background. Person B receives the message and decodes it based on B's cultural background. The partially shaded area in B suggests that B's interpreting, evaluating, and responding stages reflect B's cultural background. The feedback also symbolizes differences in culture. The amount of difference between A's intended meaning and B's interpretation of that meaning is contingent upon the degree of cultural diversity. If A is Korean and B is German, the difference undoubtedly will be great, as the two cultures are vastly different in many respects. If A is a North Korean and B is a South Korean, the difference will be slight because the two cultures are much the same.

CULTURAL DIMENSIONS

Cultures differ, but how? In this section and the next we examine principal differences between cultures. In this section we describe five main dimensions of cultural variation, and in the next we explain cultural dissimilarities that impact the perception of self, social objects, and events.

Individualism and Collectivism[13]

Much social behavior can be accounted for by the individualism and collectivism dimension. Although people in every culture have individualistic and collectivistic tendencies, the relative emphasis is toward individualism in the Western cultural world and toward collectivism in the Eastern cultural world. The United States is an example of a Western individualistic culture, and Japan illustrates the collectivism of the East.

When the characteristics of individualism and collectivism are delineated, the contrasts become more vivid. In individualistic cultures the members tend to join and belong to many groups, establishing a wide range of social relationships. Their attachments to these groups, however, normally are weak, and their own personal goals take precedence over group goals. In collectivistic cultures the members are likely to enroll in fewer groups, holding membership in one or two: in the family and at work. They have little interest in joining other groups. Their attachments, however, are strong in the groups to which they belong, and the group goals are their goals.

In an individualistic culture like the United States, all sorts of groups are available to those who are interested in affiliating. The number is staggering. Once they are old enough to walk, children can enroll in neighborhood groups of all kinds: Little

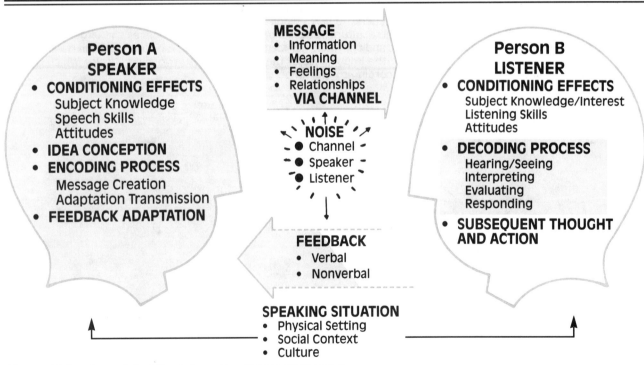

Figure 12.2. A model of the intercultural speech process.

Signs in English in Foreign Locations

American tourists have found these signs, printed in English, in foreign locations. Much is lost in translation.

Japanese hotel:	Please take advantage of the chambermaid.
Paris dress shop:	Dresses for street walking.
Bangkok cleaner:	Drop your trousers here for best results.
Tokyo bar:	Special cocktails for the ladies with nuts.
Thailand donkey ride:	Would you like to ride on your own ass?
Geneva inn:	Special today — no ice cream.
Hong Kong dentist:	Teeth extracted by the latest Methodists.
Swedish furrier:	Fur coats made for ladies from their own skin.
Hong Kong dress shop:	Ladies have fits upstairs.
Rome laundry:	Ladies, leave your clothes here, and spend the afternoon having a good time.

Status differences are rejected in the individualistic cultures, although they exist, and equalitarianism is emphasized. Authority figures such as the boss or group leader consult often with underlings and try to avoid telling or ordering. Democracy in the family, the workplace, and other kinds of groups is encouraged. In the collectivistic cultures status differences are a fact of life. They usually are accepted without question. Authority figures are paternalistic and most likely obtained their position because of age or seniority, not necessarily because of effective performance or superior knowledge. At home the eldest male rules, and each family member has a carefully defined role.

In the individualistic cultures the individual is prominent. Personal independence is valued along with personal achievement, exceptional performance, assertiveness, and material success. In the collectivistic cultures interdependence is valued as is interpersonal support. Aggressive behavior is taboo, except perhaps with strangers. Group achievement is the foremost consideration; harmonious relationships reign supreme.[14]

Nonverbal behavior differences are identifiable between the individualistic and collectivistic cultures. People in the most individualistic cultures

League teams, scout troops, boys' and girls' clubs, and other social and recreational groups as they pass through elementary and secondary school. Out of school, people can join church, political, and neighborhood improvement groups. A plethora of groups exists, open to virtually everyone who is interested: Kiwanis, Lions, Rotary, Toastmasters, Civitan, Zonta, YMCA, YWCA, PTA, Veterans of Foreign Wars, yacht clubs, golf clubs, garden clubs, Sierra clubs. Most people enroll for the personal satisfaction membership will bring, whether it be social, educational, recreational, economic, political, or religious.

In the collectivistic cultures, Japan for example, many of the sorts of groups just mentioned can be found, but the family and the work or school group can fulfill most of their interpersonal needs. The desire to affiliate with other groups is not strong. Japanese teenagers do not seek membership in non-family groups as American teenagers do.

In the individualistic cultures the members welcome conflict in social relationships. Confrontation is a means of clearing the air, and winning one's own way is a measure of personal worth. Successfully completing a task on an individual basis is highly prized. If one loses too often, other groups are open to join. Divorce is a popular option. The collectivistic cultures stress harmony in social relationships. Group success is preferable to personal success. Maintaining the family is prized, with every family member dependent on each other.

Related Terms

The following terms are related to the study of intercultural communication.

Intracultural Communication:
Communication between members of the same culture.
Example: Two Koreans talking together.

Crosscultural Communication:
Not a synonym for intercultural communication, but used when some phenomenon is compared across cultures.
Example: Comparing communication apprehension in Japan, Korea, and the U. S.

Interracial Communication:
Talk between members of different racial groups.
Example: Black and White Americans conversing.

Interethnic Communication:
Talk between members of different ethnic groups (groups distinguished by customs, characteristics, language, common history, or geographical origin).
Example: Polish-American speaking to a German-American.

Microcultural Communication:
Talk between different microculture members.
Example: Father talking to son.

(United States, Australia, Great Britain, Canada, the Netherlands, New Zealand, Italy, Belgium, and Denmark) are likely to be proximically remote and distant. Socially, they tend to stand apart, touching little. The more collectivistic cultures (Venezuela, Colombia, Pakistan, Peru, Taiwan, Thailand, Singapore, Chile, and Hong Kong) promote closeness. Being interdependent, the people tend to work, sleep, play, and live together in closer proximity. Family movements, schedules, and actions are closely coordinated.

People in individualistic cultures keep their own schedules, with family members coming and going as they please. They smile more and are friendlier than those in collectivistic cultures, practicing more affiliative types of personal behavior such as flirting, making small talk, dating, and making friends. Rock dancing is popular because each dancer does his or her own thing. People in the collectivistic cultures prefer group dancing and singing.[15]

Masculinity and Femininity[16]

Cultures are classifiable along a masculine-feminine dimension. "Masculine" in this case has nothing to do with male biological traits but instead refers to personality characteristics associated with masculinity, such as assertiveness, dominance, and achievement. "Feminine" also has no reference to female biological qualities but rather to feminine characteristics of nurturance, interest in people, and interdependence. Some cultures are highly masculine, the top ten being Japan, Austria, Venezuela, Italy, Switzerland, Mexico, Ireland, Great Britain, Germany, and the Philippines. Others are highly feminine, the top ten being Sweden, Norway, the Netherlands, Denmark, Finland, Chile, Portugal, Thailand, Peru, and Spain. The United States falls into the middle rank of masculine cultures.

Members of the masculine cultures show high levels of stress, probably because they internalize their emotions. They appear more assertive, competitive, and ambitious. The members are money- and things-oriented, and excellence in performance is important in whatever they do. They work to achieve, are independent, and exhibit *machismo* (manliness) qualities.

The feminine cultures' members more freely express their emotions and emphasize compassion, quality of life, service, and benevolence. The members are people-oriented and are concerned about the environment and the unfortunate. They work to live, not live to work and think unisex and androgyny are ideal. The mother holds the stronger position in the family.

Contact and Noncontact Cultures[17]

A third dimension of classification, contact, has to do with physical relationships: standing close, touching, maintaining eye contact. Some cultures are high-contact, and these are located mostly in the warmer climates such as the Arab, Mediterranean, and Hispanic countries and Indonesia. European and Middle Eastern Jews are high-contact people, as are many Eastern Europeans and Russians. Members of high-contact cultures touch a lot.

The low-contact cultures are found in Northern Europe (Scandinavia, Germany, and England), Japan, and the white Anglo-Saxons of the United States. In the United States people living in the warmer latitudes are more contact-prone than those living in the colder areas. Residents of Hawaii probably touch more than residents of Minnesota. Members of low-contact cultures touch less than those of high-contact cultures. The Japanese, for example, avoid touching when greeting someone. They bow instead.

High- and Low-Power Distance[18]

Power distance is a fourth way of classifying cultures showing how cultures vary one from another. Power distance refers to the degree of inequality in power between less powerful and more powerful individuals. Power is the potential to determine or direct the behavior of other persons.

High-power-distance cultures have rigid stratification. The bosses make up an elite, and the workers constitute the powerless who follow the orders of the elite. Everyone has a rightful place in high-power-distance cultures. A selected few are independent, are superior, and hold the power. Most of the people are dependent, are underdogs, and have no privileges. Privileges are restricted to the power-holders. The powerless accept the superiors as being different and realize that the distance between them and the superiors is great. The top ten high-power-distance cultures are the Philippines, Mexico, Venezuela, India, Singapore, Brazil, Hong Kong, France, Colombia, and Turkey, in that order.

Communication between the powerful and the powerless in high-power-distance cultures is limited or nonexistent. When they do interact, the powerless do not disagree with the powerful. The powerless have superiors who direct them or who are persuasive. Authoritarian leaders are preferred, and the powerless tend to conform to the desires of the powerful.

Low-power-distance cultures encourage equal rights for all people. Inequality is to be minimal, with latent harmony between the powerful and powerless. Independence is valued; obedience is not considered vital. Decisions are made with the participation of all concerned. Communication between everyone is endorsed. The ranking ten low-power-distance cultures are Austria, Israel, Denmark, New Zealand, Ireland, Sweden, Norway, Finland, Switzerland, and Great Britain. The United States ranks fifteenth.

High and Low Context[19]

High-context cultures are ones in which the messages of their members are implicit. Most of the information is either in the physical context or is internalized in the message sender. Low-context cultures are the opposite. The message is in the words uttered. It usually comes in elaborate detail and is clearly communicated.

High-context cultures include China, Japan, Korea, cultures in the southern and eastern Mediterranean areas, Latin America, Turkey, Greece, and the Arab countries. The people are highly attuned to nonverbal cues, able to read facial and bodily motions, subtle gestures, and environmental cues more meaningfully than people from low-context cultures. Little information is contained in the coded, explicit, transmitted parts of a message, requiring people to infer what was left out of a message.

Low-context cultures include Switzerland, Germany, the United States, Canada, Scandinavia, and much of the northern European area. Members of low-context cultures are not as adept at reading nonverbal cues. They come across as talkative, redundant, and unattractive to high-context people, who think low-context people talk too much.

In this explanation of the five dimensions, not every culture is mentioned, just the extremes — the highs and lows. Those not specified fall in between. The five dimensions do provide insights into people's behavior. We can expect Orientals, as people from a high-context culture, to be quiet in communication situations. The Swiss, Americans, and Canadians are going to be talkative. People from high-power-distance cultures are not going to talk much to superiors whose authority they acknowledge. Those from low-power-distance cultures will interact more freely, not only with superiors but actually with almost anyone. People from high-contact cultures will touch easily, whereas those from low-contact cultures will maintain some distance from their fellow communicators. Members of masculine cultures are more aggressive, generally speaking, than members of feminine cultures. Those from the feminine cultures, however, tend to be more concerned with the personal welfare of those they talk with. People from the individualistic cultures are more inclined toward independence, and they are more remote proximically. In contrast, collectivists are happier conversing with members of their own groups than with strangers.

CULTURAL VARIABLES

Another means of identifying cultural differences is by examining variables that make up our personal orientation system and our social institutions.

Personal Orientation System

Needs, values, beliefs and attitudes are parts of our personal orientation system that governs our behavior. In different cultures each of these parts may be dissimilar. The importance and strength of individual needs varies across cultures as do the salience, direction, and degree of values (see Chapter 4). That part of our belief system known as world view also is different, with the Eastern and the Western perspectives dividing the world. In the context of the discussion here, beliefs and attitudes merit our attention because of their impact on intercultural communication.

Beliefs

Beliefs are judgments about what is true or probable, statements we can make about our self and the world around us. Beliefs can be *experiential,* derived from direct experience, *informational,* from sources such as the media or other people, or *inferential,* inferences we draw about persons and events around us.

In developing beliefs, we reason. We sense a stimulus, and we draw conclusions about it. We reason, "Because something happened, we believe something else will happen." There are cultural variations. Germans stress logic, whereas the Japanese

---

High-Context Japanese Silently Negotiate

"The use of silence has a profound effect on cross-cultural negotiations. In the Western cultural context, silence usually means anxiety, shyness, or hostility. But in Japan, silence can mean respect for the person who is speaking, thinking over an important point or even disagreement that is not expressed. In other words, silences are not empty spaces to be filled with meaningless words."

From Kazuo Nishiyama, *Strategies of Marketing to Japanese Visitors* (Needham Heights, MA: Ginn Press, 1989), 114.

reject a logical approach, they are more intuitive and meditative. Russians practice an axiomatic, deductive sort of reasoning; the Arab world is characterized by an intuitive, affective sort of reasoning. Each culture has a reasoning process, but each employs its own process in its own way.[20]

Attitudes

An attitude is a learned tendency to respond favorably toward a given object of orientation. Although we hold thousands of attitudes, three classes are exceedingly important in intercultural communication, because they direct and specifically affect our communication with people of other cultures: ethnocentrism, stereotyping, and prejudice. These attitudes are at the heart of many misunderstandings we have with those who are not entirely like us.

Ethnocentrism. Our culture helps us decide how we should think, act, and feel. It becomes the means through which we judge the world, and it often functions unconsciously to blind us to other ways of thinking, acting, and feeling. The way our culture functions is the "natural way" to function in the world. Whatever our culture says is best, we are apt to consider as best for the rest of the world. Ethnocentrism, thus, is *the unconscious tendency to interpret or to judge all other groups and situations according to the categories and values of our own culture.*[21]

We display ethnocentrism when we fail to consider other cultures as equally workable alternatives to organizing the world. Our culture, ethnocentrics believe, is correct, natural, and superior when compared to other cultures. We may perceive cultures other than ours as odd, amusing, inferior, or immoral. Among first-time visitors to Japan, some will look askance at the Japanese custom of removing shoes before entering private homes and some public buildings.

Believing that our culture provides us with the correct way to think, act, and feel has advantages. Ethnocentrism helps maintain the integrity of our culture, makes us more homogeneous, increases cohesiveness, and aids us in surviving outside threats. Carried to extremes, however, ethnocentrism becomes detrimental. If one culture thinks its way of life is superior to all others, its leaders may decide their duty is to change the others. Wars have been fought to save the world for democracy. Missionaries have preached the gospel to save idol worshipers from everlasting punishment. Billions of dollars have been poured into governmental programs to bring civilization to "backward" nations, with little success.

Stereotyping. A stereotype is *a fixed impression of a group of people through which we then perceive specific individuals.*[22] Although the stereotypes most often are negative, they can be positive. The stereotyper consciously or unconsciously disregards any differences or distinctions that set an individual apart from the stereotyped group. A stereotype, therefore, is an attitude held about a person solely on the basis of the group to which the person belongs, as we learned from the description of the interpretation stage of perception in Chapter 5.

Stereotypes are an unfortunate but necessary part of thinking and communicating. Because we cannot respond individually to the millions of isolated elements we perceive every day, we lump them into categories and respond to the categories. Too often we stereotype when referring to members of cultural or ethnic groups; we generalize about a group of people and the individuals who make up the group.

The American Indian Historical Society studied the stereotypes attached to Indians (or Native Americans)[23], finding the following stereotypes: Indians are warlike people who are stoical and humorless, unclean and diseased, unreliable workers, uninterested in school, consumers of food unfit for human consumption, and speakers of gutteral, simple languages. These stereotypes, of course, mask individual differences in the Indian population. We see a drunken Indian, and we categorize all Indians as drunkards. Like all cultures, the Indian culture has shirkers and ignoramuses; not all Indians are noble, poor, or angelic. Indians are individuals who are to be respected for their individual attainments and criticized for their individual errors, as are the members of any group.

Stereotypes can interfere with our ability to objectively view a new acquaintance from a foreign culture. We assign the person the characteristics we have learned to associate with the group the person belongs to. Learning that a person we are introduced to is Filipino, we automatically assign to this person the characteristics we think Filipinos possess. If we believe Filipinos are sensitive, friendly, courteous, family-oriented people, we will perceive the Filipino as such a person. If we think Filipinos are hot-tempered, prone to violence, gamblers, and heavy drinkers, we will look for those behaviors in our new acquaintance. We fail to take into account the individual characteristics that make this Filipino a person in his or her own right. We apply our stereotype and perhaps judge the person unfairly. We fail to see the individual; we see the stereotype we hold of the group.

One world traveler talked of the experiences he had being stereotyped as an American:

> Basically, I am a shy, quiet individual, not given to bragging or making a sow's ear seem like a silk purse. I try to be honest and forthright but diplomatic. When I meet

people in the Orient for the first time and they learn I am American, I can sense the wheels in their heads turning, making me out to be a typical American in their way of thinking. I'm going to be loud, obnoxious, a braggart, joke-teller, back-slapper, who talks constantly. Fortunately, they will also see me as kind and generous. After they get to know me, my behavior confounds them. They don't know how to treat me.

The American was classified in a stereotypical fashion. His individual qualities were not considered, and he was judged before people knew what he was really like. Most of the people he met had few previous contacts with Americans. The stereotypes they held were based on media reports and portrayals. We form opinions about other racial and ethnic groups from what we read and what we see in the movies and on television. If we were to watch cowboy and Indian moves on Saturday television a number of times, and if we did not know better, we would picture Indians as cutthroats, despoilers of white women, thieves, and less than noble people.

Prejudice. Prejudices are *faulty, inflexible, negative attitudes an individual has about another individual or group of people.*[24] Although we can hold positive prejudices as well as negative ones toward objects and people, most prejudices are negative, and we will treat them as such here.

Prejudices are also *faulty,* because they represent generalizations without a factual basis. They are judgments made on the basis of insufficient evidence. Because they are irreversible in the face of contrary evidence, they are *inflexible.* Prejudiced people make judgments grounded in insufficient or inadequate evidence, and they will not alter their judgments when confronted by opposing facts.

For our purposes, prejudices are always *directed toward a person or group of people.* We can be prejudiced toward objects, too, but communication concerns people and the definition reflects that bias.

Prejudice takes many forms of expression. These are usually classified into three categories: verbal abuse, discrimination, and violence.

1. *Verbal abuse* is the mildest, manifested in ethnic jokes ("How many Cubans does it take to screw in a light bulb? Three — one to screw it in and two to explain to him why he's screwing it in"), name-calling (Dago, Pole, Hebe, Jap, Chink, Whitey, Hun, Katonk), and derisive talk ("I can't tell one white face from another; they all look alike to me" said the Egyptian).

2. *Discrimination* is the most frequent form of prejudice. It occurs when the group in power denies out-groups equality of treatment. Out-groups may be denied equal housing, health, protection, education, pay; freedom of movement, of religion, of residence; and peaceful association.

3. *Violence is* the severest form of prejudice. Fist fights, gang fights, vandalism, and riots are kinds of violence erupting because of prolonged discrimination against a group of people.

Social Institutions

To deal with the business of living with other people, a number of social institutions were invented and developed. We focus on the ones most responsible for our growth and the ones that most influence our lives: the family, school, religion, politics, and economics. Each functions in every culture, and each affects the way we communicate, in our own culture and with people in other cultures.

The Family

Families are the backbone of every culture. The two primary types are the *nuclear* family (a married couple and their children) and the *extended* family (the nuclear family and other relatives). Additional forms are single-parent households and households wherein a married couple is temporarily sharing living quarters with relatives. Unmarried couples with their children constitute another family relationship. In other cultures other family relationships are found. In India the wives of the Nayar live with their mothers instead of their husbands. In the Israeli kibbutz children are reared apart from their parents.

The family is important to a culture as the place of biological and social reproduction. Children are born in the family and are prepared through family instruction to assume roles in the community. The family provides love and affection for family members and offers innumerable services including child and health care, food service, shelter, education, and financial aid.

Although the family provides many of the same basic functions, worldwide, its structure changes according to culture. Marriage practices differ, for example, in form and mate selection. *Monogamy* (the marriage of one man and one woman) is most common. *Polygamy* (marriage to more than one partner of the same sex) is practiced in cultures where there is a shortage of males or females. *Polygyny* is the marriage of one man to two or more women, and *polyandry,* the marriage of one woman to several men, also occurs. Brothers sharing one wife is an example, and it happens when the brothers are too poor to afford separate households.

Most marriages are *endogamous,* between members of a certain race, religion, or social class.

Exogamous marriages, however, are on the increase, especially in pluralistic United States, where mixed marriages are commonplace. Many cultures permit their people to choose their own mates, yet in some the parents make the choice.[25]

Education

In our classrooms nowadays, we are apt to encounter field-independent learners and field-dependent learners. Though most Americans are *field-independent*, meaning that they function better as independent student achievers in competition with others, more and more are *field-dependent*, preferring to work closely with others in personal, conversational relationships. The latter include Filipino-Americans, Mexican-Americans, Thai, Vietnamese, and other minority groups.

Teaching methods vary around the world, encompassing some fifty or more. In *postfigurative* instruction, which characterizes most literate societies, an older person teaches younger, less experienced and less knowledgeable students. A few cultures follow *cofigurative* learning patterns, in which peers teach peers. Ancient Hawaiians followed this pattern. In *prefigurative* learning, gaining popularity in the Western world, older people are taught by instructors considerably younger than they are.

Nearly all American schools practice *out-of-context* learning. Students learn a body of knowledge in school that is applied out of school at a later time and place. We are taught intercultural communication in the classroom; someday we will apply that instruction in a multicultural setting. If we were taught in a real-life setting, we would be engaging in *in-context* learning, not popular in Western culture but more commonplace in nonindustrialized settings where family experts teach the children to hunt, cook, fish, sew, or whatever in the actual setting — the kitchen, field, stream. In-context instruction does take place in the United States on the job, when old-timers teach newcomers how to do a specific task.

Classroom interaction varies from culture to culture. Some cultures permit lots of talking and question-asking. Others prohibit all talking, and only the teacher talks, as in Vietnamese classes. Japanese students busily take notes while the teacher lectures. The Israeli kibbutz is noisy, and the students are interactive. Algerian students are highly critical and often debate the teacher. Mexican students are tightly controlled and learn in an authoritarian atmosphere. Italian classrooms permit lots of touching between teacher and students. In American classes, teachers who touch could be in trouble. Chinese classrooms reflect the Buddhist tradition that knowledge, truth, and wisdom come to those who allow the spirit to enter through silence.

Nothing about education is absolute. Every aspect results from cultural choice — who should be educated, how, when, in what subjects, and for what purposes. Students entering foreign classes to study often bring a naively ethnocentric attitudes and expectations. They err when they judge the new learning situation against what they learned at home. Differences should be expected as they surely will appear.[26] Figure 12.3 graphically depicts the number of students from abroad in American universities.

Religion

Religion is a strong force in intercultural communication. It is a source of personal beliefs and a powerful social force, a pervasive factor in establishing cultural patterns. The personal side of religion deals with moral values and attitudes, affecting our behavior. The decision to cheat on a test, for instance, is a personal choice that can be guided by our religious beliefs.

Religion also has a social side. One of the ten commandments, "Thou shalt not steal," is a moral principle with far-reaching implications. Religious beliefs in the ownership of property have provided moral justification for laws against stealing and have supported the actions of police forces world-wide. Religion is a social institution made up of numerous churches, temples, and community organizations, each with its customs, loyalties, and hierarchies. Many help the young, care for the old, look after the sick, and give aid to victims of natural disasters.

The primary purpose of religion is to give meaning to human existence. To do so, religions created a world view, or definition of reality, described in Chapter 4 as concerned with ontological matters such as God, humanity, lower forms of life, inanimate objects, supernatural beings, nature, and other matters relating humans to one another and to the world around them. In our previous explanation, we noted that cultures do not share the same world view: variations are many. Eastern and Western perspectives show the major distinctions.[27]

Political Institutions

When we communicate interculturally, we meet people with different backgrounds — different religious, educational, and family backgrounds. We also meet people from different political orientations. Immigrants to the United States may come from democracies such as those in northern Europe or Japan. More likely, though, they will be running away from authoritarian or totalitarian regimes, the other two major political associations.

1. *Authoritarian* states usually are ruled by a strongman or a small elite. A few are dictatorships led by

Intercultural Communication

39,530	China
36,678	Japan
33,417	Taiwan
28,935	India
23,229	Korea
18,339	Canada
13,448	Malaysia
12,633	Hong Kong
9,373	Indonesia
7,743	Pakistan

Top ten countries of origin

"1991: 407,530 Foreign Students from 193 Countries Attended Universities in the U.S.A.," *Time*, April 13, 1992.

Figure 12.3. Number of students from abroad in U.S. universities, 1991.

someone who seized illegitimate power. Most are oligarchies ruled by an aristocratic, bureaucratic, or military group that also seized power. The group stays in power through coercion, suppressing dissent of all sorts.

2. In *totalitarian* states the government controls all social institutions. The state governs every aspect of life: the family, religion, education, employment, and values. A single party run by a usually self-appointed leader holds the power over the people. An elaborate bureaucracy enforces total domination over people's minds and bodies. Individual liberties are suppressed, and conformity is enforced through propaganda and terror. The former Union of Soviet Socialistic Republics (USSR) is the classic example.

3. *Democracies* are rare, largely found in industrial countries in western Europe and North America, as well as Japan. A literate, urban population and a stable middle class seem to be necessary for a democracy. Special-interest politics with a decline in political party strength and an erosion in government authority can cause a weakened democracy.[28]

In our contacts with people from foreign countries, we will encounter individuals representing authoritarian and totalitarian governments. Depending upon the type of regime from which they came, they probably will be more reserved, a little less open in their communication, perhaps fearful of government agents listening in.

Economic Institutions

Economic systems vary from culture to culture. Most use a form of monetary exchange: dollars, pounds, marks, yen, francs, lira, pesos, won, shekels, baht, dinar, dong, among them. In parts of New Guinea the sweet potato is used. Many countries practice swapping (you clean my teeth, and I'll clean your cesspool).

The most important economic facet world-wide is people's desire to improve their living conditions. Many countries with a small industrial base have few jobs for their citizens, forcing them to move elsewhere for work. Many emigrated to western Europe and North America to find work and, when times were good, Filipino, Malaysian, Indian, Jordanian, Pakistani, and other immigrants were welcome. They worked cheaply and did menial jobs most natives would not touch. When economic conditions worsened, they were told to go home, but they were not invited back to their native countries. They were no longer needed or wanted back home. Many gave up their citizenship to go to the adopted land, and were forced to remain as wards of the adopted state, supported by welfare. Discrimination and, in a few cases, violence resulted for these people who were not welcome in their adopted land and not welcome to return home.

SUMMARY

In a multicultural nation like the United States, it is vital that we be prepared to meet and deal with cultural dissimilarities in communication situations. Talking with people from different racial and ethnic groups is normative for virtually all Americans except perhaps those living in the most isolated, rural areas of the nation. The rest of us can anticipate frequent intercultural contact, depending on what we do and where we live.

Culture consists of the artifacts, sociofacts, and mentifacts made by humans. Culture for us is everything not biological, and it is learned, shared, adaptive, and changeable. Intercultural communication is communication between persons from different cultures.

Five dimensions of cultural variation are: individualism/collectivism, masculinity/femininity, contact/noncontact, high/low power distance, and high/low context. Cultural variables include those that are part of our personal orientation system, specifically beliefs, attitudes, needs, and values (explained in previous chapters). Ethnocentric behavior, stereotyping, and prejudice play large roles in intercultural interaction. The family, education, religion, political institutions, and economic factors also impact on intercultural communication.

The United States, a pluralistic country, is composed of many cultures. The macroculture is the universal or national culture shared by many citizens. Its base is Anglo-Saxon, stemming from political and social institutions influenced by western European tradition. These institutions affect most aspects of our lives, and they provide the framework for the traits and values of much of the nation's culture. Within the macroculture are many microcultures. Most share the political and social institutions of the macroculture, yet they have distinctive cultural patterns of their own. We are a part of several of these microcultures, and they have considerable influence on our communicative behavior.

13

The Interview

The interview, we learned in Chapter 3, is a form of interpersonal communication involving two parties: interviewer and interviewee. The two parties, which can consist of any number of persons, meet to fill a predetermined purpose. They can meet to gather information, as in surveys, polls, police investigations, newspaper and television interviews, or to discuss employment opportunities, or to sell and buy products, or to appraise work performance, among other possibilities. In fulfilling their purpose, the interviewer and the interviewee rely on questions and answers, not discussion or speech-making.

This chapter focuses on the methods and techniques of interviewing, covering the topics of: preparing for an interview, questioning, organizing the interview, evaluating interview performance, and being an interviewee. It is a "how-to-do-it" chapter with practical information on conducting interviews of all sorts.

PREPARING FOR AN INTERVIEW

Both interviewer and interviewee will profit from preparation. How much time they should devote to preparation depends upon the type of interview. A pollster wanting to gather quantities of data will have to prepare carefully. A student who desires to learn more about the next assignment probably can think through the necessary questions to ask on the way to the teacher's office.

The procedure outlined next covers the eight steps necessary to prepare for the most extensive interview. This is the procedure the pollster should follow in gathering large amounts of data. The student who wants more information about the next assignment should keep the procedure in mind and use the steps that are most useful in planning his or her interview.

Determining the Purpose

The first step in preparing for an interview is to determine its general purpose and then to narrow down that purpose to a more specific goal. Six general purposes, roughly corresponding to the types of interviews, are met through the interviewing process:[1]

1. Applying for a job. The interviewer questions the applicant (the interviewee) about his or her qualifications; the applicant questions the interviewer about the job.

2. Appraising performance. The interviewer evaluates the interviewee's job performance, issues a reprimand, or asks about a grievance or complaint.

3. Persuading. The interviewer influences the interviewee to buy a product, idea, or service.

4. Counseling. The interviewer allows the interviewee to explore various alternatives to solving a personal problem.

5. Gathering information. The interviewer obtains information from the interviewee, such as in opinion polling, police interrogating, market researching, journalistic news gathering.

Persuasive interviews involve buying products, ideas, or services.

6. Solving problems. Interviewer and interviewee meet to find a solution to a mutual problem.

With the general purpose in mind, the interviewer next determines a more specific goal, one directly related to the subject of the interview. For example, the employment interviewer knows the general purpose: to interview job applicants. Next, the interviewer has to determine what job is to be filled and what qualifications are needed on the job. The interviewer narrows down the subject matter of the interview to the specific goal. A television reporter who plans to interview a local expert on traffic has the general purpose of gathering information about traffic. With only a couple of minutes of air time available, the reporter must get specific. What should the interviewer ask about traffic? The answer will determine the course of the interview.

Researching the Subject

This step entails doing background research on the specific subject of the interview and preparing an interview agenda, a list of topics to be covered.[2] For example, the employment interviewer has determined that the specific goal of the interview is to hire someone to do yard work. At this stage, the interviewer has to find answers to questions such as: What qualifications are necessary? When and where does the person work? How much will the person earn? What benefits does the person receive? The interviewer will have to do research to discover the answers.

With the answers in mind, the interviewer prepares an agenda consisting of the specific content areas to be explored in the interview. The employment interviewer's agenda might contain these topics: (a) explain duties and benefits of the job; (b) describe qualifications needed to perform the job; (c) question applicant about his or her qualifications.

Selecting Respondents

To select respondents, the interviewer determines who should be interviewed. The television reporter planning to cover the local traffic situation has to find an interviewee, preferably someone who is an expert on the matter.

Structuring the Interview

The fourth step in preparing for an interview is to decide upon an overall design or structure. The structure is influenced by the purpose of the interview and the persons being interviewed. What is the purpose? Who are the interviewees? What do they know about the subject of the interview? What are their attitudes or opinions? Will the subject be threatening to them? What is their level of motivation?

The interviewees, along with the interview's purpose, have to be considered. Some individuals may not be motivated to talk, and others might be quite eager to be interviewed. Two principal ways of structuring — directive and nondirective — take into account both the interviewees and the purpose.

We can portray the two structures as falling on opposite ends of a continuum with varying degrees of the two appearing in between. At one end is the *directive* structure; at the other, the *nondirective*, as depicted in Figure 13.1.

The *directive* design is most useful whenever an interviewer has to obtain relatively large amounts of information. It calls for a highly structured interview, with the interviewer in full control. The interviewer knows exactly where to go and what to accomplish. Opinion poll takers use this design when they gather data from vast numbers of people. The wording and sequence of the questions are predetermined, and the same questions are asked of the interviewees in exactly the same way. Everything is standardized.

The *nondirective* interview permits interviewees to respond in any manner, wherever their thoughts take them. The interviewees talk about whatever is on their mind with reference to the subject matter. Even though it is unstructured, however, it is not uncontrolled. The interviewer concentrates his or her efforts on encouraging the interviewee to speak

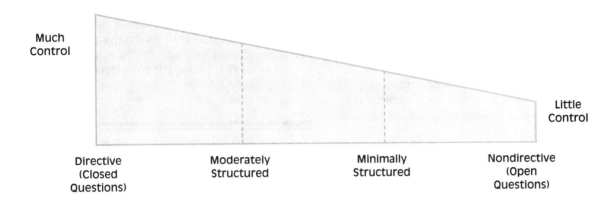

Figure 13.1. Types of interview structures.

freely, but within the time constraints and on the subject. The interviewer functions as an empathic listener and does not evaluate the interviewee's remarks until the interviewee's intended meaning is clear.[3]

The nondirective structure is most useful in interviews involving complaints, grievances, appraisals, problem solving, and counseling. Interviews initiated by the interviewee, such as medical interviews, also can be handled nondirectively, especially when the interviewer knows little about the interviewee or has little or no time to prepare.[4]

In between the directive and nondirective ends of the design continuum are structures varying in control and freedom. Near the directive end of the continuum is the *moderately structured interview,* allowing more freedom on the interviewee's part to answer questions. The *minimally structured interview* is near the nondirective end. There are no predetermined questions; the interviewer formulates the questions on-the-spot, using a list of topics as a guide.

Developing Questions

Interviewing depends heavily upon questions, and in this step the interviewer prepares a set of questions to ask, if the interview is directive or moderately structured. In nondirective interviews the interviewer comes up with the questions during the interview. The various types of questions are considered in a forthcoming section.

Planning the Physical Environment

The environment in which an interview is held contributes to the overall outcome of the interview. As explained in Chapter 9, "Nonverbal Communication," factors in the physical setting of a communicative act affect the talk taking place. Noise, temperature, light, seating arrangements, and space have an influence. For example, the work setting creates a more formal, businesslike atmosphere; a more neutral environment decreases work-related pressures. Conferring with an instructor in the instructor's office usually affords privacy, but that setting might be too formal for a frank discussion. A neutral area such as the student union, cafeteria, or coffee house may permit more freedom of expression.

Conducting an interview in the interviewee's home is an appropriate place for interviews of the information-gathering and persuasive types. If the family is present, however, the home may not provide sufficient privacy because family members may interrupt, join in, or otherwise influence the

The physical environment contributes to the success of an interview.

responses. Supervisor/employee interviews frequently take place in the boss's office, a location that tends to inhibit employee participation. Another, more neutral location may be better, especially in circumstances of employee appraisal. Noise and other forms of interruption (ringing telephones, clattering typewriters, loud talk) disrupt thought patterns and concentration, which could destroy the mood the interviewer is trying to create. Whatever location is selected, the choice should be private, comfortable, attractive, and noise-free, if possible.

Deciding on the Time

The time of day to conduct the interview should be thought through, as should the length of the interview. The main consideration is the availability of both the interviewer and the interviewee. Often the interviewer must adjust his or her schedule to accommodate the interviewee, and the interviewer must allow enough time to cover the subject.

Occasionally the goals of the interview are too extensive to achieve in a single meeting. In those cases, several meetings may have to be scheduled. Of course, everyone has certain routines and activities that could conflict with participation in an interview. For example, home interviews should avoid meal hours, Monday night TV football games, and the peak hours for housekeeping chores.

Pretesting the Interview Format

Over the years we have conducted several dozen international, information-gathering interviews. Before actually conducting the interviews (normally directive types with predetermined questions), we pretested them on small groups of people, in which we tried to include experts in the subject matter, grammarians, and individuals with knowledge about our type of research. The pretesting helped us clear

Steps in preparing for an interview:

1. Determine the purpose.
2. Research the subject.
3. Select respondents.
4. Structure the interview.
5. Prepare questions
6. Plan the physical environment.
7. Decide on time.
8. Pretest the interview format.

up any inaccuracies that may have biased the results. In the same manner, with in-person interviews, we practiced a few times, fixing the procedures firmly in mind. In like fashion, when time is available, the interviewer should run through a trial interview or two to test the interview's format.

QUESTIONING

Questions are fundamental to most interviews. Whether the interviewer is choosing a new employee, gathering information, selling a product, or appraising an employee's performance, questions have to be formulated and asked. *Using questions effectively is an important communication skill.*[5] Anybody can ask questions. Not much skill is required to do so. But not everybody can ask questions that elicit worthwhile answers. In this section we review the methods and procedures for asking effective questions.

Framing Questions

To maximize the quality of interviewee responses, the questions must be phrased appropriately. Otherwise the responses may lack completeness or honesty.[6] When framing questions, five points should be kept in mind.

1. *The language should be understandable to the interviewee.* The questions should aim toward a shared meaning between the interviewer and interviewee. Hence, the language must reflect a common frame of reference. This requires the language of the questions to be at the language level of the interviewee, not above or below.

2. *The questions must be relevant to the interview's purpose.* If the interviewer's purpose is to find out the interviewee's qualifications for a particular job, the questions should be directed to discovering what the person's qualifications are.

3. *The questions must deal with the interviewee's knowledge level on the subject.* If the interviewee is not knowledgeable about the subject or does not possess the information a specific question requests, the interviewee's answers will likely be meaningless. The interviewer, therefore, must take care in choosing who to interrogate.

4. *The questions should be simple and clear, and only one question should be asked at a time.* The interviewer should avoid complex or wordy questions, because they may confuse or frustrate the interviewee.

5. *The questions should be nonthreatening.* Many interviewees have trouble dealing with perceived threats. Questions must be phrased, therefore, to reduce the perception of threat. Rather than asking a student, for example, what he or she thinks of the instructor, a department chairperson who is evaluating the instructor might frame the question to the students more indirectly: How do the students in the class feel about the instructor's teaching style?[7]

Types of Questions

Questions are of nine types. Each has a specific purpose and a particular use in interviews. Three — open, closed, and leading — are *primary* questions because they introduce new topic areas. Six are *secondary* questions, those that probe a topic more deeply: extension, echo, confrontation, direct/indirect, summary, and repetition.

Open Questions

Broad and unstructured, open questions ask about the subject in a general way. They allow the interviewee to say as much as he or she pleases. Examples are: What's the weather in Honolulu like this time of the year? Why did you marry her? What do you think is the cause of your problem? What happens in inflation?

Open questions can vary in the broadness of their scope so that it is possible to create a series of open questions that successively narrow the subject matter. The following questions move from a very general to a very limited field of inquiry: What is the problem? What are its causes? What are its effects? What has been done to solve the problem? What is the best solution to the problem? Using a series of questions like this, the interviewer can lead the interviewee through a complete analysis of a single subject.

Ideally, open questions fit the nondirective type of interview. They tend to be easy to answer and pose little ego threat. They permit the interviewee considerable freedom in answering, encouraging the respondent to say what he or she wishes. In doing so, the interviewee reveals the depth of his or her knowledge on the subject matter.

Closed Questions

By the nature of closed questions, the interviewee is limited to an answer of just a few words. Therefore, closed questions are ideal for the directive type of interview. The restrictive quality of closed questions is seen in three variations: identification, selection, and yes/no.

1. The *identification* variation calls for naming something such as a person, place, thing, group, time, or number. The question begins with *who,*

TYPES OF QUESTIONS

Examples of primary questions appear below. Write-in the type (open, closed, leading) in the blank space. The answers are on page 243.

1. You don't believe in a silly thing like ghosts, do you? _____

2. Who do you think will win the batting title this year? _____

3. What foods do you prefer? _____

4. What do you like best, apples or oranges? _____

5. Milk is loaded with fat. You don't drink it, do you? _____

6. How did the Civil War start? _____

7. What caused the 1992 Chicago flood? _____

8. I like Eisenhower. He was a great president, wasn't he? _____

9. What happened to your boyfriend? _____

10. Are you going to the dance tomorrow? _____

Be prepared to defend your answers.

what, where, when or *how many*, as in: Who are you? What time is it? Where were you born? Each question requires only a word or two in reply.

2. The *selection* type forces the respondent to choose one of two or more answers. Examples are: In what age group do you fit: 18–21 years, 22–25 years, 26–30 years? How often do you brush your teeth: once a day, twice a day, three times a day? Do you prefer blondes or brunettes?

3. The *yes/no* variation requires either a "yes" or a "no" answer: Do you smoke? Are you a professor? Are you going to work today?

Leading Questions

Leading questions indicate that the answer is to be given in either explicit or implicit fashion. They direct the interviewee to the answer the interviewer wants. A question worded neutrally is: How do you feel about the President's handling of the topic of inflation? A leading version is: You certainly don't favor the President's inadequate way of handling inflation, do you? The neutrality disappears in the latter version. The interviewee is led into the expected answer; the interviewee is supposed to answer in the negative, thereby agreeing with the interviewer, which is what the interviewer wants.

In the following cases, each question provides a tempting way to reply: You don't smoke, do you? Most smart people avoid cholesterol — don't you? Baseball is the grand old game, don't you think? The interviewee is led to the answer the interviewer desires. A contrary answer would seem contradictory, giving the impression that the interviewer does not know what he or she is talking about.

If the respondent is subordinate to the questioner, a contradiction is likely to be viewed as a serious matter. If the instructor says authoritatively, "Our textbook's authors are certainly brilliant, don't you agree?" the student, in the subordinate role, will agree or at least will give the matter careful thought before replying negatively.

Leading questions tend to distort or bias the reply. Therefore, they are a powerful force in interviewing. Unless the interviewee has considerable personal independence, the interviewer, through leading questions, can obtain answers confirming the interviewer's viewpoint, even though they may differ from the interviewee's true feelings.

Open, closed, and leading questions are primary questions. They introduce topics. The six secondary questions explained next are used to elicit more information about a topic introduced by primary questions. When answers are vague, incomplete, ambiguous, irrelevant, or inaccurate, secondary questions can probe more deeply into the interviewee's answer.

Extension Questions

The extension, or probe, can be used to obtain additional data. The interviewer can prod the interviewee into supplying more details. For example:

Question:	Who says people fear to speak?
Answer:	Studies say so.
Question (an extension):	What studies?

Echo Questions

Echo questions mirror or restate the respondent's reply, searching for more information. For example:

Question:	What studies?
Answer:	McCroskey and Richmond's.
Question (an echo)	McCroskey and Richmond?

Confrontation Questions

This type of question checks what the respondent says; at the same time, it creates a feeling of stress or anxiety in the respondent. The respondent seems to be inconsistent or lying and the questioner confronts the respondent with the inconsistency or lie. Examples are:

Yesterday you said she had blue eyes. Today you're not sure. Are they blue or aren't they?

In your earlier testimony you said McCroskey and Richmond. Now you say Gorham and Davis. Who are the authors of the studies you know so much about?

Direct and Indirect Questions

Direct and indirect questions are considered together because they are exact opposites. With direct questions, interviewers come right out and ask what they want to know. With indirect questions, interviewers probe in a roundabout way, trying not to be threatening. An example of a direct question is: When people are apprehensive, you said they are impacted negatively. What do you mean — impacted negatively? The same question, stated indirectly, is: If I understood you correctly, you seem to suggest that apprehension has a strong impact on people. Is this something disagreeable?

Summary Questions

Summary questions recap what was said, to confirm it. An example is: Am I correct? You did say the studies of McCroskey and Richmond, didn't you? And then you said the studies of Gorham and Davis. Am I not correct?

Repetition Questions

When using this type of question, the questioner repeats a question usually because the answer was vague, evasive, or incomplete. An example is: I don't believe you answered the question. I asked "Why did it happen?"[8]

The interview is built around primary questions, but during the actual interview, secondary questions are asked as needed. If the interviewee does not answer a primary question to the interviewer's satisfaction, secondary questions are used to explore the answer further.

The Questioning Sequence

Questions usually are interconnected, not only primary with secondary questions but also primary with other primary questions. These interconnections form a sequence for the entire interview or sequences within topics and subtopics.[9] Five sequence options are considered here: funnel, inverted funnel, yes-response, who/what/where/when/why, and tunnel sequences.

The Funnel Sequence

The funnel sequence moves from the general to the specific. It starts with broad, general questions and advances to succeedingly narrow and more specific questions, like water going through a funnel. Open questions begin the sequence, and closed questions end it. Here is an example:

1. In your own words, would you please tell us what happened?

2. How much of this did you see?

3. What was each person doing?

4. What were you doing?

5. Do you think this could happen again?

The series begins with an open question, which permits the respondent to say as much as he or she wishes. The next questions are increasingly restricted. In this way, the content is narrowed to the interviewer's objective.

One of the major purposes of the funnel sequence is to prevent early questions from conditioning or biasing the responses of those that come later. The funnel sequence enables the interviewer to maintain a good relationship with the respondent, and it helps to motivate the respondent to communicate. In the early stages the interviewee can say all that is salient for him or her.

The Inverted Funnel Sequence

The funnel is inverted in this sequence. It starts with specific questions and concludes with the most general questions. An example is:

1. Do you think anyone will hit four home runs in a World Series again?

2. How did you feel when you hit the fourth?

3. How about the people around you?

4. Would you recap the whole experience for us?

The inverted sequence is especially appropriate for subjects in which the respondent is without strong feelings or on which the respondent has not formulated a point of view. In cases like this, it helps the respondent think through a topic and arrive at a viewpoint during the interview itself. In the example, the interviewee, just off the playing field after hitting the four homers, probably had little opportunity to reflect on what he had accomplished. The interviewer helped him by leading off

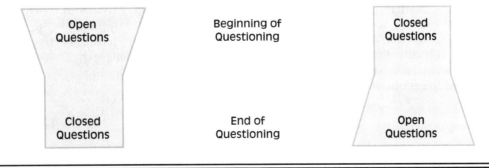

Question sequence: Funnel and Inverted Funnel

Open Questions   Beginning of Questioning   Closed Questions

Closed Questions   End of Questioning   Open Questions

with the specific question, which could be answered in a few words, and then moved toward increasingly more general questions. As the player moved through the sequence, he had time to analyze his feelings about the experience of hitting four home runs and become prepared mentally to deal with the final question.[10]

The Yes-Response Sequence

The yes-response sequence uses a series of leading questions formulated so the interviewee has to agree with what is asked. A string of simple questions, all requiring "yes" answers, leads the respondent to the key question, to which the interviewer also wants a "yes" answer. The key question usually covers a topic the interviewee is undecided about or would be against if questioned specifically about it. The interviewer's strategy, thus, is to lead the respondent to answer in the way the interviewer wants.

In the following example, the interviewer asks a series of questions calling for "yes" answers. The respondent gets into the habit of replying affirmatively and finds himself or herself trapped into a final "yes" answer.

Questioner: You do believe you should get paid a wage worthy of the work you do, don't you?

Respondent: Yes, I do.

Questioner: You would like to work in agreeable surroundings, wouldn't you?

Respondent: By all means, yes.

Questioner: You would like free parking privileges, wouldn't you?

Respondent: Certainly. I don't want to have to pay to park.

Questioner: You want a paid vacation, don't you?

Respondent: Of course. Yes.

Questioner: Then you obviously will vote for the new union contract, won't you?

Respondent: Well, uh, I guess so.

After responding "yes" a few times, especially to questions representing matters vital to the respondent, responding negatively to the key question about an issue the respondent may have been uncertain about is more difficult. Once the respondent replies in the affirmative, he or she has made a commitment that is hard to get out of.[11]

The Who/What/Where/When/Why Sequence

Often called the "journalistic sequence," this pattern consists of a series of questions that seek

Questioning sequences:
Yes, Who/What/Where, Tunnel

YES! — Definitely
YES! — Positively
YES! — Sounds great
YES! — I agree
YES! — I suppose so

Who? What? Where? When? Why? How? Which?

Questions strung together like a string of beads — all much alike

answers to questions such as: Who did it? What happened? Where? When was it done? What was the motive? Why was it done? Interviewers such as investigative reporters and police interrogators obtain the basic facts using this sequence of questions.[12]

The Tunnel Sequence

A tunnel sequence consists of a series of similar questions, either open or closed. It has value in simple, informational interviews in which the interviewer is interested in the interviewee's spontaneous reactions or when easily quantifiable data are desired. It is not useful for in-depth probing or persuasive situations. The following is an example of a tunnel sequence an employment interviewer might use to determine the qualifications of a person for a particular job, in this case, a gardener:

Have you had gardening experience in any of the following areas:

1. Mowing grass with power mowers, push types and tractor-pulled?
2. Applying fertilizer, weed-control agents, insect repellants?
3. Thatch build-up?
4. Grafting?
5. Seeding lawns?
6. Plant care?
7. Tree trimming?
8. Mulching?

9. Sprinkler system construction?
10. Irrigation?

The questions cover a list of qualifications, strung together like a string of beads. This, by the way, is another name for the tunnel sequence — the "string-of-beads."[13]

ORGANIZING THE INTERVIEW

An interview has three parts — opening, body, and closing — each of which has essential functions. The three parts constitute an interview's organization. Ideally, the pattern of development should reflect a consistent point of view on the subject of the interview and clarify the relationship among the ideas.

The Opening

The opening of the interview represents the initial face-to-face contact between the two parties. It is important because it sets the tone for the rest of the interview. If the parties start off feeling hostile, that feeling will affect the balance of the interview. Thus, the opening determines whether the mood of the parties for continued interaction will be receptive.[14] Three vital functions — establish rapport, introduce the purpose, and motivate the interviewee — are performed in the opening.

Establishing Rapport

Rapport comes when the two parties establish trust and goodwill. It begins with the way each greets the other, and through self-introductions if the two have not met before. Nonverbal immediacy behaviors accompany the verbalizations. A firm handshake, eye contact, smile, and friendly voice are examples of these behaviors.

The rapport-building process continues with a period of *phatic communion,* which might consist of discussing the latest news, weather, or gossip. The small talk should be limited time-wise, however. The session has another purpose, so the interviewer should get on with the business at hand.

Introducing the Purpose

The interviewer next explains the purpose and format of the interview. Knowing the "why" and "what" of the interview helps to reduce anxiety and increase rapport. As a result, the interviewee will be more able to see the interview as a whole and as a sequence of several segments, giving a sense of the direction the interview will take.

Motivating the Interviewee

The interviewer can tap two forms of motivation: internal and external. *Internal motivation* revolves around the pleasure the interviewee can obtain from the interaction. To elicit this motivating factor, the interviewer should try to satisfy the interviewee's needs for acceptance, security, and self-esteem. In providing a climate for internal motivation, the interviewer listens empathically, asks questions in a nonthreatening manner, and responds to the interviewee in a nonevaluative way.

External motivation stems from the interviewee's perception that the interview will be profitable. The interviewee sees the interview as a way to get something desirable: a better job, a salary increase, a solution to a worrisome problem, mention in the newspaper, and so forth.[15]

The triple task of building rapport, introducing the purpose, and motivating the interviewee may seem like a lot to accomplish during the opening minutes, but usually this is not the case. Rapport and motivation can be combined in a statement or two taking a few seconds, and the purpose statement likewise can take only a few brief moments. These two sample openings fulfill the three functions in a few words:

> Hello! I'm Jill Baxter, an economics major at the university. I'm gathering opinions for Senator Jones on what is causing unemployment locally. She needs your help to be able to attack the problem.

> Hi, Joe! I'm pleased you dropped in! Can you give me a few moments of help with a problem I'm having?

The Body

The body is the most significant part of the interview; it contains the main content. It is structured according to one of the designs mentioned earlier: directive, moderately directive, minimally directive, nondirective. The questions follow one of the questioning sequences also noted previously: funnel, inverted funnel, yes-response, who/what/where/when/why, tunnel sequences. In the body of the interview, the questions are asked and the responses are given. The body encompasses any discussion about the subject matter beyond what comes with the questioning. Because the bulk of the interview is devoted to the body, it obviously consumes the most time, perhaps all of the time except for short opening and closing statements.[16]

The Closing

The closing period ends the face-to-face relationship between the two parties. It should not be taken lightly, as it serves two major functions: to summarize the substantive parts of the interview and to suggest future accessibility. Like the other parts of the interview, the closing moments should be planned in advance.

Summarizing

In the summary the interviewer reviews what transpired during the interview, recapitulating the main points and checking these with the interviewee for verification. If discrepancies exist, they can be cleared up before adjourning. The summary has value because it reminds both parties of what was covered. The so-called law of recency may operate also: The only points we will remember from a meeting are the ones talked about last.

Considering the Future

The closing also should contain statements about what will happen next: future accessibility. Are new meetings in order? Will a report be forthcoming? Will the interviewer be available on call? Frequently this final orientation is lacking, leaving the interviewee wondering what will happen next. Will there be a follow-up of some sort? During the closing, the next steps, if any, should be clearly understood.

The summary and statements about the future should leave a positive impression on both parties. Each should express appreciation for the other's contributions, time, and cooperation. To end in a manner that will keep the relationship sound and productive is useful.[17]

A DUET, WITH EQUAL PARTS

"An interview is not a glorified quiz...a mere question and answer session.

A true interview . . . is a locking together of two . . . personalities. There is give and take on both sides. There is, if not mutual admiration or mutual respect, at least mutual recognition. The [district attorney] skilled in the art of cross-examination performs a verbal ballet sequence with the witness, in which both parties are equally important. The same with the experienced police officer. He knows the successful interview is not too far removed from a duet. A duet with equal parts. With point and counterpoint, melody and descant, harmonies and cross-harmonies. Sometimes the interviewer is on the ascendant. Sometimes the interviewee . . ."

From *Brainwash* by John Wainwright (New York: St. Martin's Press, 1979).

EVALUATING THE INTERVIEW

What went well in the interview, and what did not? The parts that went well can be continued; those that went poorly should be corrected in future interviews. The nature of the evaluation varies with the type of interview, but usually three steps — review, criticism, and correction — are involved.

1. *Review.* If the interview was recorded, listening to the tape will be helpful. A far better use of the tape, however, is to have expert interviewers review it and suggest what can be improved.[18] If it was not recorded, the interviewer should review his or her notes and think through what took place.

2. *Criticism.* The best criticism comes from experts. If one or two are available, the interviewer would do well to talk with them about what transpired. In appraising the interview, attention should be given to how well it fulfilled the purpose, how effectively the process fit the interview structure, how the question sequence worked, how well the opening and closing statements met the requirements, whether the interviewer listened empathically, and how successful the overall interaction was between the two parties.

3. *Correction.* If the interviewer encountered any problems, experts can provide suggestions about what to do in future interviews. Otherwise the interviewer has to rely on his or her own best judgment.

BEING AN INTERVIEWEE

Our focus to this point has been largely on the interviewer. We shift now to the interviewee and what that individual can do to participate more successfully.

To be successful in the interviewee role, interviewees must approach the situation with the attitude that they are not there merely to answer questions and to be passive participants. Rather, they are present as active participants with as much at stake as, or more than, the interviewer. In employment interviews, for example, a job might be at stake, so interviewees will want to sell themselves and at the same time find out how the company and the job will fit their needs. In an appraisal interview, interviewees should be willing to accept suggestions for improvement, but at the same time they want to protect their point of view. In a sales interview, interviewees should find out how the product will meet their special desires, and should learn as

A SAMPLE INTERVIEW

Counseling a Student for Graduate School

Opening

Good morning, Melanie. I'm Ruth Roberts, a graduate school advisor here at the university. I understand you're interested in attending graduate school in speech communication and want some guidance. Won't you be seated? I'll ask you questions that should make you think about yourself and about what you need to consider regarding grad school.

Body (questions arranged in a tunnel sequence)

Do you like to make your own decisions and try out new ideas?

Do you enjoy being challenged and do you thrive on competition?

Have you ever thought seriously about your personality? Does it lend itself favorably to several more years of school?

Do you have willpower and discipline to get things done on time and plan ahead?

Do you like to work? Do you understand that grad school will make you work hard and long, even on holidays and weekends?

Can you shoulder responsibility and juggle details without falling apart?

Do you realize you will not be able to satisfy all of your instructors all of the time even though they may expect you to?

Do you realize that you don't know everything about speech communication and that there are many new ideas to learn?

Can you take advice?

Are you adaptable? Can you change your methods of doing things if required?

Do you have common sense?

Do you have the financial support to attend grad school? Can you get financial help from others to cover hidden costs?

Do you realize your standard of living may be lowered until you graduate?

Do you understand that outside employment is forbidden?

Do you realize that 90 percent of grad school dropouts are due to poor management of personal time and energy?

Do you have the requisite undergraduate courses?

Do you possess the necessary writing, speaking, computing skills?

Are you aware of the advantages of graduating from college and going to work without pursuing the advanced degree?

Why do you want an advanced degree? Do you have future plans the degree will serve?

Are you able to accept the impartial thinking and judgments of fellow students?

Are you aware that you may fail?

Closing

Well, Melanie, you've answered most of the questions, but you may want to think some more about a few. I've checked them off on this list, and you may want to take it along with you and reconsider your answers. The list should serve as a summary of what we covered. This office is open to you for whatever additional guidance you may wish. If you want, we can set up another appointment right now. Or, if you'd rather think over our conversation first, you can arrange a future visit at your convenience. Thank you for dropping in! I hope I've been of help to you.

---

much about it as possible. The attitude should be to put one's best foot forward, to speak and act with skill and confidence.

Usually people are more confident in interpersonal situations such as interviewing when they know what to expect. Some of the ambiguity can be eliminated through investigation and study. Interviewees should be familiar with the communication process and aware of the communicators' roles in the process. They should be aware of the influence of language and nonverbal behavior in communication and understand the effect of listening in interpersonal interactions. An interviewing situation involves interpersonal interaction. The knowledge presented so far in this text should be applied to all these aspects of interpersonal communication. Some common-sense suggestions for participating as interviewees — in interviews in general

and in employment interviews in particular — round out the chapter.

Participating in the Interview

Each interview and each interviewer is different from others in various ways. Therefore, the interviewee must adjust to each new situation as much as possible. Despite the difference in each interview situation, the following guidelines will be useful for most interviews.

General Impression

Interviewees can give the best possible impression by applying these suggestions:

1. *Prepare.* If the interviewee has time, he or she should prepare for the interview. Preparation

may consist of reading on the subject of the interview, talking over with friends the questions that might be asked, and trying to recall information previously learned on the subject.

2. *Arrive on time.* The interviewee should be on time. Keeping the interviewer waiting leaves a negative impression. Being late is frowned upon in the United States. The interviewee is better off being a few minutes early.

3. *Be alert and maintain eye contact.* In face, tone of voice, and posture, the interviewee should convey an attitude of interest. Disinterested or bored interviewees will not create a positive image. By looking at the interviewer, the interviewee displays self-confidence and poise, characteristics that help define an agreeable impression.

4. *Think before answering.* The interviewee should think before answering unanticipated questions. A pause in which to think is better than a hasty answer that may sound foolish or inaccurate. When the interviewee does not understand a question, he or she should ask the interviewer to paraphrase it to check the meaning.

5. *Listen empathically.* Before commenting, the interviewee should try to understand the interviewer. Many listeners are preoccupied with what they are going to say to the interviewer and, thus, do not give that person their full attention. In being empathic, the interviewee listens to understand, giving the impression of an interested person.

6. *Avoid undesirable behaviors.* The interviewee should avoid behaviors that will label him or her as an undesirable person by established standards. An undesirable person lies, shows a lack of interest, is belligerent, rude or impolite, insincere, evasive, indecisive, unclear, and oversells.

Appearance

Because appearance can be considered part of the general impression that interviewees create, it could have been covered in the previous section. Appearance is singled out here, however, to emphasize its significance in interviews, especially those that are formal, planned events, rather than spur-of-the-moment happenings.

By appearance, we mean appropriate dress and grooming. How a person dresses and grooms sends strong messages about self-image and attitude. A neat, clean appearance adds to a person's believability; a sloppy one detracts. Dirty-looking, unkempt, smelly people do not generate as much confidence as tidy people do. What is appropriate in one setting, however, may not be appropriate in another, so

the interviewee should check out, before appearing for an interview, what is proper.[20]

Nonverbal Behaviors

The interviewee's nonverbal behavior often speaks louder than words, so the interviewee must pay attention to facial expressions, eye contact, and body postures. The interviewee also must carefully attend to word choice, voice sound, and rate of speech, and minimize distracting mannerisms.[21]

Nonverbal behaviors that typically communicate interest and acceptance include a warm, inviting smile and good eye contact, a voice transmitting warmth and interest with the appropriate degree of volume for the setting, an outstretched arm or welcoming wave, a firm handshake, a relaxed posture leaning slightly toward the interviewer, a good rate of delivery and fluency in language, and enthusiasm. In contrast, nonverbal behaviors that tend to communicate disinterest in the proceedings include, among others, a cold, frowning facial expression, poor eye contact (downcast, staring, peering), sloppy attire, rigid posture, shifting body, mumbling, soft, cold voice, too much silence, too many "you knows," a cold, impersonal greeting, "fishy" handshake, and lack of enthusiasm.[22]

Assertiveness

The ability to express feelings honestly and to take charge of our rights responsibly is termed *assertiveness.* Assertive individuals are self-enhancing and expressive, and they feel good about themselves. They stand up for their rights. Interviewees who are assertive suggests that they are self-assured and have a healthy respect for the rights of others.

In sharp contrast to assertiveness are two other types of behavior: nonassertiveness (apprehension) and aggression. Nonassertive people are often

---

How we express our rights:

Aggressively
- Enhance self at others' expense
- Engage in conflict with others
- Make demands

Assertively
- Enhance self at no one's expense
- Stand up for own rights
- Feel good about self

Nonassertively/Apprehensively
- Deny self
- Be pushed around by others
- Be inhibited, shy, anxious

apprehensive in communication situations, deferring to others. Unable to voice their opinions and feelings, they come across as passive, inhibited, and anxious. Nonassertive interviewees are submissive participants, saying little and acting fearful.

At the other extreme, aggressive people are domineering, easily angered, and overly self-concerned. Aggressive interviewees have been known to be obnoxious if things are not going their way. They tend to blame others for their faults, practice name-calling, and do their best to dominate the interview.

Of the three types, assertiveness obviously is the preferred behavior. This is true not only in interviews but in all other forms of interpersonal communication as well.[23]

Participating in Employment Interviews

As we have discovered, interviews are of various types. We participate in many of these much more frequently than employment interviews. The subject of this section, the employment interview, is a relatively uncommon activity, occurring only a few times during the lifespan for most of us. Nevertheless, we have singled out the employment interview for special treatment because it represents an important event in our life. For students soon to enter the job market, it is a crucial activity. Being an effective interviewee may make the difference between a satisfying job and one that just kills time.

The following guidelines will be helpful for typical employment interviews.[24] Because each interview is different and employment practices vary from company to company, however, the guidelines should be adapted to fit the specific interview situation.

1. *Know when and where the interview will take place.* The interviewee should know the company's full name, location of the interview, time it will occur, and its anticipated duration.

2. *Know the interviewer's name and how to pronounce it properly.*

3. *Be familiar with the company.* The interviewee should find out as much as possible about the company: what it manufactures or sells, how long it has been established, the location of its branches or stores, how it has grown, its future growth possibilities, its principal officers, who owns it, and so forth. If the company is large, company publications may provide such information. Or the school library or student placement office may have the pertinent details.

4. *Know the job qualifications.* The interviewee should understand the job for which he or she is applying — what the job entails and what skills are necessary to do the work.

5. *Know what you can do.* Interviewers usually ask job seekers what they can do, because many jobs require specialized abilities or knowledge. If the job requires a specific skill, the interviewee should be able to perform it. Otherwise, why apply?

6. *Prepare a resume.* A resume is a concise summary of the applicant's qualifications, carefully prepared and neat. It is attached to a letter of application. The interviewee should check with the company to find out which of the various styles of resume is preferred.

7. *Anticipate questions and prepare answers.* Many employment interviews are predictable in that they follow a certain line of questioning. Six general areas of questioning are:

   a. *Job expectations:* what the applicant wants in a job, what kind of job he or she is looking for, and whether the applicant is likely to be content in the job applied for.

   b. *Academic background:* schools attended, degrees/certificates earned, grades received, subjects taken, extracurricular activities.

   c. *Knowledge of company:* why the applicant wants to work for this firm.

   d. *Work experience:* what sort of work the applicant has done before, if he or she liked it, what the person actually did in previous jobs, why the person quit, and if previous job employers provide references.

   e. *Career goals:* where the applicant sees himself or herself ten years from now, what kind of career the person expects with the company, what the applicant's immediate objectives are.

   f. *Strengths and weaknesses:* the applicant's areas of strength and areas of weakness.[25]

8. *Prepare questions to ask.* The interviewee should have questions in mind to ask during the interview. Some possibilities are:

   a. Does my resume contain anything that is not clear?

   b. Is the work to be done similar to anything I have done before?

   c. Are any of the extracurricular activities in which I took part of interest or potential use to the company?

   d. Will the job match my needs and strengths?

   e. The salary range for the position is $_____. Is that correct?

f. What is the exact nature of the work I would be expected to do if hired?

g. Does the company plan specific changes for the immediate future?

As a note of caution, the interviewee should not express undue interest or concern in salary, benefits, working conditions, and other matters related to personal advantages. The interviewer may infer that the benefits are of more concern than the job itself.

9. *Be properly attired, neat, and clean.* The interviewee should observe the suggestions presented previously about appearance.

10. *Know your rights.* Applicants have rights protected by state and federal laws. Employers can ask only about matters directly related to the job. If questions about gender, race, religion, age, or national origin have nothing to do with the job, they are off limits. Generally, questions in the following categories are illegal: age, religious affiliations, citizenship, height and weight, marital status and household arrangements, number of children, club memberships and affiliations.[26]

SUMMARY

To prepare for an interview, this eight-step procedure is suggested:

1. Determine the purpose.
2. Research the subject.
3. Select respondents.
4. Structure the interview.
5. Prepare questions.
6. Plan the physical environment.
7. Decide on the time.
8. Pretest the interview format.

The interviewer should frame questions with the interviewee in mind. Nine types of questions are: open, closed, leading, extension, echo, confrontation, direct/indirect, summary, and repetition. Questions should be organized in some manner; five sequential options are: funnel, inverted funnel, yes-response, who/what/ where/when/why, and tunnel.

Major parts of the interview are the opening, body, and closing. A three step procedure for evaluating interviews includes: review, criticism, and correction.

As an interviewee, the person should pay attention to appearance and other nonverbal messages, and should be assertive but not aggressive. The employment interview is particularly important to students. It entails specific preparation including resume, knowledge of the interviewing firm and the position, and awareness of one's own potential contributions.

14

Group Discussion

The small group, as described in Chapter 3, consists of three or more individuals who dynamically interact about a common concern. Countless small groups are present in our society, and human beings typically belong to a number of them. In thinking of the groups of which we are members, in terms of goals, we most likely are members of casual, learning, therapeutic, problem-solving, and action groups.

Two of those groups — *learning* and *problem-solving groups* — are the topics of this and the next chapter. These are *task-oriented groups*, ones in which the members have a job to do or a task to perform. In learning groups the task is to learn something about a subject of interest. Problem-solving groups meet to make decisions and to solve problems. Often, problem-solving groups implement the solutions, and, when they do, they become action groups. Indirectly, then, we touch on a third type of group, the *action group*.

In these two chapters we examine techniques and methods for functioning more successfully in learning and problem-solving groups. This chapter focuses first on the factors that influence participation in the two types of groups and then on the roles of members and leaders, stressing how to perform these roles more effectively. Finally, we consider ways of participating in groups. The next chapter covers methods of interacting in a logical fashion in learning and problem-solving groups.

Both types of groups entail a process called *group discussion*. If we are to understand more fully how to succeed as group learners or problem solvers, we should be familiar with the discussion process.

THE NATURE OF GROUP DISCUSSION

In the Chapter 3 explanation of the nature of small groups, we described small groups in a general way, noting the characteristics that shape all types of small groups. Here our interest narrows to *only* task-directed groups, particularly learning and problem solving groups. The oral communication typifying these two types of groups is discussion, a concept we define as *an orderly, intellectual process conducted by active and cooperative participants.*[1]

Good discussion has the qualities of small-group communication noted in Chapter 3. In addition, it has characteristics uniquely its own, described next.[2]

1. *Purposeful.* Of the seven elements, the most significant probably is its purposefulness. Ideally, group members determine the goals of discussion at the outset. The members clearly define and understand these goals and keep them constantly in mind. For example, the goal of a learning group may be to comprehend the art of origami, the traditional Japanese art of folding paper to form flowers, animal figures, and so on. The group's members have agreed upon this goal, and they understand what it entails. As they meet to discuss what they have uncovered in their research about the art, that goal is always before them.

2. *Systematic and logical.* Discussion follows a *systematic and logical plan.* The plan stresses *inquiry*, a

153

Group discussion is an orderly intellectual process conducted by active and cooperative participants.

way of finding the truth or the best answers. At the same time, the plan downplays *advocacy*, a way of gaining support for a predetermined idea. Inquiry is a characteristic of discussion, whereas advocacy is a quality of debate. Discussion and debate, therefore, are different forms of communication distinguished by inquiry and advocacy. Chapter 15 describes systematic and logical patterns of interaction for learning and problem-solving groups.

3. *Facts and opinions*. Discussion requires the best evidence available, free from bias. When evidence, consisting of *facts and expert opinions*, is not available, group members have to undertake whatever research is necessary to secure it. Once the facts and opinions arc in hand, they should be tested for validity and value. Those found to be suspect should be discarded.

4. *A group process*. Discussion takes place in small groups. It is a *group process*. Hence, the interpersonal relations of the members always must be of concern. Maintaining the group's morale is of primary importance, along with sustaining the group as an entity and achieving its goals. At the same time, the needs of individual members have to be satisfied, so consideration must be given to them as well.

5. *Leadership*. Discussion implies leadership in one of two forms, designated or latent. *Designated leadership* means that a force external to the group appoints a member to be the leader. For example, the instructor selects five students to arrange a

semester-ending class picnic and designates one of them as the leader.

Latent leadership, the second form, means that the members of a group choose their own leader or share the leadership functions among themselves; no one person carries the leadership title. Ideally, members should share the leadership functions to the extent of their ability. Leadership is best when it is a cooperative function performed by more than one group member.

6. *An oral process*. Discussion is a *speaking activity*. Learning or problem solving in groups is difficult, if not impossible, without speech. Even groups that utilize written communication extensively need to talk over their written remarks. As an oral process, proficiency in oral skills is necessary if the process is to be worthwhile. Skillful use of voice, meaningful language, and purposeful content are needed in discussion.

7. *Evaluation*. Evaluation entails the frequent review of group decisions and actions to ensure that they are in the group's best interests. From time to time as a discussion proceeds, the members should reflect for a few moments about what has taken place. Questions to be asked of themselves during these times might include: Where are we? What are we talking about? How are we doing? How can we do better? By taking account of what has happened, the group should be able to keep moving toward its goal. When the discussion is completed, the group should evaluate itself once again to find out what went right and what was wrong. In that way, the group can correct its mistakes to the benefit of future meetings.[3]

FACTORS AFFECTING DISCUSSION

In previous chapters we explored in depth the various factors that generally impact on the communication process. We considered the influence of the process itself, differences in communicator personalities, self-concept, apprehension, language, nonverbal influences, listening, and a host of other factors. Because all of these affect group discussion, they must be recognized as contributors to successful or ineffective discussion. Additional factors that have special significance in group interaction include environment, norms, conformity, productivity, and conflict.

Group Environment

A group's environment, the physical facilities and arrangements of the meeting place, has a direct influence on learning and problem solving.[4] The atmosphere of a meeting room affects the comfort and motivation of a group's members. Dull, drab, dingy rooms produce fatigue, headaches, irritability, and hostility. In contrast, well-appointed rooms contribute to feelings of pleasure and comfort.

Light, temperature, and noise, also components of environment, likewise affect interaction. Extremes in all of these environmental factors tend to create fatigue and lower productivity. Too much light has about the same effect as too little light; both tend to cause irritability.

A room that is too hot or too cold affects group members' ability to concentrate. Excessive noise can lower performance levels, especially when tasks are difficult, requiring much concentration.

Furthermore, the size of the meeting room influences how closely the members will sit next to each other. An inverse relationship seems to exist between room size and distance between members. The larger the room, the closer the members sit to each other; the smaller the room, the farther apart they sit. Our observations of groups confirm this. When questioned about their seating distance, group members have strong feelings. In large rooms they feel lost and gather closely. In small rooms they feel hemmed in and, by spreading out more, experience greater personal freedom.

Also, where a person sits impacts on the group process. The placement of chairs in a room influences the patterns of interaction. If group members are seated in a circle, they tend to speak to those opposite rather than those next to them. If they are seated at a rectangular table, individuals at the corners speak less than those at the ends or in the center positions. The designated leader is expected to sit at one of the ends of a rectangular table.

Based on our analysis, several conclusions can be drawn about the physical arrangements of a meeting room. Adequate lighting, comfortable temperature, and proper ventilation should be provided in the meeting room. Preferably, the seating arrangement should be circular, permitting members to sit close together, with a writing surface available to each. If a rectangular table is the only option, members in the center positions might push their chairs out from the table, allowing eye contact among all of the members and more closely approximating a circle.[5]

Group Norms

Groups originate norms or rules of behavior that are uniquely their own. These norms are *generally agreed-upon patterns of behavior that come to be a relatively permanent and predictable part of the group's operation.* Group norms encompass a variety of member behaviors and group practices. Included among them are behaviors and group procedures such as dress

regulations, number of tolerated absences, membership fees, eligibility requirements, beginning and ending times for meetings, meeting dates, rules for discussion, and smoking regulations, among any number of other possibilities. Norms usually are not written down, nor are they imposed from an outside authority. Rather, they tend to be ideas in the minds of group members, ideas that can be verbalized, specifying what the members (or group visitors) should do or are expected to do under given circumstances. These norms are enforced by peer pressure, not by outside authorities.

When a group is first organized, it does not have a set of norms uniquely its own, but norms are established quickly. In the following press dispatch, a participant in a seminar recounted the establishment of a group's norm:

> The hotel's dining room was the scene of several welcome lunches and dinners. A pre-scribed ceremony developed. On the first night, someone on the hosts' side said, "If the ladies will give permission, the men would like to remove their coats." The ladies did not say yes or no. But the men removed their coats. On the second night, it was, "With the ladies' permission, we shall remove our coats." By the third night, and thereafter, the men just took off their coats.[6]

A norm had established itself by the third meeting.

This vignette illustrates a feature of norm development: *Norms reflect cultural beliefs about what is good or bad, proper or improper, wise or foolish.* Although the norms of a small group are new in its culture, they embody the way of life of the larger culture of which the small group is a part, the organization or society at large. When group members come together for the first time, they bring with them past experiences and expectations regarding social and cultural rules, along with the rules they observed in similar groups. From these experiences and expectations, they form the norms governing the new group.

New members of established groups have to be especially concerned about norms. To be perceived as a full-fledged member by the old-timers, a neophyte will have to learn the norms and follow them as quickly as possible.[7]

Conformity

Conformity is defined as *acting in accordance with the norms of a group and being in harmony and agreement with the members.*[8] Thus, conformity and norms are inextricably intertwined. This definition does not suggest that the members cannot have differences in opinion, that everyone should think alike, but it does mean that group members do share similar goals, have compatible needs; and follow the rules and regulations in conducting their business together.

Conformity is necessary and vital in group discussion. Without it a group's deliberations could turn into a free-for-all, with little accomplished, particularly if the norms are not followed. Not all members conform to the same extent because not all members hold similar commitments to the group's goals. The degree of commitment is influenced by the member's personality characteristics, cohesion in the group, the task, and other situational factors.[9]

Conformity

◆ Conformity reflects the group's success in getting the individuals to follow its norms.

◆ Conformity introduces order in group process.

◆ Conformity is influenced by:
 • The member's personality
 • The group's attractiveness
 • The situation

Personality Characteristics

Certain types of people conform more readily than do others. Generally, women tend to conform more than men, intelligent people more than those who are less intelligent, submissive people more than dominant ones, authoritarian individuals more than equalitarian ones, and apprehensive people more than aggressive ones.[10]

Cohesion

Cohesiveness is the "stick-togetherness" of a group. It is *the sum of all factors influencing members to remain in a group.*[11] When a group is cohesive, the positive forces of attraction toward the group outweigh the negative forces of repulsion away from the group.

The attractiveness of a group for the members causes them to conform more to the norms than members in less attractive groups.

The attractiveness of a certain group to a specific individual depends upon the individual's needs and his or her perception of the group's ability to satisfy those needs. If a group cannot satisfy a person's needs, the group will not be attractive to the person.[12] The person then will conform less to the norms.

Group Task

The sort of task a group undertakes influences conformity. The more difficult the task, the more the members conform, to a point. When the task becomes too difficult, conformity decreases and the group's attractiveness for the members lessens. At the other extreme, tasks that are too easy can be boring to the members, with a resulting loss of interest and decrease in conformity.

Situational Pressures

Crisis situations usually cause increased conformity. Attacks on a group from outside sources make the group more tightly knit. *Group size* also affects conformity. The larger the group, the greater is the chance that conformity will decrease. Discussion groups with more than five members have a tendency to form small, conflicting subgroups, or cliques, that disrupt the group's proceedings. That is one reason a five-person group is an ideal size.[13]

Productivity and Cohesiveness

Cohesiveness has a bearing on conformity, as noted, but it is influential in its own right in group discussion because of its link to productivity. Groups with members who stick together work together more successfully and accomplish much more than less cohesive groups. Cohesive groups are more productive.

A group's cohesiveness is readily discernible. Attendance is one indicator. If attendance at group meetings is consistently high, the group is probably attractive to the members, and they attend because they are benefiting from the meetings. Punctuality is a related indicator. If the members are consistently on time, the group most likely is cohesive and productive. When members are frequently absent or late for meetings, the group probably lacks cohesion.

Another indication of cohesiveness is the amount of fun the members have at the meetings. If they are enjoying themselves, the group is likely to be cohesive and productive. The trust members have for each other is an indicator, as is the amount of support they give each other.[14]

Cohesion

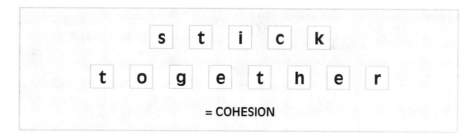

= COHESION

High cohesiveness leads most often to high productivity.

Members in highly cohesive groups:
- Support one another.
- Are attractive to each other.
- Repel outside threats easier.
- Are more satisfied.
- Are less deviant.

A group's cohesiveness can be increased in various ways. One is by *heightening the members' awareness of the benefits* they obtain from membership. Letting them know the values of membership strengthens the members' attraction to the group. Another way is to make the group more *need-satisfying;* activities that fulfill inclusion, control, and affection needs make the group more attractive. Cohesion can be increased by making the group more *prestigious,* thereby enhancing the personal status of its members. Heightening *interaction* among the members is another way of increasing cohesiveness. Arranging more satisfying activities for the members, bringing them together more, will result in a greater degree of cohesiveness. Increased cohesion should lead to increased productivity. The group that sticks together works hard together.[15]

Group Conflict

Even the most cohesive groups are not free from some degree of conflict. Actually, the more intimate and secure the group is, the more intense and frequent the conflict will be. We are likely to be more direct and hostile in groups in which we feel confident, such as our family. Conversely, we are much more reserved and tactful in groups whose members we do not know so well.

In group communication, conflict does have positive functions. It tends to encourage inquiry, promote objectivity, and sharpen analysis, and it seems to be vital to group progress. When members disagree over important issues, these disagreements cause the issues to be scrutinized more carefully. To settle the dispute, everyone involved will have to study the facts. History is replete with examples of positive results stemming from committee disagreements. The framers of the U. S. Constitution were not without internal conflict in their discussions; yet the outcome was a document that has stood the test of time.

At the other extreme, absence of conflict may signify an apathetic or indifferent group of members, who do not care what happens in the group's deliberations and readily conform to the wishes of a single authority. They avoid being involved in group decision making. Hence, the group becomes ripe for a dictatorship to develop.[16]

MEMBERSHIP ROLES

In some ways group discussion is similar to team play in athletic activities. On a basketball team, for example, each of the five players has a specific role: center, forward, or guard. When the five serve their roles well, the team functions smoothly. Similarly, for a discussion to function smoothly, group members must take on certain roles and perform them well. In athletics the roles are carefully defined and assigned to individuals. This is not so in discussion. A group member may assume only one role or more than one role. Usually each member takes on various roles. Also, several members can have the same role during the course of discussion. Still, the comparison between athletics and discussion is valuable. If a group is to function efficiently, certain roles must be performed when needed and, like successful athletic teams, the roles must be coordinated for the common good.[17]

What roles characterize group discussion? There are quite a few. To understand them better, we have classified them into three broad categories: task, maintenance, and individual roles. The first two classes encompass roles that help the group toward its goals. The third consists of self-centered roles, exhibited by individual members, which can be dysfunctional although personally need-satisfying.[18]

Task Roles

The following roles are directed toward accomplishing the group's task, whether it be to learn new information or to solve a problem.

1. *Initiator-contributor.* Suggests new ideas — goals, solutions, approaches to the problem — or new procedures for completing the task.

George: Today we're considering the question, "Should the federal government guarantee a minimum annual cash income to all citizens?" Let me suggest that we restrict our discussion to the United States even though the poverty problem is worldwide.

2. *Information-seeker.* Asks for clarification of facts presented by someone else and for new facts pertinent to the problem being discussed.

Pauline: Poverty means different things in different cultures, George. What does it mean in the United States?

3. *Opinion-seeker.* Asks for clarification of opinions presented and for additional opinions from the members.

Ruth: I'm not sure what we mean by "guarantee" and "minimum annual cash income." What do you think they mean, Candace?

4. *Information-giver.* Offers facts and opinions pertinent to the problem.

Candace: Let me try "guarantee." The dictionary says the word means a pledge or assurance that something will be done.

5. *Elaborator.* Gives details necessary to clarify someone else's information by presenting examples and definitions; helps others clarify their reasoning.

Pauline: Candy's right. But there's more to it. In our question, guarantee means the federal government formally assures our citizens that they will receive a minimum income.

6. *Coordinator.* Summarizes what has been discussed; shows the relationships among various ideas and suggestions; coordinates the group's activities.

Janis: Candace stressed old age as a cause. Ruth talked about unemployment. Actually, both are causes of poverty.

7. *Orientor.* States the position the group seems to be supporting; raises questions about where the group is going.

George: By now we have a good idea of what the terms mean, and we have some knowledge of the causes.

8. *Critic.* Evaluates the group's progress on the basis of some standard related to the group task.

Janis: But, George, we agreed at the beginning that after twenty minutes of discussion, we should be at the solution stage. We're not there yet.

9. *Energizer.* Prods the group to action; stimulates the group to greater activity.

Ruth: She's right, George. Let's get going. We need to move faster.

10. *Task-expeditor.* Performs routine tasks such as distributing materials, arranging seating, and so on.

Ann: Here are the copies of the poverty law I promised to run off for you.

11. *Recorder.* Keeps records of the group's business.

Sharon: Janis is correct, George. I have it in the minutes.

Maintenance Roles

To operate smoothly, a group requires more than task performance from the members. It benefits from a warm and friendly atmosphere, which the following functions can help develop and maintain:

1. *Encourager.* Agrees with and accepts the contributions of others; praises and commends.

Ruth: That's an excellent suggestion, one we should give further thought to.

2. *Harmonizer.* Mediates the conflicts that arise and attempts to settle them.

Secretary: They missed quite a few meetings, and they should be kicked out.

Treasurer: I disagree! They paid their dues and have a right to stay like anybody else, including you!

President: Well, let me interrupt. What you are saying, Sally, is that they've been absent quite a lot and you're wondering if they've given up their membership privileges. Karen, you're saying that dues are a reason for keeping a member in the club. I guess we can settle this by checking the Bylaws. Let's see what they say.

3. *Compromiser.* Helps to resolve a conflict in which he or she is involved by yielding status, admitting error, or agreeing to go along with the group.

Secretary: I guess I'm wrong. The Bylaws say a member may be placed on probation for missing three meetings in a row or five a semester. The members I'm talking about haven't. My apologies for not checking the facts.

4. *Regulator.* Proposes regulations on communication to permit equal speaking opportunities for the less talkative and overly talkative.

Chairperson: This issue is important, and all members should be heard. I'll call on each of you to comment. Please keep your remarks short. I'll interrupt if you get carried away.

5. *Observer.* Evaluates group members' ability to get along; keeps track of member satisfaction.

Henry: Looks like we're moving along very nicely. Everyone seems to be enjoying the meeting and at the same time contributing quite a bit.

6. *Follower.* Listens passively on occasion; accepts others' ideas; serves as an audience.

Chairperson: What do you think, Lance?

Lance: Oh! I agree 100 percent. The idea is great!

Individual Roles

Our actions in groups parallel our actions in everyday life. We praise, blame, resist, defend, seek recognition, and function in other ways to shore up our feelings of personal adequacy and security. These acts are self-oriented and directed to satisfying personal needs. Some of these behaviors are negative; some are not. In group interaction individual behaviors can operate to the group's detriment. Some behaviors block group progress; some do not. A few are useful when they come at critical times. A conflict may be developing, and a little humor may lighten the atmosphere. Here is a list of individual behaviors.

1. *Aggressor.* Deflates the status of others to inflate his or her own status; expresses disapproval of what the others do; attacks the group and its problems.

Tom: Maybe that's the way you guys do it here. Maybe that's why you do such a lousy job! The way we did it at Washington was different — and better. Here's how you should do it if you want to succeed . . . .

Member Roles

Roles group members may enact as they function together:

1. Group Task Roles:

     To facilitate and coordinate group efforts — initiator-contributor, information seeker, opinion-seeker, information-giver, elaborator, coordinator, orientor, critic, energizer, task expeditor, recorder.

2. Group Building and Maintenance Roles:

     To develop and increase cohesion, consensus, cooperation — encourager, harmonizer, compromiser, regulator, observer, follower.

3. Individual Roles:

     To satisfy highly personal motives at the expense of the group's progress — aggressor, resistor, recognition-seeker, self-confessor, playboy/playgirl, dominator, help-seeker, interest-pleader.

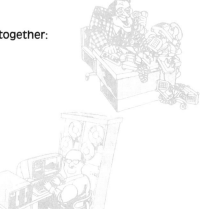

2. *Resistor.* Tends to block group progress by disagreeing and opposing without reason.

Jane:	So, I think we should have a dance.
Bill:	I don't agree.
Jane:	What's wrong with a dance?
Bill:	They're no good. Count me out of that.
Jane:	Why?
Bill:	Dances . . . phooey!

3. *Recognition-seeker.* Calls attention to himself or herself by boasting, reporting personal achievements, or acting out of line.

Joan:	Let's . . .
Jim:	Hey! Did you people hear about my new record? Broke the NCAA freestyle record! How about that!
Joan:	Great! Let's. . .
Jim:	And that's not all. The coach said I'm gonna be national champ! You haven't seen anything yet!

4. *Self-confessor.* Uses the group as an audience for his or her personal ideas, insights, feelings not related to the group task.

Jan:	Are we through? I want to tell you about a new recipe Sally gave me.

5. *Playboy/Playgirl.* Displays lack of interest by telling jokes, fooling around, and distracting the others.

Chairperson:	Is there any new business? Harry, you have your hand up.
Harry:	Yeah. Say, did you hear this one? What did Paul Revere say at the end of his ride? Give up? He said, "Whoa!" How about this one? One guy says to the other, "Are you going to take your car out in this weather?" The other guy says, "Yes, of course, it's a driving rain, isn't it?"

6. *Dominator.* Tries to manipulate the group through flattery, threats, interruptions.

Chairperson:	Does anybody else have any ideas? Steve, you talked all evening.
Harry:	Let's get this straight. Either we do it my way or I won't give the $1,000 to the building fund. As a matter of fact, I'll quit.

7. *Help-seeker.* Seeks sympathy for his or her personal problems, confusion, insecurity.

May:	Well . . . I don't know if I can. My stomach has been acting up lately . . . and

my boyfriend got laid off. I'm not sure what will happen next.

8. *Interest-pleader.* Speaks on behalf of some special interest of his or hers to the detriment of group progress.

Sam:	Let me also mention that to run a dance like that, we need insurance. My company has a policy that covers dances. It has these features . . .[19]

A group's effectiveness can be hindered by dysfunctional roles. The group should strive, therefore, to strengthen the task and maintenance functions of its members and reduce the frequency of the dysfunctional behaviors.

Learning the Roles

Any group is strengthened and enabled to work more efficiently if its members become conscious of the roles the group needs at any given time. Knowing what the needs are, the group can find out the degree to which members are helping meet these needs through what they do. One way to become aware of the needed roles and the extent to which they are being performed is to have an observer keep track of the task, maintenance, and individual role-playing of the members. The observer may be a group member who does not participate in the discussion for a meeting or two; instead, he or she sits on the sidelines and witnesses the action. After the meeting, this person reports the results to the group.

A role analysis form such as the one presented in Figure 14.1 can be used to evaluate group members' performance and to keep track of the roles being played. In using the form, the observer should have a basic understanding of the roles so he or she can identify them as they occur in the group's discussion.

After the group has determined what roles are needed but are not being performed, group members can practice building these roles into the discussions. One way of doing this is for several members to take responsibility for being sensitive to the need for the missing roles and supplying them when indicated. For example, if a group of ten members is weak in the coordinating and encouraging roles, several members might take responsibility for coordinating and several for encouraging. Another method of practicing the roles is to rotate the roles, or some of them, among the members, with each person playing his or her role when it seems appropriate. Whatever method is used, an observer should be involved, with the task of evaluating role performance.[20]

Name _____ Group # _____

Discussion Group Process Feedback
For Task, Maintenance, and Individual Roles

I. TASK ROLES	Person 1	Person 2	Person 3	Person 4	Person 5
1. Initiator-Contributor					
2. Information-Seeker					
3. Opinion-Seeker					
4. Information-Giver					
5. Elaborator					
6. Coordinator					
7. Orientor					
8. Critic					
9. Energizer					
10. Task Expeditor					
11. Recorder					
II. MAINTENANCE ROLES	Person 1	Person 2	Person 3	Person 4	Person 5
1. Encourager					
2. Harmonizer					
3. Compromiser					
4. Regulator					
5. Observer					
6. Follower					
III. INDIVIDUAL ROLES	Person 1	Person 2	Person 3	Person 4	Person 5
1. Aggressor					
2. Resistor					
3. Recognition-Seeker					
4. Self-Confessor					
5. Playboy/Playgirl					
6. Dominator					
7. Help-Seeker					
8. Interest-Pleader					

Figure 14.1 Sample role analysis form.

LEADERSHIP ROLES AND FUNCTIONS

Leadership is the *communicative behavior of any member that activates a group toward its goal.*[21] Thus, leadership, like membership, is part of the group process. Some membership roles serve leadership functions as well. Those who play the member role of activating others, for example, are engaging in a leadership role. Those who respond to or are activated by the leaders are playing nonleader membership roles at that particular time.

Characteristics of Leadership

Five characteristics are significant to the concept of leadership.[22] These are described briefly.

Meets Group Goals

Members who activate the group toward group goals have to be aware of what the members want. The activators must understand the membership well enough to know the desires of individual members and what goals they seek. The activators also must be able to supply the means or methods of moving the group to goal satisfaction. They must contribute something that will stimulate the members to move toward the goal. Members have to accept this "something"; they have to agree that whatever is being proposed is the best way available to them. Until then, they cannot be said to have been activated.

A simple illustration might clarify what this first characteristic entails: The president of the student body has appointed a committee of seven students to develop a procedure for student evaluation of faculty performance. The committee has had many meetings and has made little headway. The members' research has uncovered considerable literature on faculty evaluation, offering many procedures.

The student body president calls for a workable plan to be submitted in three days. The group panics. The members don't know what to do. Finally, one member, Lenny, suggests a meeting schedule for the next two days and a strategy for completing the group's assignment. The group accepts Lenny's suggestions.

In this example, Lenny plays the leadership role as he moves the group to satisfying its goal. Lenny provides the knowledge to move the group along.

Is Related to the Situation

Leadership is relative to the situation confronting the group at a given time. The student body committee illustration exemplifies this point. In that case, a problem existed requiring a specialized leadership function. Only a member who knew how to perform the function in that situation could lead. Lenny had the necessary understanding, so he became the leader. Situations differ, however. What works in one situation may not in another. Thus, leadership is related to the situation.

May Be Assumed by Anyone

Any member who can activate a group toward its goal of the moment can occupy the leadership position. It is not restricted to one person.

May Reside in More Than One Person

This characteristic is closely tied to the previous one. If anyone can assume leadership, it can reside in more than one person. Any member who is able to help a group achieve its goals can take on the leadership function. Most groups, however, have one leader. The person in charge is appointed by an outside force or is elected by the membership. The position usually carries definite responsibilities and authority. Among the many examples of single, central authorities are a chairperson, president, king, boss, ruler.

The person elected or appointed as the one in charge usually is perceived as having the group's goals in mind and as possessing the means to reach these goals. In most instances this perception is the reason the person is selected.

Although the person in charge usually is perceived as the group's leader, he or she may not be the one who performs the leadership function in every situation. Leadership is relative to the situation, and the person in charge may not have the capability to lead in every situation. Some other member may be better prepared to handle a specific situation. That person then becomes the leader at that time in that situation. The person with the title of chairperson, president, supervisor, director, ruler, or whatever temporarily relinquishes the leadership role.

Has Status

Leadership carries status. Whoever fills the leadership role has influence over the other members. What the members may say or do may be calculated to win the leader's approval or avoid his or her displeasure. Thus, the leader affects the conduct of the meeting and the ideas expressed.

Functions of Leadership

Our definition perceives leadership as the communicative behavior of any individual that helps a group achieve its goals. Therefore, any member can

Effective leaders offer creative and critical thinking, provide procedural help, and foster healthy relationships.

potentially be the group's leader in a given situation. The exact behavior required in a specific situation is not predictable. Sometimes a group is seeking new ideas. Other times procedural matters are causing problems. Or social and emotional leadership may be needed. These three prevailing needs can be translated into three principal functions of leadership,[23] described briefly here.

Provide Creative and Critical Thinking

Groups can profit from fresh ideas. Members who are able to supply new, promising ideas or can stimulate others to do so can fill the leadership role. Contributing new ideas is an intellectual kind of function that benefits virtually every group. Discussion is more productive when a group has one or more members who are capable of suggesting new ways to perform group functions.

Groups also profit from evaluating ideas. When the time comes to analyze the ideas being deliberated, individuals who possess the skills to do this are prime candidates for the leadership role.

Give Procedural Help

Members who are able to handle the tasks related to administration and management of a group can take over the leadership when those issues arise. Two such tasks are initiating the discussion and making agenda suggestions. Clarifying, summarizing, and verbalizing consensus or agreement also are procedural matters.

Foster Healthy Relations

A third function focuses on interpersonal relations. Members who can suggest as well as perform actions

to carry a group through emotional crises with a minimum of damage can provide valuable leadership services. Creating and maintaining a healthy, positive group atmosphere increases morale and cohesion, thereby increasing productivity.

GUIDELINES FOR SERVING AS CHAIRPERSON

In our description of the leadership process, we noted that many discussion groups select or elect a member to serve as the group's head or chairperson. In other groups the authority that appoints the members to the group also designates the chairperson(s). For example, a club may have a number of committees, of which the membership is assigned by the club president and the president designates one member of each as the chairperson.

However the chairperson gets the job, he or she has certain duties to perform, responsibilities to carry out. Most of these relate to the smooth functioning of the group, and they tend to be administrative or managerial in nature. In many organizations the group's charter or constitution spells out the duties. In other groups the chairperson follows established guidelines set forth in parliamentary procedure books such as *Robert's Rules of Order*. The person taking on a chairperson's role in a group should become familiar with the group's charter or constitution, parliamentary procedures, and any special regulations the group has for conducting meetings.

In addition to parliamentary procedures, group regulations, and the leadership functions outlined previously, several functions a chairperson can perform to keep the group running smoothly are as follows.[24]

1. *Inform the group members about each meeting.* The chairperson should have a notice sent to all members, letting them know the forthcoming meeting's date, time, place, and tentative agenda.

2. *Plan an agenda.* The agenda, which is a list of topics to be discussed or an order of business to be followed, should be planned with the input of group members.

3. *Arrange the physical facilities.* The chairperson should provide for a comfortable, well-lit and ventilated environment with optimum seating arrangements (discussed previously).

4. *Initiate the discussion.* The chairperson should assume the responsibility for calling the meeting to order and getting things started. If the group is meeting for the first time or if new members are present, the chairperson should make the proper introductions. Then he or she should state the

order of business in a way that is nonthreatening and encourages conformity and cohesion.

5. *Keep the meeting orderly and organized.* While encouraging everyone's participation, the chairperson should keep the group moving toward its goal. To help keep the discussion on track, he or she can perform the roles of summarizer, clarifier, orientor, expeditor, and critic.

6. *Encourage participation.* When a group first meets, the members must determine how to behave and what to do. Frequently they are anxious, unsure of themselves, and reluctant to participate. The chairperson should recognize these feelings. One way to encourage participation is to make the members responsible for what happens in the meeting.

   For example, after handling the formalities of starting the meeting and announcing the agenda, the chairperson could shift the responsibility by remarks such as, "So this is where we are. Where should we go from here?" Typically that question elicits little or no response at first. The chairperson should wait, giving members time to think. Quite likely, each is waiting for someone else to begin. Normally the wait is short. Someone eventually speaks up. The chairperson then should let the other members do the talking. A time finally comes when the members begin to participate freely, if the group consists of typical individuals who are interested in the group's goals. Once everyone does join in the discussion, the chairperson also can interact more freely.

7. *Close the meeting.* As a group's meeting draws to a close, several chores have to be accomplished. To wrap up what has transpired, a summary of the principal actions is needed. If no one else does this, the chairperson should. Then he or she should remind everyone of the next meeting's time and place.

GUIDELINES FOR PARTICIPATING AS MEMBERS

Just as the chairperson has to perform certain duties to keep group meetings functioning without major hassles, so, too, the members have responsibilities. All the members can carry out the seven functions listed next.[25]

1. *Be informed.* Members of a discussion group are responsible for knowing the subject matter being discussed. They should complete whatever research is necessary to participate intelligently. Often pressured by other demands on their time, members sometimes forego research, counting on the others to have done it. The others, then, are forced to carry those who have failed to prepare. Before long, those who have prepared for the meeting realize they are being taken advantage of, and they react negatively. The group's progress is impeded, with unsatisfactory results. All members should share the responsibility for being informed.

2. *Be cooperative.* Group discussion requires the cooperation of all members. Each should carry his or her full share and participate to the best of his or her ability. Although the members may disagree about information, ideas, and activities, they should search for a group outcome that will prove to be satisfactory to all. The members should willingly contribute their individual knowledge and thinking for the good of the group, considering each other as partners in the discussion process.

3. *Be open-minded.* The members should practice empathic listening, being open to the ideas of others and trying to understand them before criticizing them.

4. *Think rationally.* In the next chapter we consider ways in which group members can think logically together. Those methods are based on reflective thinking processes, enabling rational consideration of the subject matter.

5. *Participate actively.* All members should be encouraged to participate, and the quiet ones should receive special urging. Extremely vocal members may have to curb their participation to give everyone an opportunity to talk.

**Effective group members are informed.
They do their homework.**

6. *Practice the roles*. Applying the task and maintenance roles described earlier should improve group effectiveness.

7. *Be patient*. Group discussion is a time-consuming process because each member should have a chance to speak. Too, some members may not be as fully informed as others on the discussion topic, and they will need time to catch up. Better-informed members might become impatient. Those who are well-informed should try to be patient.

SUMMARY

The first of two chapters covering group discussion, this chapter deals with the discussion process in general, setting the stage for our explanation of two types of discussion — learning and problem solving — in the next chapter. Group discussion is an orderly, intellectual process conducted by active, cooperative participants. It is a purposeful speaking activity in which group members strive to reach a common goal — for us, understanding a subject more completely or solving a problem of some kind. As group members interact, they utilize facts and opinions, organized in a systematic and logical fashion, to reach their goal. Leadership is provided by a person designated or elected to carry out the leadership functions, or by the members themselves. To make sure the group is functioning properly, evaluation should take place periodically so members get a feel for how they are doing. This enables them to make improvements, if necessary.

As in all types of oral communication, several factors affect the success of discussion. In addition to the ones analyzed in previous chapters, the environment, conformity, cohesion, productivity, and conflict have an impact on discussion.

Interaction in group discussion takes place within the framework of member and leader roles. *Membership* roles can be classified into three categories: task (related to substantive issues of the discussion), maintenance (involving the emotional climate), and individual (concerning members' need satisfaction). *Leadership* is the communicative behavior of any member that moves the group toward its goal. Leadership can be assumed by anyone in the group, and can change according to the specific situation.

VOCABULARY CHECK

These terms are explained in Chapter 14. Match the proper definition with the appropriate term. The answers are on page 243.

———— 1. Aggressor

———— 2. Group discussion

———— 3. Norms

———— 4. Small-group communication

———— 5. Designated leadership

———— 6. Conformity

———— 7. Leadership

———— 8. Cohesion

———— 9. Information-giver

———— 10. Latent leadership

A. An orderly, intellectual process conducted by active and cooperative participants.
B. Members choose their own leader.
C. Generally agreed-upon patterns of behavior.
D. An external force appoints a member to fill the role.
E. Deflates the status of others, thereby inflating his/her own.
F. Three or more people in physical proximity who dynamically interact over a common concern.
G. Acting in accordance with the group's norms.
H. The sum of factors influencing members to remain in the group.
I. The communicative behavior of any member that activates a group toward its goal.
J. A person who offers facts and opinions toward a problem's solution.

15

Methods of Group Discussion

We generally use discussion in two rather different types of situations: learning and problem solving. In learning discussion, the goal is to increase understanding, improve old skills or develop new skills, discover relationships, or explore ways of applying new knowledge. In problem solving discussion, the aim is to resolve differences, determine policies, make decisions, or seek agreement. In learning discussion, the goal is to acquire new information that may have immediate or delayed benefits for the group members. In problem-solving discussion, the goal is to resolve some difficulty that might have an immediate or later influence on a group or its members.

The two types of discussion are not mutually exclusive. Learning discussions may take on some aspects of problem-solving discussions, and problem-solving discussions invariably involve some learning. Both the content and the process of learning and problem solving, however, have unique characteristics.[1]

In this chapter we describe some of the characteristics of, and the methods and procedures for, learning and problem solving in groups. In addition, we note other methods of group discussion, all of which have utilitarian value in learning or problem solving. First, however, we answer an important question: Why discuss?

WHY DISCUSS?

Why go through a process that is often time-consuming and frequently leads to unsatisfactory conclusions? Why not learn by ourselves or turn over our problems to experts to solve? Why bother with group discussion? To answer these questions, comparisons have been made between the products of group effort and of individual effort. The results are conclusive: Group effort is superior to individual effort in most circumstances. If we are looking for an accurate, reasonable, and quick answer, the group has a better chance of achieving this aim than does a single individual, other things being equal.[2]

Keeping that statement in mind, let us review the advantages of discussion. Discussion has its faults also, of course. It is not a panacea that cures every ill in learning and problem solving. Hence, we will consider the disadvantages as well.

Advantages of Discussion

Some advantages can be attributed to all forms of discussion. Several of these are directly ascribed to learning and problem solving discussion.

General Advantages

Discussion is of considerable value when the goal is to change individual attitudes and behavior. Unless we refuse to listen or all of the viewpoints of others coincide with our own, chances are that our attitudes and behavior will change when we meet with others and discuss a subject of common interest. The changes may be minor and not earth-shaking, but we can recognize them as being brought about by discussion.

Discussion is of value also in helping group members develop as individuals. Through discussion, their skills in relating meaningfully to others should improve. Groups offer individuals stimulation and reinforcement, and they provide many opportunities for developing satisfactory interpersonal relationships. Group members learn more about other people as they interact with their fellow members in situations that at times are difficult. The give-and-take of discussion usually increases appreciation of others. Discussion provides countless occasions for satisfying personal inclusion, control, and affection needs, noted earlier as needs we have to fulfill if we are to lead normal lives.[3]

Advantages of Learning Groups

When group members study together, learning occurs more quickly than it does when they study by themselves. Group members absorb information faster because the ideas contributed to the common pool in discussion add to those the individual already has learned by reading alone or by listening to classroom lectures.[4] Discussion thrusts the individual into the learning process and, because of the influence of other group members, the individual becomes an active seeker and inquirer.[5]

Student involvement and enthusiasm for learning is superior in discussion to other means of learning. As a consequence, test scores are at least equal to, and usually higher than, those obtained from studying in isolation, and evaluations of the students' work increase—if group members are reasonably able, sensible, and well-meaning. A group of unprepared and unfit members can only lead to the pooling of ignorance.[6]

Group learning apparently is effective because the group motivates individuals to do better than they would by working alone. The mere presence of the others, however, is not the motivating factor. Their evaluations of each individual's performance is the motivational element. "None of us particularly wants to be judged a dummy by the other group members. Yet those members continuously are observing our behaviors and forming impressions about us. Our concern about their judgments thus produces arousal in us."[7]

Advantages of Problem-Solving Groups

Problem solving in groups is generally superior to individual problem solving. Groups produce more and better solutions to problems than do individuals working alone, a distinct advantage.[8]

Another advantage, an important one, is that people tend to carry out the decisions they help make. They put more effort into implementing the solutions because the solutions are theirs, not ones imposed upon them. They have to make the solutions work. Otherwise they could be faulted for poor decision making.[9]

Also members' contributions can be pooled. The combined knowledge and experience of group members can produce more and better solutions. Deficiencies in evidence and reasoning can be uncovered and corrected more readily under the critical scrutiny of a number of people.

Finally, a group working together on a problem arouses greater interest in the task; the members stimulate each other to put forth more effort. Of course, group members must be able, sensible, and well-meaning people who have done their homework.[10]

Disadvantages of Discussion

Perhaps the major disadvantage of group learning and problem solving is the amount of the time required. Meetings are time-consuming unless the members are denied opportunities to explore issues and make decisions.

A second disadvantage is that discussion requires skill. A group does not automatically make superior decisions. Members have to have training in logical thinking, research, use of evidence and reasoning, group interaction, and speaking. Training takes time, involves schooling, and requires practice.

A third disadvantage stems from the tendency of many members to rely on others in the group to carry the load while they coast. Discussion dilutes

Advantages of Discussion

- Two or more heads are frequently better than one.
- People tend to carry out decisions they have helped to make.
- Discussion can change individual behavior and attitudes including motivation and enthusiasm.
- Combined knowledge produces better solutions.
- Discussion can help satisfy social needs.

Disadvantages of Discussion

- Discussion takes time.
- Discussion requires skill.
- Discussion might weaken individual responsibilities.
- Discussion doesn't work in emergencies.
- Dominant group members can take over.

individual responsibility. With others around, individual members are not as compelled to do their full share. Classroom discussion groups often are guilty of such irresponsibility; one or two students carry the discussion while the others loaf.

Also, discussion is not practical in emergency situations. Calling a group together to discuss an immediate crisis is not an intelligent course to take. Emergency situations require instantaneous action, not group deliberation. A group may arrive at a superior solution to the crisis, but if the crisis has passed, the solution is worthless.

Discussion has additional disadvantages. A dominant personality can take over a meeting and make it a one-person show. Shy, anxious people may not participate at all, denying the group their knowledge. And in-group pressures to conform can cause members to accept bad decisions for the sake of conforming to the majority.[11]

Despite the disadvantages, however, our original statement still stands. Group effort is superior to individual effort in most situations.

THE LEARNING GROUP

Learning groups constitute a major strength of our society. A great number of them are formed as people join together to learn about some aspect of the world around them. People belong to hobby groups, classes, and seminars for learning purposes. Conferences, conventions, and workshops are organized for the exchange of ideas, techniques of doing things, and the latest information. People in business, scientific fields and the professions meet regularly to obtain knowledge. For students, the learning group is an essential part of the school system.

Types of Learning Groups

Three major classes of learning groups are: experiential, enlightenment, and classroom learning groups. We will concentrate on the classroom types, but we also describe the others to note how they differ.

Experiential

Experiential groups are *small, temporary collections of people who meet with the general goal of interpersonal inquiry and personal learning.* They meet for the expressed purpose of helping people grow, develop, and mature as human beings. Thousands of such groups meet regularly in the United States, and dozens assemble daily in large cities of the country.[12]

Experiential learning groups include sensitivity training groups, T-groups ("T" stands for training),

human relations groups, self-help groups, skill-training groups, encounter groups, Gestalt groups, and theme-centered instruction groups. Each of these groups is somewhat different from the others, but the *common aim is for the participants to know themselves better and grow psychologically.* A few of these kinds of learning groups are also therapeutic in effect.

Enlightenment

Enlightenment groups meet to *exchange ideas, learn new methods, and expand knowledge.*[13] Business and professional people, teachers, and scientists are among the categories of those who regularly meet in groups to learn. Also included are hobby and craft groups, classes such as flower arranging, basket weaving, sewing, cooking, quilting, jewelry making, and others that emphasize skills training.

Classroom

The type of group that most concerns us, the classroom learning group, is one that virtually every student will take part in sometime during his or her school years. Instructors organize classroom learning groups to maximize learning. They focus on the subject matter of a course, assisting students to understand and master the course material.

In a sense, classroom learning and enlightenment groups are similar. They have the common purposes of informing and educating. The classroom group, however, is found only in the school setting, whereas enlightenment groups operate in a variety of settings. Because classroom learning groups can have a considerable effect on our lives as students, the discussion of learning groups here is restricted to this type. Classroom and enlightenment learning groups differ from experiential groups in that the first two concentrate on learning about subject matter and skills; experiential groups focus on learning about oneself.

A Format for Classroom Learning

The format for classroom learning groups, which follows, and the format for problem-solving discussion, which appears later, are models of group discussion. The procedures are presented mostly step-by-step. The steps should be practiced slavishly, at least in the process of learning them. After the procedures are learned, variations can be made as desired.

Students often are irked by the thought of rote learning. They want to be spontaneous perhaps, preferring to be creative or permissive in discussions with others. Utilizing the direction and guidance that designated formats offer, however, has value, especially in group discussion. By their very nature, groups require patterned interaction. When a number of people communicate for common purposes, direction in their thinking is necessary. Otherwise time and effort can be wasted in what might prove to be useless talk.

The steps in the learning group format are logical and systematic; they follow in order. They provide direction to a classroom group that is attempting to master a reading assignment or a textbook chapter. To bring results, however, preparation is prerequisite. Students have to do their homework. Before meeting in class to discuss, they should read the assignment for the discussion and take notes. The notes might pertain to each of the five steps, described below and shown in Figure l5.l.

1. *Define important terms.* Before discussing the subject matter, participants should know the meaning of crucial terms and concepts. Most subjects taught at the university level utilize special terms. Understanding the terms becomes an essential first step in comprehending the material. The following suggestions may be helpful in learning the terms:

   a. List the terms requiring definition.
   b. Define and explain each of the listed terms.

   c. Check with the group members to see if they understand each term.

2. *Obtain an overall meaning of the reading.* The group should try to grasp the assignment's overall purpose and identify the main topics. Here are some suggestions:

   a. Ask each member to state the meaning in his or her own words.
   b. Compare the members' statements. If they differ, decide which is most accurate.
   c. State the headings, subheadings, and major topics
   d. Decide which topics are most difficult.
   e. Formulate questions about the difficult topics that might be used to initiate discussion.
   f. List the topics and questions for all to see.

3. *Discuss the main topics.* In this step the group covers the main topics, especially the difficult ones, asking questions as necessary. Further, the members should relate what they learned in the assignment to what they already know about the subject matter, if anything. The new information becomes more

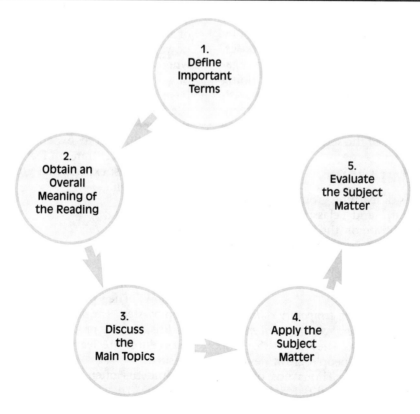

FIGURE 15.1. Steps in the learning group format.

meaningful when the old and new are related. These suggestions might help:

    a. State the information from the assignment that explains, proves, illustrates the main topics.

    b. Discuss the questions raised about the difficult topics.

    c. Consider any minor ideas or topics.

    d. Discuss how the new material relates to knowledge already acquired on the subject.

4. *Apply the subject matter.* At this point the members try to decide how to use what they have learned about the subject. They discuss the value of the new knowledge to themselves personally. Many subjects have direct personal value—for example, information on personal and public speaking, which can be applied immediately in everyday speaking situations. Other subject matter has little immediate use, but it could have future value. Some subjects supply intellectual stimulation, cultural information, or historical data that educated people ought to possess. These techniques should assist in this step:

    a. Speculate how the new material can be used.

    b. Give examples of its possible application.

    c. Compare the group's and the author's ideas, if these are stated, about how the information can be used.

5. *Evaluate the subject matter.* At this stage the members should be able to assess the material presented in the discussion assignment. As we read, we develop personal feelings about what we read. We may feel good, bad, or indifferent about it. We may enjoy the way the author writes or find the material too easy or too difficult. We may like the author's ideas, or we may think they are a waste of time. Now is the point at which to express those feelings. Some suggestions about what can be discussed are:

    a. The main ideas.

    b. Validity of the supporting materials.

    c. Usefulness of the reading.

    d. The author's writing style.

Expression of personal feelings should wait until the end of the discussion so the subject matter can be dealt with first. If group members begin voicing their feelings about the reading too soon, they may never get around to discussing it fully.[14]

To use the discussion time most satisfactorily, the group should divide the time available in this fashion:

Step 1.   defining terms: 10% of the time

Step 2.   determining overall meaning: 10% of the time

Step 3.   discussing main topics: 70% of the time

Step 4.   applying the subject matter: 5% of the time

Step 5.   evaluating the subject matter: 5% of the time

GROUP PROBLEM SOLVING

Hardly a day passes without our having to face and resolve problems of some sort. For example, we awaken in the morning and find no food in the house. We had better eat, because we are hungry. Also we have a morning exam, and we think better with food in our stomach. What should we do?

We get to class, pick up a copy of the test, and discover we have nothing to write with. How do we cope with that problem?

After class, we meet a friend and he or she wants to cut the next class, drive to town, and see a movie. Should we go?

We are almost out of cash because we have been spending foolishly. Mom or Dad won't send more until the end of the month. We've over-borrowed from our friends. What do we do?

Although these problems are not earth-shaking by any means, they are frustrating. We confront problems of this magnitude every day. We also face more serious problems, and those that are not as personal. We encounter joint problems; other people face the same problem, and we have to work together to solve it. Problem solving discussion then is in order.

Characteristics of Problems

Problems have certain similarities. First there is an *awareness* of the problem. People perceive that something is wrong and realize that something must be done about it, although they may not know what to do. When we realize something is wrong, we usually have become aware of the problem's symptoms, the manifestations of the problem. If we develop a stomach pain, we have a symptom of a problem. We just don't know what the problem is yet.

Once we become aware of a symptom and realize we have to do something, a *goal* emerges. The goal may be to solve the problem, remove an obstacle, reach an agreement, or prevent something from happening. In the case of the stomach ache, the goal might be to find out the cause and then remove the cause, thereby solving the problem.

The third similarity in problem situations is that each has *barriers* to the goal. With the stomach ache problem the barriers may be multiple. We may have to get to a doctor, but the doctor will charge a fee, and we may have to get a prescription for medication. Furthermore, we will have to skip class to go to the doctor. All sorts of barriers can arise.

In every problem these three characteristics exist; without any one of them, no problem is present. If we are not *aware* of a problem, it does not exist; something becomes a problem only when we perceive that it exists. If there is no *goal,* no problem is present; we may be *aware* that something is not right, but our awareness does not result in a problem until we decide to do something about it. If no *barriers* stop us from acting, there is no problem; we just go ahead and do what is necessary.

To be a group problem, it must have these three characteristics and in addition must affect a number of people. If it affects only one person, the problem is a personal one to be solved by the person alone. When a problem affects a number of people, problem-solving discussion can be used.[15]

Types of Problems

Problems that can be solved in groups using discussion methods are of three types: fact, value, and policy.

Problems of fact concern something that is, was, or will be so, and refer to events, happenings, or objects. There are two types of facts. *Accepted* facts are those purported to have happened and perceived to be true, but a probability issue makes them discussable. Is it true that Americans buy foreign cars because American-made cars are of poor quality? Is it true that medical care is expensive because of doctors' high fees? The second type of facts consists of those that are *verifiable.* Did it rain yesterday? We probably could find several hundred or more people who would be able to answer that question and establish its truth.

Problems of value center on the desirability or worth of an idea, a person, or an action. They are determined subjectively. "Are labor unions good for the country?" deals with values and attitudes. This type of problem is not easily solved by uncovering facts. The group's perception of labor unions and what is good is what counts. And that perception relates to the values the members hold.

Problems of policy require taking an action of some sort. To determine the kind of action, facts can be brought into the discussion, reasoning can be applied, and a solution can be found. Examples of policy questions are: What should be done about the economy? Should intercollegiate athletics be abolished? Should students be allowed to drop courses at any time? Each of those questions requires objective analysis to uncover the goals and barriers, and each can lead to possible solutions.[16]

The Standard Agenda

Group discussion is an orderly process, and orderliness is a part of the standard agenda that can be applied to group problem solving. That agenda is based on the process of reflective thinking,

---

TYPES OF PROBLEMS

These statements concern problems of *fact, value,* or *policy.* Determine which is which by writing in the name of the appropriate type. The answers are on page 244.

1. What should be done about unemployment? _____

2. Is the consumption of alcoholic beverages increasing among college students? _____

3. Should the drinking age be raised to 25? _____

4. What should be done about limiting terms of office for members of congress? _____

5. Is premarital sex moral? _____

6. Is date-rape on the increase? _____

7. Is abortion a God-given right? _____

8. What are the consequences of AIDS? _____

9. Is cheating on your mate acceptable? _____

10. Should there be a dress-code on university campuses? _____

advocated by John Dewey almost three-quarters of a century ago.

Dewey thought of reflective thinking as a scientific habit, relying on an attitude of suspended judgment until all the facts are in, and demanding mastery of the various methods of searching for materials. *Maintaining an intelligent state of doubt and practicing systematic inquiry are the ingredients of reflective thinking.*[17] Dewey's conceptualization of reflective thinking consists of five steps: (1) awareness of a felt difficulty, (2) definition of the felt difficulty, (3) formulation of possible solutions to overcome the felt difficulty, (4) analysis of the possible solutions, and (5) confirmation of the best solution.

The standard agenda (the problem-solving sequence or reflective thinking pattern) likewise consists of five steps, which we state as questions: (1) What is the problem? (2) What caused the problem? (3) What are possible solutions to the problem? (4) What is the best solution to the problem? (5) How can the best solution be implemented? The five steps roughly correspond to those Dewey set forth.

1. *What is the problem?*

When problem solving, many groups observe a common practice. They "think in reverse." Before identifying the problem or knowing the facts about it, they propose solutions. If luck is with them, a satisfactory solution might result, but these short cuts usually do not work. The problem reappears and continues to plague the group. A more sensible approach to problem solving is to begin by determining what the problem is. Usually a group undertakes problem solving because of a felt difficulty. The members perceive a perplexing situation and realize it has to be dealt with. What group members ordinarily perceive are the effects of the situation,

the signs or symptoms of a possible problem, not the problem itself. They have to ferret out the problem before they can treat it satisfactorily. To identify a problem, answers to questions like the following are helpful:

    a. What is the situation in which the problem is occurring?

    b. What in general is the difficulty?

    c. How did the difficulty arise?

    d. What is its importance?

    e. What are the meanings of any terms that require clarification?

By obtaining the answers to these questions, a group can more ably determine what the problem really is.

For classroom training purposes, the instructor often selects a problem for the students to solve. When that happens, the students do not have to spend time deciding what the problem is, but they do have to share the same understanding of it.

2. *What caused the problem?*

After the group has agreed on what the problem is, the next step is to analyze it, particularly its causes and effects. In doing this the group must try to avoid letting opinions take priority over facts. The question "What are the facts?" must be foremost in the members' minds.

Answers to these questions are helpful in locating the facts:

    a. What effects indicate that a problem exists?

    b. How serious are the effects?

    c. What is causing the problem?

What is the problem?

What caused the problem?

d. Are the causes inherent in the problem situation?

e. Have previous attempts been made to solve the problem?

Most problems have multiple causes. In Step 2 we should identify them so we can uncover a workable solution.

3. *What are possible solutions to the problem?*

After deciding what caused the problem, the group proposes solutions. These solutions preferably will not only solve the problem but also will not cause other problems to develop and make conditions worse than they already are. In the case of the stomach ache, the doctor discovers that the patient has a kidney infection. One solution is to take out the kidney, but that solution might cause more serious problems than the patient has at present. A less drastic solution may be more appropriate, perhaps a program of medication.

To ensure that a group's solution does not cause more serious problems than already exist, the proper procedure is to develop a set of criteria or conditions that an acceptable solution must meet. One criterion obviously is that the solution must correct the cause of the problem. Other general criteria worth considering are:

a. Is the proposed solution workable?

b. Is it economical?

c. Is it the best possible way to solve the problem?

d. Will it produce more benefits than disadvantages?

e. Are the benefits significant?

f. Is the proposed solution just?

g. Is it moral?

h. Will it get the job done efficiently?

i. Is it clear?

j. Will it be harmful in any way?

Having determined the criteria, the group proposes solutions to the problem. Rather than accepting the first one proposed, the members should try to think of many ways to solve the problem.

To create a list of possible solutions, the group might use *brainstorming,* a technique designed to bring forth many ideas. Three rules govern its use: (a) ideas are to be expressed freely; as an idea comes to mind, it is to be expressed without evaluation by anyone; (b) all ideas, wild or otherwise, are welcomed; (c) as many ideas as possible are voiced; quantity is the goal. When the group runs out of ideas, it evaluates those resulting from the brainstorming.

4. *What is the best solution?*

In this step the group chooses the solution that seems to meet the criteria better than any other. As a means of accomplishing this end, these questions are helpful:

a. What is the exact nature of each solution?

b. How would it correct the problem?

c. How well would it remedy the problem?

d. How well does it satisfy the criteria?

e. Would a combination of solutions be best?

Determining which of the proposed solutions is best is a decision-making process. A decision implies

What are some possible solutions?

What is the best solution?

Methods of Decision Making

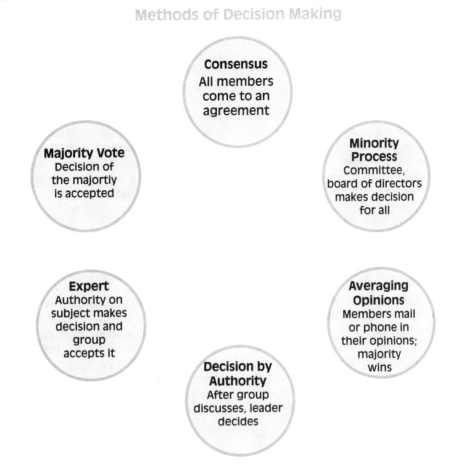

Consensus
All members come to an agreement

Majority Vote
Decision of the majortiy is accepted

Minority Process
Committee, board of directors makes decision for all

Expert
Authority on subject makes decision and group accepts it

Decision by Authority
After group discusses, leader decides

Averaging Opinions
Members mail or phone in their opinions; majority wins

that agreement to do something prevails among the group members, and the something that is agreed to is a choice among different alternatives.

Decisions can be made in many ways. Six common methods of decision making are examined briefly. Each has its values, and each fits certain circumstances. Each also has its own special consequences for the group's future functioning.[18]

Group consensus is the most satisfactory method of decision making. Everyone is in complete agreement. No vote is taken. None is necessary because all of the members arrive at the same conclusion. This is the ideal way to choose the best solution. Reaching consensus, however, is time-consuming in most circumstances. Nevertheless, consensus decisions usually enlist the support of all members, and they work together to implement it.

Majority vote is a second method of decision making. After the alternative solutions have been posed and discussed pro and con, the members vote for the alternative they prefer. The best solution is the one receiving the most votes. This method is quicker than consensus, but it has a serious drawback. If a minority is present, as is often the case, the minority

may not support the solution of the majority. Without the minority's help, the solution could be doomed.

A third common method of arriving at a decision is through the *minority process*, in which a selected group of members makes the decision for the majority. Many large groups invest the decision-making power in the hands of a committee, a board of directors, or an executive committee. This smaller group discusses the issues and selects the solution the group thinks is most appropriate. A disadvantage of this method is that the majority may not like the decision the minority makes.

Averaging individual opinions is carried out by asking each member individually — by phone or through the mail — for his or her choice. The chairperson then counts the votes and announces the decision. Because this method does not allow for discussion about the issue under question, it can create a problem.

Expert decisions are made by an individual or two who are known authorities in the problem area. The group then accepts the expert's decision. A potential problem with this method is deciding who is an expert. Care must be taken to choose the proper person.

The final method is *decision by authority*. After the group discusses the possible solutions, the chairperson or president makes the decision.

5. *How can the solution be implemented?*

The final step involves deciding how to put the solution into effect. This step has much value. First, in deciding how to execute a solution, the group may uncover possible weaknesses. What often sounds like a good decision might prove to be inoperable. The members find this out when they try to institute a plan of action. If the solution is unworkable, it can be abandoned in favor of one that is more likely to work.

Second, the group forces itself to go beyond just talking about a solution. It has to do something to carry out the solution. The adages "talk is cheap," "actions speak louder than words," and "put your money where your mouth is" apply here. Talk does not suffice in solving problems.[19]

Responsibility for executing the plan of action frequently is assigned to an individual, a subcommittee, or an action committee. If this is done, the problem-solving group outlines the general features of the action plan, which the assigned person or committee puts into operation.

In the classroom, where students are merely learning how to use the problem-solving method, Step 5 might result only in setting up a plan of action. A group to carry out the plan may not be necessary.

OTHER METHODS OF DISCUSSION

Groups can use a number of additional methods to assist in the discussion process. Ten are considered here, each of which has its own strengths. Some are most useful when audiences are present; others are restricted to private discussions.

Brainstorming

In brainstorming, a process for generating many ideas in a short time, group members can say what pops into mind without fear of evaluation. After the group has exhausted its ideas, evaluation of the ideas ensues. The aim is to eliminate premature and discussion-discouraging comments of a critical nature and thus permit more creative ideas to come to light.

The brainstorming period begins after the chairperson has stated the problem and given the necessary background information. The members are encouraged to state any ideas that come to mind, regardless of whether they seem implausible, impractical, impossible, or wild. A recorder writes these on a chalkboard for all to see. After the group runs out of ideas, each suggestion is analyzed in terms of established criteria. The criteria relate to the advantages and disadvantages of each proposal. Is it workable, economical, beneficial, just, moral, harmful, understandable, the best way to solve the problem? After the proposals have been analyzed, one or two should stand out as the best, and the group decides on the favored one.[20]

Nominal Group Technique

NGT for short, the nominal group technique gets its name from the first step in the process. During that part of the procedure, the members are a group in name only; no oral interaction takes place. The members meet, and each obtains a copy of the problem and its background information in written form. Each member then writes down his or her ideas without consulting the other members. This step permits all members to express their ideas (in writing) without fear of evaluation. Usually, lots of ideas are generated.

After the members are through writing, the papers are collected, and the ideas are written on a chalkboard or presented orally by the chairperson. The ideas then are evaluated. The ideas are not associated with the originator, making the discussion idea-centered.[21]

The Delphi Technique

Through the Delphi technique, judgments are systematically obtained from a group without the group's ever meeting. The entire process is handled through the mail. Given a problem to solve or a decision to make, the members independently and anonymously write comments, suggestions, and solutions. These are collected and combined, and a set is sent back to each contributing member. Each member reviews this set, again independently and anonymously, and returns comments, suggestions, and criticism to the sender. The process continues until a consensus develops in favor of the preferred idea, suggestion, or solution.

This technique minimizes problems associated with some sorts of members. Status-conscious members do not have to defend their ideas before their superiors. Subordinates do not have to be concerned about disagreeing with their superiors; they can say what they feel without fear of reprisal. The process takes time, however, and that is its major drawback.[22]

Problem Census

The problem census is used to find out what a group wishes to discuss at a group meeting. At the meeting's start, the presiding officer calls for suggestions for the meeting's agenda, problems the members would like to consider. After the group has exhausted the possibilities, the members vote on which problem should be considered first, second, and so on, establishing a priority of topics. These then are discussed in the order voted upon. If time runs out, the remaining topics are carried over to the next meeting.[23]

Role-Playing

Role-playing calls for members to act out a problem in human relations that is affecting the larger group. Members act out the circumstances surrounding the problem. They dramatize what it is all about.

Following the dramatization, they discuss what happened and suggest ways of dealing with the problem the role-players presented. The dramatization makes the problem easier to understand.[24]

Buzz Group

A large group or audience sometimes is divided into smaller units, or buzz groups, permitting everyone in the large group to participate. With an audience of fifty people, for example, ten groups of five people each might be formed. All members of each group then have an opportunity to speak if they desire. Typically used after an address by a speaker or lecturer, buzz groups can discuss issues brought up by the speaker. If the groups have questions, they have an opportunity to pose them to the speaker following the buzz sessions.[25]

Panel Discussion

The panel most often is composed of three to seven people pursuing a common topic in an in-

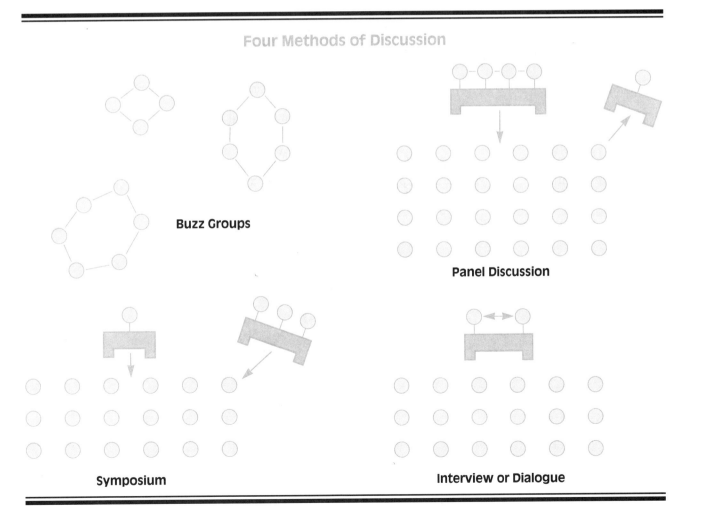

Four Methods of Discussion

Buzz Groups

Panel Discussion

Symposium

Interview or Dialogue

formal climate designed to promote spontaneous interaction. The panel normally speaks in front of an audience. A procedural leader starts off the panel discussion, keeps the talk on track, and ends the meeting. The audience may ask questions. The panel provides a novel way of informing an audience about a topic of interest.[26]

Symposium

Also staged before an audience, the symposium consists of a series of speeches delivered by three to five speakers. Each speaker covers a different aspect of the same subject, one in which he or she is an expert. A moderator controls the time, introduces each speaker, and handles the question-and-answer period following the speeches. This method is useful for informing a large group about various phases of a subject.[27]

Dialogue

In the dialogue, two people interact, discussing a topic in front of an audience. It can take different forms: a simple conversation between the two, an interview (one questions the other), or a counseling sort of session. The audience participates by asking questions at the end of the dialogue. Again, the method is used to inform an audience in a unique manner.[28]

Interview

In the interview, the interaction is restricted to questions and answers. An audience is present, listening to an interviewer question an expert on a subject area. "Meet the Press" and "Face the Nation" are television versions of this technique, another way of informing an audience.[29]

SUMMARY

Under ordinary circumstances, we can learn more and can arrive at better solutions to our problems in groups. Group discussion has disadvantages, but these are largely outweighed by the advantages. Discussion works if group members have done their homework and if the members are sensible, willing, and able.

There are three categories of learning groups: experiential, enlightenment, and classroom. The classroom learning group is the one most pertinent to students. A format for learning in groups sets forth a logical, systematic method for discussing a reading assignment or a textbook chapter.

In defining a problem, awareness, goals, and barriers must be present for a problem to exist. Problems can be of three types: fact, value, and policy. Policy problems are the sort most often discussed in small groups.

One problem-solving format is the standard agenda. It is patterned after the Dewey reflective thinking process. Its five steps help a group move through discussion of a problem, practicing systematic inquiry.

Ten additional methods of discussion that groups employ when meeting in private or before public audiences are: brainstorming, the nominal group technique (NGT), the Delphi technique, problem census, role-playing, buzz group, panel discussion, symposium, dialogue, and interview.

16

Public Speaking: Preliminary Steps

For a class assignment, students were asked to present a one- minute speech on why people should support consumer protection associations. The class listened to each speech and then selected the best one. Tom Jones garnered the most votes with this speech:

Caveat emptor! Let the buyer beware! Words are slippery things, especially in the hands of some salesmen. There was a farmer who took a truckload of fine hogs to the county fair. But he kept bragging about the one he hadn't brought. That hog, he said, was so tall that a man couldn't touch its back if he held his hand as high as he could reach. "Some tall hog," he kept saying.

Finally a stranger stepped up and said he would buy *that* hog. They agreed on a price, and the stranger paid his money. Then he went home with the farmer to get the hog. The farmer took the man into the pig pen. "There he is," he said. "That hog?" asked the man, pointing to a small, scrawny pig. "Sure," said the farmer. "You just reach up as high as you can and you can't possibly touch its back."

Some salesmen are like the farmer. They make their products sound better than they are. The consumer needs to be protected against their shyster tricks. That's why I believe we should support consumer protection associations.

Why did the students vote for this speech? They gave a variety of reasons. It took exactly one minute to deliver. It was well-organized. It clearly made the point. Many found it absurd, yet funny and interesting. They got a chuckle and learned a lesson without being lectured.

The speaker covered very well some of the rudiments of an effective speech, especially organization, clarity, and interest. More important, he won over the listeners, receiving more votes than anyone else. When quizzed about his preparation strategy, Tom replied that he had his fellow students in mind when he constructed the speech. He thought humor would be appealing to them and an anecdote would make the point better than facts and figures could with his audience. Tom's approach to the subject focused on the listeners; he was listener-centered.

Through Tom's listener-centered approach, he fulfilled the goal of public speaking: to influence the behavior of the listeners in the way the speaker desires. In Tom's case, he wanted to alert them to the need for better consumer protection and at the same time win their votes. He did this by considering their needs and interests, how they would respond to his message. As any speaker should, Tom kept in mind the qualities of effective speech construction, but foremost in his thinking was the audience: How can I win them over?

As we begin this explanation of some of the elements of speech construction, we should remember to respect our listeners. If we want to influence their behavior, we will succeed more often by directing our attention to the receivers of our messages. The key to success as a speaker is knowing what the listeners want and then satisfying those desires.

The remaining chapters of this book center on public speaking, that type of speech in which a single speaker presents a continuous discourse on a subject supposedly of interest to a sizable number of people. In these five chapters we concentrate on preparing and delivering public speeches. This chapter covers audience analysis, choice of subject and purpose, and subject analysis, as parts of the preparatory process.

ANALYZING THE AUDIENCE AND OCCASION

A colleague reports the following experience:

At one time I emceed many variety shows for clubs and organizations, and I was fairly good at it. My reputation won me a well-paid contract emceeing a dinner show for a military club. I envisioned a group of several hundred boisterous males, slightly under-the-weather, ready for laughs, especially at off-color jokes.

Imagine my surprise when I stepped out to introduce the first act to see a "family" audience—husbands, wives and children! Not knowing what to do, I stuck with my script and began as I had planned with a couple of colorful jokes, most appropriate for an all-male serviceman audience. Silence followed my humor — no laughter, no clapping, just silence. Backstage, between acts, the club director issued an ultimatum: Cut the jokes or the show stops. I cut the jokes and learned a lesson I never forgot: Know the audience and the occasion, and adapt the message to both.

Our colleague undoubtedly knew that the audience is central in speaking situations. He mentioned that he had visualized an all-male audience and planned his remarks accordingly. Of course, his thinking proved faulty and trouble resulted. He recognized the error in his thinking and vowed never to make the mistake again.

What should he have done? How can a speaker analyze an audience? The question of audience analysis is vital in public speaking because if a speaker knows the listeners' interests and attitudes, he or she can shape the speech around them. Speech-building factors such as topic selection, formulation of the speech's purpose, selection of supporting materials, and choice of language can be molded around listener interests and attitudes.

The audience analysis question is so important that considerable research has been invested in finding the answers.[1] Our purpose here is not to describe the research results but, rather, to offer a way to analyze an audience, based on the research. We recommend that the speaker analyze the audience by obtaining data on the occasion, on the common needs and interests of the listeners, and on the listeners' attitudes toward the subject and speaker.[2]

First we describe how to obtain the general kinds of data, then specify what data are pertinent in

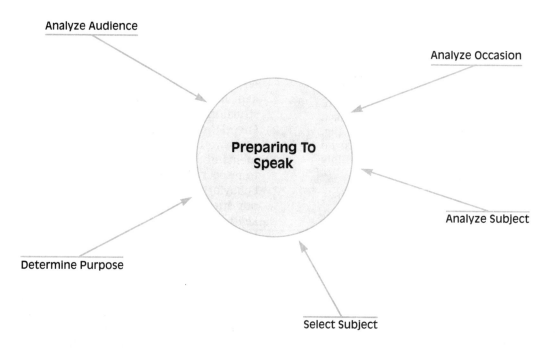

FIGURE 16.1.　Preparing to speak.

analyzing an audience, and finally describe how to use the data obtained.

Obtaining Data About Listeners

How can a speaker obtain data about an audience? The answer is twofold: by observation and by inquiry. The emcee who messed up his performance by telling off-color jokes realized afterward that he should have analyzed his audience, and he could have done so by observation and inquiry. He could have observed the audience beforehand by attending previous shows, because they were regular features of the military club. By observing them prior to his engagement, he would have gotten a fair idea of the group's composition, gender, age range, and so forth. He could have gained additional data by inquiry — asking the person who hired him. A telephone call or two would have provided him with enough details to prepare for his audience.

Of course, data can be obtained in other ways besides observing and inquiring. The members themselves can be questioned, as can others who have spoken before the group previously. Many organizations publish newsletters or magazines, and these reveal insights about the potential audience. Also, letters can be written to gather information about an audience.

In many speech classes, students learn how to analyze by polling the class members. The class constructs a questionnaire, which everyone fills out. In this manner, class members elicit useful information about the needs and interests of the class as a whole. Each student can use this information in preparing speeches for class.

Classes use two other devices for audience analysis purposes. The first measures the class's knowledge about the subject of each speech, and the second, the students' attitudes toward each subject.

To find out how much the class knows about the subject, each student speaker prepares and administers a test several days before speaking. The test contains items that bear significantly upon the topic. If the class as a whole scores low on the test, the speaker's classmates probably know little about the subject, and he or she can enlighten them in the speech. If they score high, they probably know much about the topic already, and he or she will have to adopt a different tactic; the speaker could add new knowledge or change the subject altogether. The test can be administered after the speech to measure what the students learned from it, and the before-and-after scores can be compared.

An attitude measure also can be administered before the student delivers the speech. The speaker announces the point of view to be upheld in the speech and asks class members to indicate whether they are for, against, or neutral toward his viewpoint. From the information obtained, the speaker can adapt the ideas accordingly. If the audience is favorable, the speaker's ideas will be well-received, and he or she can say what he or she wants. If the class is generally opposed or neutral, the speaker will have to adjust his or her speech to win them over.

What kind of information should a speaker obtain about an audience? A description of items that have proven to be helpful in speech preparation and delivery follows.[3]

The Occasion

When is the speech to be given? What date and hour? Is there anything unusual about the date and hour; for instance, is it a holiday? Where is the meeting — in a small town, large city, farm area? How many people will attend? Is the meeting indoors or outdoors? What size is the meeting place? What equipment is available — a speaker's platform, podium, chalkboards, audio system, movie or slide projection facilities? Is the meeting a regular meeting or a special meeting of the organization? What is the purpose of the meeting? What will the general mood or atmosphere likely be? Are other speakers on the program? Will someone introduce the speaker?

The Nature of the Audience

What is the age range of the listeners — all children, all adults, mixed? What genders are represented — all male, all female, mixed? How about family status — single, married, parents, children, mixed? What is the general economic status — low, middle, upper, mixed? What educational backgrounds are evident — elementary, high school, college, mixed? What occupations are represented — skilled, unskilled, professional, business, trade, homemakers, students, mixed? What religions have a bearing? What political beliefs are apparent — liberal, conservative, independent, radical, mixed? What memberships do the listeners hold — union, management, lodges, fraternities, sororities, clubs? What types of entertainment do they like? Where do they get their information — books, magazines, newspapers, television?

Attitudes Toward Subject

What is the prevailing attitude toward the speaker's subject? Is it favorable, opposed, undecided, indifferent?

Attitudes Toward Speaker

Do the listeners know the speaker? If so, are they favorable, neutral, or unfavorably inclined? Is the speaker like or unlike the listeners in terms of needs and interests? What are the speaker's reasons for speaking to this group? What is the speaker's reputation?

Using the Data

The data can be used to help the speaker adapt to the audience in at least four ways: (1) slanting the subject; (2) choosing supporting materials; (3) modifying delivery; (4) avoiding blunders.[4]

Slanting the Subject

Slanting the subject perhaps can be explained more clearly by citing the preparation methods of a successful politician. Reelected to state office for fourteen two-year terms, Fred Smith went into each campaign with one speech keyed to the major issues of the time. During the campaign he delivered the speech almost a thousand times, some days as often as five times.

Although the basic points remained constant, the rest of the speech changed for each new audience. For one thing, he slanted the subject to fit the audience. If he addressed an all men's group, he developed the subject around predominantly male interests — sports, business, money, politics. When he faced a rural audience, he modified his basic speech to cover the subject from the farmers' perspective. When talking to women, he stressed their primary interests as they related to the subject. The subject took on a decided football flavor in a city with a championship national league football team.

Choosing Supporting Materials

This speaker chose supporting materials in the same way, selecting those that seemed most appropriate for the specific audience. With businesspeople he was heavy on statistics and careful analysis. With union members tales of his own working days abounded.

Modifying the Delivery

Fred's voice was powerful. He could be heard in the largest hall without a microphone. But he adapted his delivery to the audience and the occasion. Before a female group, he spoke softly but loud enough to be heard. In a tavern, he blasted away, sometimes using slang.

Avoiding Blunders

Fred's strength was in avoiding blunders. He always said the right thing to each audience, being careful about the race, religion, and politics of his listeners. Rarely offending anyone, he worded his points carefully to win the votes of both Republicans and Democrats, Catholics and Protestants.

How did Fred manage to know his audiences so well? He kept a card file. Over the years he added considerable information about clubs, organizations, and people throughout the state. As he prepared, for each audience, he referred to these cards. Consequently, he usually tapped the audience's interests.

Fred earned his living knowing people. The average speaker, however, would have little use for a card system like Fred's. Nevertheless, Fred's preparation methods illustrate how to use the data obtained from audience analysis. The information assists the speaker in adapting the subject matter, supporting materials, and delivery to the audience, avoiding blunders in the process.

SELECTING THE SUBJECT

One of our colleagues headed the university speaker's bureau for three years. Upon request, the bureau provided faculty speakers for community groups. He reports: "Almost every request — and I average ten a week — was for a particular subject: 'Could you send us a speaker on population control?' 'We'd like to hear Professor Thomas lecture on abortion.' 'Do you have someone who can talk about the PLO question?'" Our colleague's point is that when we are asked to give a speech or report, most of the time we are assigned a subject area to talk about. Only in rare instances —when the speaker is famous, for instance — is the subject left to the speaker's choice. Even then the speaker might ask what the audience would like to hear. Thus, for the average speaker, choice of subject is not an issue.

Speaking in Class

For the student completing a classroom assignment, subject selection becomes an important issue. "What can I talk about?" is a common question. The obvious answer is: matters the speaker thinks are important for other people to know; subjects that could be useful, instructive, profitable, beneficial, or entertaining to the listeners; topics that are on the speaker's mind, either impressed on it by daily experience or developed through observation and reflection. The speaker ought to talk about matters with which he or she is intimately acquainted, those pertaining to schoolwork, personal life, or, if he or she works, the job.

When a student, Joelyn, asked, "What can I talk about?" we replied: "What do you do? What courses do you take? Do you participate in sports? Go to church? Work? Go steady?" She answered, "I major in psychology — taking 'abnormal' this semester. I play tennis, golf, and racquetball. I'm Catholic. I work part-time as a dental assistant. I'm engaged."

"Anything in particular about abnormal psych that fascinates you?" we inquired.

She replied: "I'm interested in personality disorders, the hysterical and cyclothymic types especially. Actually I know quite a bit about them."

"How do you feel about tennis and golf pros earning thousands?" we asked.

Joelyn answered: "I'm definitely against that. My friends say I rant and rave about them."

"As a Catholic, what's your view on abortion?" we asked her.

She answered quickly: "I could talk for hours on that subject. Woman priesthood also . . . and contraception."

Our next question was: "Do you believe in the use of gas to quiet dental patients?"

"No," she said. "The side-effects are dangerous to some people, and the dentist doesn't bother to take a patient's medical history."

Then we asked, "Do you believe in premarital sex?"

She hesitated, "Well—"

Finally we asked, "Do you have any ideas for subjects for your speech?" No answer was required. Joelyn had a half dozen subjects to talk about. Now, Joelyn wondered, "Which one would the audience be interested in?"

Joelyn's query can be answered through audience analysis, by following the procedures described in the previous section. Through her analysis she might learn, for instance, that her audience is pro-choice. A pro-life stance on her part would have to be tempered to fit her listeners' biases. Or she might discover that the audience knows absolutely nothing about hysterical personality types but are eager to learn. Maybe they don't care about dental care, so she might be wise to pass over that subject. Through inquiry and observation Joelyn can find out what interests her listeners.

Guidelines for Subject Choice

Through our questions Joelyn uncovered five or six subjects that she could talk about. Of course, she could talk about only one at a time, so she had to choose one. Listener interest should influence her choice, but additional guides might help her make up her mind.

She should pick the subject that most interests not only the audience but herself as well. Perhaps her classmates want to know her views on three subjects: premarital sex, abortion, and female priests. They seem equally interested in all three. She then has to choose, and her choice should be the one in which she is most interested and about which she has, or can acquire, more knowledge than her listeners have.

In addition, Joelyn should consider the time available and the appropriateness of the subject for the occasion. For a ten-minute speech, thorough coverage of any one of the three choices of her classmates would be impossible. Books have been written on each subject, so treating any one in depth would be impossible. Perhaps she could talk about some aspect — premarital sex for teenagers, one reason why women should be ordained as priests, or medical reasons for abortion. Difficult, obscure, technical, and complex subjects require more time, not only to talk about but also to prepare for. Thus, Joelyn would have to consider how much time she has to prepare and how long she can talk, and then stay within those limits.

The occasion also is a consideration. Almost anything in good taste is acceptable in a speech class. If Joelyn were to speak to an elementary school class, however, the wisest course would be to abandon topics on abortion, premarital sex, and priesthood for women. These subjects would not be appropriate for the audience.[5]

DECIDING ON THE PURPOSE

Having analyzed the audience and occasion and having picked a subject on which to speak, Joelyn next has to decide on the purpose of her speech. She really has to come to a decision about two purposes: a general purpose for her speech and a specific purpose relating to the subject.

From the Chapter 3 description of the types of speaking, we will recall three general purposes: to inform, to persuade, and to actuate. Speeches to inform are designed to widen listeners' knowledge on a subject. Persuasive speeches are those with the general purpose of altering the direction, intensity, or salience of listeners' attitudes toward the speaker's subject. Speeches intended to actuate expect the listeners to perform a definite overt act, to take some sort of action.

The specific purpose refers to the exact outcome the speaker intends and hopes to achieve with the particular audience and with the particular subject. The specific purpose should be stated in a single declarative sentence. It should be something that is realistically attainable within the limits of speaker, audience, occasion, and available time.[6] Here are samples:

1. *Subject of speech:* television viewing by children
   General purpose: to inform
   Specific purpose: to develop within the audience an understanding of the extent of commercialization during children's television programs

2. *Subject of speech:* government control of children's television programs
   General purpose: to persuade
   Specific purpose: to bring about the realization within the audience that children's television programming is over-commercialized

3. *Subject of speech:* government control of genetic engineering
   General purpose: to actuate
   Specific purpose: to ask the audience to vote for government control of genetic engineering because of the release of genetically engineered viruses, bacteria, and transgenic plants and animals into the environment

4. *Subject of speech:* handguns
   General purpose: to inform
   Specific purpose: to bring about an appreciation within the audience of the prevalence of handguns in American homes

5. *Subject of speech:* intercollegiate athletics
   General purpose: to persuade
   Specific purpose: to convince the audience that we should promote intramural rather than intercollegiate sports

Some public speakers attempt to do too much in a speech and, because they do, they fail. In developing the specific purpose, the speaker must consider the amount of speaking time as well as the audience and occasion. A classroom speech with a five-minute time limit cannot cover the commercialization of children's television programming in its entirety, but it can point out the extent of commercialization with a few pointed statistics and an example or two. In developing the specific purpose, the speaker must take care, therefore, not to cover too much.

The shorter the speech, the more pointed the specific purpose must be. In Example 3, the subject, genetic engineering, probably cannot be dealt with adequately in a five-minute classroom speech. The subject demands a longer speaking time. Unless the class is made up of genetic engineering students, explaining genetic engineering itself could take at least five minutes. A more specific purpose might be to inform the class, in the five minutes, of the intelligence of vegetables, an important aspect of genetic engineering, and one that can be treated in that amount of time while keeping the class highly interested.

With the specific purpose in mind, the public speaker now can move to subject analysis, the next step in preparing to speak. As the analysis proceeds, however, the speaker may uncover new insights about the subject and, as a consequence, may want to alter the specific purpose to keep it in line with the new thinking. Later, when researching the subject, the speaker again may become aware of aspects of the subject that he or she did not know about. The specific purpose may have to be changed once more. The speaker should make whatever adjustments are necessary to accommodate the new awareness.

ANALYZING THE SUBJECT

When public speakers analyze a subject, they take it apart, intellectually, to probe its meaning or to discover what topics are involved. Through analysis, they should seek not only the topics or "talking points" but also locate the main points and subpoints for their speech. Only through analysis can a speaker determine which ideas are relevant and germane to the subject and the specific purpose.

Subject analysis has added values. It enables the speaker to research the subject with discrimination and judgment, limiting the scope of the research. Knowing which points or topics are vital to the subject and purpose, a speaker can search for materials that support those points. The speaker will know what he or she needs and will be able to recognize appropriate material when it is uncovered in the research.[7]

Beginning speakers often ask which should be done first — deciding on a specific purpose, analysis, or research. The best answer, generally speaking, is that they go hand-in-hand. Some general reading is necessary at the outset to obtain a broad conception of the subject. In turn, the specific purpose can be stated in a preliminary way. After the analysis has been completed, more intense reading and research can take place. When that is done, the specific purpose can be changed if need be.

Among the many methods of analyzing a subject, three common ways—stock question, stock issues, and lines of argument— are considered here. High school and college debaters will recognize these as methods debaters use to analyze debate propositions. The first, the stock question method, is especially useful in analyzing subjects for informative-type speeches.

The information on subject analysis, by the way, applies not only to public speaking but to interviewing and group discussion as well. The interviewer and the group discussant will find the following descriptions useful in preparing a subject for interviewing or discussing purposes.

Stock Question Method

In the stock question method the speaker tries to locate answers to these questions about the subject: who, which, what, when, where, how, and why.[8]

A student, Melissa, used this method as a means of analyzing her subject, the plight of the elderly. She sought answers to these questions: Who are the elderly? Which ones are being poorly treated? What is happening to them? When does it occur? Where does it happen? How are they being mistreated? Why is this happening to them? With the answers to the questions in hand, she had a general understanding of her subject. Next she fleshed out the subject by gathering more details on the aspect she decided to concentrate on in her speech. She believed the answer to the "why" question would be most appropriate for her audience of classmates. Therefore, she built her speech around those answers, after finding more reasons why the elderly are having a difficult time.

Stock Issues Method

The stock issues method is most useful for analyzing a complex problem and arriving at a solution to that problem.[9] There are six stock issues, of which one, several, or all could constitute a speech: problem or need, inherency, plan, practicality, advantages/disadvantages, and counter plan.

1. *Problem or need.* Is there a problem to be solved? Before we change to a new way of doing things, we usually have to be convinced that something is wrong with the old way, or that the old way may cause difficulty in the future. A thorough analysis of this stock issue requires examination of the present system, including its history. The analysis ordinarily uncovers any problems related to the present, and why these problems came about. To do this, the speaker tries to find the answers to questions such as: What is the present system? What is wrong with the present system? Why do we have the present system? Whom is it likely to harm in the future?

2. *Inherency.* Is the problem, or the cause of the problem, an inherent part of the status quo? Not only must we be able to visualize a problem before we make a change, but we also must realize that we cannot overcome the problem with our present policy, whatever it may be. The issue of inherency deals with the relationship that exists between the present problem and the present policy.

   This relationship is illustrated in the following questions: Must we adopt a new policy to overcome the problem, or can we continue to practice the present policy and overcome the problem? Or can we modify the present policy in some way without adopting a new one and still overcome the problem? To adequately analyze the inherency issue, we should answer questions such as: What caused the problem we are facing? Have attempts been made already to solve this problem? If so, are they part of the present policy? Why have previous attempts at solving the problem failed?

3. *Plan.* After deciding the present policy has an inherent need for change, the speaker determines what type of policy related to the proposition can be proposed. Needs and plans must be compatible. Therefore, stock issues may be phrased as follows: Would the action the resolution suggests eliminate the inherent problem? The analysis for stock issue 3 should answer two important questions: What possible plans could be suggested in keeping with the policy we are advocating? How will these plans solve the problem? In answering the first question, the speaker should consider all possible plans.

4. *Practicality.* Is it reasonable to assume that the plan the resolution implies could be implemented if it were found to be desirable? Figuring out answers to solve problems is not too difficult, but putting these solutions into practice is quite another thing. For example, for a city government to have "an impartial Board of Control" to investigate complaints against its police department may be theoretically ideal, but finding impartial people to compose such a board might be quite a different matter.

5. *Advantages/disadvantages.* Would plans suggested by the proposition be free from serious detrimental side-effects if they were put into effect? The basis upon which many people decide to accept a new policy in preference to an old one is that they believe the effect of their decision will be

advantageous in the long run. We frequently discover inherent needs in the present system and an obvious plan that could overcome these needs, but we may find that the new program creates new harms, some of which may be worse than the current ones.

In the early 1960s, for example, the United States perceived an inherent need to do something about Castro in Cuba. One solution proposed was for the U. S. Marines to invade Cuba and throw Castro out. Most people had little doubt that Castro was a danger, that he was not going to be eliminated under the current U. S. foreign policy, and that the Marines were capable of invading Cuba and eliminating him. When the question of overall advantages and disadvantages was raised, however, this policy was rejected. The possibility that it would cause a direct confrontation between the Soviet Union and the United States deterred an invasion. Most people believed that having Castro with all of the accompanying evils was better than having war with Russia. Thus, even though the current policy was conceded to be ineffective, it was retained because it was more desirable than the alternative.

In the analysis the speaker should weigh the advantages and disadvantages of all possible plans and attempt to determine all of the advantages and disadvantages that would accrue if any one of them were adopted. In this way the speaker will be able to judge which plan is best to use and, at the same time, be able to determine the significant arguments against all plans.

6. *Counter plan.* Is the policy stated in the proposition the best way to eliminate the problem? Stock issue 6 considerably widens the scope of analysis. The speaker should determine what other solutions could be proposed for all the problems uncovered in the proposition analysis and also determine the advantages and disadvantages of these solutions.

The stock issues system seems more involved than it actually is. This system does provide a comprehensive method for analyzing a subject. It may not be worthwhile for all class speeches, but it is certainly worthy for speeches of greater importance than earning a grade to pass a course. One of our former students, a legislator, uses the stock issues method when preparing to speak at committee sessions or before his legislative peers. College debaters utilize this system when analyzing debate propositions. Businesspeople of our acquaintance follow this pattern as they get ready for public speaking engagements.

Line of Argument

A third method of subject analysis is useful for subjects related to public policy — government regulations, laws, and so forth. This method analyzes the subject through lines of argument.[10] The nine lines are justice and injustice, waste, confusion, security, morality, efficiency, strength and weakness, prestige, and destruction.

1. *Justice and injustice.* One of the primary ways we evaluate policy today is on the basis of the "justness" of that policy. The speaker should determine if an injustice is being perpetrated on any people under the present policy. In addition, the speaker should consider if the proposed policy would be unjust to anyone.

2. *Waste.* Most people consider waste to be an evil. Therefore, the speaker should examine the present system to see if there is any waste of money, manpower, and resources under this system. All proposed plans should be similarly examined.

3. *Confusion.* If a present or proposed policy is confusing in its interpretation or application, that is reason to reject it. The speaker should examine the policy to determine if confusion does or would exist.

4. *Security.* Most people consider security, whether individual, community, or world, to be a highly desirable commodity. Insecurity, or things that threaten security, are considered undesirable. Consideration of the security provided, or threatened, by the present policy and any proposed policies should be included in the analysis.

5. *Morality.* As individuals in a society, we have certain moral principles. If a policy violates these principles, we consider that policy to be bad. The speaker should examine present and proposed policies to determine their moral quality. If they are morally reprehensible on one or more grounds, that may be reason to reject them.

6. *Efficiency.* On propositions of policy, arguments often center on the relative efficiency of a proposed policy versus the inefficiency of a present one. It is often argued, for example, that the federal government should act to attain a certain goal because the fifty state governments cannot do it as efficiently. In some propositions the central issue is efficiency. To illustrate with the proposition, "The federal government should establish a program of air pollution control," the speech should focus on the question of whether the federal government can control air pollution more efficiently than the individual states can.

7. *Strength and weakness.* We want ourselves, our families, our community, and our nation to be

strong. The speaker should analyze present and proposed policies to see if they will lead to increased or decreased strength of those affected.

8. *Prestige.* One of the strongest arguments employed with some propositions is the effect it will have on people's prestige. We like to be well thought of as individuals, as communities, as states, and as a nation. Thus, a good policy enhances prestige. Most of us consider a policy that detracts from prestige to be undesirable.

9. *Destruction.* A common line of argument in policy debate concerns the destructive potential of policy. Many policies are opposed because they may lead to nuclear war or to the destruction of some aspect of our way of life. For example, a furor was raised in Hawaii when some land developers wanted to build apartments and hotels on the slopes of Diamond Head, a landmark on the island of Oahu. Those who opposed the plan argued that this policy would destroy the natural beauty of the island.

With the line of argument approach, the speaker analyzes the subject in terms of the most fitting arguments. Melissa, the student who talked about the elderly, used this method for a second speech she gave on the subject. In the first speech she employed the stock question system. As a result of that speech, she realized the elderly were being unjustly treated. For the second speech she analyzed the "justice and injustice" line of argument as it related to the subject, and her analysis gave her additional insights around which she then built the second speech.

Subject analysis ranks as a priority element in speech preparation. Through analysis the speaker determines which ideas are relevant and important to the subject. By following a system such as one of the three described, the speaker investigates the subject with discrimination and judgment. Knowing the points vital to the subject, the speaker can seek materials that amplify or support those points.

SUMMARY

The key to successful speaking is knowing what the audience wants and then adapting the speech material to fit those desires. Familiarity with the special requirements of the occasion during which the speech is to be presented will enable us to avoid mistakes in delivery. Like audiences, occasions differ, and to be successful, the speaker should be cognizant of the particular demands of the occasion during which he or she speaks.

After analyzing the audience and the occasion, the next step in preparing to speak is to select a subject. The general guidelines revolve around picking a subject that has interest to the speaker and to the audience. They also take into consideration the available time for speaking and the occasion.

The next step, deciding on the speech purpose, has two phases. The general purpose asks: Is the intent of the speech to inform, persuade, or actuate? After the speaker has made that decision, he or she should select a specific purpose. That purpose concerns the exact outcome the speaker intends for the speech, the particular audience, and the occasion.

Subject analysis helps the speaker locate "talking points," the main topics to be covered in the speech. It also helps guide research and gives further direction in deciding upon the specific purpose.

Related to subject choice, purpose selection, and subject analysis is the question: Which of these activities should come first? In most cases a preliminary analysis — based on the speaker's general reading and personal knowledge — should precede the others. As the speaker begins researching the subject, deeper analysis can take place and the specific purpose may become more pointed. Subject, purpose, analysis, and research are complementary activities; they go hand-in-hand.

Investigating
The Speech Subject

At this stage in preparing to speak, the speaker has a subject and a specific purpose well in mind. He or she has accomplished audience analysis and knows much about the occasion. The speaker has analyzed the subject somewhat so that subsequent research will not be time wasted looking for unnecessary, irrelevant information. This next step is to investigate the subject. Research is in order.

In this chapter we describe how to find materials on the speech subject. We look first at the sources the speaker can draw on for information: personal knowledge, interviews, and library resources. Then we explain what to look for — specifically, amplifying and supporting materials. As we review the suggestions and techniques for conducting speech research, we should recognize that they are useful not only in speech preparation but also can be employed for investigating subjects in interviewing and group discussion.

SOURCES OF INFORMATION

Two categories of research sources are available to a speaker: subjective and objective sources. *Subjective* sources are those the speaker is personally involved with. Two such sources — the speaker's personal knowledge and speaker-conducted interviews — are considered here. These are subjective sources because of the speaker's direct personal involvement, based on the speaker's internal judgment of the worth of the information.

Objective sources are factual materials, those similarly perceived by other people and verifiable scientifically, if necessary. Unlike subjective sources,

objective materials do not pertain to a speaker's likes and dislikes or agreements and disagreements with the information. The objective sources we will be reviewing are primarily those located in a library.[1]

Personal Knowledge

If the subject selected is one in which the speaker has a strong interest, he or she quite possibly has had direct experience with the subject. The speaker's knowledge can provide interesting and valuable material.[2] For example, Melissa chose as her subject the plight of the elderly. She drew heavily on her own experiences with her mother and father, both of whom were hospitalized for months with serious illnesses. Both died in the hospital, leaving behind several hundred thousand dollars' worth of medical bills after depleting all of their personal savings. Joelyn talked about cosmetic dentistry. Because she worked in a dentist's office, she was familiar with the pros and cons of that type of dental work. She was able to offer valuable advice about which individuals should have their teeth treated cosmetically.

As we know from our discussion of speaker credibility in Chapter 4, speakers we deem credible are ones we are most apt to believe, and they have the most influence over us. We tend to believe experts and people of authority who have high initial credibility with us. We also are influenced by those who produce a derived image of credibility because of their obvious command of the facts about their subject. Students usually have little initial credibility, but they may achieve credibility as they speak, by exhibiting solid factual knowledge. Knowledge drawn from their limited experience and background may not be very convincing. Objective, factual information usually serves them better.[3]

Interviews

Vast amounts of useful and authoritative information can be gathered by interviewing the appropriate people. If a speaker is preparing a talk on local employment practices, what better sources of information could be interviewed than the personnel directors of local businesses? Or, if the speaker plans to talk on a topic such as gun control, why not talk with police officers and with business people who sell guns? Usually, individuals who are experts in a given subject area are willing to be interviewed about it.

Proper interviewing procedures should be followed, of course, and the interviewer must be careful not to be pushy or irksome. The interviewer should make appointments in advance and should prepare for the interview by writing out the questions to ask. Too often students let such matters go until the last minute. Then they rush around, cornering professors between classes or appointments, trying to secure answers to ill-conceived questions, with poor results. Short interviews, arranged and scheduled correctly, can yield invaluable information.

Too, poll-taking can provide useful insights on a topic. For example, to find out how people will vote in an election, a common practice is to take a poll in neighborhoods in which people have voted for past winners. The residents are asked questions about whom they favor, and their favorites will more than likely win again. Poll-taking can yield samples of people's opinions on a variety of subjects. And canvassing people in a shopping center by asking several well-thought-out questions can yield interesting opinions on a variety of subjects.

Interviews can be conducted through correspondence.

In addition to being a pollster, speakers can conduct interviews by corresponding with the person whose opinion they seek. Letters requesting the desired information should be prepared and mailed early enough so the reply will arrive in time. Through correspondence, the interviewer can obtain opinions of people living in distant places.[4]

Library Resources

An important part of gathering material is learning how to use the school or community library. Almost all of the data needed for public speeches can come from books, pamphlets, periodicals, and documentary materials in libraries. In addition, the library staff can offer valuable assistance. These workers usually are willing to aid in the search for special materials, helping to procure publications from sources other than the library, and assisting in other ways.

Library research requires an understanding of the methods libraries use to organize their collections, as well as a knowledge of basic bibliographic and reference materials. Essentially, all libraries follow the same general principles in organizing their collections, and all provide similar resources for research. They follow a system of subject classification, use a card catalog, and offer bibliographic and reference materials. Of course, every school and community library arranges its materials in its own special way, and each one does not supply the identical quantity and quality of material. In spite of these variations, however, they follow the same general procedure, and certain bibliographic and reference resources are common to all.

Card Catalog

When the speaker is looking for books in a library, the card catalog is the place to begin. Normally it is housed in a centrally located, many-drawered cabinet. Many libraries have computerized the card catalog, and information is secured by typing the request onto a computer terminal.

The card catalog provides information on every book in the library. The cards are classified by title, by author, and also by subject. If the speaker knows only the title or only the author, the book's card can be found by looking under title or author. If only the subject is known, the subject catalog is the place to look.

The catalog card also supplies the information necessary to locate the publication. A "call number" appears in the upper left corner of the card. The symbols are derived from the scheme of subject classification the particular library uses. Normally, libraries post simple explanations near the card catalog of the scheme they follow.[5]

Many libraries have computerized the card catalog.

Indexes and Bibliographies

The card catalog, of course, lists only the publications available in that library. Its value, therefore, is limited to that library's collection. In doing library research, the resources of several libraries may be needed, particularly if the library is a typical, small school library. Also, the catalog does not index all materials in the library. Periodical articles are not indexed, nor are pamphlets, special collections, and government documents (although these frequently are indexed separately). Therefore, the speaker must turn to other sources such as indexes and bibliographies.

1. *Periodical indexes.* The speaker should consult one or more of the following publications for articles on specific subjects:

    a. *Reader's Guide to Periodical Literature* — articles appearing in about a hundred periodicals of general interest.

    b. *International Index to Periodical Literature* — scholarly journals and many foreign publications.

    c. *Public Affairs Information Service* — books, articles, pamphlets, and government documents in the areas of economics, political science, and sociology.

    d. *Agriculture Index* — special publications related to agriculture.

    e. *Education Index* — articles, books, pamphlets, and government documents on education.

    f. *New York Times Index* — index of the contents of the *Times.*

    g. *Facts on file* — a weekly summary of current events.

2. *Bibliographies.* The researcher also should examine bibliographies — comprehensive lists of publications issued in a given country — for all types of published materials on many subjects. *The United States Catalog* (1899 to 1934), which is kept up-to-date by the *Cumulative Book Index,* is the index to publications issued in this country since 1898. It lists these publications by author, subject, and title. Obviously it is very large, consisting of many volumes and covering many subjects. Its thoroughness actually may be a handicap because a great deal of searching is required to uncover materials on a specific topic.

Reference Books

Because of their general character, reference books cannot be indexed by subject matter in the card catalog. Yet these books — general and special dictionaries, encyclopedias, yearbooks, directories, and biographical dictionaries — are extremely valuable. Dictionaries are useful in defining terms; encyclopedias (e.g., *Encyclopaedia Britannica*) are excellent sources for a quick orientation to the subject matter and for special items of information, and biographical dictionaries (e.g., *Who's Who*) contain data about people.

Special Materials

Certain periodicals and documents contain current information on various subjects. Following are a few of the periodicals that may be useful:

Harvard Business Review
Nation's Business
Survey of Current Business
American Economic Review
Current History
American Journal of International Law
Foreign Affairs
Foreign Policy Reports
International Affairs
Law and Contemporary Problems
International Labor Review
Monthly Labor Reviews

Annals of the American Academy of Political and Social Science
American Political Science Review
Journal of Politics
Atlantic Monthly
Commentary
Harper's Magazine
Nation
New Republic
Twentieth Century
Yale Review

U.S. government documents also are rich sources of information. These are indexed in the *United States Government Publications Monthly Catalog,* which most libraries have on hand. The documents, for the most part, can be purchased from the issuing government agency or from the Government Printing Office.[6]

KINDS OF INFORMATION

Once the speaker has learned where to look for speech information, the next step is to find material that will work in the speech. To do this, he or she undertakes the specific purpose and subject analysis. Let us say the speaker's specific purpose is to inform the audience about the role of the stock broker in purchasing stocks. By now, the speaker has completed a preliminary analysis of the subject, as described in Chapter 16, and has used the stock-question analysis method (who, what, where, when, why, how). Now the speaker's notes look something like this:

Who are stock brokers?	Look for information about them.
What do they do?	Explain their job.
Where do they operate?	Obtain details about brokerage houses.
How do they operate?	Find out what they do.
Why do they exist?	Locate the details.

With a rough analysis like this, the speaker will save time. He or she will not have to read everything about stock brokers but instead can concentrate on locating the answers to the questions.[7]

The speaker should look for two types of material to flesh out the speech, amplifying and supporting materials. These materials will provide the main content of the speech. Some of it comes from library research; other material comes from personal experience and interviews.

Amplifying Materials

As the speaker develops an idea by amplifying it, he or she is seeking to explain or clarify it. The most common amplification methods are definitions, examples, comparisons, contrasts, descriptions, anecdotes, restatements, and audiovisual aids. The method that is best for a particular speech depends upon the subject, audience, and occasion.

Definitions

Many communication barriers result when the speaker and listeners fail to come to a common understanding about the terms used in a speech. These barriers can be eliminated if the speaker assumes responsibility for stating clearly what the terms mean. To help in defining terms, the speaker

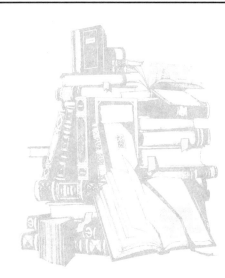

The speaker looks for amplifying and support materials.

might: (a) use the dictionary definition, (b) use examples, (c) explain what the word does *not* mean, and (d) use the term in a sentence to illustrate its meaning.

In this illustration, a teacher is lecturing to a class about the meaning of *norms*. The methods she uses are indicated by italics within brackets.

> Today, let's consider why people conform to group norms. By "conform" I mean why members of groups — church clubs, sororities, fraternities — obey club rules and regulations *[example]*. The dictionary states that group norms are standards of behavior *[dictionary definition]*. That's a fancy way of referring to rules, regulations, and social practices like dress codes *[example]*. A club's bylaws are examples of norms that club members must follow *[example]*. The bylaws usually contain items like dues — when they are due, how much, penalties if not paid. Attendance requirements are norms. So, when a member says, "You've not obeyed the attendance norm," you know you've erred *[use of term in sentence]*. Norms are not irregularities in behavior *[what norms are not]* but represent what is regular and acceptable to most people.

Examples

Examples are *specific, concrete instances* used to clarify more general or abstract statements. In the following excerpt the speaker gives a personal example of how prejudice, the subject of the speech, affected her.

The fact that prejudice creates misunderstanding and an atmosphere for distrust and hate follow easily the first two results. Let me give you a personal account. A couple of summers ago, I visited Japan. Wherever I went, people would stare and secretly whisper. I couldn't understand why because I am Japanese. I look like them. What reason do they have to treat me like that? This hurt me somewhat. However, I tried to enjoy the trip, and I did. When the time came to leave, I didn't want to. I had gotten so attached to the people. I believe they felt the same about me. But I wanted to know why the stares and whispers when I first arrived. One of my good friends said: "We had made up our minds about what you would be like before we met you. We felt you would be different because you are an American. Now that we know you, we think differently."[8]

This example provides a good explanation of what prejudice meant to the speaker. It is *factual* and cites real and personal experiences. But examples do not have to be entirely factual; the speaker can make them up. Such examples, called *hypothetical*, should be identified as figments of the imagination. To explain the high cost of medical care, one student used a hypothetical example to make his point:

Bill seemed to have difficulty hearing, so he went to his doctor, a general practitioner. The doctor said, "Oh, you have wax in your ears. Buy some wax remover; it'll clear it out." Bill bought the wax remover and used it. Unfortunately, it didn't work. In fact, it made the situation worse. So he went back to his doctor. "Oh," said the doctor, "sometimes wax remover doesn't work. It causes the wax to solidify. It melts, then hardens. That's what happened to you." Bill asked, "Can you take it out?" "No, I don't do ears," the doctor replied. "See an ear specialist." Bill did, and the ear specialist cleaned the ear in a few seconds. Besides the time Bill wasted visiting the doctors and the discomfort involved, Bill paid $50 per visit to the general practitioner and $250 to the specialist, plus $7.50 for the remover — $357.50 for a few seconds of work!

Hypothetical examples are situations that really could have happened, and they are useful for explaining or clarifying a point. Factual examples, however, are more effective because they are verifiable.

Comparisons

To clarify the new idea to listeners, speakers often find utilitarian value in comparisons. Comparisons are found in the *simile* and the *metaphor*. A simile expresses a resemblance or likeness ("My friend swings a baseball bat like my aunt swings her rolling pin"). A metaphor expresses an implied relationship between essentially different things ("His features resemble sand — coarse and grained").

Contrasts

Contrast is the opposite of comparison; the speaker amplifies an idea by showing how it is unlike another idea. Here is an example used to demonstrate the differences between American and New Zealand labor costs:

Most butter is shipped to Hawaii because very little, if any, butter is processed in the state. Butter made in Los Angeles, 2,300 miles from Hawaii, sells for approximately $2.50 a pound. Butter shipped to Hawaii from New Zealand, 4,500 miles away, is richer in butter fat content than the Los Angeles butter. It costs $1.20 a pound. Labor costs account for the difference in price.

Descriptions

Almost any subject can be amplified by describing its characteristics as they appear to our senses of sight, smell, taste, touch, and hearing. In his book about Hawaii, *Calabashes and Kings*, Stanley D. Porteus described a part of Hawaii in this paragraph:

It is mountains, mountains all the way from the time you make the last hairpin turn at the bottom of the Pali and take the akua loa's road that curls over and around spurs of the lower slopes of the ranges, past the isolated peak of Olomana, and goes straight as an arrow string across the bent bow of the Koolaus. Nowhere in the world do mountains have that strange fluted appearance, scored as they are by a hundred parallel fissures, each one narrowly separated from its fellows by a ridge running from base to summit. Some of these canyons-stood-up-on-end are so narrow and deep that looking up from the bottom, you seem to be in a vertical, nearly closed funnel.

Anecdotes

A *brief narrative used to illustrate or clarify an idea*, the anecdote may be true or untrue, funny or sad, but always related to the idea. Too often people tell jokes that have no relationship to the subject and, though they may provoke laughter, they are meaningless in a speech. A good story, well told, that illustrates an idea adds to a speaker's effectiveness.

The following example was incorporated into a speech about clarity in expressing ideas:

> Napoleon Bonaparte wanted his communications to be as clear as crystal. He had a saying that applies to many of us today: "An order that can be misunderstood will be misunderstood." The story goes that Napoleon kept an idiot sitting outside his headquarters. This person wore corporal's stripes because he served a very important purpose. Whenever Napoleon wrote an order, he would show it first to the corporal. If he understood the order, Napoleon felt it was safe to transmit it.

Restatements

This device involves *finding a new way to say the same thing.* It frequently is preceded by phrases such as, "that is to say," "in other words," "we mean by that statement," or "to state it simply." Restatement clarifies by stating an idea in words different from the ones used to express the idea in the first place.

Audiovisual Aids

Audiovisual aids are helpful in explaining and clarifying the content of a speaker's message. They also gain attention and hold interest as well as support a speaker's points. Among the visual aids are charts, graphs, cartoons, diagrams, drawings, posters, maps, globes, photographs, models, specimens, motion pictures, slides, videotapes, and filmstrips. The audio aids include stereo and tape recordings. VCRs are the newest audiovisual aid.

Using audiovisual aids does not guarantee a successful presentation. The aids must be chosen carefully, and they must be handled with skill. Criteria for choosing audiovisual aids are:

1. *Availability of sufficient equipment.* If a film or slides are to be shown, is a projector available? Can the room be darkened? Is there a screen? An electrical outlet? If a chalkboard is to be used, are chalk and erasers available? If graphs, or diagrams are to be included, is there a place to hang them where all can see?

2. *Supportiveness.* Does the audio or visual aid clarify, amplify, or prove the point under consideration? Is it attention arousing or interesting? Does it stress the point being made?

3. *Appropriateness for the user.* Can the person using the audio or visual aid handle it properly? If a photograph or projector of some sort is to be used, does the user understand its operation? If a chalkboard is to be used, does the user write legibly?

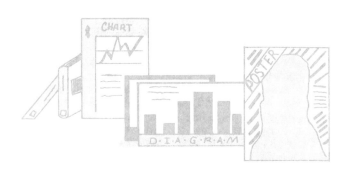

Audio and visual aids are helpful in explaining and clarifying.

4. *Availability of time.* Is enough time available to properly present the visual aid? If a film is to be shown, will there be enough time to introduce it, show it, and briefly discuss it? Has the speaker practiced the presentation beforehand to check the time needed?[9]

Some suggestions for using audiovisual aids more effectively are:

1. Introduce the audio or visual aid, and stress its importance to the subject of the speech.

2. Make sure the entire audience can see the visual aid and can hear the audio aid.

3. Emphasize the points the visual or audio is making.

4. After presenting the visual or audio aid, review the main points.

5. Restate the speech's line of reasoning amplified by the audiovisual aid.[10]

Supporting Materials

Supporting material provides the evidence and proof upon which understanding and belief rest. Supporting materials *establish the major ideas or contentions* the speaker wishes to communicate. They are the proof that confirms the speaker's arguments.[11] Four types of supporting materials are available to the speaker: tangible objects, opinions, factual examples, and statistics.[12]

Tangible Objects

Tangible objects are *real things,* capable of being seen and touched. Weapons, fingerprint impressions, books, personal letters, and other items of personal property are examples of tangible objects. In a court of law, they constitute evidence to assist in proving the innocence or guilt of someone. In a speech before an audience, they support the speaker's ideas. They provide visual testimony, functioning similarly to visual aids. For example, a student gave a speech on the merits of chocolate chip cookies. She brought samples for each class member, presenting tangible evidence of their tastiness.

Opinions

An opinion is a *statement based on one's own judgment* rather than uncertain knowledge. It is an interpretation of facts, or it is a judgment of value concerning facts. Opinions have two primary sources: authorities and lay people. Opinions of authorities are favored over those of lay people. The authorities are experts on the subject matter under discussion, or at least members of the audience consider them such. Lay people are nonexperts whose personal opinions on the subject are based on their own experiences.

Opinions of authorities are considered more valuable than those of lay people as forms of support. Further, both the opinions of authorities and of lay people are more acceptable than the speaker's assertions, unless the speaker is an expert in the subject area. In the classroom, students often rely on their personal opinions as support. Unfortunately, most students, busy with various school activities, may not have enough expertise on a subject to talk about it with authority. Consequently, students' opinions are apt to carry little weight with an audience.

Factual Examples

Factual examples are *accounts of something known to be true, to exist, or to have happened*, in the past or present. These can be verified with reasonable assurance of accuracy because they actually occurred. They are the strongest form of support. Examples are included under both amplifying materials and support because they serve both functions.

Statistics

Statistics are *a series of factual examples grouped together and reported in numerical form*. They normally appear in terms of number of cases, percentages, or rates of frequency. This example is replete with statistics: "John Wilson walked through the gate and found 4,789 people dead. Of those, 47% were male, 53% female; 90% were over sixty years of age; 97% were Caucasian. He was visiting the National Cemetery of the Pacific."

Statistics are easy to find. Any newspaper issue contains dozens of statistics, and magazines and other periodicals have many more. Statistics are easy to use, but they can be boring if too many are contained in a single speech. The speaker must take care not to overwhelm the audience with figures.

A strategy the speaker can utilize to strengthen statistics and the other forms of support is to cite their source. This advice is especially worthwhile for student speakers, because stating the source adds credibility to the speech. The source citation need not be extensive or elaborate; a simple statement will do, as in these examples: "*The New York Times*, September 4, 1992, stated . . ." "According to President Bush, in his remarks to Congress, January 22 this will . . ." "Connie Chung, CBS broadcaster, in her June 21, 1992, broadcast, said . . . ." Without source citations, students tend to treat the speaker's remarks as his or her own opinions, and they will be worth no more than the credibility the audience affords the speaker.

RECORDING THE INFORMATION

The primary purpose of research is to provide amplification and support for the ideas a speaker communicates to the audience. To be a credible speaker, he or she must be correct when reporting the content of the speech, and accurate and ethical when crediting the source of material. The speaker must record the information uncovered in the research so it is available for constructing the speech when the time comes.[13]

Often note cards are used to record information, but some speakers prefer full-size paper. Card-users can get only one idea on a card; paper-users can include much more on a single sheet. Cards can be easily sorted for speech construction purposes; papers are easier to keep track of.

Whatever is used, cards or paper, the following information should be recorded along with the notes from the source:

1. Author(s) name(s).
2. Title of book or article.
3. If article, name of periodical, volume and issue number, year of publication.
4. If book, year of publication, publisher, place of publication, edition number (if other than first edition).
5. Page numbers of quoted material.
6. Library call number, if from a library.

Notes taken from the publication can be in abstract form, summary form, or direct quotation. If a direct quotation is used, it should be identified as such on the card or note paper.[14]

The information should be filed in an orderly manner, making the information easier to locate when the time comes to organize the speech. Cards are, of course, easier to file than papers. Among several filing systems are:

1. *Time sequence.* Begin at a certain period and move forward or backward in time.

2. *Cause-effect sequence.* File together the materials related to causes of the problem and the materials related to effects.

3. *Problem-solution sequence.* Divide the materials into those that relate to the problem and those that relate to possible solutions.

4. *Topical sequence.* Arrange the materials according to topics.

5. *Introduction/body/conclusion sequence.* File together information that is introductory, materials that contain the bulk of the information, and materials that can conclude the speech.

The five sequences are similar to the patterns of organizing a speech, which will be explained in the next chapter.

Example of Note Card with Direct Quote

Donald W. Klopf, Intercultural Encounters: The Fundamentals of Intercultural Communication, 2nd ed. (Englewood, CO: Morton, 1991).

. . . culture covers a wide range of human endeavor. Virtually everthing nonbiological, in the broadest sense of the term, is part of culture. Culture is persistent, enduring and omnipresent. It influences everyday modes of behavior, including the communication practices of all people.

(pg. 39)

Example of Note Card with Summary Information

Donald W. Klopf and Ronald E. Cambra, Speaking Skills for Prospective Teachers, 2nd ed. (Englewood, CO: Morton, 1991).

Classroom lecturing, a topic in the book, explains the nature of lectures, the process of explaining, how to prepare and design lectures, and how to present them to a class. The lecture is used to give a class large amounts of information on a subject. It involves explaining the why, how, and what of the subject to give understanding.

(pg. 305-328)

OUTLINING THE INFORMATION

At this juncture, after the speaker has gathered and filed the data, he or she can develop a tentative outline to visualize the relationship of the ideas and their supporting or amplifying information.

An outline supplies a means of displaying the structure and sequence of a speaker's ideas. It is a technique for representing thought relationships. It is not a process synonymous with organization, as some persons believe, nor is it a guarantee of organization. The organization process extends beyond the outlining skill, as we shall learn from the discussion of organizing speeches in the next chapter.

The outline is a way of depicting connections between thoughts. If all thoughts would be able to stand alone or have equal importance, outlines would not be necessary. Because this usually is not the case, a device such as the outline is needed to show the relationships.

Outline Form

Outlining shows thought relationships through a set of symbols and indentations that follow specific rules. If the rules are observed, the relationships between ideas are clearly established.

The outline form uses a descending set of symbols in which numbers and letters alternate. All symbols with the same rank are placed directly under each other in straight columns. Subordinate ranks are indented equally in a staircase fashion. The number of ranks varies with the complexity of the material being outlined. The same principle holds true for the number of items within each rank. A short talk may have only a couple of ranks; a longer one will have many. The outline format looks like this:

I. _____
  A. _____
    1. _____
      a. _____
      b. _____
    2. _____
    3. _____
  B. _____
    1. _____
    2. _____
      a. _____
        (1)_____
        (2)_____
      b. _____
  C. _____

II. _____
   A. _____
   B. _____
III. _____
          _____

Rules of Outlining

The form as illustrated follows a set of rules governing outline construction:

1. A consistent form of symbols and indentation, with alternating numbers and letters, is used.

2. A symbol is assigned to each element of the outline.

3. Each point in the outline consists of a complete thought.

4. Only one symbol is used before each point.

5. Each symbol is followed by a period.

6. Only one thought is assigned to a symbol.

7. Symbols of the same rank are assigned to comparable points.

8. The symbol always stands out from the thought that follows it; hence, for thoughts longer than one line, the second line begins under the first word of the first line.

9. The symbols for subordinate subpoints are always placed under the first letter of the first word of the superordinate thought.

10. The first word of every point is always capitalized.

Types of Outlines

Three types of outlines are word, phrase, and sentence outlines. These are briefly described next.

Word Outline

The word outline consists of one or two key words for each idea, point, or subpoint. Thus, it provides little information, but it does remind the speaker of the main ideas he or she will develop more fully as the speech is presented orally. Here is a sample:

I. Gathering material
   A. Through interviews
   B. Through library reading
II. Recording information
   A. Using cards
   B. Using notebooks
   C. Using sheets of paper

Phrase Outline

The phrase outline provides more information about each point, in phrase form. Hence, this type of outline offers more assistance, giving the speaker more complete clues from which to speak. A sample is:

I. How to amplify ideas
   A. Use definitions from dictionaries, in examples, in sentences
   B. Use examples — factual or hypothetical.
   C. Use comparisons or contrasts
   D. Provide descriptions
   E. Tell jokes or stories
   F. Use restatements
II. How to support ideas

Sentence Outline

In the sentence outline the major points and subpoints are stated in sentences, making the information more comprehensible and easier to read. This outline form provides a maximum amount of information, allowing others to use it if need be. Here is an example:

I. Credibility is the attitude toward the speaker that a listener holds at a given time.

   A. It is an extremely important factor in determining the speaker's effectiveness.
      1. The speaker's credibility influences the listeners' ability to learn or to believe.
      2. The speaker's credibility influences how listeners feel about the speaker.

   B. Credibility has three primary characteristics.
      1. Expertness is the quality of being competent and intelligent.
      2. Trustworthiness is the quality of being honest and showing goodwill.
      3. Forcefulness is the quality of being a dynamic and enthusiastic speaker.

II. There are ten ways to enhance credibility.

The sentence outline follows some additional rules:

- Every point is a complete sentence.
- Every point begins with a capital letter and ends with a period.
- Every entry is matched by one or more points of equal importance. Thus, if there is an A, there has to be a B; if there is a 1, there has to be a 2.

Sentence outlines are most useful for inexperienced speakers. The thoughts and the relationships between them are outlined clearly in sentence outlines, providing speakers with excellent support when their time comes to speak.

EVALUATING THE INFORMATION

While gathering materials and later when organizing them, the speaker should evaluate what he or she has collected. The speaker should use the best evidence in the speech. What does "best" mean? The best usually can pass tests of *validity and reliability*. The speaker should apply them to his or her information. Let us consider each of these tests.

1. *Is the source of the information competent?* A competent source is someone who is in a position, by reason of training or experience, to make an accurate observation. Members of the audience have to perceive the source as competent.

2. *Is the source of the information trustworthy?* Merely being in a position to make accurate observations does not necessarily mean the person will do so. Because of personal biases, the source may record information inaccurately. The concern, therefore, is whether the listeners will perceive the source as biased or unbiased.

3. *Is there enough information?* Listeners may consider a single example or opinion sufficient. More likely, however, they will not think a single piece of information is enough. Corroboratory support, a lot of evidence, is better.

4. *Is the information consistent with other known information?* If the information the speaker intends to include is consistent with the information listeners already know, there is no difficulty. If it is not, the speaker must be prepared to explain the discrepancy or the speaker's information will be discounted as inaccurate.

S. *Does the information address the point at issue?* Does the information support or amplify the actual point being made? For information to be valuable, listeners must perceived it as relevant to the idea it supposedly is supporting or amplifying.

6. *Is the information recent?* Other things being equal, the most recent information is ordinarily the best information. In the scientific world, for example, new discoveries out-date information quickly. Material that is several years old may be suspect because of its age. If the material is not recent, the speaker should be prepared to defend it by explaining that the information has not changed since the item was created.[15]

SUMMARY

The subject chosen for the speech must be investigated. The speaker undertakes a program of research to find the information that will amplify or support the principal ideas. People participating in interviews and group discussions also need to do research. Thus, the techniques noted in this chapter are applicable to interviews and discussion as well as to public speaking.

Two categories of research sources are available to the speaker: subjective (personal experience and interviews) and objective (factual information that can be found in library resources). In the investigation the speaker should be looking for amplifying materials and supporting information. Amplifying materials include definitions, examples, comparisons, contrasts, descriptions, anecdotes, restatements, and audiovisual aids. Supporting materials (evidence) include tangible objects, factual examples, opinions, and statistics.

If the information is to be useful to the speaker, it must be recorded, either on note cards or on note paper. Whatever information the speaker obtains through the investigation, it must be the best information available, at least from the listeners' point of view. If the listeners do not consider it credible, the speaker will have wasted time and energy and the listeners will not accept the speaker's ideas. To make sure the information is the best, it must be evaluated as to validity and reliability.

18

Organizing The Speech[1]

The purposes of public speaking are to inform, to persuade, or to actuate. Before any of these goals can be reached, speakers must make some determinations and choices. They must determine, for example, at least roughly what their listeners believe about the subject, and they must offer some new ideas that the listeners might accept. The speakers then can settle on the information that will best serve them in getting their points across. Then they can assemble the information into some sort of preliminary outline.

After speakers have done these things, they are ready to consider one of the final stages of preparation: structuring and organizing the speech. Their job now is to shape the information into some kind of sensible form, so they can present what they have gathered to the listeners in an understandable and acceptable way.

Speakers who haphazardly toss their ideas at their listeners significantly limit their chances of obtaining the desired response. A speaker who fails to structure the speech in a sensible way loses the listener. The listener asks: What does all of this mean? What is the speaker driving at? What is the sense of this? *Speech structure assists in understanding.* In some cases, without structure there is no speech

If given a choice between a half-baked apple pie and a properly baked apple pie, we would choose the pie that was adequately baked. We have no trouble telling the difference between the two pies. Likewise, listeners can distinguish between disorganized and organized speeches, and they obviously prefer organized speeches. This does not mean that disorganized speeches are completely misunderstood. Unless the speech is totally chaotic, listeners are capable of imposing some structure upon speeches that come to them in a relatively disorganized manner. The careful speaker, however, does not purposely impose such a burden upon the listener. For one thing, a listener has to have a genuine interest in order to remain attentive to a disorganized speech. If we are hungry enough, we might settle for the half-baked pie. Even so, the cook who wants to please us will make sure the pie is done. And certainly the attentive cook does not expect the eater to finish baking the pie.

The sensible structuring of speeches is most important in formal speaking situations. In face-to-face and small-group settings, listeners can ask the speaker what he or she means if a lack of organization creates misunderstandings. In more formal settings, the listeners rarely have the chance to ask a speaker for clarification. As a result, whenever we face an audience in a public speaking or mass communication setting, the need for sensibly structuring our speeches is particularly acute. Because of individual differences in the ability of each person to listen and understand, large groups cannot cope with disorganized speeches as readily as small groups or a single listener can.

Structuring speeches brings to mind the often repeated story of the old preacher who had a reputation for well-organized sermons. When asked why his sermons were so effective, the preacher replied: "First, I tell them what I'm going to tell them; then I tell them; then I tell them what I told them." Through a lifetime of sermonizing, the preacher had come to recognize the three basic divisions of a speech: the introduction, the body, and the conclusion.

THE INTRODUCTION

The introduction is the speaker's "calling card." It is the listeners' first exposure to the speaker. From the introduction the listeners form their first impression of the speaker. The purpose of an introduction is to win the audience's attention and goodwill, to focus the audience's thinking on the subject, and to demonstrate how the subject will satisfy the audience's needs. An introduction succeeds if it causes members of the audience to think: "This sounds interesting. I think I want to listen to what this speaker has to say. The message sounds as if it will be timely and valuable."

Modern-day studies of audience response have added little to the advice of Aristotle, the influential Greek philosopher who died more than 300 years before the birth of Christ. Aristotle's advice to speakers goes something like this: "Listeners consider most attentively things that are vital, that concern their own interests, that are astounding, that are pleasant."

In fact, modern scholars support the traditional audience classification system, apparently established in the *Rhetoric to Alexander*, a book by an unknown author written about the time of Aristotle's *Rhetoric*. Its author developed a system describing listeners as friendly, neutral, or hostile. The unknown author advised that "there is no problem in obtaining goodwill if the listeners are friendly. If the listeners are neutral, they should be complimented for their fair evaluation of the speaker's ideas. If they are hostile, the speaker should try to discover the reasons for their hostility before he speaks. In his opening remarks, he should do whatever he can to overcome the audience's hostility." The advice of centuries ago is still relevant today. The introduction should make the audience attentive, well-disposed, and receptive.

Arousing Attention

The most important part of the introduction — and, as many experienced speakers know, the most important aspect of the speech — consists of the opening words. The first few words can make or break a speaker in the eyes of the audience. Through the opening words the listener is either hooked or lost. Once listeners are lost, they might be lost forever. The speaker might as well give up. As a general rule, most listeners become attentive and perk up their ears when opening remarks are either humorous or appeal to their personal interests and concerns. The following five devices are tried-and-true ways of successfully engaging an audience through the speaker's introductory remarks.

Examples and Anecdotes

If used intelligently and pertinently, examples and anecdotes are almost certain attention-getters. Everyone, after all, likes a good story. People also like the kind of down to earth feeling engendered by a well-chosen example. Some anecdotes are appealing because they plunge the listeners into the middle of some type of action. An apt anecdote suggests that more excitement is on the way. In a speech about the importance of reducing automobile accidents, one student plunged his audience into the midst of things by leading off with the following:

> The debris from two cars that crashed in a head-on collision on normally peaceful Conway Street scattered across lawns and even reached the houses themselves. One car's wheel flew through the picture window of the Thomas Madison home and instantly killed six-year old Debbie Madison, playing in the living room. The flying hood of the other car severed pedestrian Leonard Moore's leg from his body. Flaming gasoline sprayed over John McCormick's parked car and set it afire. Glass fragments pelted onlookers and caused minor cuts. The drivers of the two cars were not injured.

Startling Facts

Speakers frequently employ startling facts in their introductory remarks. The aim of this type of attention-getter is to shake up the listeners. An astounding fact or a dramatic statement captures their interest. Here are two examples from classroom speeches:

> The bad news first: According to the latest reports, one of every five college students will become diabetic. One of seven will suffer a heart attack. One of ten will be afflicted with gout. Arthritis will attack one of ten. Healthwise, we don't have much to look forward to. Now, the good news! All four of these cripplers can be controlled by proper diet. The secret of the good life: a well-balanced diet.

> Students agitate against many things. But what do they do about the nation's greatest killer of humans? Nothing! Every five minutes an American dies from a car accident. Every three seconds someone is injured. Protest against our greatest enemy? Nonsense! There's no glory in fussing about accidents.

A Question or Series of Questions

A question, or series of questions, frequently serves as an effective opening device. Questions imply that the audience is to respond. Questions tend to involve an audience. Usually the response expected is a silent one. The speaker who begins with a question seeks a mental or an emotional response from the audience.

The following example illustrates the use of questions in introductory remarks. The questions are designed to arouse attention and stimulate thought:

> What is the number one killer of humankind? Is it heart disease? Auto accidents? War? Pestilence? No, it is . . . .

A Striking Quotation

Another effective way of opening a speech is to use a striking quotation. Ideally, the quotation should be memorable and to the point. It should be the utterance or writing of someone who commands respect. If the quotation is startling, well-phrased, and to the point, and if it fits the audience's interests, it will be more effective. Two examples taken from students' speeches are:

> "When I'm getting ready for an argument with a man, I spend one third of the time thinking about myself and what I'm going to say, and two-thirds thinking about him and what he is going to say." Lincoln's words get right to the heart of speech preparation: Be listener-centered.

> "Six-figure incomes come from six-figure thinking and six-figure effort." Most of us have heard those words before, but I wanted to repeat them because they spell out the bottom line of my talk today.

Familiar References

Many speakers get off on the right foot with a particular audience by referring specifically to familiar events the listeners have witnessed or taken part in, or to experiences the listeners have had. A speaker also might refer to people whom members of the audience know and hold in high esteem, or to ideas and interests they share. By using such references, the speaker seeks to establish a bond with the audience. He or she does this to develop a feeling among the listeners that "the speaker is one of us" or "the speaker knows our problems." For example, one speaker who addressed the members of a local Kiwanis Club began his talk by elaborating upon his former membership in that community service organization:

> Mr. President and Kiwanians. Through your generous welcome, you've made me feel as though I were home among friends once again, even though I am far from home. As I took part in your opening ceremony, I recalled similar ceremonies that I enjoyed during my ten years of attendance at Kiwanis meetings. Before I retired as an active member, I served my club as secretary, vice president, and president and had the honor of being president when the club won the highest performance record of any club in our district. Mostly, I recall the enjoyable moments of working and playing together with my fellow members. Today seems like a homecoming for me — to be present with those who form a valued part of the community — even if only for a few hours.

Introductions differ. They come in all forms and have content of various kinds. The types we have reviewed here are quite common, but successful introductions do not always appear in a pure form; they frequently appear in combined form. For example, an introduction could feature an anecdote, but the anecdote could at the same time contain questions or quotations. Or it could be a story with which the members of a particular audience are personally familiar. In any case, all good introductions get the audience interested in what the speaker is going to talk about.

Preview of the Speech

The preview follows immediately after the opening remarks, which were designed to secure the audience's attention. The preview focuses the listener's attention upon the specific subject of the speech and outlines for the listener the main divisions of the talk. The purpose of the preview is to help the audience follow what the speaker will say. It serves as a brief "table of contents" for the speech.

The following preview is taken from a student speech on the makeup of the United Nations. Immediately after the opening remarks, the speaker announced the topic of the talk and then identified the six specific agencies of the United Nations, which were to be discussed next:

> The United Nations, the topic of my talk, functions through various bodies, six of which I would like to describe and explain. They are the General Assembly, Security Council, International Court of Justice, Economic and Social Council, Secretariat, and Trusteeship Council. I'll try to show at the end how each relates to and depends upon the other.

Typically, a preview begins with a *statement of purpose*. The statement announces the speech's content and states the speaker's intent. The purpose statement normally is followed by what we might call a *partition statement*, an overview of the major points to be covered in the body of the speech. The partition statement ticks off the speech's major subdivisions. The following sample previews incorporate purpose statements and partition statements. The purpose statements appear in italics. The remaining part of each preview is the announcement of the major subtopics to be discussed:

> *How to find materials in the library is the topic of my report.* Three steps are involved: first, understanding the general layout of the library; second, using the card catalog; and third, checking special sources.

> *This morning I'd like to describe what one nutritionist claims is a plan for healthy eating.* The plan requires eating at regular hours, eating a well-balanced diet, and eliminating snacks.

> *Permit me to show you the safety features on our latest model in the Galaxy series:* disc brakes, the orbital suspension system, and the three-point seat belt.

The preview is an optional element in a speech. No speech absolutely has to include one. In fact, in persuasive speeches especially, speakers sometimes are better off remaining silent about the purpose. They want to convince the audience. If they tell the listeners at the outset that they are going to convince them of something, they run the risk of losing the listeners before they start. A door-to-door encyclopedia salesperson wants to persuade a customer to buy a set of books but never announces this intent the moment the door is opened. The salesperson hopes instead for a chance to talk, expecting that, in the course of the talk, he or she can win a customer. Thus, a preview might not be desirable for all occasions. Nevertheless, most beginning speakers find the partition statement to be as much of an aid to them as it is to the audience. If speakers state the divisions of their talk, they have a basic outline to follow.

In some speeches it is difficult to speak of the preview as a separate part. Note the following example of an introduction. In it the speaker establishes the fact that he is in a position to know what he is talking about. He wins the audience's attention by demonstrating that he is familiar with the topic. He also announces his topic — the advantages and disadvantages of local and dormitory colleges — in the introduction.

> Your principal asked me to talk with you today about the advantages of attending a local college so you can live at home. I was asked, I believe, because I may have the qualifications to speak on the subject. Let me tell you what they are. As an undergraduate, I went to school in my home town and lived at home those four years. Then I began work on a master's degree. As a graduate student, I had to go away to school. This meant college dormitory living for a year and an apartment for another. I lived both at home and away during my six-year college career. So I know some of the advantages and disadvantages of each. Let me share my experience with you.

THE BODY

A speaker can prepare a compelling introduction that truly grabs the listeners and forces their attention. The speaker also can forcefully announce the purpose and effectively outline the main divisions of the talk. By themselves, however, these elements are of minor importance, for the body of the speech is where the payoff comes. The body of the speech carries the freight. It is the meat of the talk. In the body of the speech, the speaker seeks to gain the listeners' support. In the body the speaker presents his or her arguments and provides the evidence he or she hopes will convince the listeners to think as the speaker thinks. In the body of the speech, therefore, structure is extremely important.

Many patterns are used to structure ideas in the body of a message. Here we will examine the most common patterns of content arrangement. These patterns are common simply because they naturally lend themselves to the content of most speeches. The patterns are: *time, space, topical, causal, problem-solution,* and *motivated-sequence.*

Time Pattern

In the time pattern, ideas are arranged in the order in which they occurred in time, or in such a way that the time sequence of events is obvious. Ordering ideas in this fashion usually is dictated by the subject matter. Certain subjects lend themselves to time patterning. A speaker who describes how to grow wheat can recount the events chronologically, beginning with the first step, broadcasting the seed, and then describing the next step and each succeeding step in the order in which they actually happen. This type of arrangement is extremely easy for listeners to follow because idea follows idea in a normal chronological fashion.

The following excerpts are from a talk to the American people by then U.S. President Franklin D. Roosevelt in September, 1941, during the onset of

World War II. Notice how the speaker employs the time pattern to develop his contention that Nazi Germany was engaged in a deliberate effort to sink the ships of what were at that time neutral nations.

> The Navy Department of the United States has reported to me that on the morning of September 4 the United States destroyer *Grier*, proceeding in full daylight toward Iceland, had reached a point southeast of Greenland. . . . She was then and there attacked by a submarine. Germany admits that it was a German submarine. . . .

> A few months ago an American flag merchant ship, the *Robin Moor*, was sunk by a Nazi submarine in the middle of the South Atlantic, under circumstances violating long-established international law and violating every principle of humanity.

> In July, 1941, nearly two months ago, an American battleship in North American waters was followed by a submarine which for a long time sought to maneuver itself into a position of attack upon the battleship.

> Five days ago a United States ship on patrol picked up three survivors of an American-owned ship operating under the flag of our sister republic of Panama. In view of the established presence of German submarines in this ship's vicinity, there can be no doubt of who sunk her. . . .

> Also five days ago another United States merchant ship, the *Steel Seafarer*, was sunk by a German aircraft in the Red Sea 220 miles south of Suez. She was bound for an Egyptian port.

> So four of the vessels sunk or attacked flew the American flag and were clearly identifiable. Two of these ships were warships of the American Navy.

In his talk, Roosevelt began with the most recent occurrences in time and then went back to trace the chronological sequence of the events. The listeners were always aware of the time sequence, which helped the President demonstrate that those occurrences were on the increase.

Space Pattern

As the name implies, the structure imposed by the space pattern corresponds to the relationships of the parts to the whole as they exist in space. In using this pattern, the speaker proceeds systematically in describing how something looks or functions. If a speaker wants to describe how something looks, he or she proceeds from left to right or from bottom to top. In describing a house, for example, the speaker talks about the various features, beginning, perhaps, with the foundation and then moving up to the roof. The speaker does not jump around from point to point, moving from foundation to chimney and then back to the first floor.

Note the space pattern imposed upon the following student talk. Impressed by ships, the student is describing the *World Duchess*, a mammoth oil tanker:

> The *World Duchess* has a cruiser stern, a bow shaped pointedly which permits the ship to cut cleanly through the water. The hull in back of the stern is smoothly tapered for the entire length of the vessel. The contour of the hull is designed to provide minimum resistance and to permit maximum propulsion of the ship through the water. At the stern, the sides sweep gracefully but sharply upward, maintaining the basic "V" design.

> The pilot house is located about thirty yards behind the ship's prow. It rises to the equivalent height of a four-story apartment building. The first level houses the computer equipment which guides the ship's navigational system. The second level contains the equipment which energizes the radar system. A chartroom dominated by an enormous map table occupies the third level. The wheelhouse sits on the top level.

> The open deck — the length of four football fields — stretches behind the pilot structure. A narrow catwalk runs down the center for the ship's entire length. The enormous tank covers stretch out on either side of the walkway. Below the covers are the enormous tanks, capable of holding a full load of 200,000 tons of oil.

> The crew's living quarters are aft. This six story complex . . .

Notice how the speaker stayed with the space pattern. He took things as they came. He moved logically from place to place, enabling the listener to easily follow and formulate a mental picture of the vessel being described.

Topical Pattern

The topical pattern evolves from the natural parts or divisions of the subject. For example, if a speaker wants to talk about the new Germany, he or she might organize the message into five parts. The speaker can talk about the political, social, economic, cultural, and religious forces in the nation. If the subject is the government of Japan, the speaker might talk about the Emperor, the Diet, the Prime Minister and his Cabinet, and the Courts. These institutions constitute the Japanese government.

In the following excerpt, Karl Menninger, the noted psychiatrist, organized a speech about mental health into four topics, which grew naturally out of his general topic, mental health:

> I want to report four observations to you. The first observation is that mental illness is something that may occur in the lives of any of us. It always develops rather unexpectedly. Nobody plans to get mentally ill. Nevertheless, mental illness does come. It may come to any of us.
>
> Now for a second observation. The general notion has long prevailed that once mental illness has appeared, the victim is doomed. . . . Most attacks of mental illness subside; most of the patients recover. . . .
>
> The third observation . . . is that some of those afflicted with mental illnesses seem to recover for a while and then stop, others recover slowly, and still others may recover more rapidly but have recurrences. . . .
>
> The fourth observation . . . is that some patients may even get "weller." I mean they get better than they ever were. . . . Take an instance familiar to all of you. Abraham Lincoln was undoubtedly a far more productive, a far bigger man, and a far broader and wiser man after his attack of mental illness than he was before.

Notice that the division of the general topic into four separate categories enabled the speaker to focus attention on these basic considerations alone. This allows an audience to easily follow the talk.

Causal Pattern

The causal pattern normally is divided into two parts. The first sets forth the causes of a problem. The second describes the effects. The message becomes an explanation of the causal factors and their effects. For example, in a speech about traffic problems, the speaker might utilize the causal pattern in this fashion:

Cause: New York has an inadequate number of freeways.

Effect: The lack of freeways has resulted in terrible traffic congestion during daylight hours.

The pattern can be reversed, with the effects presented first and the causes identified later:

Effect: The streets of New York are packed with cars during the day.

Cause: New York's mass transit system is inadequate.

The following excerpt is taken from a segment of a television discussion on health problems. Note the overall structure:

> Simply stated, diabetes is caused by an inability to digest sugar. Technically, the cause is more complex, but it boils down to the fact that one of every five of us, according to the latest estimates, cannot use the sugar we consume daily. . . .
>
> The effects vary with most diabetics. Generally speaking, frequent urination, drowsiness, fatigue are common signs. One high school football player, in excellent physical condition otherwise, dragged himself back to the locker room after every practice and game. A bottle of soda quickly revived him. Hearing that story, I ordered a glucose tolerance test and found him to be a diabetic. The effects are insidious . . . .

In this excerpt, the cause-and-effect structure is obvious. Notice that the structure allowed the listeners to follow the discussion and to see the relationship between the two basic parts of the explanation.

Problem-Solution Pattern

The problem-solution pattern seems appropriate for situations in which the audience faces a problem and the speaker proposes to solve it. The speaker first describes the problem and then offers a practical and desirable plan to eliminate it. The plan, of course, must be capable of being put into operation, and it must eliminate the problem without introducing new and worse difficulties of its own.

For example, a speaker might select the topic of tooth decay. Tooth decay is a problem that most people confront. Most have suffered the pain and discomfort that result from tooth decay. Most recognize that treatment of tooth decay is necessary to dental health and personal well-being. The speaker presents the problem and then offers a solution. He or she devotes the rest of the speech to discussing fluoridation of the water supply, pointing out that fluoridation offers a safe and economical solution to the problem of tooth decay.

The following excerpts are from a student speech dealing with the problem of environmental deterioration. The speech employs the problem-solution pattern:

> Someday there may be more truth than fiction in the story plot of an episode in the old television series "Time Tunnel." The plot concerned two beings from another

world who came to earth to amass protein. Their own supply depleted long ago, the gatherers moved from planet to planet, universe to universe, harvesting protein to sustain life in their own world. Each year as they drained another planet's supply, they roamed farther and farther away from home, and found protein becoming scarcer and scarcer.

Contemporary earth people soon may be facing a similar deficiency of life sources, cry some alarmists, and in several centuries, according to one prognosticator, humans will be living on other, more fertile planets, or in artificial spaceships, which will wander the cosmos collecting raw materials wherever these materials are available. . . . The nation has grown increasingly anxious over the ruin of once-fertile lands, the plunder of natural resources, pollution of air and water, the destruction of wildlife. Environmental deterioration no longer burdens only the conservationists; economists, architects, urban planners, and other concerned citizens foresee environmental devastation ahead. Protein harvesting on other planets may indeed become a necessity . . . .

Something has to be done, and it appears to be the lot of the ordinary person to resolve these problems of conservation. . . .

In this excerpt the speaker identified the problem in some detail. Then she offers a solution (that ordinary people must conserve), which will help alleviate the problem she is discussing.

Motivated-Sequence Pattern

The motivated-sequence pattern provides a basic framework for organizing almost all topics in a meaningful fashion. The various parts of the pattern can be lengthened, shortened, or entirely omitted, depending upon the nature of the topic to which it is applied. The pattern consists of four parts.

1. *Needs.* After the introductory remarks the speaker identifies a need. The speaker indicates the existence of a problem and focuses attention on the extent of the problem. In this section the speaker identifies something that has to be dealt with.

2. *Satisfaction.* The speaker offers some possible solutions. He or she cites examples of actions that might satisfy the need expressed in the first section of the pattern.

3. *Visualization.* The speaker presents concrete examples that vividly show how the solutions suggested in the preceding section would help to reduce the problem.

4. *Action.* The speaker issues a call for action. He or she asks the audience to do something, to join in the fight to solve the problem spoken about.

Here are excerpts from a speech using the motivated-sequence pattern. They illustrate only the four parts of the pattern as they appear in the body; the introduction and conclusion are not given.

Need:	A problem confronts America today: what to do about our senior citizens. Unable to exist on social security, they are not eligible for welfare because they have incomes. Let me describe their plight. . . .
Satisfaction:	We can do something to alleviate the problem of the aged. First, we can remove mandatory retirement ages. Second, we can. . . .
Visualization:	By removing the mandatory retirement ages, those who are able to work can continue to earn a living wage. By. . . .
Action:	I urge all of you to write to your Congresspersons and ask them to remove the mandatory retirement age, to . . .

The full need-satisfaction-visualization-action structure of the motivated-sequence pattern may not be evident in all speeches structured in this basic way. Some speeches utilize only the first two parts, especially when the speaker merely wishes to stimulate the audience's thinking. Other speeches use all four parts and treat each to varying degrees. If a speaker knows an audience understands the problem well, he or she might treat the first part rather superficially and concentrate instead on the second part.

As its name implies, the motivated-sequence pattern is particularly appropriate for topics that require the audience to do something, those that require the audience to take some action. Almost every speech using the motivated-sequence pattern emphasizes the final part — the call to action — to some extent.

The six patterns of organization discussed here should be thought of as *general structural patterns*. They represent typical methods of structuring the parts of the body of a speech. If we say that the body of a speech follows a time pattern, what we mean is that the major units of the body conform to a time sequence; the time pattern is the structure most evident in the body of the speech. The major divisions of the speech are arranged in chronological order. But, as we shall learn next, each element of the body also must be structured in some sensible way. In the examples presented in this section, we selected as examples only the major elements in speeches. The next section takes a close look at the smaller units of the body that make up these major sections.

STRUCTURING UNITS OF THE BODY

To ensure successful communication and to bring about the kind of change the speaker tries to induce, the entire body of a speech must be arranged in a sensible way. Some pattern of organization, as we have seen, must shape the body of the speech. The major segments must be arranged so they add up to an understandable whole. Each major section of a speech's body also must be organized so it makes sense to the listener.

The general formula for each individual unit matches the formula for the speech as a whole. The speaker tells the listeners what they will hear. The speaker then must deliver on the promise and provide the content of the message. Finally, the speaker summarizes for the listeners what the listeners have been told.

More specifically, the formula for organizing each of the major units of a speech consists of five steps:

Step 1. S = Statement of the idea to be discussed in the unit.

Step 2. R = Restatement of that idea in different language.

Step 3. S = Support material for explaining the idea.

Step 4. R = Restatement of the ideas as a summary.

Step 5. T = Transition to the next unit.

Through the S-R-S-R-T formula, each major unit of a speech becomes a unified whole and is linked to every other unit by a transition. This unit of a student's speech illustrates the formula's use:

Statement:

The first reason why we should change our approach to the teaching of foreign languages is a practical one. It's concerned with speaking face-to-face with foreigners in their own language. Our foreign language courses should prepare us to talk in ordinary conversation with those in foreign countries.

Restatement:

By that first reason I mean that the foreign language student should be able to converse with people in day-to-day situations.

Foreign language students should learn the language of the street so they can speak the ordinary language of ordinary people.

Support:

Let me explain. I studied conversational German. The textbook was written by an American teacher twenty years ago. He had never been to Germany, although he was an authority on German literature. My teacher's qualifications? She studied the language in college and toured Germany for two weeks. She took lots of slides. She showed them every time she forgot to prepare a lesson. I went to Germany and practiced my German. I should have stuck to "good morning." I knew that well since we had to say it first thing every day in class. But I tried to speak the language I learned. What a horror! I asked for green tea and got a green wastepaper basket! I asked to use an iron to press my clothes. I got an old-fashioned charcoal-burning one after a long wait. My textbook was written before electric irons were invented, I guess. I asked for a steak and got a slap in the face — I'm not sure why! Yet I had spent hours in conversational drill on those and similar expressions.

Restatement:

I was short-changed in my foreign language course. Those courses should prepare us to converse in the idiom the people of the country currently use.

Transition:

That's the first reason. Now for the second.

This example illustrates the general plan for structuring the individual units of the body of a speech.

THE CONCLUSION

The primary purpose of the conclusion of a speech is to summarize what has been said in the speech's body. This is the "I tell them what I told them" part of the speech. The basic purpose of the conclusion can be accomplished by a simple restatement of the purpose statement along with the partition statement. A secondary purpose of the conclusion is to memorably sum up what has been said, leaving the audience with the speech's purpose powerfully presented. Many speakers, therefore, try to end a speech by using one of the attention-getting devices of the introduction to capture the audience. In devising a conclusion, it's a good idea to keep the title of one of Shakespeare's plays in mind: *All's Well That Ends Well.*

The following conclusions illustrate various ways of ending speeches. The first employs a general summary to touch once again on the main points covered in the body of the speech:

> In summary, then, in this speech I have asked and answered the question about what to do to help the aged. I have suggested that we first eliminate the mandatory retirement age; second, provide free medical care for those over 65 years; third, establish a minimum cost-of-living allowance for those whose retirement pay does not reach the minimum; fourth, provide a free-meal program.

The next example of a conclusion offers a summary and also includes an attention-gaining device. It is taken from a eulogy delivered by Adlai Stevenson at a memorial service for Winston Churchill.

> The great aristocrat, the beloved leader, the profound historian, the gifted painter, the superb politician, the lord of language, the orator, the wit — yes, and the dedicated bricklayer — behind all of them was the man of simple faith, steadfast in defeat, generous in victory, resigned in age, trusting in loving providence and committing his achievements and his triumphs to a higher power.
>
> Like the patriarchs of old, he waited on God's judgment and it could be said of him — as of the immortals that went before him — that God "magnified him in the fear of his enemies, and with his words he made prodigies to cease. He glorified him in the sight of kings and gave him commandments in the sight of his people. He showed him his Glory and sanctified him in his faith."

The third example bases its impact on an anecdote. It also includes a restatement of the speech's purpose:

> I close with a story. It may not at first seem relevant to what I've said. But it does illustrate the main thrust of my talk: — a plea for understanding youth. After all, making false judgments, jumping to conclusions before all the facts are known, is a common human failing.
>
> A man was walking up and down the aisle of a train in the dead of night, carrying a crying baby in his arms. For an hour he walked until a man snapped, "Why don't you take the child to its mother?" The man replied, "I wish I could, but the mother lies in a casket in the baggage car."

The final example comes from a speech by the late General of Armies, Douglas MacArthur. The speech was delivered to a military audience. The conclusion refers to the speaker's years of military service and describes the end of his career. It contains a number of references that would be familiar to his military listeners:

> The shadows are lengthening for me. The twilight is here. My days of old have vanished — tone and tints. They have gone glimmering through the dreams of things that were. Their memory is one of wondrous beauty watered by tears and coaxed and caressed by the smiles of yesterday. I listen vainly, but with thirsty ear, for the witching melody of faint bugles blowing reveille, of far drums beating the long roll.

SUMMARY

For the person who has yet to speak before an audience, this chapter provides considerable help in how to put together a speech. Once the speaker has decided on a subject and gathered the necessary material to properly support his or her point of view, the speaker has to organize the material in some sensible way.

Thousands of years ago speech teachers believed that speakers must arouse the audience's attention and introduce the subject before they would discuss the main ideas. After the speakers made whatever points they wanted to make, they had to summarize what was said and leave the audience with a few concluding thoughts. That advice is essentially what this chapter is all about: the speech's introduction, body, and conclusion.

Each part has to fulfill certain tasks. The speaker supplies the material to fulfill them. He or she seeks attention-arousing material to begin the speech, then decides on a way to pattern the body of the speech. Six patterns are: time, space, topical, causal, problem-solution, and motivated-sequence. The pattern provides the speaker with a procedure for organizing the data gathered in research. Finally, the speaker concludes the talk, rephrasing the main points in summary fashion, ending with a well-chosen final remark.

During this process the speaker should remember that his or her remarks should resemble the latest Paris fashion: long enough to cover the subject and short enough to be interesting. Above all, the talk should not be like steer horns — a point here, a point there, and a lot of bull in between.

19

Informing and Persuading

"What's up, Ken?"

"Not much. I'm off to class. The prof's gonna lecture on collectivism. Then, I gotta see Peg. She wants to go to Pittsburgh to listen to the symphony. I'm not sure I wanna go."

"So — you're gonna be informed and persuaded, right?"

"Dave, you've been taking too many speech classes."

Dave is correct. Ken is going to be informed by the professor and Peg most likely is going to try to persuade Ken to go to the symphony. As students we probably have been listening to years of informative speeches, or lectures, from our teachers and, as partners in relationships, we probably have done some persuading and have been persuaded by friends. Much of our daily communication revolves around informing and being informed and persuading and being persuaded.

In Chapter 3 we mentioned the three goals of speaking: to inform, to persuade, and to actuate. Because speeches to actuate include persuasive elements, we include them as part of the persuasive goal. In this chapter we describe informative and persuasive speaking, principally from the public speaking viewpoint, recognizing that the characteristics we analyze could apply in interviews and group discussion as well.

SPEAKING TO INFORM

In his lecture on collectivism, Ken's professor intends to widen Ken's range of knowledge regarding the subject matter. The professor is hoping he will make Ken and the other students understand the subject, so he provides them with the information needed for that understanding. The professor's lecture is an informative speech, a speech designed to increase an audience's knowledge and understanding of a topic.[1]

Forms of Informative Speaking

Informative speeches take varied forms. Three merit attention here because they are so commonly used: oral reports, oral instructions, and informative lectures.[2]

1. *Oral reports* are common in business and professional organizations. Speakers present scientific reports, committee reports, executive reports, and informational accounts of similar ilk. Research experts announce their findings at conventions and conferences. Committees investigate and report their results to the membership. Department heads explain their progress in weekly reports to the rest of the staff.

2. *Oral instructions* include class instructions, job instructions, and instructions for special group efforts. Teachers tell students how to prepare class assignments. Supervisors inform their subordinates how to carry out a job assignment. Doctors instruct their patients about their health needs.

3. *Informative lectures.* Like the professors who lectured on collectivism, all sorts of people, not only teachers, are invited to share information or knowledge with groups. Informative talks are given to community organizations and associations. Public lectures are presented at church gatherings, luncheon clubs, and neighborhood

study groups. Visiting speakers appear at business and professional institutes.

In each case the speaker's goal should be to make certain the audience understands clearly and fully the ideas offered. Clarifying a topic is important, and the speaker also has to be interesting and provide significant information. Some devices we noted in previous chapters — examples, anecdotes, descriptions, audio-visual aids — can help make speeches interesting. The speaker can attach significance to the information by pointing out to the listeners why they need to know about the subject of the speech. The introduction is the place to do this. The listeners' attention will be captured if they perceive the relevance of the subject to their lives. Nonetheless, the major goal is to make the report clear, to have the instructions understood, or to ensure a proper grasp of the lecture's content.[3]

Successful Informative Speaking

How do informative speakers know if their messages are successful? One teacher answers the question this way: "I find out quickly if my lectures were understood by giving a quiz or asking questions. If the responses are pretty good, I know I've gotten the message across." Other informative speakers likewise can check their effectiveness by seeking overt feedback from the listeners. Overt feedback can come from immediate behavioral responses to the message.

At one university years ago, speech class students found out how effective they were by "before" and "after" tests. Before they spoke, they questioned the student listeners about the listeners' knowledge on the subject matter. If the response was negligible, the speakers knew the subject was unfamiliar to the listeners. After they spoke, the speakers questioned the listeners again, expecting more positive responses. If the listeners responding to the "before" version obviously knew much about the subject, the speakers then introduced more sophisticated materials, information the listeners were ignorant about.

Speakers can measure immediate behavioral responses in additional ways. The basketball coach instructing players on the proper method of shooting free throws can check her effectiveness by having the players shoot free throws. The English teacher can check his effectiveness in instructing students how to write an essay by having them write an essay. Sometimes enthusiastic applause and positive feedback are measures of effectiveness, especially with large audiences, when other measures are impractical. "After I report on my unit's progress

during the week," a supervisor said, "I'm aware of my success if the boss and the other department heads accept my report."

Presenting the Content

As informative speakers, we should review Chapter 16 on speech preparation, recognizing as we do so that analyzing the audience, the occasion, and the subject are important preliminary steps. A review of Chapter 17, investigating the speech subject, is equally essential, as is the material in Chapter 18 on organizing the speech. Our minds refreshed with this information, we should keep the following points before us as we prepare our lecture, report, or set of instructions.[4]

1. *Create a need for the information.* In the introduction we can create a desire to listen by showing the subject's significance to the listeners. This can be done in a few simple phrases. A beauty products salesperson called her listeners' attention to her topic's importance in this manner: "My report is about cultural variations among our customers. If we realize that blacks have different skin needs than whites do, we will adjust our sales message to fit the needs of each group — and make more sales." The basketball coach, instructing players on free throw shooting, created interest in this manner: "Let's face it. Most games are won on the free throw line. It's important for us to know how to shoot free throws. We can win games that way. Anyone can stand on the line to shoot, but not everyone can make 'em. We have to learn how."

2. *Use relevant information.* When choosing a subject and picking the information on the subject to speak about, we should select pertinent materials, information bearing upon the listeners' needs and desires. Audience analysis is in order. A speech on what suntan lotion to use would have relevance to vacationers bound for Hawaii's sunny shores, but irrelevant to a group of Finns who plan to spend January at home. Why we pay taxes would be of greater interest to taxpayers than to teenagers interested in the latest popular music.

3. *Select informative information.* Listeners tend to remember and understand generalizations and main ideas rather than specific details and lots of facts. Speakers are well-prepared if they limit their content to a few main points — four or five in a ten-minute speech, for example. Listeners cannot remember many more.

Then, too, simple words and concrete ideas are better retained than more complex materials. One student was heard to remark after a guest lecture, "I was impressed . . . his language . . . the big words and so many foreign phrases. I wrote down his reference to 'la belle dame sans merci causing perverted cutaneous sensations.' He used it so much. I want to look it up. I thought he was supposed to speak about cocaine." The student perhaps would have understood the message if the lecturer had simply said, "Cocaine is like a beautiful lady without mercy. Users feel like they have bugs under their skin."

Humor enlivens, humanizes, and enriches factual material, but it does not help retain information. It can make a dull speech more interesting. Tossing in irrelevant jokes for a few laughs may get a few, yet add little to the listener's knowledge.

Asking the listeners to react in an overt fashion increases understanding. "One of my teachers made us participate whenever he wanted us to remember something", the student recalled. "He'd have us repeat after him important words, key ideas. Tests — he'd give us the date and the chapters to study. Then we had to recite these aloud, and sometimes stand up while we did it. We never forgot." Methods of audience participation are explained in Chapters 14 and 15, on group discussion. Buzz groups, brainstorming, and role playing are among the means an informative speaker can use to actively involve an audience.

4. *Use signposts.* Signposts are verbal expressions that signal the importance of forthcoming statements. "Now get this," "Here's a point to remember," "Pay attention to this; it'll be on the test," "The most important point is" are signposts, indicating material of great importance. Repetition also helps. Repeating key ideas stresses their significance.

Organizing the Informative Speech

In the previous chapter we cautioned against jumping into the content of the speech without first properly introducing it. That admonition holds for the informative speech. We want to lead our listeners into the body of the speech. We do this through a proper introduction.

Introduction

For us, the introduction consists of an attention-arousing step and a preview of the body's content, with the goal of interesting our listeners in the subject matter. To refresh our memories, the attention-getting devices are examples and anecdotes, startling facts, a question or series of questions, striking quotations, and familiar references. By using one or even several of these tools, we hope to capture our audience's immediate interest, try to establish our credibility as a subject matter expert, and build goodwill.

Presenting a short classroom speech on the advantages of travel, one student began by quoting Mark Twain: "*In Innocents Abroad*, Mark Twain wrote these powerful words, 'Travel is fatal to prejudice, bigotry, and narrow mindedness, and many of our people need it sorely. . . . broad, wholesome, charitable views...cannot be acquired by vegetating in one's little corner of earth.'" The speaker then went on to cite his credentials as a travel expert and offered a quick preview of his speech, in which his purpose was to show how travel gives us a broader perspective on life, and helps us understand how people live in other parts of the world.

The preview introduces the purpose of the speech and gives an outline of the main topics to be covered. In no more than a minute or two, it climaxes an introduction for a ten-minute speech. Whether the informative speech is an oral report to business associates, a major lecture, or a set of instructions, the introduction is an essential part.

Body

The speech's body contains the meat of the message. In it the speaker presents the information itself, and does so in a clear, concise manner. The largest part of the speech, comprising from three-fourths to nine-tenths of the whole, the body is organized in one of the patterns described in the previous chapter, specifically the topical, chronological, spatial, or problem-solution pattern, whichever seems to be suited best for the subject matter at hand.

Regardless of the pattern used, each segment of the body must be arranged sensibly. In the previous chapter, we suggested a formula for doing just that: S-R-S-R-T (*state* the main idea of each segment, *restate* it in slightly different fashion, the repetition making clear the idea to be discussed, *support* the idea with information gleaned through research, *restate* the idea in a quick summary, and end with a *transition* to the next point.

Again, even though the informative speech may be an oral report, a set of instructions, or a major lecture, we should follow the procedure outlined. By doing so, we can clarify our ideas to our listeners, whether they are students listening to a class lecture, business associates listening to a supervisor's unit report, or a basketball team getting coaching on how to shoot baskets.

Conclusion

Once we have presented the information covering our topic, we summarize it, stating once again the main points around which the speech was built. We leave the listeners with those key ideas fresh in their minds. It is a good idea also to offer a concluding attention-arouser — a short example, anecdote,

Outline of a Sample Informative Speech
Innocence Abroad

Introduction

I.   Quotation from Mark Twain's *Innocents Abroad* [Attention arouser]

II. Travel is enlightening [Purpose]

    A. I've traveled to almost every country in the world [Credibility builder]

    B. Traveling helps overcome prejudices, narrow-mindedness [Motivator]

    C. These points will be covered [Preview]

        1. Bathhouses

        2. Foods

        3. People

Body [Topical arrangement]

I.   Public bathhouses are common world-wide [Statement of the idea to be discussed in this unit]

    A. Found in Korea, Japan, Philippines, China— any place where plumbing, water is scarce or expensive [Restatement]

    B. Ones I went to were mixed sex, au naturel [Support material]

        1. Scrubbed before soaking

        2. Male/female scrubbers

        3. Layers of dirt come off

        4. Soak in steaming water

        5. Talk while soaking

        6. Dry off

        7. Cleansed and rosy pink

        8. American friends shocked

        9. Mixed, au naturel bathing sinful to them

        10. Clean and healthy to foreigners

    C. Public bathing is normal in much of world [Restatement as summary]

    D. Public bathing may seem odd—how about eating sheep's eyeballs? [Transition to next idea]

II. A variety of foods eaten around the world [S-R-S-R-T formula is followed to develop this idea.]

III. People do strange things in other places in the world [The S-R-S-R-T formula is followed to develop this idea.]

Conclusion

I.   People in other lands practice strange customs [Summary]

    A. Bathe differently than we do

    B. Eat different foods

    C. Have odd behavior

II. When we travel, we learn about different customs — and reduce our prejudice and narrow-mindedness [Restate purpose]

III. Quote from Myung-seok Park [Memorable closing statement] startling statement, question, quotation, or familiar reference — to end the speech, leaving the audience with a powerful reminder of what was said.

The student reporting to the class on his travel experiences closed his informative speech with this concluding attention-arouser:

> Myung-seok Park, a famous Korean educator, writes: While it is difficult for a stranger to muddle through the superficial customs and attitudes which are different between cultures, once he does he gets to the real core which all humans share. People in every culture feel the same emotions, share the same dreams and ambitions for themselves and their children, and desire the same comforts and knowledge which make life worth living. If the stranger can do this with determination and cultural sensitivity, he will be a better person for it.

SPEAKING TO PERSUADE

After listening to the professor's lecture, Ken, whom we met in the first lines of this chapter, faces Peg. She charms him into a visit to Pittsburgh and an evening at the symphony. On the way to the concert hall, he recalls what friend Dave had said. Dave thought the professor's lecture would be an informative speech and Peg's plea a persuasive one. Dave was right; Ken was informed and persuaded.

Persuasive speaking, Ken recalls, has as its goal a desire to change the direction, intensity, or salience of listener attitudes toward a speaker's subject[5] (see Chapter 3). Ken's attitude toward the symphony and driving to Pittsburgh was at best neutral. His neutrality was not strong, and the idea of making the excursion was not important in his life. Thus, Peggy convinced him to go. After listening to Peggy, Ken became more favorable toward the trip. His neutral position became more positive, and he perceived the journey as more important to his relationship with Peggy. How did Peggy convince him? An explanation of persuasive speaking provides insights.

Behavioral Responses

A change in attitude — the goal of persuasive speaking — can be covert or overt. If we do not smoke and have a neutral attitude toward it, speeches against smoking may make our attitude unfavorable. If we never speak outwardly against smoking, the change is *covert;* it remains hidden within us. The change occurred and we know it did, but at no time do we openly display our opposition against smoking. Change also can be *overt.* Anyone can perceive the attitude change from neutralism to unfavorableness. We speak against smoking whenever we have the opportunity, chiding friends to stop and rebuking smokers in our vicinity.

Four overt responses have been linked to persuasion: adoption, discontinuance, deterrence, and continuance.[6]

1. *Adoption* calls for accepting a persuasive message and indicating acceptance by overt behavior. Peg wants Ken to accompany her to the symphony, and Ken accepts her plea and takes her to the symphony. A candidate for elected office wants you to vote for her, and when you do, you demonstrate an overt behavioral response.

2. *Discontinuance* means that listeners stop doing something they now do. When the listeners cease doing what they were told not to do, the response is overt.

3. *Deterrence* requires listeners to avoid some activity. A speaker tells us that if we want to live a healthy life, we shouldn't smoke. The speaker's goal is reached when we overtly avoid smoking.

4. *Continuance* means persuading the listeners to do as they now are doing. The behavioral response is for the listeners to continue their present behavior. Athletic club boosters are demonstrating continuance when they respond favorably to entreaties calling for booster club membership renewals.

Means of Persuasion

Various means of persuasion are at our disposal, and we identify here those that can lead to success. No set of rules guarantees success, however, and no formula ensures effectiveness. Therefore, the variables we mention increase our chances for achieving our persuasive objectives, but they do not assure it.

Credibility

We are most likely to be persuasive when our listeners like, trust, and have confidence in us. In Chapter 4 we ranked credibility as the speaker's most potent means of persuasion. Reviewing the section on credibility there will help you understand the persuasive power of credibility. Here we underline its importance: speaker credibility has a major effect on listeners' beliefs and attitudes.

Because we cannot know all there is to know about everything, when we need information or have a problem to solve, we turn to people we can trust and are experts in the area of our concern. We rely on their judgments. To us they are individuals of high credibility.

Credibility stems from varied speaker characteristics. We lump these into three main groupings: expertness, trustworthiness, and forcefulness.

1. *Expertness* involves the speaker's qualification or capability. We perceive an expert to be a speaker who is knowledgeable about the subject area — actually so well-versed as to be proficient in it. Obviously the expert knows more than we do.

2. *Trustworthiness* concerns the mental and ethical traits that make up the speaker's character. We probably will trust and believe in individuals we perceive as honest, industrious, dependable, strong, and steadfast. We are less likely to trust individuals who we know stretch the truth, who are lazy and unreliable, and who are fickle, always changing their mind.

3. *Forcefulness* revolves around a person's behavioral and emotional tendencies while speaking, the impression the person makes on us. If the speaker is lively and enthusiastic, we respond with interest to what the person says. If he or she is dull and boring, we react in like manner. Our feeling tends to be positive to a speaker who is intense and ardent in expression. If a speaker is too enthusiastic, bordering on zealousness or fanaticism, however, we are apt to perceive the person as too extreme, a zealot. We then harbor reservations about the person's credibility, seeing the individual as unbelievable.

Logicality

We are more likely to be persuasive when we show our listeners logical reasons for their support. Reasons answer the question "why?" Why should Ken go to the symphony with Peg? Why should we study for exams? Why should we vote Republican? Why should we buy insurance? Some reasons come easily, given a little time to think about the subject. Others require research, especially if we know hardly anything about the subject. Chapter 17 offers help on investigating a subject.

After we have thought about the subject and completed the needed research, we can draw up a set of possible reasons why the listeners should accept our viewpoint. From the list we then select the ones that best meet the following standards.[7]

1. *The reasons that most adequately prove our point of view.* Imagine that Peggy, in her attempt to get Ken to go to the symphony, lists these reasons: You'll enjoy excellent music. You'll do me a favor. You won't have to study today. You'll have a pleasant day in my company. You'll get away from school. Most of the reasons are persuasive. If Peg were to think about the third one, "You won't have to study today," she would drop it.

Ken would only be postponing study until the next day, and he might be in trouble if he has assignments due that day.

2. *The reasons that can be supported factually.* Supporting materials provide the evidence and proof upon which persuasion logically rests. Opinions, factual examples, statistics, and tangible objects are the supporting materials speakers need to prove their points. Without that support, they should not give reasons.

3. *The reasons that meet listeners' needs.* To be persuasive, we should know our listeners' needs, and this requires audience analysis. If Peggy understands Ken's needs and knows he does not like symphony music, dislikes driving, and wants to study, she should not use these reasons even though they sound like good ones. Ken would not be persuaded by them. Maybe he desires female companionship. That being the case, Peggy has a reason that is persuasive to him.

The world does not operate by logic and evidence alone. Sometimes we think irrationally; in such circumstances our feelings are not based on evidence. A persuasive speaker might come up with excellent arguments for dining on raw fish without changing our attitudes on that subject. We do not like raw fish, and the speaker's logic is not going to change our mind.

A colleague amasses reasoning and evidence to win his arguments, but fails to deal with the emotions of those he is trying to persuade. Insensitive to their feelings, he is unsuccessful, a poor persuader. Because he is the boss, however, his power carries him through. His subordinates expect him to treat them badly if they do not comply. The best evidence, therefore, may not win over listeners.

Emotional Appeals

Persuasion relies on emotional appeals as well as logic and credibility. Emotional appeals are appeals to listeners' feelings, emotions, or needs. Humans have an infinite number of needs, and the list in Chapter 4 covers a considerable amount. We remember from that chapter that needs are the physical and psychological feelings that give rise to tensions and hence motivate people to act in a way so as to overcome the tensions. To persuade listeners, the persuasive speaker taps their needs. Audience analysis is required to know the listeners' needs and, once they are known, the speaker has powerful persuasive appeals to use.

We have to satisfy three interpersonal needs — inclusion, control, and affection — if we are to live normal lives. When appealing to Ken to take her to Pittsburgh, Peggy would be wise to tap these needs.

If Ken is in need of female companionship (a need for inclusion or affection), Peggy has a strong persuasive appeal at her command.

The Maslow hierarchy of needs (see Chapter 4) also provides us with strong emotional appeals. A candidate for public office during a time of high unemployment can win votes by appealing to voters' safety needs. They want the security and stability employment can bring. They do not want to worry about money to buy food, clothing, and shelter. By favoring ways of increasing employment, the candidate can garner votes for his or her election.

Among the other needs listed in Chapter 4, speakers can find the means for convincing their listeners by knowing the values, beliefs, and attitudes of their listeners. Knowing that Americans are patriotic, political office candidates often "wave the flag," appealing to Americans' pride in their country. Keeping in mind that most Americans are religious, appeals to reverence can add persuasive force to our messages.

In using emotional appeals and, for that matter, logical ones, we should avoid being blatant, too obvious, or overly aggressive. Subtlety is more

OUTLINE OF A SAMPLE PERSUASIVE SPEECH
Power-Packed
Introduction

I.   The Jetson diet—a futuristic feast of prefab pellets containing all the nourishment we will need in the 21st century [Attention arouser]

II. We're still in the 20th century, and university students have problems with proper nourishment [Purpose introduced and related to audience]

Body [Motivated-sequence Pattern]

I.   What are the problems? They relate to our eating habits [Need step]

   A.   School cafeterias serve fatty foods

   B.   Eating off-campus, students consume too much pizza, tacos, red meat, bakery products

   C.   Students do not eat enough vegetables, fruit — five servings a day essential

   D.   Students often do not eat breakfast

   E.   Students eat meals at irregular times

   F.   Too much snacking

   [Each point is organized in S-R-S-R-T fashion]

II. How can students obtain more crucial nutrients in their diet? [Satisfaction step]

   A.   Eat more vegetables and fruits, eliminate fat

   B.   Supplement their diet with vitamins

      1. Evidence suggests vitamins play an important role in assuring vitality and optimal health

      2. The important vitamins and what they do

   C.   Vitamins help students stay healthier longer

III. Significant results are obtainable with vitamins [Visualization step]

   A.   Vitamins have established benefits

   B.   Research shows additional benefits not known before now

Conclusion

I.   Supplement diet with vitamins [Action step]

II. University students have nutritional problems, and these can be solved with regular doses of vitamins [Summary]

III. Quotation: You need vitamins for optimal health and the prevention of some chronic diseases [Attention-arousing ending]

[Speaker offers adequate support for each point and cites sources of these factual data] effective. Fund-raisers seeking money for new buildings on university campuses couch their appeals in language that respects their listeners' intelligence and sensitivity. Rather than to offensively state, "Give us a couple of million dollars and we'll name the building after you," they suggest, through their descriptions and illustrations, that the contributor will be supporting a worthwhile endeavor and will gain the sincere appreciation of all the people who use the building.

Organization

Chapter 18 provided details on organizing speeches. After a review of that chapter, note that the problem-solution and motivated-sequence patterns probably fit the persuasive speech the best. The others explained in the chapter are more appropriate for informative speeches.

The introduction in the persuasive speech should interest the listeners in the subject matter and establish the speaker's credibility. A preview probably is not necessary because it often is wiser to slowly lead the listeners into the speaker's purpose, not hit them over the head with it.

The body of the speech is developed around the chosen organizational pattern, either the problem-solution or motivated sequence as we suggested. The S-R-S-R-T formula is applied carefully so each main idea is properly conceived.

The conclusion provides a summary and closes with an attention-arouser, leaving the listeners interested in what was said. The purpose can be announced, with care. Too many beginning persuasive speakers conclude with remarks such as, "Today I tried to persuade you to vote for George Washington for president." This sounds offensively obvious. A subtler approach, "A vote for George Washington is a vote for union," softens the attempt. Persuasion is a seductive kind of speaking. Our goal is to convince the listeners to accept our position. We ought not try to beat them into submission.

SUMMARY

Public speakers speak to inform or persuade. When the talk is *informative*, the speaker expects to increase the audience's knowledge and understanding of a subject. The *persuasive* speaker intends to change the direction, intensity, or salience of listeners' attitudes toward the speaker's subject. For both types of speaking, the audience, occasion and subject have to be analyzed, the subject has to be researched, and the research material the speaker gathers has to be organized in a coherent fashion.

After those preparatory steps have been completed, the speaker decides whether to inform or persuade and then follows the details outlined in this chapter for whatever type is selected, being attentive to the listeners' needs and interests. If the speaker is to be effective, the listeners must be perceived as central. The speaker must know what the listeners want and design and deliver the speech to meet those desires.

VOCABULARY CHECK . . .

Match the terms with the correct explanation chosen from the past five chapters. Answers are on page 244.

_____ 1. Consensus

_____ 2. Minority process

_____ 3. Delphi

_____ 4. Inherency

_____ 5. NGT

_____ 6. Brainstorming

_____ 7. Charts

_____ 8. Cause-effect

_____ 9. Credibility

_____ 10. Mark Twain

A. No oral interaction takes place in the first step.
B. Many ideas are generated in a short time.
C. Audiovisual aids.
D. A pattern of speech organization.
E. All members come to agreement.
F. A mail method for obtaining judgments from a group.
G. A potent means of persuasion.
H. Travel is fatal to prejudice.
I. A committee decides for the group.
J. An essential characteristic of a problem.

20

Delivering The Speech

Anyone who has listened to people speak probably can draw up a list of boring, uninspired, and tiresome speakers. The list is apt to contain the name of a colorless, uninteresting teacher or two, the type who for years has dryly regurgitated the same lectures. Perhaps a religious leader is on the list, one who ponderously preaches sermons straight out of the latest book of theological discourse. A politician likely is included, a blustery person who is anxious to save society with our money. A few fellow students are bound to be on the list, especially the ones who failed to prepare and then stumble through a jumble of ideas.

Chances are that most of these people are on the list because they either did not prepare or took too lightly the oral presentation of their materials. Often the culprit is delivery; they had a good speech on paper but could not get it across to the audience. Delivery significantly affects a speaker's persuasiveness and the listeners' ability to comprehend. By itself, however, a superbly delivered speech will not guarantee success. When a well-prepared speech is coupled with an excellent presentation, however, the speaker is in the best possible position to influence an audience. Having an audience respond in a positive way takes skill, and it is a skill that has to be learned.[1]

Speech delivery is the emphasis of this chapter. It begins by noting the qualities of good delivery. The role of the voice and body movement in transmitting ideas orally is described, as well as methods of delivery and rehearsal techniques. Throughout, we offer suggestions for improving delivery.

CHARACTERISTICS OF GOOD DELIVERY

A student, Sharon, prepared what she believed was a good speech. She had analyzed her student audience well and selected a subject having much appeal to the students. The speech was chock full of interesting information and was perfectly organized. Yet as she presented it, she knew the speech was falling on deaf ears. It was a flop. Tearfully, she asked the instructor what went wrong. The instructor replied:

> Remember when you went to the board to draw a diagram to illustrate one of your points? Well, when you did that, you talked at the board. No one could hear you beyond the first row. At several points your voice was muffled as you bent your head to check your notes. Perhaps you aren't aware of it, but you have a habit of rubbing your hand across your mouth. When you do that, you block the sound. At a few places in your talk, you became rather excited about the need for the programs you were describing. When you did that, you spoke at an extremely fast rate. It was impossible for your audience to follow what you were saying.

Sharon had prepared an "A" speech, but its delivery earned an "F." Delivery cannot be overlooked in public speaking.

Qualities of good delivery:

Clear organization
Precise language and wording
Audible, pleasant voice and articulation
Direct eye contact
Enthusiasm indicated by an alert body and mind
Controlled, yet flexible bodily action
Clearly stated ideas

Qualities of bad delivery:

Obvious lack of preparation and knowledge
Vagueness
Mumbling of words
Monotonous delivery
Too many verbalizations — ahs, uhs, you-knows
Too many mispronunciations; poor grammar
Stiff body; lack of eye contact
Lack of enthusiasm
Obvious nervousness and fidgeting

What are the characteristics of good delivery? The two we consider — naturalness and conversational style — are closely related. They are the qualities of speech we practice when we talk face-to-face with friends. They just have to be carried over to public speaking situations.

Naturalness

Simply stated, naturalness is a *delivery that does not call attention to itself.* Any aspect of voice or body that causes listeners to attend to it rather than to the speaker's message is unnatural. The speaker's content — not the speaker's extraordinary voice range or elegance of gestures — should be what holds the listeners' attention.

Most of us employ a natural delivery in our everyday talk with friends and relatives. In those instances we speak *spontaneously*; the talk flows out. If the subject interests us, we probably will speak with enthusiasm. There is no artificiality. We are not trying to be golden-throated orators — just ourselves.

The trick is to bring that unpretentious delivery style to public speaking situations. To relax and be ourselves is difficult in these settings. Yet that is what is necessary to be natural. The listeners must feel we are speaking from the heart.

Conversational Style

When we speak naturally, we most likely are using a conversational style. We speak as we do when we are having a conversation with someone else. It conveys the feeling that we are talking *with*

the listeners rather than *at* them.[2] This is the proper style to use in public speaking.

In speaking conversationally, we are personal, clear, and unassuming. We use much repetition and restatement. Common, nontechnical words make up our messages. Sprinkled throughout conversational talk are personal pronouns (I, me, you, us, we), reflecting a feeling of immediacy with the listeners. Simple sentences and relaxed grammar are part of the style. Specific, concrete words add to the accuracy of the ideas being expressed. We use actual names, places, and dates to transmit a clearer picture of what we mean. Because polysyllabic words frequently confuse our listeners, simple, short words should be used to aid understanding. We should speak to an audience as we would when talking to a friend.[3]

THE VOICE

A powerful instrument, the voice can be varied to get almost any effect the speaker desires. A person can speak in a loud voice one second, then drop to a whisper in the next. A speaker can speed up to go through unimportant details quickly and slow down to emphasize key ideas. A speaker can alter voice pitch to suggest differences in meaning and can change voice quality slightly to suggest different characters.[4] The ways in which we vary our voices can be better understood by studying rate, volume, pitch, and quality. Enunciation has an impact also, although it is indirectly related to the voice itself.

Rate

Some people seem to believe, unfortunately, that rapid delivery is a sign of a great speaker. Perhaps the belief arises from the mistaken notion that people who are able to use words quickly must be able to control and exploit them expertly. Actually, the faster one speaks, the less the listeners will understand, although a rapid speaker (one who speaks 195 or more words per minute) does create an impression of vigor. When such a speaker talks about a subject of vital concern to the listeners, they might try extra hard to follow. In contrast, a slow speaker (one who speaks 120 or fewer words per minute) runs the risk of boring the listeners. The slow speaker also may be considered a bit too deliberative, sluggish, and conservative. The happy medium falls between 120 and 195 words per minute. At this speed, listening is comfortable for the audience, and talking is comfortable for the speaker.[5]

Delivery is governed by the marriage of pause and duration. Pause — *the silence between words* — gives the speaker a chance to breathe, to vocally

Using the pause:

As punctuation

"John hit Bill" = Bill was hit by John

"John, hit Bill." The comma means that John is being asked or ordered to hit Bill. In spoken language, the comma becomes a pause.

In reading aloud, we normally pause when coming across a punctuation mark.

As emphasis:

"All we have to fear is (pause) fear itself."

"He (pause) is truly the greatest man alive."

From Wayne H. Oxford, *The Fundamentals of Effective Oral Expression* (Tokyo: Eichosha, 1979)

punctuate his or her thoughts, and to give dramatic emphasis. Too many pauses, however, slow down the rate of speech, especially when each pause lasts more than a second or two. Conversely, the fewer the pauses, the faster the rate will be. Duration refers to *length of time each sound is held.* If a sound is held for a long time, the rate slows down. If a sound is held for a short time, the rate increases.[6]

Pause

Some speakers act as if they fear silence. To them, a soundless pause is to be avoided at all costs. They talk continuously until they run out of breath, and their words blend together into a hardly distinguishable mass: "Fourscoreandsevenyearsagoourfathersbroughtforthonthiscontinent (gasp) anewnation conceivedinlibertyanddedicatedtothepropositionthatallmenarecreatedequal (gasp)." Or they may revert to vocalized pauses when they need time to think about or formulate the next idea: "Four score and — er, uh — and seven years ago our — er, ah — fathers brought — uh, mm — forth . . ." "Uh," "ah," and "er" are examples of vocalized pauses, meaningless sounds uttered to eliminate silence.

Pause is a useful device for emphasis and effect.[7] Notice how pause is used in the following passage; it makes the statements more forceful and offers the listeners a second or two to reflect upon their meaning:

The team has fifteen men over thirty years old (pause), and all were passed up by other teams in the league. (pause) Yet we are told we have a pennant winner (pause) but (pause) the team has already lost more than it's won. (pause) Is anyone impressed by the management's championship claims?

(pause) Has anyone been impressed by the lack of speed, (pause) lack of defense, (pause) lack of pitching? (pause) Does anyone believe the team will win?

Vocalized pauses — sound segments such as "uh," "er," "um," "mm" — disrupt the fluency and smoothness of speech. These pauses can be eliminated once we realize what causes them. Often they are used to take up time while the speakers decide what they want to say next. More careful preparation helps to eliminate vocalized pauses caused by indecision. Frequent practice aloud before delivery should build familiarity and eliminate indecision.[8]

When speakers fail to select suitable transition statements in advance of their talk, they are more likely to use vocalized pauses to serve that purpose. "Ah," "um," and "er" function as transitions.[9] Preparation and practice of the speech can help overcome this problem.

Duration

Like pause, duration can be used to a speaker's advantage. Lengthening and shortening the duration of sounds can heighten the dramatic effect. "Tonight we have a big show for you" can make the show sound even more impressive by lengthening sounds: "Tonight we have a biiiig show for you." The extended duration of the "i" in "big" makes the show sound *really* big.

Similarly, we can lengthen the duration of a key word in a sentence to underscore the importance of the idea we are talking about or the word we are using. By saying, "Four scooorrre and seven years ago . . .," no one should mistake the length of time we are talking about. It is not "four years ago"; it is "four *score* years ago.[10]

In contrast, the shortening of duration speeds up the rate of speech to create an impression of action and excitement. A sportscaster describing the action in a basketball game can shorten the sounds, thereby increasing the rate of delivery in concert with the speed of the unfolding action. Most sportscasters vary duration automatically, speeding up and slowing down as the action dictates. Public speakers can do the same, shortening the duration of sounds to increase delivery rate. By doing so, they can build interest, suspense, or a sense of urgency.

Volume

Volume means *how loud we speak.* It influences delivery in several ways. We can manipulate the volume of our voice to add variety to our delivery. Instead of droning along at the same sound level and putting our listeners to sleep at the same time, we can vary volume just as we vary rate to add interest to what we are saying. We can stress key ideas by raising our volume slightly, making the key ideas stand out, and at the same time cutting down on the monotony of our delivery.[11]

In public speaking situations volume is a crucial factor. Speakers must talk loud enough so all the listeners can hear. Just how loud a person must speak depends upon the size of the room, the number of people in it, and the presence of competing noises. In a large room, with the sound of outside traffic filtering in, the speaker will have to increase the volume so all can hear. If a speaker is addressing ten people in a small, soundproof room, he or she can talk in a normal voice, varying volume slightly to emphasize key materials.[12]

Volume

A basic rule: *We must increase our loudness as the distance between us and our listeners increases.*

Can you project? Projection is the ability to increase loudness to compensate for increasing distance. Here is a test for projection:

In a quiet space, ask a friend to stand 3 feet away while you talk. If your friend can hear you, gradually increase the distance between you — to 6 feet, 12 feet, 24 feet, 48 feet. If you can be heard clearly at *all* of these distances, you can project.

From Wayne H. Oxford, *The Fundamentals of Effective Oral Expression* (Tokyo: Eichosha, 1979)

The public speaker has to vary volume to meet changing circumstances. Audiences tire of habitual shouters and stop listening to continual whisperers. Variation is in order. Unvaried volume can be deadly monotonous, a major enemy of good delivery.

Pitch

Pitch is determined by the vibrations of the vocal folds, two masses of muscle located at the Adam's apple. These muscles are liplike tissues that vibrate when air passes through them. The rate of vibration, along with the length and thickness of the folds, produces the pitch, *the position or location of the voice on the musical scale.*[13]

Pitch usually is described in terms of "highness" or "lowness." Pitch is said to go up or down. Variations in direction indicate differences in meaning, at least in English. Downward shifts are said to suggest determination, confidence, decisiveness, or annoyance. Upward shifts suggest suspense, indecision, and questioning.[14] Changes in pitch clarify meaning, as discussed in Chapter 8, on verbal communication, and extreme variations can add emphasis and color.

Pitch can express:

Boredom (a total lack of emotional involvement) — achieved by speaking in a monotone.

Sadness, dejection, solemn and deep feelings — achieved by using subtle, very slight variations in pitch

Excitement, enthusiasm, joyful surprise, anger — achieved by using a pitch range of about two octaves, raising the pitch level

Sarcasm — achieved by using exaggerated pitch changes

From Wayne H. Oxford, *The Fundamentals of Effective Oral Expression*, (Tokyo: Eichosha, 1979)

Speakers who do not vary voice pitch drone on monotonously. As a result of listening to a droner, members of an audience will lose interest in what is being said, seriously weakening the speaker's persuasive ability. They will see the speaker as dull, lifeless, and uninteresting.

Quality

The quality of a voice is produced by the shape and size of the throat, mouth, and nose cavities. Quality variations among people stem partially from differences in the shape and size of these cavities, or *resonators.* Quality is determined also by the way a person tenses the muscles used in voice production and by the person's general health.[15]

When we pick up the telephone and hear a familiar voice, vocal quality is our clue to the person's identity. We may recognize one person's voice by its harshness, another by its hoarseness, and another by its dullness. Voices may be shrill, muffled, raspy, childish, nasal, breathy, resonant, full, brilliant, melodious, among others. Blindfolded, we can differentiate between the talk of friends by the distinctive qualities of their voices.

Good quality comes from the absence of negative tonal characteristics. These negative qualities, which are apt to create unpleasant listening experiences, include breathiness (because of inadequately controlled breath), denasality (from obstructions in the nasal passages, which obliterate the nasal sounds "m," "n," and "ng"), and nasality (from too much breath passing through the nasal passages).[16]

Negative characteristics of the voice are difficult to overcome, especially if the fault is of long standing. A speech therapist can help, though. Under a therapist's instruction, suitable exercises often improve quality. In cases of injury, disease, or inflammation, a physician's advice is needed.

Quality

Eliminating unpleasant vocal qualities is a vastly complex task. Some can be reduced by *relaxation,* especially those resulting from negative emotions (fear, anxiety, anger). Here are some relaxation exercises:

1. Sit comfortably on a chair, relax the whole torso, bend forward with drooping shoulders and limply hanging arms. Let the head drop forward toward chest, relaxing neck and throat muscles. Rotate the head slowly, from right to left. Reverse the rotation. If the jaw muscles are relaxed, the jaw should fall open. Repeat.

2. Relax the jaw by vocalizing words and syllables ending in "a," allowing the jaw to fall open. Here are "a" sounds: ya, fa, ba, ka, ga, sa, ta. Repeat each a number of times: ya-ya-ya-ya-ya-ya-ya-ya.

3. Take a deep breath and sigh while letting the air out of the lungs quietly. Relax while sighing. Repeat.

4. Take a deep breath and sigh audibly while pronouncing the vowel sound "a." Repeat.

5. Simulate a yawn, or actually yawn. Try to retain the feeling of throat relaxation that follows.

(From Wayne H. Oxford, *The Fundamentals of Effective Oral Expression* (Tokyo: Eichosha, 1979)

Few of us has a perfect voice, one that makes listeners fall at our feet. We have to be content with what we have and use it to our advantage. Louis Armstrong comes to mind. He was a great trumpet player, but his voice quality was gravelly at best. He did sing, however, and he made millions of dollars in the process. He used what he had to his best advantage and became famous.

Enunciation

Enunciation consists of articulation and pronunciation. *Articulation* concerns the skill in pronouncing letters in words correctly. *Pronunciation* is the *ability to sound out the whole word.* Good enunciation is vital to understanding. A misarticulated or mispronounced word can cause problems.[17] The following anecdote offers an example:

> One day two men were taking an auto trip together. As they passed through the pretty little town of Wesley, one said: "What town is this?"
>
> "I think this is Wednesday," said the other in reply.
>
> "Oh, I thought it was Thirsdy," answered the first.
>
> "So am I," agreed the other. "Let's stop and have a drink."

Errors in articulation and pronunciation fall into four broad categories. The most frequently occurring is the *failure to pronounce certain sounds,* as in "makin" for *making,* "libray" for *library,* "nothin" for *nothing.* Another problem, *improper stress,* occurs when the wrong syllable is emphasized in a word. A third common error consists of *adding unnecessary sounds,* as when someone pronounces *athletic* as *athaletic* or *statistics* as *stastistics. Sound substitution* is a fourth error. An example is "feesh" instead of *fish.*[8]

Unclear articulation and mispronunciation are not major problems for most people. When they do exist, they usually are caused either by a misunderstanding of what is proper or by the speaker's carelessness. Most of us do have difficulty with a few words, but we can easily isolate these words and work toward overcoming whatever trouble we have with articulation and pronunciation. This is a worthwhile chore because faulty articulation and pronunciation are barriers to communication.

Occasionally, faulty articulation is traceable to an illness or a disease that impairs the function of muscles, jaws, lips, or palate. If this is the case, the speaker may not be able to make all sounds properly, and a trained therapist can be of assistance.

BODY MOVEMENT

In public speaking situations nonverbal behavior is part of the communicative act along with verbal behavior. Nonverbal behavior is discussed in Chapter 9, and we do not want to repeat everything we said in that chapter. We should point out, however, some characteristics of nonverbal behavior as they impact on public speaking. Eye contact, posture, movements, gestures, and facial expressions are considered here.

Eye Contact

In the public speaking situation, we have to be audience-oriented. Direct eye contact helps us do this. Direct eye contact makes audience members feel a part of the action. By looking them directly in the eye, the speaker gives the impression of talking with them, of showing concern for their interests. If the speaker looks elsewhere — out the window, at the ceiling, at a spot on the back of the room — the impression of interest will likely vanish, and the listeners may wonder what the speaker is looking at.[19]

A speech manuscript can come between audience and speaker if the speaker reads directly from it without many glances at the audience. The vital direct eye contact is missing when the speaker reads a manuscript word-for-word.

A good way to maintain eye contact is to scan the audience and look directly into the eyes of individual listeners. We should be in eye contact with the audience about 90 percent of the time. This causes members of the audience to pay more attention. The speaker must scan the entire audience, not just parts here and there. He or she should make a conscious effort to take in all parts of the audience.[20]

Posture

Not everyone is blessed with a strong, athletic build, and not all people are well-shaped. Those who are do have an advantage in speaking to the public. They are impressive to look at, adding to their credibility as speakers. Yet, we can make the most of our build and shape by standing "comfortably erect" when speaking. This communicates confidence and poise.

Standing comfortably erect does not necessarily mean standing at military attention, nor does it mean lounging against the speaker's stand. Stiffness and slouchiness both are to be avoided. This can be done by resting the body weight equally on both feet, with one positioned slightly ahead of the other and the feet spread twelve or so inches apart. The body should be held straight, and it should be relaxed.[21]

On occasion circumstances might call for a more informal posture than being comfortably erect. If the speaker is talking to a small group of five or six people gathered closely together, the speaker is better off to join them — either to sit down with them or to stand close to them, perhaps in somewhat of a leaning position.

Movements

For the public speaker, movement revolves around walking and moving about in front of the audience. The confident speaker rises when introduced and moves coolly to the rostrum. Reaching the appropriate spot behind the rostrum, this speaker pauses for a moment, looks over the audience, and begins. During the speech, the confident speaker moves around a bit and does it with ease.

In contrast, the uncertain speaker takes a few steps toward the speaker's stand when called upon, hesitates, maybe checks his or her notes, then finally moves forward. During the speech, some uncertain speakers stand rigidly. Others fidget or shift around. Then there is the pacer. The pacer begins to walk back and forth in front of the audience, and the listeners are forced to follow the action like watching the ball at a tennis match in slow motion.

When skillfully used, movement can be employed to emphasize ideas, add variety, and aid in making transitions from point to point in the speech. A few steps toward the audience adds emphasis to an idea. A few steps backward suggests that something of lesser importance is being explained. Movements from side to side suggest a shift from one idea to another. Slight changes in position from time to time add variety to the presentation.[22]

Also, the manner of approaching and leaving the rostrum leaves impressions. The speaker should do both with confidence and poise, neither hurrying nor hesitating. Inexperienced speakers, when leaving, often are so anxious to get the speech over with that they deliver the final few words on their way back to their seat. To display confidence, the speaker can pause for a second after concluding, look at the audience, then move calmly back to the seat.

Gestures

Gestures are movements of individual parts of the body such as the arms, hands, head, and shoulders. Most people in face-to-face interaction use gestures in a way that is natural for them. Their gestures reflect their emotional state at the moment. The angrier they are, the more numerous and violent the gestures are apt to be. The funnier the joke, the more pronounced the gestures probably will be.

In a public speaking situation, contrived or artificial gestures can be disconcerting to the audience; they lack naturalness. A friend recalls his elementary school days, and gesturing:

> In our grade school we had some sort of convocation about once a month at which we recited poetry or short prose bits to help us develop confidence. We'd have to memorize these, and, so we wouldn't look like wooden statues, we were taught gestures. At a certain point, we'd have to raise our hand. At another, we'd be taught to move slightly. We were taught a whole bunch of these to include with the recitation. We had two jobs then: to remember the words and to remember to gesture at the proper times. Usually the two never coincided. We said the crucial words and then we'd remember to gesture — too late to stress the important point. We looked like robots in our movements. Our parents and others in the audience tried not to laugh, but sometimes we looked hilarious, punctuating the air in a meaningless way with our gestures.

In this example, the teacher's attempts to incorporate gestures in the students' speeches were well-meaning. But a person has to be a good actor to make artificial gestures look natural.

Perhaps the best advice for public speakers regarding gesturing is to forget about it. Instead, the speaker should exhibit a genuine interest in the speech subject and let the gestures take care of themselves.

Facial Expressions

Facial movements are difficult to change because they closely mirror our feelings. If we feel sad, our face likely expresses that feeling. If we are happy about something, our face probably gives us away. Facial expressions arise automatically from our emotional state.[23]

As with gestures, the public speaker should forget about facial expressions. Instead, the speaker should concentrate on the message, realizing that enthusiasm for the content will be mirrored on his or her face. Likewise, the face will show lack of interest in the message if that is the speaker's feeling. Unless speakers are trained actors, they find it difficult to facially express an emotion they do not feel. Shakespeare put it this way: "Suit the action to the word, the word to the action; with this special observance, that you o'er step not the modesty of Nature."

METHODS OF DELIVERY

Just as good delivery depends upon effective use of the voice and bodily movement, it depends on the speaking method used to transmit the speaker's ideas. A part of speech preparation is to decide on a method of presentation. Of the four methods — extemporaneous, impromptu, manuscript, and memory — the one selected (if the speaker has a choice) should fit the audience, occasion, and speaker's ability to speak.[24]

The Extemporaneous Method

Usually a speaker knows well in advance when and where the speech is to be given, so the message can be carefully prepared. When that is the case, the extemporaneous method is best. In this method the *speaker delivers the speech from notes.* The main ideas and perhaps the introduction and conclusion may be committed to memory, but the body of the speech comes from the notes.

This method has several advantages. First, the speaker can be flexible, adapting his or her ideas to the listeners' reactions. If they look puzzled, the speaker can go back over the part that is causing trouble and try to clear up the difficulty. If the listeners seem bored, the speaker can increase audience interest by voice or gesture, by adding an

---

Sample Speaking Outline
Brief Version

Introduction

1. More than 100,000 students debate annually
2. Why? Debate is beneficial
3. Beneficial because: learn research, think clearly, express ideas well

Body

1. Learn research — example of John Smith
2. Think clearly — quote research study
3. Express ideas well — quote study and relate to my own experience

Conclusion

1. Summarize three reasons
2. 100,000 students can't be wrong

---

example or two held in reserve, or by using the chalkboard to illustrate the ideas. The extemporaneous method lends itself nicely to natural delivery and a conversational style.[25]

The extemporaneous speaker has a set of speaking notes in hand, either the speech outline described previously or a briefer version of it. The briefer version, illustrated here, can be placed on a small card or two. Hence, it is less noticeable than the detailed outline. It can be held in hand or placed on the podium, if one is available.

In the sample speaking outline, note that the speaker uses quotations twice, once to support item 2 in the body and once again to support item 3. The actual quotations do not appear on the outline itself. Instead, the speaker has put these quotations on separate cards. When the speaker needs them, he or she picks up the appropriate cards and reads the quoted material. By following this procedure, the speaker does not have to try to recall specific facts but simply reads the facts aloud.

Because the extemporaneous speaker has time to prepare, some of this time should be devoted to rehearsal. The following suggestions may be helpful in rehearsing:

1. *Rehearse often.* Within the preparation time available, practice the speech until it can be delivered using no more than the brief version of the speaking outline.

2. *Rehearse aloud.* Silent practice is not adequate. Practice aloud — before other people if possible. Time the practices. Cutting or adding material may be necessary to meet the time requirements for the speaking engagement.

3. *Seek competent criticism.* Whenever possible, have the speech instructor or another qualified person listen to several of the rehearsals and critically evaluate the performance. Ask the critic to suggest areas for improvement.

4. *Express ideas in different language.* Avoid the tendency to express ideas in exactly the same language for each practice. Consciously try to use new and different language each time. This technique helps to keep the language spontaneous and to avoid the urge to memorize.

5. *Avoid too much rehearsal.* Too much practice of a single speech may eliminate spontaneous expression. How much is too much? When the ideas are being expressed with the same words, it probably is wise to temporarily discontinue rehearsal for a day or two.[26]

The extemporaneous speaker should devote about two-thirds of the preparation time to development of the speech content and about one-third to rehearsal. If the speaker has two weeks of preparation time, for example, approximately ten days might be utilized in preparing the speech and four days in rehearsing it, with an hour or so a day in practice. Each speaker, of course, will have to discover how best to allocate the time. As a general guide, the "two-thirds development, one-third practice" formula is helpful.

The extemporaneous delivery method has a lot to recommend it to the average person. It encourages a natural, conversational manner and allows audience adaptation and directness. Without some rehearsal, however, the extemporaneously delivered speech in inexperienced hands could result in an exercise in poor speech-making. Nevertheless, its advantages outweigh the disadvantages, and a speaker should utilize it whenever possible.

The Impromptu Method

Occasionally we are called upon to speak on the spur-of-the-moment. We don't have any time to prepare; we must get up and talk. This can happen at school, on the job, and in community organizations. For example: A student sitting in class may be called upon without warning to report on some aspect of a reading assignment. At a staff meeting, the boss may ask a worker for a report on the spur of the moment. A club president may unexpectedly request a financial report from the treasurer. In these examples the person asked to speak gives an impromptu speech, one *made up at the moment of delivery.*

Although the speaker has virtually no preparation time, he or she usually has a few seconds to think — the time it takes to stand up or to move to the podium. That brief time can be well-spent if the speaker is properly trained in impromptu speaking.

In the few seconds available the speaker can think of a subject, if one is not assigned. Under normal circumstances, the speaker is asked to talk on a specific subject, in which case choosing one isn't necessary. The next thing to do is to pick a speaking plan. This is where the training comes in. Several organizational plans have been devised for just such purposes as giving impromptu speeches. They are comparatively simple and, if speakers know them, that knowledge will stand them in good stead.

The speaker picks the plan that is best suited to the subject matter, provided that he or she is familiar with the plans. Then, as the speaker talks, he or she lets the plan provide the speech's direction. The four plans are:[27]

1. *Past-present-future.* The speaker talks about the three main chronological divisions of the subject, beginning with its past history, then moving to the present, and finally talking about what could happen in the future.

2. *S-E-S-S.* S = State, E = Explain, S = Support, and S = Summarize. The speaker begins by stating the purpose of the speech. Next he or she explains the main ideas. Each of the principal ideas then is supported with whatever the speaker can muster: examples, opinions, facts, statistics. Finally, the speaker summarizes what was said.

3. *Reasons.* If the subject allows the speaker to take a stand for or against something, this plan is appropriate. The speaker either agrees, and gives the reasons for agreeing, or disagrees, and offers reasons for disagreeing.

4. *Problem-solution.* When a subject seems to involve a problem, the speaker explains it and then suggests a solution. In the explanation of the problem, the causes and effects should be brought out. The solution should suggest how it will eliminate the causes and effects.

Obviously, the four plans require quick thinking on the speaker's part. The possibilities are good, however, that the speaker will know something about the subject on which he or she is being asked to speak. The speaker's major concern, therefore, is to organize his or her thinking. The four plans can be useful in that regard.

What about delivering the impromptu speech? Here are some suggestions:

1. Walk deliberately to the speaker's stand (if there is one) and pause for a moment. Use the time involved to decide on the purpose and plan.

2. Keep the focus on the subject while talking, and don't worry about the audience's reaction. Rather, think about the subject.

3. Consider using the chalkboard, if one is available, to illustrate the ideas through diagrams or drawings.

4. Talk directly to the audience and adapt to audience feedback.

5. Be brief and to the point. Guard against rambling and the temptation of trying to say too much about the subject.

The Manuscript Method

Manuscript speaking refers to a speech that is *written out word-for-word* and the speaker reads the manuscript aloud. The manuscript should be a perfect piece of speechcrafting, the product of writing, revising, and rewriting. The speaker uses the best possible ideas and expresses them in the best possible language. The manuscript method demands excellence, the greatest the speaker can do.

This method is advantageous when exact timing is necessary. The speech can be read aloud during practice sessions, and additions or deletions can be made to fit the time limits. Because it requires pre-planned wording, the manuscript speech is preferred by people who are invited to speak on sensitive matters and want control over what they say. Copies of the speech can be made and distributed, lessening the chances of being misquoted.

Manuscript speakers have to be concerned about sounding spontaneous. Most listeners do not like to be read to. It causes them to lose interest quickly. Experienced manuscript readers usually are skilled in reading, but beginners may have trouble acting natural and conversational with manuscript in hand. Then, too, feedback is a problem; the manuscript user cannot adapt to negative listener reactions.[28]

The Memory Method

The memory method is like the manuscript method in all ways except that the speech is not read aloud. Rather, it is committed to memory and then given from memory at the time of delivery. It is preplanned, written out completely, and then memorized. It requires a speaker who is good at memorizing and at remembering what was committed to memory.

Under the pressure of the speaking situation, a speaker could forget some part of the speech and ruin the whole effort. Otherwise this type of speech has the same advantages as the manuscript speech: It can be well-crafted and designed to fit a specific time frame. The same disadvantages are apparent also: Feedback adaptation is not possible, and it is difficult to deliver a memorized speech in a natural, conversational mode.[29]

SUMMARY

Speech delivery is the oral transmission of the speaker's ideas to the listeners. The speaker may have conceived, on paper, one of the greatest of speeches, but if the speech is delivered poorly, it could fall on deaf ears. Delivery should receive as much attention from the speaker as all of the other preparation stages.

Good delivery is natural and conversational. The speaker should consider the audience as a small group of friends with whom he or she is sharing ideas. By speaking naturally and conversationally, the speaker transmits the feeling that he or she is talking with the listeners rather than at them.

Voice and body movement have an impact on delivery. A speaker can control speech rate, volume, pitch, and quality to add variety to the message. This keeps up audience interest. Rate, pitch, and volume can be altered for purposes of stress, dramatic effect, and interest. Enunciation (articulation and pronunciation) is vital to understanding. Improperly pronounced and stressed sounds can hinder comprehension of the speaker's message, as can sound substitutions and the addition of unnecessary sounds. Good body movement includes eye contact with the audience, a comfortably erect posture, movements suggesting confidence and poise, and meaningful gestures and facial expressions.

The speaker has a choice of four ways of delivering the speech: extemporaneous (the best for the typical person), impromptu, manuscript, and memorization.

The chapter's principal points may be summed up this way: Speeches are like babies — easy to conceive and hard to deliver. This entire book can be summed up in the words of Demosthenes: As a vessel is known by its sound, whether it be cracked or not, so men are proved, by their speeches, whether they may be wise or foolish.

LEARNING CHECK

These multiple choice items reflect materials in the past five chapters. Circle the correct answer. The answers are on page 244.

1. *Amplifying/supporting* materials explain or clarify ideas.

2. *Factual/hypothetical* examples are figments of imagination.

3. *General/specific* speech purpose refers to the exact outcome the speaker intends.

4. *Objective/subjective* sources supply factual material.

5. *Time/space* pattern deals with chronology.

6. *Topical/motivated sequence* is better for persuasive speeches.

7. *SRSRT/SESS* is a pattern to follow in impromptu speeches.

8. *Memory/impromptu* speaking method requires much advance preparation.

9. *Adoption/deterrence* requires listeners to avoid some sort of activity.

10. *Informative/persuasive* speeches have as their goal increasing listeners' knowledge.

Notes

Chapter 1 ♦ Communicating Competently

1. *Communication*, 4 (July 1975): ii–xi.
2. Stewart L. Tubbs and Sylvia Moss, *Human Communication*, 5th ed. (New York: Random House, 1987), 4.
3. The following represent a few of the studies historically investigating American communication habits, concluding that Americans spend much of the day communicating: Paul T. Rankin, "Listening Ability: Its Importance, Measurement, and Development," *Chicago Schools Journal*, 12 (1930), 177–79; F. J. Roethlisberger, *Management and Morale* (Cambridge, MA: Harvard University Press, 1941); Donald E. Bird, "This Is Your Listening Life," *Journal of the American Dietetic Association*, 32 (1956), 534–36; Lila R. Brieter, *Research in Listening and Its Importance to Literature*, unpublished Brooklyn College paper, 1957; Charles S. Goetzinger and Milton Valentine, "Communication Channels, Media, Directional Flow and Attitudes in an Academic Community," *Journal of Communication*, 12 (1962), 23–26; Larry A. Samovar, Robert D. Brooks, and Richard E. Porter, "A Survey of Adult Communication Activities," *Journal of Communication*, 19 (1969), 301–307; Satoshi Ishii and Donald Klopf, "A Comparison of Communication Activities of Japanese and American Adults," *English Language Education Council Bulletin*, 53 (1976), 22–26.
4. Donald Klopf, "Business and Professional Communication in Hawaii," *Speech Education*, 5 (1977), 79.
5. Ibid.
6. Ibid.
7. S. Bernard Rosenblatt, T. Richard Cheatham, and James T. Watt, *Communication in Business* (Englewood Cliffs, NJ: Prentice-Hall, 1977), 196.
8. Ole K. Harlem, *Communication in Medicine: A Challenge to the Profession* (Basel, Switzerland: S. Karger, 1977), 10.
9. Harold P. Zelko and Frank E. X. Dance, *Business and Professional Speech Communication* (New York: Holt, Rinehart and Winston,1965), 161.
10. Donald Klopf, *Interacting in Groups*, 3d ed. (Englewood, CO: Morton Publishing Co, 1988), 3.
11. Rosenblatt et al., 242.
12. James C. McCroskey, "Communication Competence and Performance: A Research and Pedagogical Perspective," *Communication Education*, 31 (1982), 1–7. McCroskey distinguishes between competency, skill, and effectiveness. Other scholars view competence as including both knowledge and skill; see Brian H. Spitzberg and William R. Cupach, *Interpersonal Communication Competence* (Beverly Hills, CA: Sage, 1984, 64–65). The McCroskey distinction best suits our purposes.
13. Ronald E. Bassett, Nilwon Whittington, and Ann Staton-Spicer, "The Basics in Speaking and Listening for High School Graduates: What Should Be Assessed?" *Communication Education*, 27 (1978), 294–303.
14. See Bassett et al.; Speech Communication Association, *Speaking and Listening Competencies for Sophomores in College* (Falls Church, VA: SCA, 1985); *Communication for Careers* (Falls Church, VA: SCA, 1978); Rebecca B. Rubin, "Assessing Speaking and Listening Competence at the College Level: The Communication Competency Assessment Instrument," *Communication Education*, 31 (1982), 19–32. For a short bibliography, see William Work, "ERIC Report," *Communication Education*, 31 (1982), 82–91.
15. *Speaking and Listening Competencies for Sophomores in College*.
16. Ibid.
17. Rosenblatt et al., 15.
18. William D. Brooks, *Speech Communication*, 4th ed. (Dubuque, IA: Wm C. Brown, 1981), 6–8.
19. William C. Schutz, *The FIRO Scales* (Palo Alto, CA: Consulting Psychologists Press, 1967).
20. Brooks, 6–8.

Chapter 2 ♦ The Nature of Speech Communication

1. James C. McCroskey, Virginia P. Richmond, and Robert A. Stewart, *One on One: The Foundations of Interpersonal Communication* (Englewood Cliffs, NJ: Prentice Hall, 1986), 1.
2. Stephen W. Littlejohn, *Theories of Human Communication*, 2d ed. (Belmont, CA: Wadsworth, 1983), 5.
3. James C. McCroskey, *An Introduction to Rhetorical Communication*, 4th ed. (Englewood Cliffs, NJ: Prentice Hall, 1982), 4.

4. Frank E. X. Dance and Carl Larson, *The Functions of Human Communication: A Theoretical Approach* (New York: Holt, Rinehart and Winston, 1976), 171–92.
5. McCroskey et al., 2.
6. William D. Brooks, *Speech Communication* (Dubuque, IA: Wm C. Brown, 1981), 6.
7. David K. Berlo, *The Process of Communication* (New York: Holt, Rinehart and Winston, 1960), 23–28. Also see B. Aubrey Fisher, *Perspectives on Human Communication* (New York: Macmillan, 1978), 300–307.
8. Dean C. Barnlund, "A Transactional Model of Communication," in Kenneth K. Sereno and C. David Mortensen, editors, *Foundations of Communication Theory* (New York: Harper and Row, 1970), 88.
9. James C. McCroskey and Lawrence R. Wheeless, *Introduction to Human Communication* (Boston: Allyn and Bacon, 1976), 15.
10. Richard Swanson and Charles Marquardt, *On Communication* (Beverly Hills, CA: Glencoe Press, 1974), 16.
11. Barnlund, 89.
12. Saundra Hybels and Richard L. Weaver, II, *Communicating Effectively* (New York: Random House, 1986), 14–16.
13. Barnlund, 93.
14. Ronald L. Applbaum, Karl Anatol, Ellis R. Hays, Owen O. Jenson, Richard E. Porter, and Jerry E. Mandel, *Fundamental Concepts in Human Communication* (San Francisco: Canfield Press, 1973), 6.
15. C. David Mortensen, *Communication: The Study of Human Interaction* (New York: McGraw-Hill, 1972), 29–65.
16. Berlo, 29.
17. Mortensen, 36–37.
18. Wilbur Schramm. "How Communication Works," in Jean M. Civikly, editor, *Messages: A Reader in Human Communication* (New York: Random House, 1974), 6–13.
19. Applbaum et al., 43–46.
20. McCroskey, 8.
21. McCroskey, 10.
22. Richard L. Weaver, II, *Understanding Interpersonal Communication*, 2d ed. (Glenview, IL: Scott, Foresman, 1981), 22–23.
23. Donald W. Klopf, *Intercultural Encounters* (Englewood, CO: Morton, 1987), 212–13.
24. McCroskey, 12.
25. McCroskey and Wheeless, 25–26.
26. Fisher, 284.
27. McCroskey and Wheeless, 149–56.
28. John W. Keltner, *Interpersonal Speech-Communication: Elements and Structures* (Belmont, CA: Wadsworth, 1970), 10–11.
29. R. R. Allen and Constance K. Knop, "Teaching the Uses of Language," *Communication*, 10 (1981), 4.

Chapter 3 ◆ Types of Oral Communication

1. R. Wayne Pace, Brent D. Petersen, and M. Dallas Burnett, *Techniques for Effective Communication* (Reading, MA: Addison-Wesley, 1979), 15–17.
2. Dean C. Barnlund, *Interpersonal Communication: Survey and Studies* (Boston: Houghton Mifflin, 1968), 10.
3. William W. Wilmot, *Dyadic Communication: A Transactional Perspective* (Reading, MA: Addison-Wesley, 1975), 6–8.
4. Pace et al., 26.
5. Michael J. Beatty, *Romantic Dialogue: Communication in Dating and Marriage* (Englewood, CO: Morton, 1986), 35–36.
6. John R. Dickman, *Get Your Message Across: How to Improve Communication* (Englewood Cliffs, NJ: Prentice Hall, 1979), 58–60.
7. Beatty, 37–38.
8. E. F. Elson, and Alberta Peck, *The Art of Speaking*, 2d ed. (Boston: Ginn, 1966), 307–11.
9. Charles T. Brown and Paul W. Keller, *Monologue to Dialogue: An Exploration of Interpersonal Communication* (Englewood Cliffs, NJ: Prentice Hall, 1979), 306.
10. Pace et al., 27.
11. Beatty, 88–89.
12. Dickman, 107–11.
13. Pace et al., 38.
14. L. S. Harms, *Human Communication: The New Fundamentals* (New York: Harper and Row, 1974), 90.
15. A. W. Siegman and B. Pope, editors, *Studies in Dyadic Communication* (Elmsford, NY: Pergamon Press, 1972), 29.
16. Donald W. Klopf, *The Art of Interviewing* (San Jose, CA: Lansford, 1979). (Audio lecture).
17. Stephen A. Richardson, Barbara Snell Dohrenwend, and David Klein, *Interviewing: Its Forms and Functions* (New York: Basic Books,1965), 32–55.
18. John Keltner, *Interpersonal Speech-Communication: Elements and Structures* (Belmont, CA: Wadsworth, 1970), 264.
19. Richardson et al., 59–87.
20. Joseph P. Zima, *Interviewing: Key to Effective Management* (Chicago: Science Research Associates, 1983), 59–80.
21. Robert L. Kahn and Charles F. Cannell, *The Dynamics of Interviewing: Theory, Technique and Cases* (New York: John Wiley,1957),316–27.
22. Donald W. Klopf, *Interacting in Groups: Theory and Practice*, 3d ed. (Englewood, CO: Morton, 1989), 3.
23. Bernard Berelson and Gerald Steiner, *Human Behavior: An Inventory of Scientific Findings* (New York: Harcourt, Brace and World, 1964), 325.
24. Klopf, *Interacting in Groups*, 6.
25. Dean C. Barnlund and Franklyn S. Haiman, *The Dynamics of Discussion* (Boston: Houghton Mifflin, 1960), 16–31.
26. Klopf, *Interacting in Groups*, 31–32.
27. The four phases are drawn from the following theories of group development: W. Braden and E. Brandenburg, *Oral Decision-Making* (New York: Harper and Brown, 1959), 28–29; Bruce Tuckman, "Developmental Sequence in Small Groups," *Psychological Bulletin*, 63 (1965), 384–99; B. Aubrey Fisher, "Decision Emergence: Phases in Group Decision Making," *Speech Monographs*, 37 (1970),53–60; R. B. Caple, "The Sequential Steps of Group Development," *Small Group Behavior*, 9 (1978), 470–76.
28. Harold P. Zelko and Frank E. X. Dance, *Business and Professional Speech Communication* (New York: Holt, Rinehart and Winston,1965), 161.
29. Alan H. Monroe and Douglas Ehninger, *Principles and Types of Speech Communication*, 7th ed. (Glenview, IL: Scott, Foresman, 1974), 123.
30. Monroe and Ehninger, 123–54.
31. Roderick P. Hart, Gustav W. Friedrich, and William D. Brooks, *Public Communication* (New York: Harper and Row, 1975), 23.
32. Hart et al., 18.
33. Stewart L. Tubbs and Sylvia Moss, *Human Communication*, 5th ed. (New York: Random House, 1987), 18.
34. Hart et al., 22.
35. Douglas Ehninger, Alan H. Munroe, and Bruce Gronbeck, *Principles and Types of Speech Communication*, 8th ed. (Glenview, IL: Scott, Foresman, 1978), 56–59.
36. Tubbs and Moss, 291.
37. James C. McCroskey, *An Introduction to Rhetorical Communication*, 4th ed. (Englewood Cliffs, NJ: Prentice Hall, 1982), 131.
38. McCroskey, 44.
39. Ehninger et al., 59.

Chapter 4 ◆ The Communicators

1. E. P. Hollander, *Principles and Methods of Social Psychology*, 3d ed. (New York: Oxford, 1976), 27.
2. Donald Klopf, *Interacting in Groups: Theory and Practice*, 3d ed. (Englewood CO: Morton, 1988), 61–72.
3. John K. Brilhart, *Effective Group Discussion*, 3d ed. (Dubuque, IA: Wm C. Brown, 1986), 50–51.
4. James C. McCroskey, Virginia P. Richmond, and Robert A. Stewart, *One on One: The Foundations of Interpersonal Communication* (Englewood Cliffs, NJ: Prentice Hall, 1986), 112.
5. McCroskey et al., 114–15.
6. Marvin E. Shaw, *Group Dynamics: The Psychology of Small Group Behavior*, 3d ed. (New York: McGraw-Hill, 1983), 167–68.
7. Shaw, 194–95.
8. E. A. Mabry and R. E. Barnes, *The Dynamics of Small Group Communication* (Englewood Cliffs, NJ: Prentice Hall, 1980), 50–51.
9. Mabry and Barnes, 34.
10. James C. McCroskey, *Quiet Children and the Classroom Teacher* (Urbana, IL: ERIC Clearinghouse, 1977), 1.
11. McCroskey et al., 115.
12. Donald Klopf and Myung-Seok Park, *Cross-Cultural Communication: An Introduction to the Fundamentals* (Seoul, Korea: Han Shin, 1982), 13.
13. David Krech and Richard S. Crutchfield, *Theory and Problems of Social Psychology* (New York: McGraw-Hill, 1948), 29.
14. Michael D. Scott and William G. Powers, *Interpersonal Communication: A Question of Needs* (Boston: Houghton Mifflin, 1978), 20.
15. Klopf, 65.
16. Norman L. Munn, *Psychology: The Fundamentals of Human Adjustment*, 2d ed. (Boston: Houghton Mifflin, 1951), 259–60.
17. Klopf, 66–67.
18. A. H. Maslow, "A Theory of Human Motivation," *Psychological Review* 50 (1943), 87.
19. William Schutz, *The FIRO Scales* (Palo Alto, CA: Consulting Psychologists Press, 1967), 5.
20. Krech and Crutchfield, 68–69.
21. Klopf and Park, 72.
22. K. S. Sitaram and Roy T. Cogdell, *Foundations of Intercultural Communication* (Columbus, OH: Merrill, 1976), 180–92.
23. Myung-Seok Park, *Communication Styles in Two Different Cultures: Korean and American* (Seoul, Korea: Han Shin, 1979), 42–45.
24. Klopf and Park, 52.
25. Larry Samovar, Robert Porter, and Nemi Jain, *Understanding Intercultural Communication* (Belmont, CA: Wadsworth, 1981), 39–40.
26. Carley H. Dodd, *Dynamics of Intercultural Communication* (Dubuque, IA: Kendall/Hunt, 1977), 72–79.
27. Klopf and Park, 87.
28. James C. McCroskey and Lawrence R. Wheeless, *Introduction to Human Communication* (Boston: Allyn and Bacon, 1976), 125–26.
29. McCroskey et al., 86–87.
30. James C. McCroskey, *An Introduction to Rhetorical Communication*, 5th ed. (Englewood Cliffs, NJ: Prentice Hall, 1986), 62.
31. Donald Klopf and Ronald Cambra, *Speaking Skills for Prospective Teachers* (Englewood, CO: Morton, 1983), 225–29.
32. James C. McCroskey, *The Fundamentals of Rhetorical Communication* (Tokyo: Eichosa, 1973), 39–40.
33. McCroskey et al., 74–76.
34. Ibid., 76–80.
35. Ibid., 77–79.

Chapter 5 ◆ Perception

1. Ludy T. Benjamin, Jr., J. Roy Hopkins, and Jack R. Nation, *Psychology* (New York: Macmillan, 1987), 99.
2. Bernard Berelson and Gerald Steiner, *Human Behavior: An Inventory of Scientific Findings* (New York: Harcourt, Brace and World, 1964), 88.
3. Julian E. Hochberg, *Perception*, 2d ed. (Englewood Cliffs, NJ: Prentice Hall, 1978), 9.
4. Donald W. Klopf, *Intercultural Encounters: The Fundamentals of Intercultural Communication* 2d ed. (Englewood, CO: Morton, 1991), 49.
5. Douglas A. Bernstein, Edward J. Roy, Thomas K. Srull, and Christopher D. Wickens, *Psychology* (Boston: Houghton Mifflin,1988), 165–66.
6. William Haney, *Communication: Patterns and Incidents* (Homewood, IL: R. D. Irwin, 1960), 13–17.
7. William D. Brooks, *Speech Communication*, 4th ed. (Dubuque, IA: Wm C. Brown, 1981), 43.
8. Alfred Kuhn, *The Study of Society: A Unified Approach* (Homewood, IL: R. D. Irwin, 1963), 107.
9. Hochberg, 3.
10. Norman L. Munn, *Psychology: The Fundamentals of Human Adjustment* (Boston: Houghton Mifflin, 1951), 546.
11. Brooks, 29–30.
12. Munn, 410.
13. Michael D. Scott and William G. Powers, *Interpersonal Communication: A Question of Needs* (Boston: Houghton Mifflin, 1978), 126.
14. Edward C. Stewart, *American Cultural Patterns: A Cross-Cultural Perspective*. (Washington, DC: Society for Intercultural Education, Training and Research, 1972), 15.
15. Berelson and Steiner, 100.
16. Benjamin, et al., 101.
17. Benjamin, et al., 101.
18. Benjamin, et al., 102.
19. Benjamin, et al., 103.
20. Bernstein, et al., 175.
21. Rudolph F. Verderber and Kathleen S. Verderber, *Inter-Act: Using Interpersonal Communication Skills*, 2d ed. (Belmont, CA: Wadsworth, 1980), 24.
22. Benjamin, et al., 105.
23. Ernest R. Hilgard, *Theories of Learning*, 2d ed. (New York: Appleton-Century-Crofts, 1956), 228.
24. Sharon Ruhly, *Intercultural Communication*, 2d ed. (Chicago: Science Research Associates, 1982), 16.
25. Joseph A. DeVito, *The Interpersonal Communication Book*, 2d ed. (New York: Harper and Row, 1980), 321–22.
26. Joseph A. DeVito, *Communicology: An Introduction to the Study of Communication*, 2d ed. (New York: Harper and Row, 1982), 92–96.
27. Blaine Goss, *Communication in Everyday Life* (Belmont, CA: Wadsworth, 1983), 84.
28. Scott and Powers, 122.
29. DeVito, *Communicology*, 92–96.
30. Satoshi Ishii, "The American Male Viewed by Japanese Female Students of English: A Stereotype Image," *Otsuma Joshi Daigaku Bungakubu Kiyo*, 8 (1976).

Chapter 6 ◆ The Concept of Self

1. William D. Brooks, *Speech Communication*, 4th ed. (Dubuque, IA: Wm C. Brown, 1981), 43.
2. Brooks, 43.
3 Donn Byrne, *An Introduction to Personality: Research, Theory, Application*, 2d ed. (Englewood Cliffs, NJ: Prentice Hall, 1974), 271.

4 Byrne, 275.
5. Donald P. Cushman and Dudley D. Cahn, Jr., *Communication in Interpersonal Relationships* (Albany: State University of New York Press, 1985), 36–41.
6. Edward C. Stewart and Milton J. Bennett, *American Cultural Patterns: A Cross-Cultural Perspective*, revised (Yarmouth, MA: Intercultural Press, 1991), 129.
7. Stewart and Bennett, 130.
8. Donald W. Klopf, *Intercultural Encounters: The Fundamentals of Intercultural Communication*, 2d ed. (Englewood, CO: Morton, 1991), 144.
9. Ronald E. Bassett and Mary-Jeanette Smythe, *Communication and Instruction* (New York: Harper and Row, 1979), 30-31.
10. Blaine Goss, M. Thompson, and S. Olds, "Behavioral Support for Systematic Desensitization for Communication Apprehension," *Human Communication Research*, 4 (1978), 158–63.
11. Pamela J. Cooper, *Speech Communication for the Classroom Teacher* (Dubuque, IA: Gorsuch Scarisbrick, 1981), 27.
12. Joseph Luft, *Of Human Interaction* (Palo Alto, CA: National Press Books, 1969). 145.
13. Stephen W. Littlejohn, *Theories of Human Communication*, 3d ed. (Belmont, CA: Wadsworth, 1989), 161.
14. Luft.
15. Robert Bolton, *People Skills* (Englewood Cliffs, NJ: Prentice Hall, 1979), 179.
16. Littlejohn, 162.

Chapter 7 ◆ Communication Anxiety

1. "What are Americans Afraid Of?" *Bruskin Report* (New Brunswick, NJ: Bruskin Associates, 1973), 1.
2. Virginia P. Richmond and James C. McCroskey, *Communication: Apprehension, Avoidance, and Effectiveness* (Scottsdale, AZ: Gorsuch Scarisbrick, 1985), 34.
3. James C. McCroskey, "Measures of Communication-Bound Anxiety," *Speech Monographs* 37 (November 1970), 269–77. The reader should recognize that apprehension, stage fright, tenseness, anxiety, reticence, and shyness are not synonyms for the fear of speaking. Each term has its own, somewhat different, meaning. In common parlance, however, the terms frequently are used to mean the same thing.
4. James C. McCroskey, "Oral Communication Apprehension: A Summary of Recent Theory and Research," *Human Communication Research*, 4 (1977), 79–80.
5. Nancy J. Metzger, "The Effects of the Rhetorical Method of Instruction on a Selected Population of Reticent Students," *Communication*, 4 (1976), 93.
6. James C. McCroskey, "The Communication Apprehension Perspective," John A. Daly and James C. McCroskey, editors, in *Avoiding Communication: Shyness, Reticence, and Communication Apprehension* (Beverly Hills, CA: Sage, 1984), 16.
7. Richmond and McCroskey, 33.
8. McCroskey, "The Communication Apprehension Perspective," 16–17.
9. Richmond and McCroskey, 36–38.
10. McCroskey, "The Communication Apprehension Perspective," 18–19.
11. McCroskey, "Measures of Communication-Bound Anxiety."
12. J. C. McCroskey and J. F. Andersen, "The Relationship Between Communication Apprehension and Academic Achievement Among College Students," *Human Communication Research*, 3 (Fall 1976), 73–81.
13. J. C. McCroskey and R. W. McVetta, "Classroom Seating Arrangements: Instructional Communication Theory Versus Students Preferences," *Communication Education*, 36 (March 1978), 99–111.
14. M. D. Scott, M. Yates, and L. R. Wheeless, *An Exploratory Investigation of the Effects of Communication Apprehension in Alternative Systems of Instruction*, International Communication Association convention paper, Chicago, 1975.
15. McCroskey, "Oral Communication Apprehension," 86.
16. A. N. Weiner, *Machiavellianism as a Predictor of Group Interaction*, M. A. Thesis, West Virginia University, Morgantown, 1973.
17. F. M. Jablin and L. Sussman, *Correlates of Individual Productivity in Real Brainstorming Groups*, Speech Communication Association convention paper, San Francisco, 1976.
18. D. Merrill, *Reference Survey Profile* (Denver: Personal Predictions and Research, 1974).
19. J. C. McCroskey, J. A. Daly, V. P. Richmond, and R. L. Falcione, "Studies of the Relationship Between Communication Apprehension and Self-Esteem," *Human Communication Research*, 3 (Spring 1977), 269–277.
20. H. R. Witteman, *The Relationship of Communication Apprehension to Opinion Leadership and Innovativeness*, M. A. Thesis, West Virginia University, Morgantown, 1976.
21. J. C. McCroskey and J. Daly, "Teachers' Expectations of the Communication-Apprehensive Child in the Elementary School," *Human Communication Research*, 3 (Fall 1976), 67–72.
22. McCroskey and Andersen, 78.
23. H. T. Hurt, R. Priess, and B. Davis, *The Effect of Communication Apprehension of Middle-School Children on Sociometric Choice, Affective and Cognitive Learning*, International Communication Association convention paper, Portland, 1976.
24. McCroskey and Andersen, 78.
25. V. P. Richmond, *Communication Apprehension and Success in the Job Applicant Screening Process*, International Communication Association convention paper, Berlin, 1977; and J. A. Daly and S. Leth, *Communication Apprehension and the Personnel Selection Decision*, International Communication Association convention paper, Portland, 1976.
26. J. A. Daly and J. C. McCroskey, "Occupational Choice and Desirability as a Function of Communication Apprehension," *Journal of Counseling Psychology*, 22 (August 1975), 309–13.
27. M. D. Scott, J. C. McCroskey, and M. E. Sheahan, "Measuring Communication Apprehension," *Journal of Communication*, 28 (Winter 1978), 106.
28. R. L. Falcione, J. C. McCroskey, and J. Daly, "Job Satisfaction as a Function of Employee's Communication Apprehension, Self-Esteem, and Perceptions of Their Immediate Supervisors," *Communication Yearbook* 1, edited by Brent D. Ruben (Brunswick, NJ: Transaction Books, 1977), 363–75.
29. Scott, McCroskey, and Sheahan, 106.
30. J. C. McCroskey and M. E. Sheahan, "Communication Apprehension, Social Preference and Social Behavior in a College Environment," *Communication Quarterly* (1978), 26.
31. J. C. McCroskey and M. M. Kretzschmar, *Communication Apprehension and Marital Relationships of College Graduates*, Eastern Communication Association convention paper, New York, 1977.
32. J. C. McCroskey and T. Leppard, *The Effects of Communication Apprehension on Nonverbal Behavior*, Eastern Communication Association convention paper, New York, 1975.
33. M. E. Sheahan, *Communication Apprehension and Electoral Participation*, M. A. Thesis, West Virginia University, Morgantown, 1976.
34. J. C. McCroskey and V. P. Richmond, *Self-Credibility as an Index of Self-Esteem*, Speech Communication Association convention paper, Houston, 1975.

35. J. C. McCroskey, J. A. Daly, and G. A. Sorensen, "Personality Correlates of Communication Apprehension." *Human Communication Research*, 2 (Summer 1976), 376–80.

36. McCroskey, Daly, and Sorensen, 376–80. Even though the research presented here supports the position that communication apprehension offers disagreeable consequences, we should recognize that apprehensive individuals themselves may not share this viewpoint. Most apprehensive persons, especially adults, quite likely have adjusted to their lives and have made choices in job, housing, and mate that are compatible with their apprehension level. As a consequence, they may be quite happy. And we also should recognize that low apprehensives do not necessarily live ideal lives; they may be so success-oriented that they have become unhappy in the process.

37. McCroskey, "The Communication Apprehension Perspective," 23.

38. Ibid., 23–24.

39. James C. McCroskey and Virginia Richmond, *The Quiet Ones: Communication Apprehension and Shyness* (Dubuque, IA: Gorsuch Scarisbrick, 1980), 6–7.

40. McCroskey and Richmond, *The Quiet Ones*, 7.

41. Vicki S. Freimuth, "Communication Apprehension in the Classroom," in *Communication in the Classroom*, edited by L. L. Barker (Englewood Cliffs, NJ: Prentice Hall, 1982), 137.

42. McCroskey and Richmond, *The Quiet Ones*, 7.

43. Ibid.

44. James C. McCroskey, *Quiet Children and the Classroom Teacher*, (Urbana, IL: ERIC Clearinghouse, 1977), 6.

45. McCroskey, "The Communication Apprehension Perspective," 26–30.

46. McCroskey and Richmond, *The Quiet Ones*, 8-9.

47. Ibid., 36.

48. Gustav Friedrich and Blaine Goss, "Systematic Desensitization," in *Avoiding Communication*, edited by John Daly and James C. McCroskey, pp. 173.

49. William J. Fremouw, "Cognitive Behavioral Therapies for Modification of Communication Apprehension," in *Avoiding Communication*, edited by Daly and McCroskey, 211–14.

50. Lynne Kelly, "Social Skills Training as a Mode of Treatment for Social Communication Problems," in *Avoiding Communication*, edited by Daly and McCroskey, 189–207.

51. Norman L. Munn, *Psychology: The Fundamentals of Human Adjustment*, 2d ed. (Boston: Houghton Mifflin, 1951), 344–53.

52. Valentine K. Larson, "Improving English thru Choral Speaking," *Communication*, 2 (1973), 61–74.

Chapter 8 ◆ Verbal Communication

1. Mario Pei, *The Story of Language* (New York: New American Library, 1965), 107.

2. David K. Berlo, *The Process of Communication* (New York: Holt, Winston, 1960), 172–73.

3. Wallace C. Fotheringham, *Perspectives on Persuasion* (Boston: Allyn and Bacon, 1966), 105–109.

4. C. D. Hockett, "The Origin of Speech." *Scientific American*, 3 (1960), 93. Also Fotheringham, *Newsweek* (May 23, 1988), 52–59, reveals scientific findings about animals' ability to think and communicate.

5. Joseph A. DeVito, *Communicology*, 2d ed. (New York: Harper and Row, 1982), 120–25.

6. Hockett, 93.

7. Ibid.

8. Bernard Berelson and Gary Steiner, *Human Behavior: An Inventory of Scientific Findings* (New York: Harcourt, World and Brace, 1964), 46.

9. Stewart L. Tubbs and Sylvia Moss, *Human Communication*, 5th ed. (New York: Random House, 1987), 100–101.

10. DeVito, 123.

11. Pei, 108–109.

12. Stephen W. Littlejohn, *Theories of Human Communication*, 2d ed. (Belmont, CA: Wadsworth, 1983), 111.

13. Sharon Ruhly, *Intercultural Communication*, 2d ed. (Chicago: Science Research Associates, 1982), 21.

14. Littlejohn, 112.

15. Ibid.

16. Berlo, 187.

17. Ibid., 178.

18. Ibid., 178–82.

19. Ibid.

20. Ibid., 178–82.

21. Hubert G. Alexander, *Language and Thinking* (Princeton: D. Van Nostrand, 1967), 77.

22. Saundra Hybels and Richard L. Weaver, II. *Communicating Effectively* (New York: Random House, 1986), 81.

23. Robert L. Oliver, *Making Your Meaning Effective* (Boston: Holbrook Press, 1971), 147.

24. Michael Osborn, *Orientations to Rhetorical Style* (Chicago: Science Research Associates, 1976), 15.

25. Gregory Cowan and Elizabeth Cowan, *Writing* (New York: John Wiley, 1980), 637–38.

26. Myung-Seok Park, *Communication Styles in Two Different Cultures: Korean and American* (Seoul: Han Shin, 1979), 19.

27. William V. Haney, *Communication Patterns and Incidents* (Homewood, IL: R. D. Irwin, 1960), 84.

28. Irving J. Lee and Laura Lee, *Handling Barriers in Communication* (New York: Harper, 1957), 13.

29. Lee and Lee, 13.

30. Haney, 22.

31. Lee and Lee, 51.

32. Haney, 56–62.

33. Ibid.. 75–84.

34. Ibid., 78–79.

35. Ibid., 83–84.

36. DeVito, 159.

37. Haney, 131.

38. Ibid., 101.

Chapter 9 ◆ Communicating Nonverbally

1. Ray L. Birdwhistell, *Kinesics and Context: Essays on Body Motion Communication* (Philadelphia: University of Pennsylvania Press, 1970).

2. Mark L. Knapp, *Nonverbal Communication in Human Interaction*, 2d ed. (New York: Holt, Rinehart and Winston, 1978), 20–26.

3. Albert Mehrabian, *Silent Messages: Implicit Communication of Emotions and Attitudes*, 2d ed. (Belmont, CA: Wadsworth, 1981), 75–78.

4. Mehrabian, 77.

5. Ibid., 44–49.

6. Peter Andersen and Janis Andersen, "Nonverbal Immediacy in Instruction," in *Communication in the Classroom*, edited by Larry Barker (Englewood Cliffs, NJ: Prentice Hall, 1982), 100.

7. Virginia P. Richmond, James C. McCroskey, and Steven K. Payne, *Nonverbal Behavior in Interpersonal Relations* (Englewood Cliffs, NJ: Prentice-Hall, 1987), 10–12.

8. Edward T. Hall, *The Hidden Dimension* (Garden City, NY: Doubleday, 1966), 1.

9. Hall, 114–129.

10. Ibid.

11. Andersen and Andersen, 108.
12. Richmond et al., 111–116.
13. Ibid., 173.
14 Marianne La France and Clara Mayo, *Moving Bodies: Nonverbal Communication in Social Relationships* (Monterey, CA: Brooks/Cole, 1978), 153.
15. James C. McCroskey, *An Introduction to Rhetorical Communication*, 4th ed. (Englewood Cliffs, NJ: Prentice Hall, 1982), 108–109.
16. Julius Fast, *Body Language* (New York: Evans, 1970), 145–149.
17. Flora Davis, *Inside Intuition* (New York: New American Library, 1973), 57–61.
18. Andersen and Andersen, 107.
19. Davis, 43–54.
20. Dale G. Leathers, *Nonverbal Communication Systems* (Boston: Allyn and Bacon, 1976), 34.
21. Andersen and Andersen, 104.
22. Nancy M. Henley, *Body Politics: Power, Sex and Nonverbal Communication* (Englewood Cliffs, NJ: Prentice Hall, 1977). 171–78.
23. Ibid.
24. McCroskey, 109.
25. Henley, 96–101.
26. Davis, 81–82.
27. Andersen and Andersen, 103.
28. Richmond et al., 45–46.
29. Birdwhistell.
30. McCroskey, 111–12.
31. Richmond et al., 41–43.
32. LaFrance and Mayo, 3.
33. Henley, 75–76.
34. McCroskey, 115.
35. Knapp, 340–49.
36. Ibid., 349–353.
37. Ibid., 353–55.
38. Ibid., 355–63.
39. Leathers, 98–102.
40. Ibid., 88–90.
41. Richard L. Weaver, II, *Understanding Interpersonal Communication* (Glenview, IL: Scott, Foresman, 1978), 164–65.

Chapter 10 ◆ Listening

1. Sperry Corp., "Your Listening Profile," in *Small Group Communication: A Reader*, edited by Robert S. Cathcart and Larry A. Samovar, 5th ed. (Dubuque, IA: Wm C. Brown, 1988), 378.
2. Ralph G. Nichols and Leonard A. Stevens, *Are You Listening?* (New York: McGraw-Hill, 1957), 6–7.
3. Robert Bolton, *People Skills* (Englewood Cliffs, NJ: Prentice Hall, 1979), 29.
4. Roger Brown and Richard J. Herrnstein, *Psychology* (Boston: Little, Brown, 1978), 345–69.
5. Brown and Herrnstein.
6. Bolton, 32.
7. Ibid.
8. Norman L. Munn, *Psychology: The Fundamentals of Human Adjustment*, 2d ed. (Boston: Houghton Mifflin, 1951), 385–98.
9. Ibid.
10. Larry L. Barker, *Listening Behavior* (Englewood Cliffs, NJ: Prentice Hall, 1971), 9.
11. Charles M. Kelly, "Empathic Listening," in *Small Group Communication*, edited by Cathcart and Samovar, 2d ed, (Dubuque, IA: Wm C. Brown, 1974), 340–52.
12. For a more thorough understanding of empathy, see Robert L. Katz, *Empathy: Its Nature and Uses* (New York: Free Press, 1963); George Gunkel, "Empathy: Implications for Theatre Research," *Educational Theatre Journal*, 15

(1963), 15–23; Gerald R. Miller and Mark Steinberg, *Between People: A New Analysis of Interpersonal Communication* (Chicago: Science Research Associates, 1975), 167–94.
13. Kelly, 340–52.
14. Barker, 9.
15. Barker, 10–11.
16. Barker, 11–13.
17. Robert O. Hirsch, *Listening: A Way to Process Information Aurally* (Dubuque, IA: Gorsuch Scarisbrick, 1979), 36–41.
18. Hirsch.
19. Barker, 50–52.
20. Barker, 52.
21. Jack R. Gibb, "Defensive Communication," *Journal of Communication*, 9:3 (1961), 141–148.
22. Thomas Gordon, *P.E.T.: Parent Effectiveness Training: The Tested New Way to Raise Responsible Children* (New York: P. H. Wyden, 1970), 41–45.
23. Ibid.
24. Gibb, 375.
25. Gibb, 375–380.
26. Jane Gibson and Richard Hodgetts, "The Listening Environment," in *Small Group Communication*, edited by Cathcart and Samovar, 5th ed., 370–71.
27. Gibson and Hodgetts, 373.
28. Gibb, 375–380.
29. Ibid.
30. Kelly, 356.
31. E. F. Elson and Alberta Peck, *The Art of Speaking*, 2d ed. (Boston: Ginn, 1966), 101.
32. Elson and Peck, 103.
33. Bolton, 51–52.
34. Ibid., 52–54.
35. Ibid., 57–59.
36. The suggestions are drawn from these principal sources: Andrew D. Wolvin and Carolyn G. Coakley, *Listening* (Dubuque, IA: Wm C. Brown, 1982); Bolton; Barker; Gordon; Dominick Barbara, *How to Make People Listen To You* (Springfield, IL: Charles C Thomas, 1971); Carl Weaver, *Human Listening: Processes and Behavior* (Indianapolis: Bobbs-Merrill, 1972); James J. Floyd, *Listening: A Practical Approach* (Glenview, IL: Scott, Foresman, 1985).

Chapter 11 ◆ Interpersonal Relationships

1. Jessie G. Delia, "Some Tentative Thoughts Concerning the Study of Interpersonal Relationships and their Development," *Western Journal of Speech Communication*, 44 (1980), 97–103.
2. Ibid.
3. Donald W. Klopf and Satoshi Ishii, *Communicating Person-to-Person* (Tokyo: Kirihara, 1988), 56.
4. James C. McCroskey, Virginia P. Richmond and Robert A. Stewart, *One-on-One: The Foundations of Interpersonal Communication* (Englewood Cliffs, NJ: Prentice Hall, 1986), 160.
5. Ibid., 160–63.
6. Ibid., 143–57.
7. Ibid., 143.
8. Ibid., 144–49.
9. Ibid., 151.
10. Ibid., 154.
11. Ibid., 154–57.
12. Mark L. Knapp, *Social Intercourse: From Greetings to Goodbye* (Boston: Allyn and Bacon, 1973), 35–44.
13. McCroskey et al., 171–75.

14. Knapp, 35–44.
15. Ibid.
16. McCroskey et al., 171–75.
17. Knapp, 35–44.
18. Robert Bolton, *People Skills: How to Assert Yourself, Listen to Others, and Resolve Conflicts* (Englewood Cliffs, NJ: Prentice Hall, 1979),
19. Bolton, 259–62.
20. Ibid.
21. Saundra Hybels and Richard L. Weaver, II, *Communicating Effectively* (New York: Random House, 1986), 161.
22. Bolton, 270.
23. John P. Fieg, *Thais and North Americans.* (Yarmouth, ME: Intercultural Press; 1980), 33
24. Margaret K. Nydell, *Understanding Arabs: A Guide for Westerners* (Yarmouth, ME: Intercultural Press, 1987), 19–25.
25. George W. Renwick, *A Fair Go for All: Australian/American Interactions.* (Yarmouth, ME: Intercultural Press, (1991), 31–35.
26. Hu Wenzhong and Cornelius L. Grove, *Encountering the Chinese: A Guide for Americans* (Yarmouth, ME: Intercultural Press, 1991), 59–63.
27. Theodore Gochenour, *Considering Filipinos* (Yarmouth, ME: Intercultural Press, 1990), 56–57.
28. C. Nakane, *Japanese Society* (Berkeley: University of California Press, 1970).
29. Yale Richmond, *From Nyet to Da: Understanding the Russians* (Yarmouth, ME: Intercultural Press, 1992), 105–109.
30. Bolton, 209.
31. Thomas Gordon, *P.E.T.: Parent Effectiveness Training: The Tested New Way to Raise Responsible Children* (New York: Wyden, 1970), 196–97.
32. David W. Johnson, *Reaching Out: Interpersonal Effectiveness and Self-Actualization* (Englewood Cliffs, NJ: Prentice Hall, 1972), 203.
33. William D. Brooks, *Speech Communication*, 3d ed. (Dubuque, IA: Wm C. Brown, 1978), 208–209.
34. Donald W. Klopf, *Attacking Conflict — Methods of Management and Resolution* (Tokyo, Japan: Tok En, 1978), 4.
35. Brian Betz, "Managing Conflict in Interaction," in *Speech Communication and Human Interaction*, by Thomas M. Scheidel, 2d ed. (Glenview, IL: Scott, Foresman, 1976), 279.
36. Alan C. Filley, *Interpersonal Conflict Resolution* (Glenview, IL: Scott, Foresman, 1975), 7–18.
37. Ibid.
38. Karen Horney, *Our Inner Conflicts* (New York: Norton, 1954), 27.
39. Donald W. Klopf, *Interacting in Groups: Theory and Practice*, 3d ed. (Englewood, CO: Morton, 1989), 114.
40. Filley, 22–30.
41. McCroskey et al., 208–209.

Chapter 12 ✦ Intercultural Communication

1. Sidney M. Jourard, "Education as dialogue" in N. Colangelo, D. Dustin, and C. Foxley, editors, *Multicultural Nonsexist Education: A Human Relations Approach*, 2d ed. (Dubuque, IA: Kendall Hunt, 1985), 5.
2. Kenneth Cushner, "Cross-cultural psychology and the formal classroom" in R.W. Brislin, editor, *Applied Cross-Cultural Psychology* (Newbury Park, CA: Sage, 1990), 98–120.
3. Phillip R. Harris and Robert T. Moran, *Managing Cultural Differences*, 3d ed. (Houston: Gulf, 1991), 3–23.
4. Edward S. Glenn and Edward C. Stewart, "Intercultural Communication," *Communication* 3 (1974), 10.

5. Bernard Berelson and Gerald A. Steiner, *Human Behavior: An Inventory of Scientific Findings* (New York: Harcourt, Brace and World, 1964), 175.
6. Donald W. Klopf, *Intercultural Encounters: The Fundamentals of Intercultural Communication*, 2d ed. (Englewood, CO: Morton, 1991), 31–36.
7. George Murdock, The Common Denominator of Cultures," in Ralph Linton, editor, *The Science of Man in World Crisis* (New York: Columbia World Press, 1945), 50.
8. Murdock.
9. Donna M. Gollnick and Phillip C. Chinn, *Multicultural Education in a Pluralistic Society*, 3d ed. (New York: Merrill, 1990), 12.
10. Gollnick and Chinn, 14–15. Other terms used instead of microculture include *subculture* and *co-culture*. Subculture suggests that the members of subcultures are lower than or subordinate to the dominant culture, the macroculture. Co-culture suggests that the co-culture group is equal in size or number of members to the dominant culture. Typically, this is not true. Hence, our choice is the terminology employed by Gollnick and Chinn.
11. Jack Daniel, "The Poor: Aliens in an Affluent Society: Cross-Cultural Communication," in L. A. Samovar and R. E. Porter editors, *Intercultural Communication: A Reader*, 3d ed. (Belmont, CA: Wadsworth, 1982), 220.
12. Klopf, 40.
13. Geert Hofstede, *Culture's Consequence.* (Beverly Hills, CA: Sage, 1984), 148–175.
14. Hofstede, 148–175.
15. P. Andersen, "Explaining Intercultural Differences in Nonverbal Behavior," in Samovar and Porter, 6th ed. (1990), 290.
16. Hofstede, 176–210.
17. E. T. Hall, *The Hidden Dimension* (New York: Doubleday, 1966), 25.
18. Hofstede, 65–104.
19. E. T. Hall, *Beyond Culture* (Garden City, NY: Doubleday, 1976), 30.
20. Hofstede, 254.
21. W. G. Sumner, *Folkways* (New York: New American Library, 1906), 6.
22. J. A. DeVito, *Communicology: An Introduction to the Study of Communication*, 2d ed. (New York: Harper and Row, 1982), 111.
23. Gollnick and Chinn, 19–20.
24. D. W. Klopf, *Prejudice: Parts I and II* (San Jose, CA: Lansford, 1974).
25. D. M. Kennedy Center for International Studies, *Culturgrams: The Nations Around Us, I–II* (Provo, UT: Kennedy Center, 1986–86).
26. J. F. Andersen and R. Powell (1991). "Intercultural communication and the classroom," in Samovar and Porter, editors, 6th ed. (1991), 213.
27. Klopf, *Intercultural Encounters*, 126–127.
28. Klopf, 127–128.

Chapter 13 ✦ The Interview

1. Larry A. Samovar and Susan A. Hellweg, *Interviewing: A Communicative Approach* (Dubuque, IA: Gorsuch Scarisbrick, 1982), 6–7.
2. Cal W. Downs, G. Paul Smeyak, and Ernest Martin, *Professional Interviewing* (New York: Harper and Row, 1980), 40–41.
3. Gary M. Richetto and Joseph P. Zima, *Interviewing*, 2d ed. (Chicago: Science Research Associates, 1982), 27–28.
4. Donald W. Klopf, *The Art of Interviewing* (San Jose, CA: Lansford, 1979). (Recorded lecture program)
5. Downs et al., 41.
6. Samovar and Hellweg, 13.

7. Ibid., 13–14.
8. Stephen A. Richardson, Barbara Snell Dohrenwend, and David Klein, *Interviewing: Its Forms and Functions* (New York: Basic Books,1965), 127–236.
9. Charles J. Stewart and William B. Cash, Jr., *Interviewing: Principles and Practices*, 3d ed. (Dubuque, IA: Wm C. Brown, 1982), 95–101.
10. Robert L. Cahn and Charles F. Cannell, *The Dynamics of Interviewing* (New York: John Wiley and Sons, 1957), 158–160.
11. Klopf.
12. Ibid.
13. Joseph P. Zima, *Interviewing: Key to Effective Management* (Chicago: Science Research Associates, 1983), 109.
14. Samovar and Hellweg, 14.
15. Zima, 116.
16. Downs et al., 60–67.
17. Ibid., 66–67.
18. Michael E. Stano and N. L. Reinsch, Jr., *Communication in Interviews* (Englewood Cliffs, NJ: Prentice Hall, 1982), 47–48.
19. Rudolph F. Verderber, *Communicate!*, 4th ed. (Belmont, CA: Wadsworth, 1984), 180–181.
20. Zima, 51.
21. Ibid., 47.
22. Ibid., 48–49.
23. Klopf.
24. The guidelines came from these sources: Melvin W. Donaho and John L. Meyer, *How to Get the Job You Want* (Englewood Cliffs, NJ: Prentice Hall, 1976), Jason Robertson, *How to Win in a Job Interview* (Englewood Cliffs, NJ: Prentice Hall, 1978), Saundra Hybels and Richard Weaver, II, *Communicating Effectively* (New York: Random House, 1986), Zima, Downs et al.; Stewart and Cash; Richetto and Zima.
25. Hybels and Weaver, 198–200.
26. Hybels and Weaver, 201: see also Shirley Biagi, *Interviews That Work* (Belmont, CA: Wadsworth, 1986), 157–71.

Chapter 14 ◆ Group Discussion

1. Donald W. Klopf, *Interacting in Groups: Theory and Practice*, 3d ed. (Englewood, CO: Morton, 1989), 10.
2. David Potter and Martin Andersen, *Discussion in Small Groups: A Guide to Effective Practice*, 3d ed. (Belmont, CA: Wadsworth, 1976), 1–2.
3. Ibid.
4. John K. Brilhart, *Effective Group Discussion*, 5th ed. (Dubuque, LA: Wm C. Brown, 1986), 76–78.
5. Brilhart, 77.
6. *Mainichi Daily News*, June 10, 1975.
7. Brilhart, 109–111.
8. Donald W. Klopf, *Interacting in Groups: Discussion and Leadership* (Tokyo, Japan: Gaku Shobo, 1978), 70.
9. Marvin E. Shaw, *Group Dynamics: The Psychology of Small Group Behavior*, 3d ed. (New York: McGraw-Hill, 1981), 281.
10. Shaw, 281.
11. Dorwin Cartwright and Alan Zander, *Group Dynamics: Research and Theory* (Evanston, IL: Row, Peterson, 1953), 78.
12. Leon Festinger, "Group Attraction and Membership," in *Group Dynamics*, edited by Cartwright and Zander, 92–100.
13. Lawrence B. Rosenfeld, *Human Interaction in the Small Group Setting* (Columbus, OH: Merrill, 1973), 71–74.
14. Ernest G. Bormann and Nancy C. Bormann, *Effective Small Group Communication*, 2d ed. (Minneapolis: Burgess, 1976), 49.

15. Cartwright and Zander, 80–82.
16. Donald W. Klopf, *Conflict Resolution* (San Jose, CA: Lansford, 1977). (Audiovisual learning program)
17. Klopf, *Interacting in Groups*, 187.
18. K. D. Benne and P. Sheats, "Functional Roles of Group Members," *Journal of Social Issues*, 4 (1948), 41–49.
19. For more on the roles, see G.M. Beal, J. M. Bohlen, and J. N. Raudabaugh, *Leadership and Dynamic Group Action* (Ames, IA: Iowa State University Press, 1962), 206–213, and *Adult Leadership*, 1 January 1953), 6–23.
20. *Adult Leadership*.
21. Klopf, *Interacting in Groups*, 149–150.
22. Ibid., 168–74.
23. Dean C. Barnlund and Franklyn S. Haiman, *The Dynamics of Discussion* (Boston: Houghton Mifflin, 1960), 283–88.
24. Brilhart, 138–47.
25. Ibid.

Chapter 15 ◆ Methods of Group Discussion

1. David Potter and Martin Andersen, *Discussion in Small Groups: A Guide to Effective Practice,* 3d ed. (Belmont, CA: Wadsworth,1976), 93.
2. James Davis, *Group Performance* (Reading, MA: Addison-Wesley, 1969), 43.
3. R. Victor Harnack, Thorrel Fest, and Barbara Schindler Jones, *Group Discussion: Theory and Techniques*, 2d ed. (Englewood Cliffs, NJ: Prentice Hall, 1977), 13–19.
4. John E. Baird, Jr. and Sanford B. Weinberg, *Communication: The Essence of Group Synergy* (Dubuque, IA: Wm C. Brown, 1977), 126.
5. Elizabeth W. Flynn and John F. LaFaso, *Group Discussion as a Learning Process* (New York: Paulist Press, 1972), 102–103.
6. William Fawcett Hill, *Learning thru Discussion* (Beverly Hills, CA: Sage, 1969), 15–16.
7. Baird and Weinberg, 125.
8. Davis, 34.
9. Harnack et al., 15.
10. Davis, 40.
11. Harnack et al., 19–21.
12. Kjell Eric Ruestan, "The Experiential Group," *Small Group Communication: A Reader*, Robert S. Cathcart and Larry Samovar, editors, 5th ed. (Dubuque, IA: Wm C. Brown, 1988), 104.
13. Dean C. Barnlund and Franklyn S. Haiman, *The Dynamics of Discussion* (Boston: Houghton Mifflin, 1960), 24–26.
14. Hill, 22–31.
15. Potter and Andersen, 93–94.
16. Donald W. Klopf, *Interacting in Groups: Theory and Practice*, 3d ed. (Englewood, CO: Morton, 1989), 219–20.
17. Raymond S. Ross, *Speech Communication*, 5th ed. (Englewood Cliffs, NJ: Prentice Hall, 1980), 358.
18. Klopf, 205–209.
19. William M. Sattler and N. Edd Miller, *Discussion and Conference* (Englewood Cliffs, NJ: Prentice Hall, 1954), 105.
20. Bobby R. Patton and Kim Giffin, *Decision-Making Group Interaction*, 2d ed. (New York: Harper and Row, 1978), 149–52.
21. C. M. Moore, *Group Techniques for Idea Building* (Beverly Hills, CA: Sage, 1987), 24–36.
22. A. L. Derbecq, A. H. Vanderven, and D. H. Gustafson, *Group Techniques for Program Planning* (Glenview, IL: Scott, Foresman, 1975), 83–106.
23. H. Proshansky, "Why a Problem Census?" *Leadership Pamphlet #6*, Adult Education Association, 1955, 33–35.
24. Chris Argyris, *Role Playing in Action*, New York State School of Industrial and Labor Relations, Bulletin 16, 1951, 1–22.

25. Potter and Andersen, 175–77.
26. G. M. Beal, J. M. Bohlen, and J. N. Raudabaugh, *Leadership and Dynamic Group Action* (Ames, IA: Iowa State University Press, 1962), 206–13.
27. Gerald M. Phillips, *Communication and the Small Group*, 2d ed. (Indianapolis: Bobbs-Merrill, 1973), 94–95.
28. Lawrence Rosenfeld, *Now That We're All Here . . . Relations in Small Groups* (Columbus, OH: Merrill, 1976), 87.
29. Ronald L. Applbaum, *Group Discussion*, 2d ed. (Chicago: Science Research Associates, 1981), 18.

Chapter 16 ◆ Public Speaking: Preliminary Steps

1. Theodore Clevenger, Jr. *Audience Analysis* (Indianapolis: Bobbs-Merrill, 1966), 5.
2. Milton Dickens and James McBath, *Guidebook for Speech Communication* (New York: Harcourt Brace Jovanovich, 1973), 69–71.
3. Ibid., 70–71.
4. Ibid., 69.
5. Glen E. Mills, *Message Preparation: Analysis and Structure* (Indianapolis: Bobbs-Merrill, 1966) 1–22.
6. Frank E. X. Dance and Carol C. Zak-Dance, *Public Speaking* (New York: Harper and Row, 1986), 112.
7. Mills, 23–25.
8. Ibid., 26.
9. Donald W. Klopf and James C. McCroskey, *The Elements of Debate* (New York: Arco, 1969), 66–69.
10. Ibid., 68–69.

Chapter 17 ◆ Investigating The Speech Subject

1. Frank E. X. Dance and Carol C. Zak-Dance, *Public Speaking* (New York: Harper and Row, 1986), 83–87.
2. Saundra Hybels and Richard L. Weaver, II, *Communicating Effectively* (New York: Random House, 1986), 283.
3. Donald W. Klopf and James C. McCroskey, *The Elements of Debate* (New York: Arco, 1969), 99.
4. Alan H. Munroe and Douglas Ehninger, *Principles and Types of Speech Communication*, 7th ed. (Glenview, IL: Scott, Foresman, 1974), 289–90.
5. Hybels and Weaver, 284.
6. Gerilyn Tandberg, *Research Guide in Speech* (Morristown, NJ: General Learning Press, 1974), 73–150.
7. Hybels and Weaver, 294–96.
8. From a speech by Kay Fujii, University of Hawaii.
9. Tandberg, 46–48.
10. Walter Wittich and Charles Schuller, *Audio-Visual Materials: Their Nature and Use* (New York: Harper and Row, 1967), 71–123.
11. Munroe and Ehninger, 300.
12. Klopf and McCroskey, 50–55.
13. Dance and Zak-Dance, 91–92.
14. Ibid., 92.
15. James C. McCroskey, *The Fundamentals of Rhetorical Communication* (Tokyo, Japan: Eichosha, 1973), 84–85.

Chapter 18 ◆ Organizing The Speech

1. Much of the information in this chapter is derived from the article, "Patterns of Public Communication," *Communication* 2 (January 1973), 1–6.

Chapter 19 ◆ Informing and Persuading

1. S. L. Tubbs and S. Moss, *Human Communication*, 5th ed. (New York: Random House, 1987), 291.
2. A. H. Monroe and D. Ehninger, *Principles and Types of Speech Communication*, 7th ed. (Glenview, IL: Scott, Foresman, 1974), 487.
3. J. C. Pearson and P. E. Nelson, *Understanding and Sharing: An Introduction to Speech Communication*, 5th ed. (Dubuque, IA: Wm C. Brown, 1991), 432–433.
4. Pearson and Nelson, 440–443.
5. J. C. McCroskey, *An Introduction to Rhetorical Communication*, 4th ed. (Englewood Cliffs, NJ: Prentice Hall, 1982), 131.
6. Pearson and Nelson, 461.
7. R. F. Verderber, *Communicate!* 4th ed. (Belmont, CA: Wadsworth, 1984), 327–329.

Chapter 20 ◆ Delivering The Speech

1. Frank E. X. Dance and Carol C. Zak-Dance, *Public Speaking* (New York: Harper and Row, 1986), 161.
2. Saundra Hybels and Richard L. Weaver, II, *Communicating Effectively* (New York: Random House, 1986), 340.
3. Donald W. Klopf, *Public Speaking* (San Jose, CA: Lansford, 1973). (A visual program)
4. Hybels and Weaver, 349.
5. Horace Rahskopf, *Basic Speech Improvement* (New York: Harper and Row, 1965), 270.
6. Paul Heinberg, *Voice Training for Speaking and Reading Aloud* (New York: Ronald Press, 1964), 220.
7. Alan H. Munroe and Douglas Ehninger, *Principles and Types of Speech Communication* (Glenview, IL: Scott, Foresman, 1974), 198–99.
8. Ibid., 199.
9. Rahskopf, 60–61.
10. Theodore D. Hanley and Wayne L. Thurman, *Developing Vocal Skills*, 2d ed. (New York: Holt, Rinehart and Winston, 1970), 158–60.
11. Heinberg, 212–13.
12. Ibid., 206–208.
13. Ibid., 181.
14. Rahskopf, 273–77.
15. Wayne H. Oxford, *The Fundamentals of Effective Oral Expression* (Tokyo, Japan: Eichosha, 1979), 48.
16. Rahskopf, 284.
17. Hybels and Weaver, 350.
18. Helene Wong, *Articulation and Pronunciation* (Tokyo, Japan: Eichosha, 1973), 2–20.
19. R. R. Allen and Ray E. McKerrow, *The Pragmatics of Public Communication* (Columbus, OH: Merrill, 1977), 25.
20. Hybels and Weaver, 347.
21. Stanley G. Rives, *The Fundamentals of Oral Interpretation* (Tokyo, Japan: Eichosha, 1981), 50–51.
22. Ibid., 52–53.
23. Allen and McKerrow, 24.
24. Donald W. Klopf and Takehide Kawashima, *The Bases of Public Speaking* (Tokyo, Japan: Sansyusya, 1975), 60–63.
25. Hybels and Weaver, 343–45.
26. Donald W. Klopf, *Coaching and Directing Forensics*, 2d ed. (Skokie, IL: National Textbook, 1982), 231–32.
27. Klopf, Coaching, 233–34.
28. Klopf and Kawashima, 62.
29. Ibid., 62–63.

Bibliography

Adult Leadership 1 (1953).

Alexander, H. G. *Language and Thinking.* Princeton, NJ: D. Van Nostrand, 1967.

Allen, R. R., and Knop, C. K. "Teaching the Uses of Language." *Communication 10* (1981).

Allen, R. R., and McKerrow, R. E. *The Pragmatics of Public Communication.* Columbus, OH: Merrill, 1977.

Andersen, P., and Andersen, J. "Nonverbal Immediacy in Instruction." In *Communication in the Classroom*, edited by L. L. Barker, Englewood Cliffs, NJ: Prentice Hall, 1982.

Applbaum, R. L. *Group Discussion*, 2d ed. Chicago: Science Research Associates, 1981.

Applbaum, R., Anatol, K., Hayes, E. R., Jenson, O. O., Porter, R. E., and Mandel, J. E. *Fundamental Concepts in Human Communication.* San Francisco: Canfield Press, 1973.

Argyris, C. *Role Playing in Action.* New York State School of Industrial and Labor Relations *16* (1951).

Baird, J. E., Jr., and Weinberg, S. B. *Communication: The Essence of Group Synergy.* Dubuque, IA: Wm C. Brown, 1977.

Barbara, D. *How to Make People Listen to You.* Springfield, IL: Charles C. Thomas, 1971.

Barker, L. L. *Listening Behavior.* Englewood Cliffs, NJ: Prentice Hall, 1971.

Barnlund, D. C. "A Transactional Model of Communication." In *Foundations of Communication Theory*, edited by K. K. Sereno and C. D. Mortensen. New York: Harper and Row, 1970.

Barnlund, D. C. *Interpersonal Communication: Survey and Studies.* Boston: Houghton Mifflin, 1968.

Barnlund, D. C., and Haiman, F. S. *The Dynamics of Discussion.* Boston: Houghton Mifflin, 1960.

Bassett, R. E., and Smythe, M. J. *Communication and Instruction.* New York: Harper and Row, 1979.

Bassett, R. E., Whittington, N., and Staton-Spicer, A. "The Basics in Speaking and Listening for High School Graduates: What Should Be Assessed?" *Communication Education 27* (1978).

Bassett, R. E., Whittington, N., and Staton-Spicer, A. *Speaking and Listening Competencies for Sophomores in College.* Falls Church, VA: Speech Communication Association, 1985.

Beal, G. M., Bohlen, J. M., and Raudabaugh, J. N. *Leadership and Dynamic Group Action.* Ames: Iowa State University Press, 1962.

Beatty, M. J. *Romantic Dialogue: Communication in Dating and Marriage.* Englewood, CO: Morton, 1986.

Benjamin, L. T., Hopkins, J. R., and Nation, J. R. *Psychology.* New York: Macmillan, 1987.

Benne, K. D., and Sheats, P. "Functional Roles of Group Members." *Journal of Social Issues 4* (1948).

Berelson, B., and Steiner, G. *Human Behavior: An Inventory of Scientific Findings.* New York: Harcourt, Brace and World, 1964.

Berlo, D. K. *The Process of Communication.* New York: Holt, Rinehart and Winston, 1960.

Bernstein, D. A., Roy, E. J., Srull, T. K., and Wickens, C. D., *Psychology.* Boston: Houghton Mifflin, 1988.

Betz, B. "Managing Conflict in Interaction." In *Speech Communication and Human Interaction*, edited by T. M. Scheidel, 2d ed., Glenview, IL: Scott, Foresman, 1976.

Biagi, S. *Interviews That Work.* Belmont, CA: Wadsworth, 1986.

Bird, D. E. "This is Your Listening Life." *Journal of the American Dietic Association*, 32 (1956).

Birdwhistell, R. L. *Kinesics and Context: Essays on Body Motion Communication.* Philadelphia: University of Pennsylvania Press, 1970.

Bolton, R. *People Skills.* Englewood Cliffs, NJ: Prentice Hall, 1979.

Bormann, E. G., and Bormann, N. C. *Effective Small Group Communication*, 2d ed. Minneapolis: Burgess, 1976.

Braden, W., and Brandenburg, E. *Oral Decision-Making.* New York: Harper and Brown, 1959.

Breneman, L. N., and Breneman, B. *Storytelling Handbook.* Tokyo, Japan: Gaku Shobo, 1977.

Brilhart, J. K. *Effective Group Discussion*, 3d ed. Dubuque, IA: Wm C. Brown, 1986.

Brilhart, J. K. *Effective Group Discussion*, 5th ed. Dubuque, IA: Wm C. Brown, 1986.

Brooks, W. D. *Speech Communication*, 3d ed. Dubuque, IA: Wm C. Brown, 1978.

Brooks, W. D. *Speech Communication*, 4th ed. Dubuque, IA: Wm C. Brown, 1981.

Brown, C. T., and Keller, P. W. *Monologue to Dialogue: An Exploration of Interpersonal Communication.* Englewood Cliffs, NJ: Prentice Hall, 1979.

Brown, R., and Herrnstein, R. J. *Psychology.* Boston: Little, Brown, 1978.

Bruskin Associates. *The Bruskin Report*. New Brunswick, NJ: Bruskin Associates, 1973.

Byrne, D. *An Introduction to Personality: Research, Theory, Application*, 2d ed., Englewood Cliffs, NJ: Prentice Hall, 1974.

Cahn, R. L., and Cannell, C. F. *The Dynamics of Interviewing: Theory, Technique and Cases*. New York: John Wiley, 1957.

Caple, R. B. "The Sequential Steps in Group Development." *Small Group Behavior 9* (1978).

Cartwright, D., and Zander, A. *Group Dynamics: Research and Theory*. Evanston, IL: Row, Peterson, 1953.

Clevenger, T., Jr. *Audience Analysis*. Indianapolis: Bobbs-Merrill, 1966.

Cooper, P. J. *Speech Communication for the Classroom Teacher*. Dubuque, IA: Gorsuch Scarisbrick, 1981.

Cowan, G., and Cowan, E. *Writing*. New York: John Wiley, 1980.

Cushman, D. P., and Cahn, D. D., Jr. *Communication in Interpersonal Relationships*. Albany, NY: State University of New York Press, 1985.

Cushner, K. "Cross-Cultural Psychology and the Formal Classroom." In R. W. Brislin, editor, *Applied Cross-Cultural Psychology*. Newbury Park, CA: Sage, 1990.

Daly, J. A., and Leth, S. *Communication Apprehension and the Personnel Selection Decision*. International Communication Association convention paper, Portland, 1976.

Daly, J. A., and McCroskey, J. C. "Occupational Choice and Desirability as a Function of Communication Apprehension." *Journal of Counseling Psychology 22*, 1975.

Dance, F. E. X., and Larson, C. *The Functions of Human Communication: A Theoretical Approach*. New York: Holt, Rinehart and Winston, 1976.

Dance, F. E. X., and Zak-Dance, C. C. *Public Speaking*. New York: Harper and Row, 1986.

Davis, F. *Inside Intuition*. New York: New American Library, 1973.

Davis, J. *Group Performance*. Reading, MA: Addison-Wesley, 1976.

Delia, J. G. "Some Tentative Thoughts Concerning the Study of Interpersonal Relationships and Their Development." *Western Journal of Speech Communication 44* (1980).

Derbecq, A. L., Van de Ven, A. H., and Gustafson, D. H. *Group Techniques for Program Planning*. Glenview, IL: Scott, Foresman, 1975.

DeVito, J. A. *Communicology: An Introduction to the Study of Communication*, 2d ed. New York: Harper and Row, 1982.

DeVito, J. A. *The Interpersonal Communication Book*, 2d ed. New York: Harper and Row, 1980.

Dickens, M., and McBath, J. H. *Guidebook for Speech Communication*. New York: Harcourt Brace Jovanovich, 1973.

Dickman, J. R. *Get Your Message Across: How to Improve Communication*. Englewood Cliffs, NJ: Prentice Hall, 1979.

Dodd, C. H. *Dynamics of Intercultural Communication*. Dubuque, IA: Kendall/Hunt, 1977.

Donaho, M. V., and Meyer, J. L. *How to Get The Job You Want*. Englewood Cliffs, NJ: Prentice Hall, 1976.

Downs, C. W., Smeyak, G. P., and Martin, E. *Professional Interviewing*. New York: Harper and Row, 1980.

Ehninger, D., Monroe, A. H., and Gronbeck, B. *Principles and Types of Speech Communication*, 8th ed. Glenview, IL: Scott, Foresman, 1978.

Elson, E. F., and Peck, A. *The Art of Speaking*, 2d ed. Boston: Ginn, 1966.

Falcione, R. L., McCroskey, J. C., and Daly, J. A. "Job Satisfaction as a Function of Employees' Communication Apprehension, Self-Esteem, and Perceptions of Their Immediate Supervisors." *Communication Yearbook*, edited by B. D. Ruben. Brunswick, NJ: Transaction Books, 1977.

Fast, J. *Body Language*. New York: Evans, 1970.

Festinger, L. "Group Attraction and Membership." In *Group Dynamics: Research and Theory*, edited by D. Cartwright and A. Zander. Evanston, IL: Row, Peterson, 1953.

Fieg, J. A. *Thais and North Americans*. Yarmouth, ME: Intercultural Press, 1980.

Filley, A. C. *Interpersonal Conflict Resolution*. Glenview, IL: Scott, Foresman, 1975.

Fisher, B. A. "Decision Emergence: Phases in Group Decision Making." *Speech Monographs 37*, (1970).

Fisher, B. A. *Perspectives on Human Communication*. New York: Macmillan, 1978.

Floyd, J. J. *Listening: A Practical Approach*. Glenview, IL: Scott, Foresman, 1985.

Flynn, E. W., and LaFaso, J. F. *Group Discussion as a Learning Process*. New York: Paulist Press, 1972.

Fotheringham, W. C. *Perspectives on Persuasion*. Boston: Allyn and Bacon, 1966.

Freimuth, V. A. "Communication Apprehension in the Classroom." *Communication in the Classroom*, edited by L. L. Barker. Englewood Cliffs, NJ: Prentice Hall, 1982.

Fremouw, W. J. "Cognitive Behavioral Therapies for Modification of Communication Apprehension," in *Avoiding Communication: Shyness, and Communication Apprehension*, edited by J. A. Daly and J. C. McCroskey. Beverly Hills, CA: Sage, 1984.

Friedrich, G., and Goss, B. "Systematic Desensitization," in *Avoiding Communication: Shyness, Reticence, and Communication Apprehension*, edited by J. A. Daly and J. C. McCroskey. Beverly Hills, CA: Sage, 1984.

Gibb, J. R. "Defensive Communication." *Journal of Communication 9* (1961).

Gibson, J., and Hodgetts, R. "The Listening Environment." *Small Group Communication: A Reader*, 5th ed., edited by R. S. Cathcart and L. A. Samovar. Dubuque, IA: Wm C. Brown, 1988.

Glenn, E. S., and Stewart, C. "Intercultural Communication," *Communication*, 1974.

Gochenour, T. *Considering Filipinos*. Yarmouth, ME: Intercultural Press, 1990.

Goetzinger, C. S., and Valentine, M. "Communication Channels, Media, Directional Flow, and Attitudes in an Academic Community," *Journal of Communication 12*, (1962).

Gollnick, D. M., and Chinn, P. C. *Multicultural Education in a Pluralist Society*, 3d ed. Columbus, OH: Merrill, 1990.

Gordon, T. *P.E.T.: Parent Effectiveness Training: The Tested New Way to Raise Responsible Children*. New York: P. H. Wyden, 1970.

Goss, B., Thompson, M., and Olds, S. "Behavioral Support for Systematic Desensitization for Communication Apprehension." *Human Communication Research 4* (1978).

Goss, G. *Communication in Everyday Life*. Belmont, CA: Wadsworth, 1983.

Gunkel, G. "Empathy: Implications for Theater Research." *Educational Theater Journal 15* (1963).

Hall, E. T. *Beyond Culture*. New York: Doubleday, 1976.

Hall, E. T. *The Hidden Dimension*. Garden City, NY: Doubleday, 1966.

Haney, W. D. *Communication: Patterns and Incidents*. Homewood, IL: R. D. Irwin, 1960.

Hanley, T. D., and Thurman, W. L. *Developing Vocal Skills*, 2d ed. New York: Holt, Rinehart and Winston, 1970.

Harlem, O. K. *Communication in Medicine: A Challenge to the Profession*. Basel, Switzerland: S. Karger, 1977.

Harms, L. S. *Human Communication: The New Fundamentals*. New York: Harper and Row, 1974.

Harnack, R. V., Fest, T., and Jones, B. S. *Group Discussion: Theory and Techniques*, 2d ed. Englewood Cliffs, NJ: Prentice Hall, 1977.

Harris, P. R. and Moran, R. T. *Managing Cultural Differences, 3*d ed. Houston: Gulf, 1991.

Hart, R. P., Friedrich, G. W., and Brooks, W. D. *Public Communication.* New York: Harper and Row, 1975.

Heinberg, P. *Voice Training for Speaking and Reading Aloud.* New York: Ronald Press, 1964.

Henley, N. M. *Body Politics: Power, Sex, Nonverbal Communication.* Englewood Cliffs, NJ: Prentice Hall, 1977.

Hilgard, E. R. *Theories of Learning,* 2d ed. New York: Appleton-Century-Crofts, 1956.

Hill, W. F. *Learning thru Discussion.* Beverly Hills, CA: Sage, 1969.

Hirsch, R. O. *Listening: A Way to Process Information Aurally.* Scottsdale, AZ: Gorsuch, Scarisbrick, 1979.

Hochberg, J. E. *Perception,* 2d ed. Englewood Cliffs, NJ: Prentice Hall, 1978.

Hockett, C. D. "The Origin of Speech." *Scientific American* 3 (1960).

Hofstede, G. *Culture's Consequences.* Beverly Hills, CA: Sage, 1984.

Hollander, E. P. *Principles and Types of Social Psychology,* 3d ed. New York: Oxford, 1976.

Horney, K. *Our Inner Conflicts.* New York: Norton, 1954.

Howell, W. S., and Borman, E. G. *The Process of Presentational Speaking,* 2d ed. New York: Harper and Row, 1988.

Hu, W., and Grove, C. L. *Encountering the Chinese: A Guide for Americans.* Yarmouth, ME: Intercultural Press, 1991.

Hurt, H. T., Priess, R., and Davis, B. *The Effect of Communication Apprehension of Middle-School Children on Sociometric Choice, Affective and Cognitive Learning.* International Communication Association convention paper, Portland, OR, 1976.

Hybels, S., and Weaver, R. L., II. *Communicating Effectively.* New York: Random House, 1986.

Ishii, S. "The American Male Viewed by Japanese Female Students of English: A Stereotype Image." *Otsuma Joshi Daigaku Bungakubu Kiyo* 8 (1976).

Ishii, S., and Klopf, D. W. "A Comparison of Communication Activities of Japanese and American Adults." *English Language Educational Council Bulletin* 53 (1976).

Jablin, F. M., and Sussman, L. *Correlates of Individual Productivity in Real Brainstorming Groups.* Speech Communication Association convention paper, San Francisco, 1976.

Johnson, D. W. *Reaching Out: Interpersonal Effectiveness and Self Actualization.* Englewood Cliffs, NJ: Prentice Hall, 1972.

Jourard, S. M. "Education as Dialogue," in N. Coulangelo, D. Dustin, and C. Foxley, editors, *Multicultural Nonsexist Education: A Human Relations Approach,* 2d ed. Dubuque, IA: Kendall-Hunt, 1985.

Katz, R. L. *Empathy: Its Nature and Uses.* New York: Free Press, 1963.

Kelly, C. M. "Empathic Listening." *Small Group Communication: A Reader,* 2d ed., edited by R. S. Cathcart and L. A. Samovar, Dubuque, IA: Wm C. Brown, 1974.

Kelly, L. "Social Skills Training as a Mode of Treatment for Social Communication Problems." In *Avoiding Communication: Shyness, Reticence, and Communication Apprehension,* edited by J. A. Daly and J. C. McCroskey. Beverly Hills, CA: Sage, 1984.

Keltner, J. W. *Interpersonal Speech-Communication: Elements and Structures.* Belmont, CA: Wadsworth, 1970.

Klopf, D. W. *The Art of Interviewing.* San Jose, CA: Lansford, 1979.

Klopf, D. W. *Attacking Conflict—Methods of Management and Resolution.* Tokyo: Tok En, 1978.

Klopf, D. W. "Business and Professional Communication in Hawaii." *Speech Education* 5 (1977).

Klopf, D. W. *Coaching and Directing Forensics,* 2d ed. Skokie, IL: National Textbook, 1982.

Klopf, D. W. *The Components of Small Group Interaction.* San Jose, CA: Lansford, 1973.

Klopf, D. W. *Conflict Resolution.* San Jose, CA: Lansford, 1977.

Klopf, D. W. *Interacting in Groups: Discussion and Leadership.* Tokyo, Japan: Gaku Shobo, 1978.

Klopf, D. W. *Interacting in Groups: Theory and Practice,* 3d ed. Englewood, CO: Morton, 1989.

Klopf, D. W. *Intercultural Encounters: The Fundamentals of Intercultural Communication,* 2d ed. Englewood, CO: Morton, 1991.

Klopf, D. W. "Patterns of Public Communication." *Communication* 2 (1973)

Klopf, D. W. *Prejudice* (Parts I & II), San Jose, CA: Lansford, 1974.

Klopf, D. W. *Public Speaking.* San Jose, CA: Lansford, 1973.

Klopf, D. W. *Twenty Do's and Don'ts For Beginning Speakers.* San Jose, CA: Lansford, 1972.

Klopf, D. W., and Cambra, R. E. *Academic Debate: Practicing Argumentative Theory,* 2d ed. Englewood, CO: Morton, 1979.

Klopf, D. W., and Cambra, R. E. *Speaking Skills for Prospective Teachers.* Englewood, CO: Morton, 1983.

Klopf, D. W., and Ishii, S. *Communicating Effectively Across Cultures.* Tokyo, Japan: Nan'Un-Do, 1984.

Klopf, D. W., and Ishii, S. *Communicating Person-to-Person.* Tokyo, Japan: Kirihara, 1988.

Klopf, D. W., and Ishii, S. *Communicating Without Words.* Tokyo, Japan: Nan'Un-Do, 1987.

Klopf, D. W., and Kawashima, T. *The Bases of Public Speaking.* Tokyo, Japan: Sansyusya, 1975.

Klopf, D. W., and McCroskey, J. C. *The Elements of Debate.* New York: Arco, 1969.

Klopf, D. W., and Park, M-S. *Cross-Cultural Communication: An Introduction to the Fundamentals.* Seoul, Korea: Han Shin, 1982.

Klopf, D. W., Park, M-S., and Cambra, R. E. *Elements of Human Communication.* Seoul, Korea: Han Shin, 1983.

Knapp, M. L. *Social Intercourse: From Greetings to Goodbye.* Boston: Allyn and Bacon, 1973.

Krech, D., and Crutchfield, R. S. *Theory and Problems of Social Psychology.* New York: McGraw-Hill, 1948.

Kuhn, A. *The Study of Society: A Unified Approach.* Homewood, IL: R. D. Irwin, 1963.

LaFrance, M., and Mayo, C. *Moving Bodies: Nonverbal Communication in Social Relationships.* Monterey, CA: Brooks/Cole, 1978.

Larson, V. K. "Improving English through Choral Speaking." *Communication* 2 (1973).

Leathers, D. G. *Nonverbal Communication Systems.* Boston: Allyn and Bacon, 1976.

Lee, I. J., and Lee, L. *Handling Barriers in Communication.* New York: Harper, 1957.

Littlejohn, S. W. *Theories of Human Communication,* 3d ed. Belmont, CA: Wadsworth, 1989.

Loganbill, G. B., and Kawashima, T. *The Bases of Voice, Articulation, and Pronunciation.* Tokyo, Japan: Sansyusya, 1974.

Luft, J. *Of Human Interaction.* Palo Alto, CA: National Press Books, 1969.

Mabry, E. A., and Barnes, R. E. *The Dynamics of Small Group Communication.* New York: Prentice Hall, 1980.

Maslow, A. H. "A Theory of Human Motivation," *Psychological Review* 50 (1943)

McCroskey, J. C. "The Communication Apprehension Perspective." In *Avoiding Communication: Shyness, Reticence, and Communication Apprehension,* edited by J. A. Daly and J. C. McCroskey, Beverly Hills, CA: Sage, 1984.

McCroskey, J. C. "Communication Competence and Performance: A Research and Pedological Perspective." *Communication Education* 31 (1982).

McCroskey, J. C. *The Fundamentals of Rhetorical Communication*. Tokyo, Japan: Eichosha, 1973.

McCroskey, J. C. *An Introduction to Rhetorical Communication*, 4th ed. Englewood Cliffs, NJ: Prentice Hall, 1982.

McCroskey, J. C. "Measures of Communication Bound Anxiety." *Speech Monographs* 37 (1970).

McCroskey, J. C. "Oral Communication Apprehension: A Summary of Recent Theory and Research." *Human Communication Research*, 4 (1977)

McCroskey, J. C. *Quiet Children and the Classroom Teacher*. Urbana, IL: ERIC Clearinghouse, 1977.

McCroskey, J. C., and Andersen, J. F. "The Relationship Between Communication Apprehension and Academic Achievement Among College Students." *Human Communication Research* 3 (1976).

McCroskey, J. C., and Daly, J. A. "Teachers' Expectations of the Communication Apprehensive Child in the Elementary School." *Human Communication Research* 3 (1976).

McCroskey, J. C., Daly, J. A., Richmond, V. P., and Falcione, R. L. "Studies of the Relationship Between Communication Apprehension and Self Esteem." *Human Communication Research* 3 (1977).

McCroskey, J. C., Daly, J. A., and Sorensen, G. A. "Personality Correlates of Communication Apprehension." *Human Communication Research* 2 (1976).

McCroskey, J. C., and Kretzschmar, M. M. *Communication Apprehension and Marital Relationships of College Graduates*. Eastern Communication Association convention paper, New York, 1977.

McCroskey, J. C., and Leppard, T. *The Effects of Communication Apprehension Nonverbal Behaviors*. Eastern Communication Association convention paper, New York, 1975.

McCroskey, J. C. and McVetta, R. W. "Classroom Seating Arrangements: Instructional Communication Theory Versus Student Preferences." *Communication Education* 36 (1978).

McCroskey, J. C., and Richmond, V. P. *Self-Credibility as an Index of Self-Esteem*. Speech Communication Association convention paper, Houston, 1975.

McCroskey, J. C., and Richmond, V. P. *The Quiet Ones: Communication Apprehension and Shyness*. Scottsdale, AZ: Gorsuch and Scarisbrick, 1980.

McCroskey, J. C., and Wheeless, L. R. *Introduction to Human Communication*, Boston: Allyn and Bacon, 1976.

McCroskey, J. C., Richmond, V. P., and Stewart, R. A. *One on One: The Foundations of Interpersonal Communication*. Englewood Cliffs, NJ: Prentice Hall, 1986.

McCroskey, J. C., and Sheahan, M. E. "Communication Apprehension, Social Preference and Social Behavior in a College Environment." *Communication Quarterly* 26 (1978).

Mehrabian, A. *Silent Messages: Implicit Communication of Emotions and Attitudes*, 2d ed. Belmont, CA: Wadsworth, 1981.

Merrill, D. *Reference Survey Profile*. Denver: Personal Predictions and Research, Inc., 1974.

Metzger, N. J. "The Effects of the Rhetorical Method of Instruction on a Selected Population of Reticent Students." *Communication* 4 (1976).

Miller, G. R., and Steinberg, M. *Between People: A New Analysis of Interpersonal Communication*. Chicago: Science Research Associates, 1975.

Mills, G. E. *Message Preparation: Analysis and Structure*. Indianapolis: Bobbs-Merrill, 1966.

Monroe, A. H., and Ehninger, D. *Principles and Types of Speech Communication*, 7th ed. Glenview, IL: Scott, Foresman, 1974.

Moore, C. M. *Group Techniques for Idea Building*. Beverly Hills, CA: Sage, 1987.

Mortensen, C. D. *Communication: The Study of Human Interaction*. New York: McGraw-Hill, 1972.

Munn, N. L. *Psychology: The Fundamentals of Human Adjustment*, 2d ed. Boston: Houghton Mifflin, 1951.

Murdock, G. "The Common Denominator in Cultures." In R. Linton, editor, *The Science of Man in World Crisis*. New York. Columbia World Press, 1945.

Nakane, C. *Japanese Society*. Berkeley: University of California Press, 1970.

Newsweek, May 23, 1988.

Nichols, R. G., and Stevens, L. A. *Are You Listening?* New York: McGraw-Hill, 1957.

Nydell, M. K. *Understanding Arabs: A Guide for Westerners*. Yarmouth, ME: Intercultural Press, 1983.

Oliver, R. L. *Making Your Meaning Effective*. Boston: Holbrook Press, 1971.

Osborn, M. *Orientations to Rhetorical Style*. Chicago: Science Research Associates, 1976.

Oxford, W. H. *The Fundamentals of Effective Oral Expression*. Tokyo, Japan: Eichosha, 1979.

Pace, R. W., Petersen, B. D., and Burnett, M. D. *Techniques for Effective Communication*. Reading, MA: Addison-Wesley, 1979.

Park, M-S. *Communication Styles in Two Different Cultures: Korean and American*. Seoul, Korea: Han Shin, 1979.

Patton, B. R., and Griffin, K. *Decision-Making Group Interaction*, 2d ed. New York: Harper and Row, 1978.

Pearson, J. C., and Nelson, P. E. *Understanding and Sharing: An Introduction to Speech Communication*, 5th ed. Dubuque, IA: Wm C. Brown, 1991.

Pei, M. *The Story of Language*. New York: New American Library, 1965.

Phillips, G. M. *Communication and the Small Group*, 2d ed. Indianapolis: Bobbs-Merrill, 1973.

Potter, D. and Andersen, M. *Discussion in Small Groups: A Guide to Effective Practice*, 3d ed. Belmont, CA: Wadsworth, 1976.

Proshansky, H. "Why a Problem Census?" *Leadership Pamphlet #6*, Adult Education Association, 1955.

Rahskopf, H. *Basic Speech Improvement*. New York: Harper and Row, 1965.

Rankin, P. T. "Listening Ability: Its Importance, Measurement and Development." *Chicago Schools Journal* 12 (1930).

Renwick, G. W. *A Fair Go For All: Australian/American Interactions*. Yarmouth, ME: Intercultural Press, 1991.

Richardson, S. A., and Dohrenwend, B. S., and Klein, D. *Interviewing: Its Forms and Functions*. New York: Basic Books, 1965.

Richetto, G. M., and Zima, J. P. *Interviewing*, 2d ed. Chicago: Science Research Associates, 1982.

Richmond, V. P. *Communication Apprehension and Success in the Job Applicant Screening Process*. International Communication Association convention paper, Berlin, 1977.

Richmond, V. P., and McCroskey, J. C. *Communication: Apprehension, Avoidance and Effectiveness*. Scottsdale, AZ: Gorsuch Scarisbrick, 1985.

Richmond, V. P., McCroskey, J. C., and Payne, S. K. *Nonverbal Behavior in Interpersonal Relations*. Englewood Cliffs, NJ: Prentice Hall, 1987.

Richmond, Yale. *From Nyet to Da: Understanding the Russians*. Yarmouth, ME: Intercultural Press, 1922.

Rives, S. G. *The Fundamentals of Oral Interpretation*. Tokyo, Japan: Eichosha, 1981.

Robertson, J. *How to Win in a Job Interview*. Englewood Cliffs, NJ: Prentice Hall, 1978.

Roethlisberger, F. J. *Management and Morale*. Cambridge, MA: Harvard University Press, 1941.

Rosenblatt, S. B., Cheatham, T. R., and Watt, J. T. *Communication in Business*. Englewood Cliffs, NJ: Prentice Hall, 1977.

Rosenfeld, L. *Now That We're All Here . . . Relations in Small Groups*. Columbus, OH: Merrill, 1976.

Rosenfeld, L. B. *Human Interaction in the Small Group Setting.* Columbus, OH: Merrill, 1973.

Ross, R. S. *Speech Communication,* 5th ed. Englewood Cliffs, NJ: Prentice Hall, 1980.

Rubin, R. B. "Assessing Speaking and Listening Competence at the College Level: The Communication Competency Assessment Instrument." *Communication Education* 31 (1982).

Ruestan, K. E. "The Experiential Group." In *Small Group Communication: A Reader,* edited by R. S. Cathcart and L. Samovar. Dubuque, IA: Wm C. Brown, 1988.

Ruhly, S. *Intercultural Communication,* 2d ed. Chicago: Science Research Associates, 1982.

Samovar, L. A., Brooks, R. D., and Porter, R. E. "A Survey of Adult Communication Activities." *Journal of Communication* 19 (1969).

Samovar, L. A., and Hellweg, S. A. *Interviewing: A Communicative Approach.* Dubuque, IA: Gorsuch Scarisbrick, 1982.

Samovar, L. A., and Porter, R. E., editors, *Intercultural Communication: A Reader,* 6th ed. Belmont, CA: Wadsworth, 1991.

Samovar, L., Porter, R. E., and Jain, N. *Understanding Intercultural Communication.* Belmont, CA: Wadsworth, 1981.

Sattler, W. M., and Miller, N. E. *Discussion and Conference.* Englewood Cliffs, NJ: Prentice Hall, 1954.

Schramm, W. "How Communication Works." In *Messages: A Reader in Human Communication,* edited by J. M. Civikly. New York: Random House, 1974.

Schutz, W. C. *The FIRO Scales.* Palo Alto, CA: Consulting Psychologists Press, 1967.

Scott, M. D., and Powers, W. G. *Interpersonal Communication: A Question of Needs.* Boston: Houghton Mifflin, 1978.

Scott, M. D., McCroskey, J. C., and Sheahan, M. E. "Measuring Communication Apprehension." *Journal of Communication* 28 (1978).

Scott, M. D., Yates, M., and Wheeless, L. R. *An Exploratory Investigation of the Effects of Communication Apprehension in Alternative Systems of Instruction.* Chicago: International Communication Association convention paper, 1975.

Shaw, M. E. *Group Dynamics: The Psychology of Small Group Behavior,* 3d ed. New York: McGraw-Hill, 1983.

Siegman, A. W., and Pope, B., editors. *Studies in Dyadic Communication.* Elmsford, NY: Pergamon Press, 1972.

Sitaram, K. S., and Cogdell, R. T. *Foundations of Intercultural Communication.* Columbus, OH: Merrill, 1976.

Speech Communication Association. *Speaking for Careers.* Falls Church, VA: 1978.

Sperry Corp. "Your Listening Profile." In *Small Group Communication: A Reader,* 5th ed., edited by R. S. Cathcart and L. A. Samovar, Dubuque, IA: Wm C. Brown, 1988.

Spitzberg, B. H., and Cupach, W. R. *Interpersonal Communication Competence.* Beverly Hills, CA: Sage, 1984.

Stano, M. E., and Reinsch, N. L., Jr., *Communication in Interviews.* Englewood Cliffs, NJ: Prentice Hall, 1982.

Stewart, C. J., and Cash, W. B. *Interviewing: Principles and Practices,* 3d ed. Dubuque, IA: Wm C. Brown, 1982.

Stewart, E. C. *American Cultural Patterns: A Cross-Cultural Perspective.* Washington, DC: Society for Intercultural Education, Training and Research, 1972.

Stewart, E. C., and Bennett, M. J. *American Cultural Patterns: A Cross-Cultural Perspective,* revised. Yarmouth, ME: Intercultural Press, 1991.

Sumner, W. G. *Folkways.* New York: New American Library, 1906.

Swanson, R., and Marquardt, C. *On Communication.* Beverly Hills, CA: Glencoe Press, 1974.

Tandberg, G. *Research in Speech.* Morristown, NJ: General Learning Press, 1974.

Tubbs, S. L., and Moss, S. *Human Communication,* 5th ed. New York: Random House, 1987.

Tuckman, B. "Developmental Sequence in Small Groups." *Psychological Bulletin* 63 (1965).

Verderber, R. F. *Communicate!* 4th ed., Belmont, CA: Wadsworth, 1984.

Verderber, R. F., and Verderber, K. S. *Inter-Act: Using Interpersonal Communication Skills,* 2d ed. Belmont, CA: Wadsworth, 1980.

Weaver, C. *Human Listening: Process and Behavior.* Indianapolis: Bobbs-Merrill, 1972.

Weaver, R. L., II. *Understanding Interpersonal Communication.* Glenview, IL: Scott, Foresman, 1978.

Weaver, R. L., II. *Understanding Interpersonal Communication,* 2d ed. Glenview, IL: Scott, Foresman, 1981.

Weiner, A. N. *Machiavellianism as a Predictor of Group Interaction.* M.A. Thesis, West Virginia University, 1973.

Wilmot, W. W. *Dyadic Communication: A Transactional Perspective.* Reading, MA: Addison-Wesley, 1975.

Witteman, H. R. *The Relationship of Communication Apprehension to Opinion Leadership and Innovativeness,* M.A. Thesis, West Virginia University, 1976.

Wittich, W., and Schuller, C. *Audio-Visual Materials: Their Nature and Use.* New York: Harper and Row, 1967.

Wolvin, A. D., and Coakley, C. G. *Listening.* Dubuque, IA: Wm C. Brown, 1982.

Wong, H. *Articulation and Pronunciation.* Tokyo, Japan: Eichosha, 1973.

Work, W. "ERIC Report." *Communication Education* 31 (1982).

Zelko, H. P., and Dance, F. E. X. *Business and Professional Speech Communication.* New York: Holt, Rinehart and Winston, 1965.

Zima, J. P. *Interviewing: Key to Effective Management.* Chicago: Science Research Associates, 1983.

Answers

Learning Check (Chapter 2)

1. usually
2. negative
3. complementary
4. interpersonal
5. encoding
6. aesthetic
7. foggy thinking
8. irreversible
9. Aristotle
10. communications

Vocabulary Check (Chapter 4)

1. B
2. D
3. C
4. H
5. F
6. I
7. G
8. J
9. E
10. A

Grouping Check (Chapter 5)

1. C (the action is continuous)
2. B (the three persons are similar, standing out from the Japanese, the natives)
3. A (the three are standing near each other at the sign)
4. D (the persons are in the same position in relation to the environment)

Mountain Talk (Chapter 8)

1. E
2. F
3. H
4. G
5. C
6. I
7. J
8. B
9. D
10. A

Learning Check (Chapter 8)

1. T
2. F
3. T
4. T
5. T
6. T
7. F
8. T
9. T
10. F

Vocabulary Check (Chapter 9)

1. B
2. F
3. D
4. G
5. J
6. A
7. C
8. E
9. H
10. I

Listening Types (Chapter 10)

1. A. Deliberative   B. Empathic
2. A. Empathic   B. Deliberative
3. A. Deliberative   B. Empathic
4. A. Empathic   B. Deliberative

Defensive Behavior (Chapter 10)

1. Name-calling, ridiculing/Reassuring, sympathizing
2. Warning, admonishing/Teaching, giving logical arguments
3. Ordering, directing/Advising, giving suggestions
4. Judging, criticizing/Interpreting, diagnosing
5. Exhorting, moralizing/Praising, agreeing

Types of Questions (Chapter 13)

1. Leading
2. Closed
3. Open
4. Closed
5. Leading
6. Open
7. Open
8. Leading
9. Open
10. Closed

Vocabulary Check (Chapter 14)

1. E
2. A
3. C
4. F
5. D
6. G
7. I
8. H
9. J
10. B

Problem Types (Chapter 15)

1. Policy
2. Fact
3. Policy
4. Policy
5. Value
6. Fact
7. Value
8. Fact
9. Value
10. Policy

Vocabulary Check (Chapter 19)

1. E
2. I
3. F
4. J
5. A
6. B
7. C
8. D
9. G
10. H

Learning Check (Chapter 20)

1. Amplifying
2. Hypothetical
3. Specific
4. Objective
5. Time
6. Motivated sequence
7. SESS
8. Memory
9. Deterrence
10. Informative

Index